HOT AIR

Also by Howard Kurtz

Media Circus:
The Trouble with America's Newspapers

HOWARD KURTZ

HOT AIR

ALL TALK,
ALL THE TIME

T I M E S 𝕿 B O O K S

R A N D O M   H O U S E

To Lenny Kurtz,
who taught me how to talk,
and Marcia Kurtz,
who taught me how to listen

ACKNOWLEDGMENTS

I am indebted to Peter Osnos, the publisher of Times Books, who grew excited about this project after eight or nine seconds, and to my editor, Jonathan Karp, who provided a steady stream of valuable suggestions. My thanks as well to all the people in television and radio who generously made time for interviews, and particularly to those programs that allowed me an unusual degree of behind-the-scenes access. I'd also like to thank my colleagues at *The Washington Post* who assisted me with the stories that gave rise to this effort. Most of all, I'm grateful to Mary, Judy, and Bonnie for putting up with me once again during the writing of this book.

CONTENTS

HOT AIR

THE TALKATHON CULTURE

A merica is awash in talk. Loud talk. Angry talk. Conspiratorial talk. Raunchy talk, smug talk, self-serving talk, funny talk, rumor-mongering talk. A cacophony of chat fills the airwaves from coast to coast, from dawn to dusk and beyond, all talk all the time.

The richest and most prominent talkers include a wide assortment of pundits, commentators, experts, hacks, and hucksters, some of them cloaked in the thinnest journalistic garb. They analyze, interpret, elucidate, expound, pontificate, and predict, an unprecedented barrage of blather and bluster that has dramatically ratcheted up the noise level of political debate.

But many of the talkers are ordinary Americans, aggrieved, frustrated, flooding the switchboards of television and radio studios to register their dissent. Gradually, with little warning, this has produced a high-decibel revolution in the way we communicate with each other and with our leaders. We have become a talk show nation, pulsating with opinions that are channeled through hosts and reverberate through the vast echo chamber of the airwaves.

The Old Media—the big newspapers, magazines, and network newscasts—still cling to some vestige of objectivity, the traditional notion that information must be checked and verified and balanced with opposing views before it can be disseminated to the public. But the talk shows revel in their one-sided pugnacity, spreading wild theories, delicious gossip, and angry denunciations with gleeful abandon. Anyone can say anything at any time with little fear of contradiction. It is raw, it is real, and it is immensely popular. The gatekeepers of the elite media have been cast aside and the floodgates thrown open.

There is, however, a price to be paid for this unending marathon of talk. As the talk show culture has exploded, the national conversation has been coarsened, cheapened, reduced to name-calling and finger-pointing and bumper-sticker sloganeering. Television has little time for context, subtlety, or caveats. Seat-of-the-pants judgments—up or down, yes or no, who won and who lost and who committed the outrage of the week—have become a driving force behind the shrill and often mean-spirited politics of the 1990s.

Outlandish opinion-mongers on the left and right tend to drown out everyone else. Extremism in the pursuit of ratings is no vice. The middle ground, the sensible center, is dismissed as too squishy, too dull, too likely to send the audience channel surfing. Rhetoric heats up and consensus melts away. There was a time when "Jane, you ignorant slut!" was a great late-night gag; now the parody cuts uncomfortably close to reality. The whole point of the talk show business is not so much to persuade as to posture, to slam-dunk opponents and to build audience share.

Let's face it: Talk is cheap. The armchair warriors defuse world crises, wipe out budget deficits, and solve the welfare mess, all before the commercial break: And it's all make-believe. They don't have to build coalitions or crunch numbers or live with the consequences of their errors. If they screw up, there's always next week's show to test-drive new theories.

With so many talkers talking around the clock, the news cycle is permanently stuck on fast-forward. Events are chewed over as they unfold, snap judgments race by in a blur, conventional wisdom hardens like so much ready-mix cement. Quick: Did Bill Clinton do the right thing or fall on his face? Will the Republicans gain the upper hand next week? On a scale of zero to ten, what are the chances that Congress will solve the health care crisis? Balance the budget? Find a cure for cancer? Complicated national and international issues are tossed into this journalistic Cuisinart and churned into high-speed pronouncements.

When Clinton ordered a bombing strike against Iraq in 1993, White House officials were stunned to see the pundits on *The Capi-*

tal Gang debating the political fallout even before the administration knew whether the bombs had landed. The talk had preempted the action itself. It is a dizzying process that provokes and titillates and entertains but, with some exceptions, rarely illuminates. And this mentality is increasingly spreading to print journalism, as exemplified by *Newsweek*'s "Conventional Wisdom Watch" and *Time*'s "Winners and Losers" column.

This is bad news for journalism, but more important, it's frequently bad for the country. The talk culture affects the business of governance in insidious ways. After the Sunday talk shows, senior White House advisers—George Stephanopoulos, James Carville, Paul Begala—get on the phone and assess whether the administration did well or got creamed that morning. Politicians of every persuasion grow obsessed with "winning the week," as reflected by the scorecard mentality of the weekend shows. Short-term maneuvering becomes more important than long-term policy. The political effort to "sell" an initiative on the talk circuit begins to overshadow the substance of the proposal itself. The talk show environment has given us a talk show government, presided over at the moment by the talkiest president of modern times. Journalists and politicians jabber at each other while the country slowly sinks into a morass of social and economic problems. The spectacle has fueled the cynicism of an electorate that sees the yawning chasm between this unceasing talk and the lack of tangible progress in their daily lives.

The triumph of talk has also produced the rise of the talk show candidate. Only in late-twentieth-century America would Patrick Buchanan, whose primary experience is popping off on radio and television, be treated as a serious presidential candidate, a status conferred in part by his appearances on the very shows for which he previously played the role of journalist. Buchanan was joined in the 1996 presidential race by Alan Keyes, a Baltimore radio talk show host and former Reagan administration official who stayed on the air for months even while campaigning, and by Representative Robert Dornan, a former California radio personality and regular Rush Limbaugh substitute. Ross Perot sought the presidency in 1992 almost exclusively by making the talk show rounds and spending part of his fortune on television ads. Talking, campaigning, and governing have become almost indistinguishable in this chattering age.

The hypercritical talk climate is not entirely new, of course; much of the press has been abusive and ill-mannered toward political leaders for more than two centuries. Thomas Jefferson was accused by Federalist newspapers of keeping a slave girl, Sally Heming, as his mistress, and the Connecticut *Courant* said his election would mean that "murder, robbery, rape, adultery and incest will openly be taught and practised." Abraham Lincoln was called an "ape," a "gorilla," and a "monster." Andrew Johnson was described as an "insolent, clownish creature" by the *New York World*. Grover Cleveland had to own up to reports that he had fathered an illegitimate child. Franklin Roosevelt was assailed on the radio by Father Charles Coughlin as a "liar," "betrayer," "scab," and "anti-God." John Kennedy was so incensed by the *New York Herald Tribune* that he canceled his subscription.

But news traveled more slowly in the pre-CNN era. Lincoln and FDR didn't have to worry about winning the week. Imagine what *The McLaughlin Group* would have said after Union troops were routed at Manassas, or how *The Capital Gang* would have jumped on the bombing of Pearl Harbor. Kennedy defused the Cuban missile crisis in 1962 by ignoring a harsh diplomatic note from Nikita Khrushchev and answering a second, more conciliatory letter. Today someone would leak word of the first note, one hundred White House reporters would demand a response, and Ted Koppel would race on the air with a "Cuba Held Hostage" special. "The constant drumbeat of news has an incalculable effect on the process of decision making," Stephanopoulos says. The political imperative is to do something—anything—to seize the initiative and quiet the catcalls, at least until the following week.

In some ways, the rise of the opinion-mongers represents a return to the era of an openly partisan press. From the earliest days of American history, newspapers were openly allied with political parties and wielded as weapons by their publishers. William Randolph Hearst could use the power of his presses to start a war and, a few years later, run for president. Only since World War II have newspapers strived to present an "objective" picture of the news, leaving raw advocacy to the editorial pages. The talk show culture is a throwback to the days of fierce partisanship, its practitioners doing noisy battle for their avowedly liberal and conservative viewpoints.

The grating tone of the talk shows reflects a broader degradation of the culture itself. There was a time when intellectuals and academics, waging rhetorical warfare in the pages of *The New Yorker* and *Partisan Review,* were considered to occupy the highest plane of public discussion. They were depicted as glamorous figures, however arcane and self-important their literary squabbles. Now middlebrow culture reigns supreme, and the political debate, reduced to its sound-bite essence, unfolds in loud bursts on television and radio. Serious ideas are still explored in books and newspapers and journals of opinion, but they cannot be popularized unless a simpler, punchier version is reenacted on the talk circuit. Authors must hawk their weighty tomes in six-minute television interviews. All this amounts to a profound cultural shift in the nature of communication. Tina Brown worries as much about getting her *New Yorker* writers on television as getting their five-thousand-word pieces in the magazine. Writers can stir the intellectual pot, but it is talk shows that create the buzz.

The evolution can be viewed in generational terms. In the early 1970s, Irving Kristol, the neoconservative writer and college professor, was invited to dine with President Richard Nixon and assemble some academicians to help the White House develop a social agenda. Nixon took a liking to Kristol after reading his book, *On the Democratic Ideal in America.* Kristol had made his sociocultural mark by writing for *Commentary* and editing *The Public Interest.*

Two decades later, his son, William Kristol, wielded great influence by firing off memos to journalists and appearing on *Crossfire, The Capital Gang, Nightline,* and *This Week with David Brinkley.* And he draws attention at the highest levels. During the 1994 campaign, Kristol suggested on *Meet the Press* that the Republicans might reduce farm subsidies. Clinton, Vice President Gore, and other White House officials promptly began warning of a "secret" GOP plan to devastate farmers. In Iowa, the president said of Kristol: "You probably never heard of him. He tells them what to think up there in Washington." The Republican Party strategist has perfectly calibrated his message for the talk culture of the '90s.

By appearing on talk shows, Kristol says, "you do have a certain name ID with .01 percent of the American people. This morning I got in a cab and the driver, some right-wing immigrant, said, 'Mr. Kristol, it's really great to have you in my cab.' You can see why Pat Buchanan thinks he can run for president. You go through an airport and someone says, 'You were great on *Crossfire*' and you say, Hey, I'm famous. You can deceive yourself that you really have influence because you're on television, when all you're doing is being a pundit. You're like one of those guys on *Hollywood Squares*."

Kristol arguably had more clout when he was Vice President Dan Quayle's chief of staff, but he was an anonymous staffer, almost never on television. When he launched a seven-person Republican advocacy group, he used the talk shows to make himself a player. During the height of the debate over health care reform, *The Mac-Neil/Lehrer NewsHour* did a twelve-minute segment on a Kristol memo that argued against universal health insurance, followed by a debate between Mark Shields and Paul Gigot. That, in turn, led more newspaper writers to quote the memo. Soon Kristol was on the cover of *The Washington Monthly* and the *Los Angeles Times Magazine*.

"If I were never on CNN or the Sunday shows, I'd be thought to be less influential in Washington," he says. "Part of being influential is being invited on *Inside Politics*. The fact that I did *Face the Nation* several times helped give my memos more visibility." Even Mario Cuomo, after twelve years as governor of New York, says he got more public feedback after an appearance on *Meet the Press*. "It's magic," he says. "If you're on TV, more people stop you the next day."

In the world of opinion magazines and op-ed pages, it is the boldest thinkers and most provocative writers who rise to the top. But the talk show culture rewards the ability to play to the camera. It is a genre that values glibness and brevity above all. Too many dependent clauses might drive precious viewers away.

"Television can only pay attention long enough for you to skim the surface," says Margaret Carlson, the *Time* columnist and *Capital Gang* regular. "What I write in *Time* magazine are things I've thought through, I've studied, I've gotten every point of view. What

do I know about Haiti? I know what everyone else knows and maybe
a little bit more. Nobody can be a specialist on five subjects every
week. Maybe you're a specialist on domestic politics and haven't
got a clue what managed competition is.

"What's good TV and what's thoughtful analysis are different.
That's been conceded by most producers and bookers. They're not
looking for the most learned person; they're looking for the person
who can sound learned without confusing the matter with too much
knowledge. I'm one of the people without too much knowledge. I'm
perfect!"

The explosion of talk shows is part of an information revolution
that now processes more news and commentary than ever before.
People read newsletters hot off the fax machine, watch congressional hearings on C-SPAN, scan databases on wafer-thin CD-
ROMs, sound off on America Online bulletin boards, download
files from the Internet. Yet in early 1995, only half of Americans
could identify the relentlessly publicized Newt Gingrich as speaker
of the House, while 64 percent knew that Lance Ito was the judge
in the O. J. Simpson trial. We are drowning in information, increasingly unable to make sense of the waves of onrushing data. The talk
shows are merely the loudest element, overloading our circuits with
chatter that ranges from profound to profoundly trivial.

The talk culture has been further vulgarized by the popularity
of tabloid television, which increasingly has set the agenda for the
mainstream media. Marla Maples discusses her love life with Diane
Sawyer on *Prime Time Live*. Paula Jones dishes to Sam Donaldson.
Gennifer Flowers is carried live on CNN. Tonya Harding appears
on *Inside Edition* and *Eye to Eye with Connie Chung*. John Bobbitt
does *American Journal* and *Now with Tom Brokaw and Katie Couric*.
Lorena Bobbitt tells her penis-chopping tale to *20/20*. All the shows
compete for the endless parade of O.J. relatives, friends, lawyers,
and hangers-on, and finally for Simpson himself, despite all the
evidence that he committed two brutal murders.

In this tawdry environment, criminals become just another kind
of celebrity to be booked, interviewed, and promoted. Diane Sawyer
chats up Charles Manson on *Prime Time Live,* just as Geraldo Rivera
and others have over the years. *Dateline NBC* debriefs Jeffrey
Dahmer. Paul Hill, who killed a doctor and his bodyguard at a

Florida abortion clinic, turns up with Phil Donahue and Vladimir Pozner. Colin Ferguson, who shot up a Long Island commuter train, gets his moment in the spotlight on *Today* and *Larry King Live*. On the talk circuit, even mass murderers are stars. The more gruesome the crime, the better the ratings.

The high priests of talk—Larry King, John McLaughlin, Rush Limbaugh, Don Imus, Phil Donahue, Oprah Winfrey, Ted Koppel —wield unprecedented power, reaching millions with their daily gabfests. While commentators in the age of Walter Lippmann or James Reston sought mainly to influence the governing elite, the new talkmeisters play to the masses. Presidents and prime ministers and putative leaders rush to appear on their programs because the hosts are presumed to be in touch with the public, as measured by Nielsen and Arbitron numbers that certify who is hot and who's not.

Yet the range of "debate" that unfolds on most television programs is almost laughably narrow. Few panelists challenge the underlying assumptions of official Washington; any argument that lacks significant support in Congress is blown off the radar screen as irrelevant. Problems that fall out of fashion with the Beltway establishment (say, homelessness) cease to exist on television, while issues that are in favor (say, family values) consume plenty of airtime. Problems ignored by Congress (say, the savings and loan crisis) hit the talk circuit only after they explode into scandal.

Many of those who yak for a living exist in a hermetically sealed cocoon, rubbing shoulders only with other affluent insiders and leaving town only to speak to paying audiences. They pontificate about welfare but have never actually spoken to a welfare mother. They hold forth on the decline of manufacturing but have never set foot in a factory, except perhaps with a politician on a handshaking tour. Firsthand knowledge or shoe-leather reporting is not a prerequisite in the talk world. With a few notable exceptions, such as *Charlie Rose* or *Nightline,* just popping off fills the bill quite nicely.

The pundit lineup tilts noticeably to the right: Michael Kinsley is charged with upholding the liberal cause on *Crossfire,* though he is not nearly as far to the left as Pat Buchanan is to the right. But Christian conservatives and far-right spokesmen are also largely excluded. Few blacks and Hispanics fill the regular pundit chairs, and the relative handful of women underscores their token status. The punditocracy is a testosterone-driven calling.

To be sure, many of those who blab for a living are smart and savvy folks, yet they must tailor their performances to the imperatives of the camera and the microphone. I understand the seductions of this culture all too well, as we will see, for although I make my primary living behind a word processor, I have gradually become part of the endless parade of talking heads. I have basked in the ego-warming glow of the klieg lights, struggling to sound sage while wrestling with the limitations of the format.

No corner of human behavior has been untouched by the talk culture. There is sports talk, health tips, financial advice, religious inspiration, call-in psychiatry. Radio, as an inherently local medium, offers a much wider range of debate and provides a home for a broad array of subcultures. Blacks in New York, Cubans in Miami, Latinos in L.A., and Christians across the country have their own radio stations. New cable channels, meanwhile, are sprouting like wildflowers—America's Talking, CNBC, National Empowerment Television, NewsTalk Television—and more are on the way. Everyone, it seems, has a talk show, from Newt Gingrich to Joan Rivers, from Tom Snyder to Susan Powter, from Charlie Rose to Charles Grodin, from Wolf Blitzer to Aleksandr Solzhenitsyn, from Kato Kaelin to Tammy Faye Bakker. *Crossfire* and *Capital Gang* have cloned themselves with new weekend versions, largely staffed by panelists from other talk shows. This proliferation of chat shows has created a seemingly insatiable market for journalists and other blowhards who can fill up the time with the sound of gab. And the politicians have become masters at exploiting the new formats. It's no accident when Bob Dole, seeking to soften his prickly image, unofficially launches his '96 presidential candidacy by yukking it up with David Letterman. Or when Senator Arlen Specter takes his long-shot White House campaign to Howard Stern's show. Or when Colin Powell launches his book-tour-as-presidential-flirtation with Barbara Walters, Katie Couric, and Jay Leno. Out-of-work candidates from Jesse Jackson to Ross Perot have also found the talk circuit an ideal place to stay in the public eye while contemplating the next campaign.

The oh-so-serious programs are simply less important in an age of news-by-Disney, when politics and pop culture seem to have merged. When Gennifer Flowers was peddling her book about Bill Clinton in 1995, nearly all the mainstream talk shows, having had their fill of her well-worn tale, refused to book her. But she briefly became a staple of Jay Leno's monologue, which underscored the message of Clinton-as-philanderer without the merest mention on the Sunday shows or *Crossfire*.

Leno on Flowers's description of Clinton's favorite fantasy: "For her to dress up like Hillary and pretend he was in charge." Leno on Flowers calling the president "kinky": "Clinton is pretty kinky. The other night he blindfolded Hillary, then tied her up, then he went out with another woman." Every two-bit political strategist knows an issue is cutting when it becomes fodder for the late-night comics.

Even talk show hosts themselves must cross-pollinate their way across the field, freshening the public's interest by displaying lighter facets of their well-known personas. That's why Ted Koppel rollerbladed his way onto Letterman's *Late Show*, Oprah Winfrey mused about giving up sleaze with Larry King, King joked about his serial marriages with Jay Leno, George Will chatted amiably with Don Imus, Geraldo Rivera held forth on the O.J. trial with Leno, and Letterman joshed about his lackluster Academy Awards performance with King. The guest ritual has become mandatory even for the mightiest talkers.

The idea that anyone in America can pick up the phone and sound off on C-SPAN, trade dittos with Rush, or question the president on *Larry King Live* is a liberating one, even if only 2 or 3 percent of the audience actually seizes the opportunity. For too many years, a handful of giant media corporations controlled the flow of news, engaging mainly in one-way communication, a few letters to the editor notwithstanding. One of the magnetic attractions of talk show democracy is the sense that it gives voice to views and information that big-shot media executives deem inappropriate for public consumption. This sort of information is often unfair, unrealistic, and unsubstantiated, but perhaps that is part of its appeal. The danger is when millions of viewers and listeners treat all the hot air as absolute truth.

There is danger, too, in the political perception that talk show audiences are an accurate barometer of public opinion. Almost by definition, those who call radio and television shows are the most angry, most outspoken, most politically energized members of the electorate. Many are insightful, others woefully ignorant. Yet the talk circuit acts as a huge megaphone, amplifying their grievances out of proportion to their numbers.

The rise of the radio megastars, thanks to the magic of satellite and syndication, has been accompanied by an equally dramatic surge in harsh rhetoric and out-of-bounds satire. Radio has become an anything-goes arena where one host assails "feminazis" and uses a vacuuming sound to perform "caller abortions" (Rush Limbaugh); another calls a United States Senate candidate "a waste of a vagina" (Howard Stern); another denounces federal agents as "bottom-dwelling slugs" and says that "shooting back is reasonable . . . I have counseled shooting them in the head" (G. Gordon Liddy); another plays the sound of a car skidding and a person gurgling underwater when invoking Ted Kennedy (Don Imus); yet another suggests that black criminals are "subhuman scum" and "savages" (Bob Grant).

The way to get attention, to climb the ladder of talk success, is to shout, to polarize, to ridicule, to condemn, to corral the most outrageous or vilified guests. When White House chief of staff Leon Panetta wanted to attack Newt Gingrich, the strongest insult he could muster was to accuse the House speaker of acting like "an out-of-control radio talk show host."

The ugliness reached a point that by 1995 pundits and politicians were openly debating whether talk radio had become hate radio, feeding a climate of intolerance that encouraged such extremist violence as the terrorist bombing in Oklahoma City. While it is obviously unfair to draw a direct link between rage on the airwaves and lawlessness in the streets, there can be little doubt that the most inflammatory hosts—and some of their listeners—are poisoning the atmosphere with their talk of government as a tyrannical "enemy" that must be taken down at all costs. It is a bit too easy for commentators on both the left and the right to deny that their incendiary words may have consequences they did not intend. In an era when citizen militia leaders, neo-Nazis, and other fringe characters can speak of armed revolution on their favorite radio shows, talk clearly matters. At the very least, like violence-soaked movies, sex-saturated sitcoms, and the more virulent strains of rap music, trash talk helps degrade a culture that is slowly sinking into the gutter.

While radio talk shows excel at turning up the volume, it is the television pundits who have the loudest megaphone of all. A political charge—say, that Clinton is a foreign policy bumbler—is leveled by Pat Buchanan on *Crossfire* Friday night, seconded by Robert Novak on *Capital Gang* Saturday night, and kicked around by Tim Russert and David Brinkley and Bob Schieffer on Sunday morning. By the time *Newsweek* and *Time* and *U.S. News & World Report* hit the streets Monday, they are carrying headlines like "Clinton's Foreign Policy Mess" and "Can He Recover?" This in turn provides fodder for Al Hunt on *Today* and Chris Matthews on *Good Morning America* and Fred Barnes on *CBS This Morning*.

In short, the most dedicated consumers of political talk shows are other journalists, who fertilize and spread the latest fodder down through the media food chain. No good idea goes uncopied. A mega-story like the O. J. Simpson case is processed and merchandised into dozens of "trend" pieces—spouse abuse, violent athletes, race and justice, media overkill, illegal search and seizure, jury selection, favoritism toward celebrities—and the same well-tailored guests are recruited to make the same points on *Larry King Live* and *Entertainment Tonight,* on *20/20* and *48 Hours,* on *Geraldo* and *Oprah.*

It seems to matter not at all that these oracles of the airwaves are often wrong, or wrongheaded, for news races along so quickly that no one cares what was said last month or last week. Words of wisdom vanish into the ether, forgotten even by those who have spoken them. Somalia gives way to Rwanda, which is superseded by Haiti, replaced by North Korea, and elbowed aside by Iraq and then Chechnya. The health care crisis explodes like a supernova and burns itself out, a black hole immediately filled by the welfare crisis, the Cuban refugee crisis, the juvenile crime crisis, the Mexican peso crisis, and the always-reliable crisis of confidence in Washington. In a talk show nation, hot topics streak across the sky—the House Bank scandal, Bob Packwood, the federal budget deficit, Woody and Mia, reinventing government, Heidi Fleiss, illegal immigration, Amy Fisher, the Los Angeles riots, the Menendez brothers—and briefly light up the media landscape until they are utterly talked out. The problems linger while the producers search for new issues, new scandals, new outrages.

The new talk culture is spectacularly ill-suited to dealing with complicated subjects. The national debate over health care that consumed the first two years of the Clinton presidency was, in the end, simply overwhelmed by talk. The Clinton plan was fatally flawed, but any attempt at reform was destroyed by a blizzard of half-truths and misinformation on radio and TV talk shows, in thirty-second attack ads, in rhetorical broadsides by every conceivable interest group. Much of the public lost track of all the competing proposals. Outright falsehoods, such as the claim that the Clinton plan would bar patients from choosing their own doctors, were repeated on the air so often that they hardened into reality. The result was a deafening roar that simply overloaded the circuits of the talk show environment. The public threw up its hands and nothing, absolutely nothing, got done. It was, in the end, all talk. The talk shows are not entirely to blame for this meltdown, of course, but they are a central element of a polarized society in which all sides practice the politics of distortion.

The political use of talk has come to resemble the Senate filibuster as a blunt instrument. It is far easier to stop something—a health plan, a controversial nomination, a congressional pay raise— than to forge a consensus among competing interests. Time is too fleeting for the talkers to seriously weigh the value of health maintenance organizations, or the benefits of job-training programs, or long-term proposals for fixing Social Security. Radio hosts rile people up about welfare and immigration and affirmative action, but anger has its limits as a public policy tool. At some point the country has to stop talking and start acting.

All the yammering out there undoubtedly reflects a populace fixated on the new and the novel, remote controls firmly in hand, grazing across the land of talk. It is a society in which the famous and not-so-famous are trotted out to discuss their sexual hang-ups and neuroses, where pathetic souls peddle their trash for cash, where people lay bare their darkest secrets for the amusement of the mass audience. The culture of news, once the straitlaced, buttoned-down preserve of Walter Cronkite and Huntley-Brinkley, has merged with the relentlessly glitzy world of entertainment, producing one great, roaring Oprahfied ooze of headlines and hype. The most prominent print journalists of our era have eagerly enlisted in this shouting-head society, electronic court jesters determined to reap the rewards of maximum exposure. They are talking their way into the heart of America, wrapping their words around each passing fad and obsession, their voices merging into a vast harmonic convergence of talk.

On October 25, 1991, Senator Edward Kennedy took the podium at Harvard University for a long-awaited address about his personal conduct.

It was days before the rape trial of William Kennedy Smith, and the Massachusetts senator, who had woken his nephew for a post-midnight bout of alcoholic revelry that fateful evening in Palm Beach, was attempting to make public amends. He spoke of "individual faults and frailties," of "my own shortcomings" and "the faults in the conduct of my private life."

At that point, CNN cut away from live coverage and returned to its Washington studio, where anchor Lou Dobbs and analyst William Schneider, armed with an advance text, held forth on the significance of a speech that was still unfolding.

It had finally happened: What journalists said about the news had become more important than the news itself. The age of perpetual punditry had arrived. Can it really be just twenty-five years since Spiro Agnew berated the networks for providing "instant analysis" after a president's speech? Nowadays we serve up our stunningly insightful interpretations even before the news has taken place. While the Kennedy episode was an obvious blunder—"bad judgment," says CNN President Tom Johnson—it was emblematic of a fundamental journalistic shift in which our talk is more important than their talk.

During the 1992 Democratic convention, the party's brightest luminaries took the stage at Madison Square Garden on behalf of Bill Clinton. But the Big Three networks, which limited their coverage to an hour or two a night, had other ideas. Jimmy Carter and Jesse Jackson were not carried because they appeared early in the evening. Only CBS aired Mario Cuomo's speech live. Other Democrats—Jay Rockefeller, Tom Harkin, Kathleen Brown—were reduced to brief blips. One network replayed just a few seconds of Aretha Franklin's rendition of the national anthem: the first singing sound bite.

What we got instead was wall-to-wall talk: *"Well, Dan—," "It seems to me, Peter—," "The interesting thing here, Tom—."* The network anchors orchestrated the show from their high-priced skyboxes ten stories above the convention floor. The proceedings themselves were reduced to a colorful backdrop for the musings of Jack Germond, John Chancellor, Tim Russert, George Will, William Schneider, David Gergen, Mark Shields, Ken Bode, David Brinkley, Cokie Roberts, and friends. As if that weren't enough, a battalion of print journalists was rushed in as reinforcements: Joe Klein of *Newsweek* on CBS. Michael Barone of *U.S. News* on ABC. Al Hunt of *The Wall Street Journal* on NBC. David Broder of *The Washington Post* and Gloria Borger of *U.S. News* on CNN. No wonder Peter Jennings worried aloud "that we're going to analyze this thing to death."

Many viewers were understandably annoyed by the endless commentary. Why spend millions of dollars covering the thing if it isn't worth putting on the air except in short snippets? Why not let viewers hear for themselves (what a concept) what the Democrats had to say? If the event itself was meaningless, then why cover it? It was as if Rather, Brokaw, and Jennings were the stars and the presidential nomination merely a pretext for broadcasting the accumulated wisdom of the nation's top journalists. For four nights at Madison Square Garden, and again the following month at the Houston Astrodome, the talk show culture reigned supreme.

Time and again, the television talkers drown out everything in their wake. In 1995, when House Majority Leader Richard Armey referred to his colleague Barney Frank as "Barney Fag," he compounded the blunder with two critical errors. First, he uttered the offending phrase into a radio microphone, so there was a recording that could be endlessly replayed. Second, he said it on a Friday, just in time for the weekend wave of punditeers to seize upon the gaffe.

"It's hard to believe this isn't the first time that this phrase . . . has passed his lips," Eleanor Clift said.

"It's clear to me that he made that slip because he talks like that all the time," Nina Totenberg said.

"I draw the conclusion that the explanation was patently dishonest. That is a lie," Michael Kinsley said.

"This was not a slip of the tongue, if you listen to it, and Armey's explanation was preposterous," Margaret Carlson said.

"He intended to say Barney Fag. He knew what he was doing," Mark Shields said.

"This business about the slip of the tongue has really received an inordinate amount of attention," Mona Charen said. For that, she could thank her talk show colleagues.

In the world of talk, almost any spark can ignite a prairie fire. On March 10, 1994, such a blaze swept Wall Street during the height of the Whitewater affair. Stocks, bonds, and the dollar all took a beating after rumors that White House lawyer Vincent Foster had committed suicide in a private Virginia apartment used by White House officials, and that his body was later moved to Fort Marcy Park, where it was found. Rush Limbaugh inadvertently embellished this unconfirmed report on his radio show, saying the word was that Foster had been murdered and moved to an apartment owned by Hillary Clinton.

The source of the false report was a newsletter published by Johnson Smick International, a consulting firm headed by a former Reagan administration official. The newsletter attributed its report to the staff of Senator Daniel Patrick Moynihan, which denied it. Research firms often peddle rumors to their clients, but this one got a powerful enough boost from Limbaugh and company to move the markets, and *The Washington Post* and other papers repeated the rumor the next day to explain the dip in the Dow. For talk radio listeners, of course, wild conspiracy theories about Foster's death were nothing new: One survey found that 49 percent of the audience was familiar with the Foster case, compared to 22 percent of the general public.

Sometimes it is the guest who makes inflammatory statements, as Tom Leykis learned on his Los Angeles radio show in January 1995. Leykis was interviewing private investigator Tom Grant, who had been hired by Courtney Love to investigate the death of her husband, rock singer Kurt Cobain, nine months earlier. Police had

ruled Cobain's death a suicide, but Grant accused Love on the air
of conspiring to murder her husband. After being contacted by
Courtney Love's lawyers, Westwood One Entertainment, which
distributes Leykis's show to 116 stations, issued a public retraction
and apology. "We have discovered no substantial evidence to support Mr. Grant's accusations," the company said. But the charge
had already been broadcast to hundreds of thousands of listeners,
some of whom may never have heard the retraction.

It would surely be unfair to blame the talk shows for the decline
of American civilization and other assorted sociological ills. This is,
after all, a country in which politicians run vicious attack ads calling
each other liars, weasels, tax cheats, hypocrites, and soft on murderers and rapists. It is a media-saturated world in which the leader of
the free world feels compelled to announce on MTV that he wears
briefs, not boxers. It is a culture in which people prattle on before
the cameras about their experiences with adultery, incest, impo-
tence, and child abuse. Talk shows simply mirror the best and worst
of society.

But they have also become a powerful vehicle that trumpets the
most extreme and polarizing views, that panders to sensationalism,
that spreads innuendo and misinformation with stunning efficiency.
Talk shows have altered the nature of journalism, shifting the center
of gravity from those who ask questions to those who seem to have
all the answers. They have become a primary conduit for political
operatives who want to spread dirt or influence legislation with little
accountability. They have become an alternative message-delivery
system for conservatives determined to bypass the mainstream
media, for blacks trying to circumvent the dominant white culture,
and for an assortment of fringe characters who would otherwise
remain on the margins of society.

The power of talk has changed the very fabric of the country.
What was once a rather stodgy collection of middle-aged media men
engaged in polite debate has become a raucous and hugely profitable
business whose collective racket seems to grow more deafening each
week. And one of those most responsible for this transformation is
a former Jesuit priest who doggedly defended Richard Nixon in the
final days of Watergate.

CHAPTER TWO

THE ART
OF THE BLURT

I t is the Friday afternoon before the 1994 elections and John McLaughlin is barking questions at his four soothsayers in the cavernous expanse of Studio A on Nebraska Avenue in Washington.

"Issue One: It could be a blowout . . . What's the likelihood of the Republicans winning at least 218 seats in the House, the number they need for a takeover? . . . I ask you, Freddy 'Give 'em Hell' Barnes."

Barnes says the Republicans will fall short. Eleanor Clift says the Republicans will fall short. Jack Germond says the Republicans will fall short.

Wronnngg. McLaughlin and Morton Kondracke (who argued the opposite a week earlier) are the only panelists who successfully predict the Republican capture of the House of Representatives. But their record will remain untarnished only a few seconds longer.

In his staccato, drill-sergeant style, McLaughlin demands to know the fate of the embattled House speaker, Tom Foley.

"I think he's going to win," Clift says.

"I haven't the foggiest idea, but I'll guess Foley," Germond says.

"I guess Foley, too," Kondracke says.

Next up is the Virginia Senate race. Barnes says Oliver North will win. Germond says Oliver North. Kondracke says Ollie. McLaughlin says Ollie.

The talk turns to Mario Cuomo, struggling for a fourth term as

New York governor. "Mario Cuomo will win," Barnes says. "Cuomo wins," Clift says. Germond and Kondracke also pick Cuomo.

In the Florida governor's race, McLaughlin, Barnes, Germond, and Kondracke all agree that Jeb Bush, the son of the former president, is headed for victory.

Four days later, Foley, North, Cuomo, and Bush all lose. But the McLaughlin combatants have lost none of their bravado when they convene for another round of verbal fisticuffs. In television, the past is always prologue.

If any one man is responsible for turning political chat shows into a rip-roaring, finger-pointing, towel-snapping exercise, it is John McLaughlin, a onetime sex lecturer, failed Senate candidate, and radio talk show host. With his owlish face, dictatorial manner, and mock-serious demeanor, McLaughlin serves as ringmaster of the circus-like program that has spawned a dozen imitators and forced even its stodgiest competitors to add a few bells and whistles.

The show is fun to watch, as long as you don't confuse it with journalism. McLaughlin refereeing the endless squabbles, announcing "let's get out," declaring that everyone else is wrong and he is right—it is far better theater than most of the droning highbrow shows where agreeable people agree to disagree with the utmost politeness.

For all its fast-paced bluster, *The McLaughlin Group* relies on a cadre of serious print journalists who ply their trade for first-rate news organizations. Yet they are happy to don the television equivalent of clown suits for the weekly shouting match that has turned them into celebrities who command lucrative fees on the lecture circuit.

"It's like a situation comedy and everyone plays their role," Clift says. "The public likes that. They root for their characters."

"Does *The McLaughlin Group* use gimmicks? Sure," Barnes says. "They work on TV. Do we try to appear to know more than we do? Yep. I guess that's a little phony, but I can live with it."

"It's like a bunch of friends who get together every Friday and have one too many drinks," Kondracke says. "Is it oversimplified? Sure. You don't have much time to think."

"God knows, *McLaughlin* is not something you take seriously,"

Germond says. "I am not comfortable with any of this, but I do it for the money. When you get to your mid-forties, either you become an editor or you have to find a way to become a mini-conglomerate if you want to have control of your schedule. If you want to make enough money, you have to do television. If I didn't have to pay alimony, I wouldn't do it."

The appeal of a sitcom, of course, is that the characters clash in predictable ways. McLaughlin likens the show to *Cheers*. He is the overbearing, opinionated father, presiding over an unruly brood. Fred Barnes is the preppy-looking favorite son, toeing the conservative line and constantly teasing his younger sister, Eleanor. Eleanor Clift is the lonely liberal straining to be heard among the boys' perpetual clamor. Mort Kondracke is the strait-laced brother-in-law, mercilessly taunted by the patriarch. Pat Buchanan is the pugnacious uncle who goes off to fight in the wars and comes staggering home, battered but wiser, waiting for the next battle. Occasionally one of the young brats will rise up and challenge the father figure himself. The occasional guests—Clarence Page, Michael Barone, Christopher Matthews, Mort Zuckerman—form an extended family of cousins, each with his own personality quirks.

"John is a genius about television," Barnes says. "He's a genius in the persona he's created. And he's created these personas for us: Freddy 'The Beadle' Barnes, Eleanor 'Rodham' Clift, Jack the racetrack guy, Mort the eternal Pilgrim."

The problem with *McLaughlin,* and all the food-fight programs it has inspired, is not just that the panelists are frequently off the mark. Nor does all the posturing and bellowing pose any great threat to the republic. The trouble is the omniscient tone that requires professional journalists to pretend they are dispensing biblical wisdom from a televised Mount Olympus.

"We have topics that none of us knows anything about, except what's in *The New York Times,*" Germond admits. "The only thing I really know anything about is politics. I know more than the guy on the corner about GATT or Bosnia, but not as much as I should." When Germond gives a speech, he often brushes aside arcane questions by pleading ignorance. "You can't do that on television. It drives McLaughlin crazy when I do that. He acts like it's serious information we're passing on."

Indeed, McLaughlin sees himself as a teacher and communicator and speaks of the "scholarship" of the program. "I'm interested in getting a large audience for educational reasons," he says. "It's like giving a lecture. If you don't have some occasional humor and wit, people start thinking about picking up their dry cleaning."

While at times he appears to be just "batting his gums," McLaughlin says, he packs as much raw information as possible into his videotaped introductions, hoping to reach beyond the "issue zombies" in the audience to those who don't pay much attention to news. "The polarities of the issue are put with such force, with such lucidity and power, that it has to engage the mind," he says in a voice that reverberates through his spacious Connecticut Avenue office. "It's like the hook of the harpoon that gets into the back of the whale."

As for those who dismiss him as a mere entertainer, McLaughlin retorts: "Give me a break! The image of a journalist as the self-important herald, the high priest of news, the mystique—it's been demythologized. And you know what? *People love it!* They see how unrealistic and how bogus is the identity of the journalist as the purist, the high priest. You could argue journalists have been cut down to size. They have become human. What I do is humanize. But the journalistic elitists will hold up their noses and 'tut tut' and 'Isn't it a shame: Look at McLaughlin, deflowering the virginity of our profession!' " He throws back his head and roars with laughter.

In the world according to McLaughlin, any issue, no matter how fraught with complexity, can be reduced to its sound-bite essence. On one program, McLaughlin asked whether Clinton would "rue" or "relish" an invasion of Haiti; not a lot of room for nuanced discourse there. He demanded to know what the president's public approval rating would be two months hence. On another occasion he had the panelists compare the Whitewater scandal to a physical ailment. Eleanor Clift picked "hangnail" or "toe-stub."

"The nature of these shows is you say things more provocative than you would in print," Clift says. "People know there's an entertainment factor, so they don't hold you personally liable for things. The danger is it turns us all into stereotypes, because you don't have time to express the *ifs, ands*, or *buts*."

The prominence bestowed by the program is hardly an umixed

blessing. Once, Mort Kondracke recalls, veteran diplomat Sol Linowitz took him to lunch and warned: "I don't think that show is
good for your image. You're a serious journalist."

"Do you ever watch the show?" Kondracke asked.

"Oh, every week," Linowitz replied.

Barnes concedes that the program has a certain "slam-bang
quality." Whenever he tries to explain something in more than a
few seconds, he sees McLaughlin waving his arms. "A two-part
idea doesn't work on TV. A lot of times I haven't been able to
complete the thought and wound up saying something incoherent."

But coherence is obviously not the drawing card. "People were
tuning into McLaughlin for the same reason people were going to
stock car races: not to see who wins but to see who crashes," says
Robert Novak, one of the original panelists.

Some guests regret joining the demolition derby. "I felt quite
literally soiled by the experience, not just by the show but sort of
embarassed by even the things I had said," says author William
Greider, who appeared on *McLaughlin* twice. "The format brought
out the worst in everybody. It made you more nasty and provocative
and half-baked. I have that quality within me, and I try to suppress
it most of the time."

While John McLaughlin bills the program as "completely spontaneous and unrehearsed," that may be a tad overstated. Christopher Hitchens, the British-born liberal columnist for *The Nation,*
once appeared on the show and later marveled at the level of stage
managing.

"There were four stages to be gone through," Hitchens says.
"First, an interview with the beaming McLaughlin himself. Second, a long talk with his 'researcher' about the order in which
questions and topics would be raised, and the order in which one
would be invited to comment on them. Third, a telephone call from
headquarters on the morning of the taping day . . . Finally,
a rehearsal along the same lines just before we moved into the
studio."

"Everything was all scripted," says Kara Swisher, who worked
as a ghostwriter for McLaughlin in 1986 and is now a *Washington
Post* reporter. "He would very elaborately organize the show on
these little blue index cards. He'd spend a lot of time preparing

things like 'on a scale of one to ten.' He'd think of his insults. He had everything planned in advance. He would sit in the office and practice." At tapings, "I always knew what was going to come next."

As for McLaughlin's political analysis, "None of it was based on original reporting. He would read *The Washington Post* and *New York Times* and some newsletters. He was talking about things he had no clue about. He would say, 'What should be my prediction this week?' "

The range of political ideas on the program generally runs the gamut from A to B. Since each question tends to be framed around the never-ending battles between the White House and Congress, the debate is circumscribed in a way that excludes unorthodox or unpopular notions.

"It's tremendously weighted toward the big-mouth right," Hitchens says. "You need to have shared assumptions for these quick-fire shows. John McLaughlin has got to be able to say, 'Is it in our interest to invade Venezuela?' If you don't think there's such a thing as 'our interest,' you're literally out of the action. I wouldn't accept the ground rules of that question. So who needs me?"

Richard Cohen, a liberal *Washington Post* columnist who appeared on *McLaughlin* once, has a similar view of such programs. "It's ridiculously simplified," he says. "The imperative is always to keep it moving. Two minutes goes by, and you have to ratchet it up. You can't develop a thought, because it's boring. It always has to be bang bang bang.

"Conservatism is rooted in the status quo: Are you for punishment or for coddling criminals? By the time you explain what 'coddling' is, one million people have clicked you off. The case for reform is always more complicated."

The scales are tilted in another way. Germond sees Barnes and Buchanan as "doctrinaire" conservatives who never ceased to defend Ronald Reagan, while he often feels compelled to admit that Bill Clinton has "fucked up royally."

"The truth is, I am probably as liberal as Buchanan is conservative," Germond says. "But I feel some restraint, except on a few issues, about taking far-out positions on the air that go beyond what I'm willing to take as a writer."

Even within the constricted parameters of Beltway politics, *McLaughlin*-type shows often display a groupthink mentality. This was painfully evident in January 1993, when Zoe Baird's nomination as attorney general was in trouble after she admitted hiring an illegal immigrant as a baby-sitter and failing to pay the proper Social Security taxes. The *McLaughlin* gang breezily dismissed this as a minor flap.

"It's not going to sink her nomination," Clift said.

"It's not a large enough ethical or moral lapse to warrant her being denied," Barnes said.

"If this is all there is to it, she'll be confirmed," said Germond.

"This is a misdemeanor, not a high crime," Kondracke agreed.

McLaughlin settled the matter: "Barring anything further, she will be confirmed. We'll be right back with spanking Saddam."

One week later, Baird withdrew her nomination after a firestorm of opposition ignited by radio talk shows. It turned out that radio hosts across the country were more in touch with popular sentiment on the Nannygate affair than the affluent Washington journalists who dominate the tube.

Week after week, the political-journalistic community forges a consensus that is faithfully trumpeted on the talk show circuit. In June 1994 McLaughlin, Germond, and Clift all agreed that Clinton would sign a health care reform bill into law by year's end. "There will be a health care bill enacted this year, and it will be built around something called a soft trigger," McLaughlin declared. Only Kondracke disagreed. Three months later, health reform was dead.

Under pressure to be clever and provocative, the panelists sometimes use uncorroborated information they would never dare publish without further checking. "You blurt out things, and they come out stronger than you wanted," Barnes admits. He once charged on the air that House Democratic Leader Richard Gephardt had been involved in spreading malicious rumors that Speaker Tom Foley was gay. "It was wrong, and I had to correct it and apologize the next week," Barnes says. "I had heard it from one person. That was very embarrassing."

Clift made a similar blunder when she criticized an *Elle* magazine reporter for overhearing a "rant in a restaurant" by Hillary Rodham Clinton and publishing it as if it were an interview. In fact, the First Lady had granted *Elle* an official White House interview;

Clift was repeating a garbled, secondhand account from another *Newsweek* reporter. She apologized the following week. "It is my fault that I didn't check it out," she says.

Snap judgments are also easy to regret. "I said some gratuitously nasty things about Joe Biden when he was running for president," Kondracke says. "I sent him a note and said I've been too nasty and I'm sorry."

The closing ritual of each show—predictions—underscores the fraudulent nature of showbiz journalism. No longer are reporters merely commenting on the news; now they must peer into the future. Most viewers instinctively know that a journalist predicting election results is only slightly more reliable than a coin flip. After all, both McLaughlin and Barnes predicted that George Bush would win a second term, while Germond flatly declared that Jesse Jackson would become mayor of Washington. But the highly specific forecasts on *McLaughlin,* delivered with utter certainty, suggest an insider's knowledge that is part of the illusion of talk television.

On one show in the mid-'80s, McLaughlin even predicted that Washington Mayor Marion Barry would be indicted—and this was several years before prosecutors finally nailed Barry on drug charges. When the others convinced him that this was injudicious, McLaughlin retaped his prediction.

Fortunately for the panelists, no one remembers their bum steers. During 1994, McLaughlin predicted that the trade embargo against Cuba would be lifted. Eleanor Clift, Jack Germond, and Clarence Page all predicted that Henry Foster would be confirmed as surgeon general. Tony Snow said that Jack Kemp would run for president in 1996. McLaughlin predicted that Edouard Balladur would be elected president of France. Clift predicted that Commerce Secretary Ron Brown would resign if a special prosecutor was named to investigate his finances. McLaughlin and Fred Barnes predicted that Congress would pass a balanced budget amendment to the Constitution. Page said that NAACP executive director Benjamin Chavis would hold on to his job despite allegations of misconduct. Larry Kudlow predicted a sudden, 350-point plunge in the stock market. Mort Zuckerman, the owner of *U.S. News* and the New York *Daily News,* predicted an "economic collapse" in Russia. Not one of those developments actually transpired.

"We're often wrong," Kondracke says, conceding the obvious.

Sometimes, of course, a panelist lucks out. In 1986 Jack Germond bumped into Charles Mathias, the veteran Maryland senator, and noticed that he seemed a bit down. On the program that week, Germond didn't have a prediction, so he boldly declared that Mathias wouldn't run for reelection. A few days later, to Germond's amazement, the senator announced his retirement.

"I didn't know shit," Germond says.

The world of Washington talk shows was a rather sedate place when John McLaughlin decided there was room for a faster, more confrontational program.

In the spring of 1982, Paul Duke was in his fifteenth year hosting *Washington Week in Review,* a relentlessly civilized reporters' roundtable on public television. Martin Agronsky was in his thirteenth year at *Agronsky & Company,* a slow-moving gabfest in which working reporters gently chewed over the news but rarely offered blunt opinions. NBC's *Meet the Press* was doing business roughly the way it had when Lawrence Spivak moved the show from radio to television in 1947: A panel of reporters sat stiffly questioning some newsmaker or other, usually a top government official. CBS's *Face the Nation,* launched in 1954, used much the same format. The only innovation was at ABC, where David Brinkley, recently hired away from NBC, was assembling a livelier group for a full hour of chitchat.

John McLaughlin was an obscure figure at the time. The son of a Providence furniture store owner, he had bounced around the edges of politics, religion, and the media. As a young man, McLaughlin entered a small Jesuit novitiate in New England, training for the priesthood. He later earned a master's in English and philosophy at Boston College and a doctorate in communications at Columbia University. As the editor of a Jesuit magazine, he began to travel and lecture on such subjects as "Intimacy Before Marriage: The Swedish Experience." He even did some television specials in New England, examining, among other things, the mass migration of women into the workforce.

In 1970 McLaughlin plunged into the midterm elections as a Republican. He ran against Rhode Island's Democratic senator,

John Pastore, as a critic of the Vietnam War, but was trounced by a 2-to-1 margin. As a consolation prize, he landed a low-level speech-writing job in the Nixon White House with the help of Pat Buchanan, one of Nixon's most loyal aides. The appointment drew fire from Robert Novak, the conservative commentator who shared a syndicated column with Rowland Evans. Novak assailed McLaughlin as a "peacenik Republican."

When the Watergate scandal enveloped the White House, McLaughlin got his big break. As author Eric Alterman has recounted, McLaughlin stepped into the breach when administration officials had trouble finding anyone to publicly defend the president. He began giving television interviews in his animated style, hailing Nixon as "the greatest moral leader of the last third of this century." He did *Donahue*. He did Tom Snyder. He did Dick Cavett. He also did a series of televised debates with Bob Novak, who was a regular commentator for Washington's Channel 5.

"It was really a food fight, shouting like children," Novak says. But one night, over drinks at a nearby Italian restaurant, McLaughlin confided that he wanted to launch a talk show "with more of a conservative twist" and asked if Novak would be a panelist. It was 1974, and Novak thought nothing would ever come of it.

The rest of the press, meanwhile, could not help but observe that McLaughlin did not exactly live a life of Jesuit deprivation, residing in the posh Watergate and earning more than $30,000 a year. McLaughlin's Jesuit superior, the Very Reverend Richard Cleary, summoned him for consultations and publicly questioned whether McLaughlin understood his vow of poverty. Still, after Nixon resigned, McLaughlin tried to hang on in the Ford White House.

Fred Barnes recalls interviewing McLaughlin during this period. "He was just like he is now, overbearing, outspoken," Barnes says. "He was still wearing his collar. You didn't have to ask a question to get an answer." The White House banished McLaughlin after Novak, based on a leak from Ford's staff, reported that "the notorious Father John McLaughlin" was still on the presidential payroll.

McLaughlin renounced his vow of celibacy and married a long-time friend, Ann Dore, who had managed his Senate race and later

worked for the Nixon administration. The newlyweds opened a
political consulting firm. But McLaughlin could not resist the limelight, and in 1980 he signed on with a Washington radio station,
WRC, as a talk show host.

"He was terrible," says Bob Novak, who appeared on the show.
"He didn't listen to the guest or the callers."

Fred Barnes also appeared as a guest. "McLaughlin kept trying
to put answers in my mouth about Jimmy Carter, who he was
always bashing," Barnes says. "He wanted me to give the worst
possible interpretation of Carter. McLaughlin did most of the talking. We waited the entire time for call-ins and nobody called." The
station fired McLaughlin after a year.

McLaughlin became the Washington editor of *National Review,*
an old-line conservative magazine, but he was determined to pursue
his vision of a new kind of television show. He didn't think much of
shows like *Meet the Press,* where he would appear eight times as a
panelist in the early '80s.

"The shows had become frightfully stilted," McLaughlin says.
"It was formalized, bloodless. There was no challenging, no interac-
tion, no disagreement, no alternate views. The journalists were artificially handcuffed. These same journalists would go out to a bar, a
saloon, and they'd have fantastic conversations where you'd get the
real skinny . . . These stuffed shirts who appear on these programs,
they don't engage the viewer. We don't all have to behave like Peter
Jennings."

McLaughlin wanted his show to have that saloon quality. He
got financial backing from a wealthy friend, Richard Moore, who
had also worked in the Nixon White House and became the show's
associate producer. For the pilot, he chose two newspaper columnists, Jack Germond and Bob Novak (who ironically had hastened
his departure from government service). Rounding out the ensemble were Judith Miller of *The New York Times* and Chuck Stone of
The Philadelphia Daily News, both of whom were quickly dropped.
McLaughlin replaced them with Pat Buchanan, his former White
House colleague, and Mort Kondracke of *The New Republic*. The
talk show culture would never be the same.

• • •

It was just over a year since Ronald Reagan had taken office, and the *McLaughlin* lineup mirrored the capital's new conservative mood: Five white men, three of them aggressively right-wing, two of them former Nixon aides. While journalists at other talk shows would dispassionately sift through the issues, McLaughlin generally supported Reagan in bombastic fashion and ridiculed the Democratic opposition. His wife, Ann Dore McLaughlin, was an assistant Treasury secretary in the Reagan administration; she would later become undersecretary of Interior and secretary of Labor.

"I try to present the issues without slant," McLaughlin would insist. "Sometimes I have crossed the line."

It was a measure of the new ethos in Washington that no one found it the slightest bit odd that McLaughlin could sound off in favor of Reagan policies week after week while his wife was a major player in the administration. McLaughlin visited Reagan in the private White House quarters, and the president once had dinner at the McLaughlin home. The lines between politics and punditry were becoming increasingly blurred.

At first, even the panelists were skeptical about the show's chances. "I thought this thing was never gonna go anywhere," Germond says.

"I remember thinking, This will last six weeks, this can't fly," Kondracke says. "It was so noisy. Novak was bullying his way around, McLaughlin was talking over all of us, nobody could get a word in. Someone said it was like inviting a couple over for dinner and watching them fight on your couch the whole night."

But there was a method to McLaughlin's maddening style. "There's a pressure cooker working," he says. "The intensity of the environment is such so that if people are hesitant to say something, they find themselves saying it anyway. My theory is people say under pressure for the most part what they really mean. In a confrontational situation, you'll get their gut. And I want their gut! And that's why people watch this show!

"Journalists almost always blurt," McLaughlin says, his ruddy face turning redder. "*Blurting is good! We want blurting!* It eliminates withholding and it eliminates slanting. The public wants it totally straight, and the journalists who provide this are esteemed more than the politician, who's got an angle. People *want* that! It's called intellectual honesty!'' He is shouting and slamming the table now. ''The panel may be biased to the viewer, but they're getting it straight, *bias and all!''*

The McLaughlin Group caught on, blurting and all, in large measure because of the larger-than-life personalities that filled the screen.

Bob Novak was known as the Prince of Darkness for his scowling visage and snarling style of debate. A native of Joliet, Illinois, Novak was a hardworking Capitol Hill reporter for *The Wall Street Journal* when he joined forces in 1963 with Rowland Evans, a patrician from Main Line Philadelphia. Their first column, about an alliance between Nelson Rockefeller and Barry Goldwater to thwart the presidential ambitions of George Romney, turned out to be wrong. The sobriquet ''Errors and No Facts'' soon stuck like tarpaper. But while their scoops sometimes seemed inflated or tinted by ideology, the column was almost always based on shoe-leather reporting.

The duo began as Rockefeller Republicans but soon lurched sharply to the right. They supported the Vietnam War and charged that some civil rights groups were being infiltrated by Communists. They issued dark warnings about the Soviet menace. They were sympathetic to Arab nations, at one point prompting a letter-writing campaign calling them anti-Israel (''the facile charge so often leveled against those who displease Israel's political friends in this country,'' they wrote).

A typically breathless lead, from 1971: ''Deepening dependence by Richard Nixon on his role as peace president to give him a second term in the White House is now causing well-concealed anxiety among some of his top-level foreign policy experts that he may unwittingly make himself a hostage in Moscow hands.''

Novak and his partner touted their favorite GOP congressman, Jack Kemp, and became cheerleaders for Kemp's tax-cutting nostrums. After Reagan was elected, the columnists often served as a bulletin board for right-wingers who found the Gipper too ''pragmatic.''

Germond recalls an evening at Novak's Delaware beach house in the late '70s. ''Bob and I were on the porch, looking out at the ocean with the remains of a half-gallon of wine, and he gave me a drunken lecture on supply-side economics. He's a master showman, but he believes all this stuff."

Evans and Novak grew into a cottage industry, with their own newsletters, CNN interview show, and off-the-record seminars with top officials, where guests were charged $350 a head. Novak became the public face of the column because he did more television. An engaging man in private, he came across on the tube as a merciless pit bull. One television critic described him as "looking as warm and friendly as a tax collector right out of Dickens."

Jack Germond, a grizzled teddy bear of a man, had been pounding the pavement since joining the Jefferson City, Missouri, *Post-Tribune* in 1951. At Gannett Newspapers, he slowly climbed the journalistic ladder—Rochester, Albany, New York City—before arriving in Washington at the start of the Kennedy administration. He flew around the country with presidential contenders—Barry Goldwater, Nelson Rockefeller, Hubert Humphrey, Bobby Kennedy—in the days when reporter and candidate could still have a Scotch-soaked chat in the front cabin.

A hard-drinking, chain-smoking reporter who could down prodigious amounts of food, Germond was the inside baseball man, the veteran scout who would spot the minor-league phenom with the great arm. He got to know Bill Clinton even before he ran for Arkansas attorney general in 1976. Younger reporters were in awe of Germond's stamina. Once, after a late-night drinking bout, recalls Baltimore *Sun* columnist Roger Simon, "I woke up at two the next afternoon with a tremendous hangover. Jack was up at seven-thirty visiting county chairmen."

Germond occasionally blew a call. He wrongly predicted that Ronald Reagan had no chance to win the 1976 North Carolina primary, but willingly ate crow in a follow-up column. "I got more response to that column than anything I ever wrote because you tell the reader, 'I fucked up. I'm not infallible,' " he says. It was a lesson he would carry to the world of television.

Some younger reporters criticized Germond for being too cozy with the pols, and there were obvious trade-offs. After a dinner party with Reagan in the '70s, Germond declined to report that Reagan was spreading some damaging gossip about Ted Kennedy.

"I didn't take a cheap shot, and I had some access," Germond says. "I could see him when he was president."

After joining *The Washington Star* in the early 1970s, Germond teamed up with old buddy Jules Witcover to write a political column, which they took to the Baltimore *Sun* when the *Star* folded in 1981. Germond became a regular pundit for the *Today* show and began to overshadow Witcover for the same reason that Novak had eclipsed Evans. "You could write your damn fingers off for twenty-five years and never have the same reach as television," Germond says. "Television is just a monster."

Pat Buchanan had never been one to duck a fight, not since his Irish father had taught him to box in the basement of their northwest Washington home. Just before his twenty-first birthday, Buchanan was kicked out of Georgetown University for a year after getting into a brawl with police officers who gave him a speeding ticket. "I was ahead on points until they brought out the sticks," says Buchanan, who pleaded guilty to assault.

After graduating from the Columbia School of Journalism, where his credits included "sucker punching" a fellow student in front of the dean, Buchanan interviewed for a job at *The Washington Post* but got into "a foolish argument with the *Post* editor over their biased coverage of everybody from Joe McCarthy to Richard Nixon," he says.

Buchanan soon found his conservative voice. As an editorial writer for the St. Louis *Globe-Democrat,* he penned attacks on Martin Luther King, Jr., with unsigned material, handed him by the publisher, that Buchanan believes was supplied by the FBI. He left journalism to work for former vice president Nixon in 1965. After Nixon won the White House, Buchanan became a presidential speechwriter, scripting Vice President Agnew's attacks on the liberal media as "a small and unelected elite."

Buchanan's hostility toward the press was unrelenting. In a November 10, 1972, memo after Nixon's reelection, Buchanan called for an "unapologetic" attack on the networks, including "a strategy against their monopoly control, and a thought-out program for cleaning out public television of that clique of Nixon-haters."

Like McLaughlin, Buchanan defended Nixon to the bitter end during Watergate. His White House tenure propelled him to new prominence as a columnist and radio and TV commentator. Buchanan always had a knack for the polarizing phrase. He described AIDS as "nature . . . exacting an awful retribution" on homosexuals, whom he called "sodomites." He dismissed feminists as "the Butch Brigade." He assailed the Supreme Court ruling banning prayer in public schools as part of "the systematic de-Christianization of America."

Rounding out the group was Mort Kondracke, another Joliet native who had known Novak since high school. Kondracke spent fourteen years as a *Chicago Sun-Times* reporter, a traditional liberal who warranted a spot on the Nixon enemies list. But he turned more conservative after becoming executive editor of *The New Republic* in 1977.

A few years later, Kondracke found himself paired with McLaughlin in a daily left-right faceoff on WRC radio. They got along well as they taped the commentaries over and over to make them exactly two minutes long. But Kondracke increasingly seemed miscast as a liberal spokesman, and by 1984 he would announce in a column that he was considering voting for Ronald Reagan.

Kondracke knew his role on the television show was to serve as a foil for McLaughlin, who called him "Mor-TAHN" and made fun of his hair. "McLaughlin used to give me little quizzes about things to make me look like a jerk," he says.

McLaughlin had a different take: "People write to me, 'Why do you pick on Mort?' And I write back: 'Because he loves to be the victim.' Then Millie, his wife, gets after him, and he fights back."

It was just a local show at first on Washington's WRC, but the program soon became part of the Beltway culture, a must-see for political insiders. It was offered free to PBS stations, and three hundred of them would pick it up, along with network affiliates in New York, Boston, and Los Angeles. President Reagan even dropped by the show's third-anniversary party, reading a speech written by Buchanan. Reagan declared the show "the most tasteful programming alternative to professional wrestling."

With Novak as the lead attack dog, the rhetorical combat could be brutal. When Christopher Hitchens was on the show, Novak referred to Cuban drug runners as Hitchens's "friends."

On another occasion, Novak demanded that Eleanor Clift apologize for saying that Oliver North should not have worn his military medals when testifying before Congress. Novak said she had impugned North's military career.

"Novak used to accuse me of being a Zionist agent," Kondracke says. "It was nasty kind of stuff. Novak, when he gets in a tizzy, exudes an odor. It's like a musk ox. It was physically intimidating. When he's in his ideological zone, he becomes the troll under the bridge of American journalism. I'm pro-Israeli, but I'm not even Jewish! I used to leave the show every week with my stomach in knots."

"I went a little over the line with Mort," Novak admits.

For all the locker-room insults, McLaughlin would lecture the panelists: "This is a fundamentally serious program, and we have to be accepted as serious commentators. We can rag each other, we can exhibit what we hope will be regarded as wit, but let's not kid ourselves that we are comedians. We are journalists."

There were constant arguments off the set as well. Germond and Novak would spar with McLaughlin over which topics to pick for the show. "You couldn't argue with him because he was so fucking sure he was right about everything," Germond says. "He is the most arrogant son of a bitch in the world."

The sitcom needed recasting when Buchanan left to become Reagan's communications director in 1985. McLaughlin refused to fill "the Buchanan chair," expecting him back eventually, and began using Fred Barnes and Eleanor Clift on a rotating basis. The group finally had a woman.

Clift, who grew up in the back of her father's deli in Queens, had started at *Newsweek* in 1963 as "a rather mousy secretary," as her onetime boss put it. She eventually worked her way up to reporter and was sent to the Atlanta bureau, where she was assigned to long-shot candidate Jimmy Carter. When Carter won the presidency, Clift followed him to the White House. She started doing shows like *Washington Week in Review* in the early '80s, usually to talk about women's issues. "I found it absolutely terrifying initially," Clift says. She even felt compelled to take a public speaking course.

When McLaughlin first called Clift for a tryout, he peppered her with a series of questions. When she hesitated, "he sort of barked at me: 'If you want to be on this show, you better get some opinions.' "

As the token blonde, Clift felt as if she had invaded an all-male sanctuary. She had to learn to raise her voice when the others tried to talk over her. But she developed a strong following; Clarence Page says his wife roots louder for Eleanor Clift than she does for him. "Most people get a kick out of the fact that a woman can hold her own," Clift says.

Fred Barnes had grown up across the river in Arlington, the son of a military man so conservative he wouldn't allow *The Washington Post* in the house. After a stint at the Charleston *News and Courier* in South Carolina, Barnes returned home, taking graduate courses and bagging groceries at Safeway. In 1967 he wangled a job as a dictationist at *The Washington Star,* typing stories phoned in by reporters in the field. As the only man on the dictation bank, Barnes was soon promoted to reporter. "I'm sure sex discrimination had something to do with it," he says.

Barnes caught the eye of Jack Germond, the paper's assistant managing editor, who elevated him to the White House beat in 1974. While Barnes had been a liberal in college, marching against the Vietnam War, he embraced conservatism during the '70s and later became a committed Christian.

Barnes jumped to the Baltimore *Sun,* and in 1984 he was one of the panelists in the first televised debate between Ronald Reagan and Walter Mondale. That moment in the spotlight led to a phone call from McLaughlin, whose show Barnes had never seen. "I waited to be called on and didn't say much," he says. That changed after Barnes became *The New Republic*'s White House correspondent, putting him in what he calls "the opinion business." (He later became executive editor of *The Standard,* a new conservative magazine.)

When Buchanan left the Reagan White House in 1987 and rejoined the show, its popularity was still on the rise. But McLaughlin's high-handed style was causing all kinds of off-camera problems. He complained that Bob Novak was talking too much, even ordered his staff to conduct word counts of each transcript, which confirmed that Novak was indeed the most verbose panelist.

"He became increasingly authoritarian and abusive," Novak

says. "Things really deteriorated . . . I think he always considered me a threat. Some people would call it Novak's show, which drove him nuts."

The tensions erupted on one program in early 1988 when Novak said it looked like McLaughlin was positioning himself for a Dukakis administration. "We go to a commercial and McLaughlin goes ape-shit," Germond recalls. "He starts screaming at Novak. McLaughlin was out of his head. Novak was pissed. I thought they were gonna go at it."

Novak calmed down and finished the show, but when McLaughlin tried to bump him from the following week's show, Novak announced he was quitting. He later backed off, but when he tried to talk things over with McLaughlin on a trip to Dallas—they were staying in the same hotel for a live appearance by the group—he was told McLaughlin was too busy to see him. Novak finally quit the program in the fall of 1988 and formed his own show, *The Capital Gang.* He wrote McLaughlin that their relationship had "proved mutually beneficial for all of its rocky aspects."

Novak wasn't McLaughlin's only target. Michael Kinsley, then the editor of *The New Republic,* appeared on the show more than twenty times. But when the magazine was preparing an article on how McLaughlin's columns for *National Review* were ghostwritten, he sent word that Kinsley could forget about future appearances if the article ran. Kinsley published it anyway and was banished from the show. (McLaughlin says he has no recollection of such a ban.)

That same year, McLaughlin's former executive assistant, Linda Dean, sued him for sexual harassment and sex discrimination, saying she had been fired for complaining about his behavior toward herself and other women in the office. McLaughlin denied the charges and settled the $4-million suit out of court. He and his wife Ann were divorced a couple of years later.

McLaughlin "had all these young women working like dogs for him" and often "screamed and yelled" at them, Kara Swisher says. She calls him "incredibly intelligent," but adds; "He was really in love with the idea that he was powerful, sort of a caricature of Washington. He would throw parties and do these elaborate guest lists." When she tried to get his attention before one such soiree, he snapped: "Don't you realize the collective power of the people that are going to be in that room?"

Another source of friction was McLaughlin's method of dividing up the cash for the group's live appearances before paying audiences, which were far more lucrative than the $600 fee for each program. The panelists were getting $2,500 apiece to stage the mock debates, but Germond became infuriated after learning that McLaughlin was keeping $7,000 to $8,000 for himself. Germond has been boycotting the road shows ever since.

"He is an impossible person to deal with," Germond says. "But he needs me, and I need the show."

As the program moved into the '90s, it lost the hard edge of the Novak days and sometimes dissolved into self-parody. But the pressure to play a role by taking predictable positions remained unabated. Sorting through issues on a case-by-case basis is increasingly seen as bad television.

"There was a time when I felt like a wimp for being a moderate," says Kondracke, now executive editor of *Roll Call,* a Capitol Hill newspaper. "One week you say something nice about Clinton and the next week you say something nasty about Clinton, and the Clintonites don't know whether you're on their side or not."

Still, *The McLaughlin Group* has brought its members a measure of fame that none could have imagined a decade ago. They have played themselves in the hit movie *Dave.* They have made a commercial for NBA basketball. On one particularly lavish boondoggle, Pepsi flew the group on a private plane to Acapulco, where they stayed in a villa before staging a debate.

McLaughlin has reaped the benefits of celebrity. He acquired the multimillion-dollar home in northwest Washington and the Florida condo and was ferried around town by limousine. He appeared on *Saturday Night Live, Cheers, Alf,* and David Letterman. He launched a separate interview show, *John McLaughlin's One on One,* and for a time hosted a third show on CNBC. And he insists it hasn't gone to his head. "If you start believing you are your persona, you're in deep shit," he says. "It's part of the game."

John McLaughlin has a bit of a dilemma.

"Do you think I should quote from my own testimony on Cuba?" he asks his staff.

"Why not?" says writer Ed Korenman.

McLaughlin and three young assistants are standing in a cluttered hallway outside Studio A in the NBC Washington bureau, where the show is taped each week. The host looks sharp in a navy suit and blue striped shirt, despite the fact that he was at the Capitol at six that morning for a *One on One* interview with Newt Gingrich.

McLaughlin had testified before a House subcommittee a year earlier that the U.S. trade embargo against Cuba should be lifted. It is one of his pet issues. Now he is preparing a segment on that very subject for *The McLaughlin Group,* which will give him a chance to sound off again. And he is wondering whether to cite his favorite expert: himself.

It is late Thursday afternoon. The regular Friday taping is tomorrow. McLaughlin is taping an extra show today to air the following weekend so he can get away over Easter vacation. He has never missed a show in fourteen years, and he does it by taping these "evergreen" programs before leaving town. Occasionally he has to junk the show and fly back for retaping if major news breaks out.

"What are the issues today?" McLaughlin asks. He is a bit confused because he has spent the morning working on tomorrow's show. He looks over his "guidance cards," as he calls his oversized index cards, and underlines key phrases with an orange marker.

McLaughlin slips into the control room and practices reading his introductions from a monitor. He has already recorded the taped setups at the office.

"We'll be right back with Killing the IRS," his voice booms from a speaker.

"You think if I ask Jack, 'By the way, what's the IRS doing about your track earnings,' he'll be pissed?" McLaughlin asks.

"Go for it," a staffer says.

Three of the panelists have assembled in the green room, as all television waiting rooms, regardless of color, are called. Jack Germond is reading the Baltimore *Sun* sports section. Mort Kondracke is buried in *The Wall Street Journal.* Fred Barnes is looking over a scholarly article on South Africa, one of the afternoon's topics.

They seem nonchalant and slightly bored, as if they are waiting for the spin cycle to end at the local Laundromat. They were faxed the program topics and exit questions yesterday but haven't done much preparation. Kondracke read some clips on Cuba and called an expert, whom he didn't reach. Barnes read a political newsletter and called Jeff Bell, a conservative Republican strategist, and Ed Gillespie, the spokesman for House Republican Leader Dick Armey. Germond finished writing his column, on the tax-cut battle in Congress, and went to the dentist. He doesn't have a prediction yet.

Barnes says he hasn't studied one of the issues, on a court ruling involving gays in the military. "I'll fake it," he says.

"If you can't fake it on this show, where the hell can you fake it?" Germond says.

The fourth panelist, Mort Zuckerman, is flying down from New York on his private jet, but the plane is delayed. Germond starts on the *New York Times* crossword puzzle.

Zuckerman finally arrives. After a quick trip to the makeup room, the panelists file into Studio A. Germond asks Zuckerman if the *News* has hired a racing handicapper yet. They take their places on the plush lavender swivel chairs. An assistant fetches McLaughlin some coffee.

The gang starts chatting about ethnic slurs by politicians. McLaughlin says the Irish are still stereotyped. "Booze and brawling—that's the way we're portrayed every Saint Patrick's Day," he says.

As the music comes up and McLaughlin's taped introduction begins, the five men continue to shoot the breeze, as if they were sitting around the kitchen table and not under the klieg lights. The taping is suddenly halted. The control room is having a problem with the audio. A second attempt yields another false start.

Zuckerman complains that the *New York Post* has been attacking him because the *News* has been running critical stories about the business dealings of Rupert Murdoch, the *Post*'s owner.

"It's great publicity," McLaughlin says.

As the technicians scramble, McLaughlin returns to the question of ethnicity. "Here's a joke," he says. "There's a new black owner of Toys R Us. What does he call it? We Be Toys. Is that denigrating?" The other panelists groan.

"You don't think blacks will laugh at that?" McLaughlin demands. "What is wrong with black dialect?"

"Try it on the air," Kondracke says.

The taping begins again. This time the on-set chatter goes on a beat too long; McLaughlin's mike picks up Kondracke's voice just as McLaughlin begins to speak.

The chatting resumes. Germond says he is writing his memoirs. "What are you getting?" McLaughlin says. "A hundred? Two fifty?" Germond mumbles a figure in between.

"I have five book offers on my desk," McLaughlin says.

The delay drags on. Zuckerman recalls a recent dinner party for Gingrich at Henry Kissinger's Manhattan apartment. Katharine Graham, owner of *The Washington Post,* was there. So was Larry Tisch, the chairman of CBS, Bob Wright, the president of NBC, Tom Murphy, the president of Capital Cities/ABC, and CNN President Tom Johnson. "I thought Gingrich was fabulous. Absolutely fabulous," Zuckerman says.

"I didn't get an invitation," McLaughlin sniffs.

Finally the taping is under way. Issue one is South Africa under Nelson Mandela. McLaughlin calls on Freddy "Easter Bunny Beadle" Barnes. There is rare unanimity on the set; everyone agrees that Mandela is a political giant. "A majestic figure," says Kondracke. "Unique moral stature," says Zuckerman. McLaughlin, for no apparent reason, notes that the most popular talk show host in the country is an Afrikaaner cross-dresser.

The floor director, Randy Stafford, wearing a red kerchief on his head, holds up a sign that says "30 SECONDS." McLaughlin uses the time cards because he doesn't like anyone talking in his ear. Stafford holds up a sign that says "15 SECONDS." He holds up the "commercial" sign. Then he switches to "1 MINUTE OVER."

McLaughlin ignores him. "Exit question: On a probability scale of zero to ten—zero meaning zero probability, ten meaning metaphysical certitude—what's the probability that the peaceful progress now being made in South Africa will continue?" Five, says Barnes. They agree that all bets are off once Mandela is gone. "We'll be right back with 'Killing the IRS,' " McLaughlin says.

A short break. The gang is discussing exercise equipment. "I'm at my highest weight ever, 218," McLaughlin confides. "I've lost my willpower."

Issue two is what McLaughlin, with a bit of hyperbole, calls "a rapidly expanding grassroots coalition" launching "a populist crusade to abolish the *loathed* federal income tax," which would be replaced by a flat tax or a national sales tax. McLaughlin recently read a *National Journal* article on the subject and obviously thinks it is a great idea. He likes to get out in front of issues before the tidal wave of publicity hits.

No namby-pamby balance here; McLaughlin blatantly stacks the deck in his intro. A graphic lists only the benefits of a national sales tax. But when he puts the question to Germond—"What do you think of this *revolutionary* idea?"—the columnist lets loose with a belly laugh.

"I think you shouldn't have resurrected it, John," Germond guffaws. "There've always been a few nuts around who thought we were gonna abolish the federal income tax."

McLaughlin retorts that Gingrich, "in a brilliant interview conducted by me," said he would consider a flat tax. At another point he says: "Bear in mind, seven billion dollars to underwrite that IRS bureaucracy!"

McLaughlin winds up the segment by asking whether the IRS will actually be abolished. When three of the four panelists say no way, he overrules them in a rising voice. "The answer is, we will see the elimination of the income tax *in our lifetime!*"

Issue three: Cuba. "The argument has taken hold that the best way to get rid of Fidel Castro is to lift the embargo," McLaughlin says. This, as it happens, is precisely the argument McLaughlin had made before Congress, although it shows few signs of "taking hold" with the Clinton administration.

Fred Barnes insists that Castro is "on the edge of being toppled." McLaughlin dismisses this as a "dream" and urges Barnes to "wake up . . . Are your libertarian instincts not outraged by the fact that you as an American citizen are prohibited from traveling to Cuba?"

"My libertarian instincts are outraged by the fact that I cannot get a Havana cigar," Germond says. "Legally."

Time is running short. Stafford holds up a sign that says "SEN-ATE." He waves it urgently. McLaughlin is supposed to switch to the fourth topic, the Republicans' prospects for increasing their Senate majority in 1996. But he keeps on going. Fred Barnes says he has changed his mind and now opposes any easing of trade sanctions against Cuba. McLaughlin argues with him. Michele Remillard, the associate producer, bursts from the control room and gives McLaughlin the windup sign. But he has already decided there is not enough time left to talk about the Senate. He plows ahead on Cuba.

"Exit question: When will the Cuban embargo be lifted?" Brushing aside the panelists' views, McLaughlin supplies the answer: "In the first term of Bob Dole or whoever the Republican is who's elected president next time, in the second year. We'll be right back with predictions."

The cameras are off. "We blew the Senate," Kondracke says.

"We can do the Senate till we're blue," says McLaughlin, unperturbed. He turns to Barnes and lectures him like a wayward student about Cuba. "I'm surprised at you," he says. "You really are a flip-flopper."

Stafford says they have seventeen seconds apiece for predictions. "Jeez, an eternity," Kondracke says.

Barnes predicts the Senate will strengthen a House bill on individual property rights. He got the information from an aide to Representative John Boehner, chairman of the House Republican Conference, while researching a speech last week to the American Petroleum Institute in San Francisco. Zuckerman predicts that Dan Quayle will run for governor of Indiana. Germond predicts that Clinton will not veto the congressional tax-cut bill. This is just his gut feeling; if he knew it for sure, Germond says, he would write about it. Kondracke predicts that Senator Phil Gramm will attach a balanced-budget measure to federal debt legislation over the summer. Kondracke has a pretty good source—Gramm himself—and has already written the story in his *Roll Call* column. McLaughlin makes a vague prediction about worsening Anglo-American relations.

The show appears to be over, but there is still the PBS segment. McLaughlin adds an extra topic each week for PBS stations, which have extra time to fill because they don't run commercials. The group had planned to do gays in the military.

"Let's do the Senate," Barnes says. "We've done the gays so many times." McLaughlin decides to switch to the Senate segment that was squeezed out of the main show.

The break drags on. "Mort, how many millions have you paid in income tax this year?" McLaughlin asks.

"A lot," Zuckerman says.

Stafford announces that there is a minute and thirty-five seconds remaining after the taped intro.

"What? That's all?" McLaughlin says, seemingly oblivious to the fact that he ignored all the earlier time cues.

McLaughlin throws the Senate question to Kondracke, but not before needling him. "Your hair looks good," he says. "You went to a barber. Who's cutting your hair now—Kato Kaelin's hairdresser?" They race through the final minute. Germond casually suggests that Senator Bill Bradley may not seek reelection. He had said the same thing on a CNN talk show weeks earlier, but it is news to McLaughlin.

"Bradley? Not run?" McLaughlin says in amazement. But there is no time for follow-up. The show is over. McLaughlin apologizes to Zuckerman for not having time to call on him in the final segment.

Now the group stages a thirty-second mini-debate to advertise the show. Will the country adopt a flat tax? Everyone gives a four- or five-second answer. "We've got to get rid of the horrors of the income tax," McLaughlin declares.

The taping is over. Germond is less than pleased with the result. "It was terrible because we were talking about bullshit," he says. "We all agreed that Nelson Mandela is a hell of a guy."

The panelists unhook their mikes and amble toward the exit. McLaughlin still has to do a series of promos for this show and for a future program, which will lead off with affirmative action. Each ad must be progressively shorter for the convenience of local stations. It is a ritual that seems to reduce the talk show culture to its barest essence.

The thirty-second spot: "Hi, I'm John McLaughlin. The so-called white males are angrier than ever. Affirmative action, they say, is taking jobs away from them . . ."

The ten-second spot: "Hi, I'm John McLaughlin. Affirmative aciton will be a hot-button issue in 1996."

The four-second spot: "Is affirmative action dead? Sunday at eleven-thirty."

• • •

By transforming news into entertainment, John McLaughlin has managed to draw people who would never dream of watching *Face the Nation* or *Washington Week in Review*. His supporting cast members have become media stars. Even the rotund Germond is a cult figure of sorts, pronounced the sexiest man alive by actress Dana Delany.

"I'm amazed by the number of lower-income black people who watch the show," Germond says. "I go to a parking garage in New Orleans and the black kid who takes my car knows me from the PBS station down there. It's scary that it has that kind of impact."

"It has an incredible viewership," Kondracke says. "Nigerian cabdrivers all watch the show."

But fame, of course, has its price. *McLaughlin* may have turned Eleanor Clift into the most recognizable woman pundit on television, but that has made her a highly visible target. "Shut up, you bitch," one letter writer told Clift. "You should be home barefoot and pregnant," another offered. A third accused her of "testosterone envy."

Clift has become a lightning rod because of her steadfast defense of Bill and Hillary Clinton. Ever since she predicted in early 1992 that Clinton would win the Democratic presidential nomination, she has been seen as a Clinton champion, defending him against the harsh onslaught of the *McLaughlin* conservatives. Clift insists that perception is unfair, but if the show is a sitcom, as she describes it, she clearly has been cast in the pro-Clinton role.

"The reporter who is perceived as being soft is immediately de-legitimized, portrayed as being in the tank," Clift says. "It's not comfortable to be singled out as someone who is somehow a cheerleader. That's the last thing any reporter wants to be considered. What I've said holds up under the banner of fair analysis . . . I don't want to be seen as someone who will defend the Clintons at any length."

Given the boundaries of *McLaughlin*-style debate, however, that is precisely how she is seen. Fred Barnes, who frequently baits Clift on the show, recognizes the box his friend has placed herself in. "It's how Eleanor defines her role," he says. "Whenever anybody

criticizes Clinton, she thinks she has to come and defend him."
When Clift interviewed Hillary Clinton about Whitewater, she
sounded so sympathetic ("Washington likes to burn a witch every
three months," Clift told the First Lady) that McLaughlin mocked
her questions on the air.

Fairly or unfairly, Clift's reputation followed her wherever she
went. When she did a radio talk show, one caller said: "You almost
have a love affair with the Clinton administration." Said another:
"I wonder why Eleanor is such an apologist for Clinton, no matter
how big a fool he makes of himself."

Clift's role on *McLaughlin* soon eroded her standing at *Newsweek*. The magazine had assigned her to the White House after
Clinton's election, but many staffers complained that she was putting *Newsweek* in a compromising position by staunchly defending
the man she was supposed to be covering. Her editors suggested
that she relinquish the beat, but she resisted. In the summer of
1994, after months of delicate negotiations, Clift gave up the prestigious post and became a part-time contributing editor. Television
had made her larger than a mere newsmagazine. Punditry, and all
its attendant rewards, had become more important than the reporting that had made Clift a star.

Eleanor Clift is hardly alone in drawing detractors. Even the
gruff, likable Germond gets his share of abuse from letter writers.

"I have some regulars who just hate my guts, and they all start
out 'Dear Fatso,' " he says. Germond blames the transitory nature
of modern society in which television is the only common link.

"There are huge numbers of people who have no other outlet
for their views," he says. "They can't go to the Rotary Club every
Tuesday and hold forth. They turn on the TV and here's this fat
son of a bitch shooting off his mouth every week. They get mad at
you for it, and I don't blame them."

All right, let's get out. Exit question: Is *The McLaughlin Group*
bad for political discourse? On a scale of zero to ten—zero being
slime, the absolute bottom of the television barrel, and ten being an
awe-inspiring, highly educational and socially redeeming experience—where does the show rate?

As a sitcom, *Roseanne* has nothing to worry about, but let's be
generous and give it a nine. For the quality of its political ideas, a

five at best. As a journalistic forum . . . well, it's not journalism. If people wanted high-minded journalism, more of them would watch Jim Lehrer. In a talk show nation, as John McLaughlin understands all too well, viewers want to be entertained. On that score, he has delivered in a way that has changed the very nature of talking-head television. The cardinal sin in the Age of McLaughlin is to be boring.

CHAPTER THREE

DAYTIME DYSFUNCTION

Phil Donahue is in his element: Outrageous, self-righteous, and smack in the center of a publicity storm.

He is devoting his program to his latest "cause": A demand that he be allowed to televise the execution of one David Lawson, a convicted murderer from North Carolina who wants to leave this world in a blaze of talk show glory. It is the summer of 1994, and Donahue has filed suit for access to Lawson's execution by gas or injection, which the white-maned host would turn into a TV spectacle. It would be a new wrinkle for a genre that has arguably seen it all: death as entertainment.

Donahue, not surprisingly, has wrapped this revolting idea in the moralistic garb of the people's right to know, touting the alleged deterrent effect on future bad guys. "The death penalty . . . is most certainly the business of the people and should be subjected to the full scrutiny of the press, including television," he tells his audience. With full-throated indignation, Donahue denies that he is interested in sensationalism, in milking the event for mere ratings. But he is clearly reveling in the attention surrounding his latest crusade. He goes on *Crossfire* to argue that state-sanctioned killing belongs on television—more particularly, on *Donahue*.

"Phil, come on," Pat Buchanan says. "What's the problem here, the lesbian midgets not pulling anymore?"

The episode is too much even for some of Donahue's talk show brethren. "The height of tackiness," says Geraldo Rivera. "The most disgusting idea I've ever heard," says Sally Jessy Raphael. The Raleigh *News & Observer* dismisses Donahue's proposal as "old-fashioned, bring-'em-in-the-tent showbiz . . . The problem with Phil is, one minute he's hosting strippers, the next minute he's hosting presidential candidates, knitting that brow and calling himself a journalist." The courts reject the Donahue lawsuit.

In the beginning, before Oprah, Sally, Geraldo, Joan, Maury, Jenny, Ricki, Rolonda, Leeza, and Montel, there was Phil. Phil wearing a skirt for a show on cross-dressing. Phil climbing into a casket to interview an undertaker. Phil milking a goat. Phil in a gorilla costume. Phil boxing and wrestling and belly dancing. Phil tossing condoms to the crowd. Phil bouncing around the stage, chatting up transvestites and incest victims, prostitutes and movie stars, nudists and neo-Nazis and nymphomaniacs.

For nearly thirty years, Donahue has explored the frontiers of bad taste on television. Yet it would be a mistake to dismiss him as a mere showman. He has periodically grappled with serious issues, from the Persian Gulf War to the Whitewater affair to the GATT trade agreement. More broadly, he has repeatedly touched a nerve in exploring matters of sexual mores, homosexuality, and personal relationships—nerves so raw that they were long considered taboo in the respectable press. The emergence of a spate of younger, sassier, bolder imitators in recent years suggests that the onetime altar boy from Cleveland knew his audience.

"Years ago, when we were doing stories on date rape, artificial insemination, homophobia, sex bias crimes, and spousal abuse, serious news programs wouldn't touch them," he says. "Now they're doing these kinds of stories routinely, and they're giving them quite a bit of time, too."

Donahue is quick to dismiss what he calls "the self-anointed and -appointed wooden soldiers and talking-head mainstream journalists who continue to believe they are morally superior to everyone and sneer at Louise-from-Omaha."

Donahue always believed in Louise. Believed that those in the studio audience and the callers at home—ridiculed by some critics as a bunch of know-nothing housewives—had something to say, and that he could give them the platform to say it. The whole array of interactive media in the '90s—from talk radio to C-SPAN—

stems from the example that Donahue set as he went racing up the aisles, wireless mike in hand, to put a face on the faceless masses by giving them access to a nationwide audience.

If it wasn't for all those male strippers, Donahue might even command a little respect from the media establishment.

In truth, much of the Donahue genre these days is unadulterated trash, designed to tease and titillate, to air all kinds of dirty laundry that most of us could do without ever seeing or sniffing. But some of it fills a vacuum left by the elite press, which in any event has been following Phil and his many offspring into the great tabloid swamp populated by the likes of Heidi Fleiss and Lorena Bobbit and Tonya Harding and Paula Jones.

Some of Donahue's less edifying shows have included "My Stepchild Is Ruining My Marriage," "Promiscuous Teens and Their Moms," and that eternal classic, "Incredible Love Triangle: Man Marries His Mother-in-Law." One program explored the psyche of Sabrina Aset, who claimed to have had sex with 2,686 men. Some of the highest-rated shows in recent years include an interview with Joey Buttafuoco, "Women Who Married Their Child's Friend," and "Women Wins Eight-Year Battle to Care for Disabled Lesbian Lover." And then there was the transvestite shopping spree, the highest-rated *Donahue* of 1991.

Phil's got plenty of company these days.

Oprah Winfrey has done subservient women, paternity fights, satanic abuse, infidelity, man-hunting, threesomes, wife beaters, shopaholics, and mothers and fathers who kill. Sally Jessy Raphael has done "Homewrecking Babysitters," "Necrophilia," "Women Who Catch Their Husbands in Topless Bars," "When Your Best Friend Is Sleeping with Your Father," "Sisters Who Strip," "Big-Breasted Women," and "Married to a Mama's Boy." Jerry Springer has done men who live as women, a woman who says she and Elvis are from Venus, and once had two women smear themselves with baby oil and go at it ("Jell-O Wrestling: Is It Sexist?"). Rolonda has hosted an ex-hooker named Kathy and her hooker daughter ("I don't look at her as a prostitute. It's just her job," Kathy says). Ricki Lake, the twentysomething phenom, has done "I Have the Hots for a Coworker" and "Mom, When My Boyfriend Gets Out of Jail I'm Taking Him Back." Maury Povich has done women who leave husbands for other women, student-teacher affairs, and a woman who says she was gang-raped at fourteen. Geraldo Rivera has done transsexuals and their families, teen prostitutes, mud-wrestling women, swinging sexual suicide, power dykes, girls impregnated by their stepfathers, serial killers, kids who kill, and battered women who kill.

A single edition of *Oprah,* beginning with Nicole Brown Simpson's endlessly replayed 911 call to police, featured the following guests: Lynnie (SAW FATHER SHOOT MOTHER), Sylvia (FATHER KILLED MOTHER), Steve (USED TO ABUSE WIFE), Elizabeth (FATHER ABUSED HER MOTHER), Janice (FATHER STABBED MOTHER TO DEATH), Brad (AGE 6, MOTHER BEATEN BY STEP-FATHER), Josh (AGE 11, MOTHER KILLED BY STEPFATHER). It's as if a lone tragedy will no longer hold the audience's attention. Producers now layer pathetic guests, one atop the other, in six-minute segments.

This proliferation of talk show smut has upped the ante for attracting a daytime audience. "You can no longer just put prostitutes on," says Ed Glavin, a *Donahue* producer. "It has to be prostitutes who are sex addicts."

"It's not enough to have a husband and the wife he cheated on," says Laura Wiley, a *Geraldo* producer. "You've got to have the mistress, maybe her boyfriend. You take things as far as they'll go."

Sally Jessy Raphael defends the seamy stuff with an age-old argument. "Nobody wants to watch anything that's smarmy or tabloid or silly or unseemly—except the audience," Raphael says. Still, she says, "Am I ashamed of some of the shows? Yeah . . . I do not like to do male strippers . . . I get embarrassed by some of those things." No less a figure than Hillary Rodham Clinton has assailed the increasingly revolting genre. "I think that the talk shows, combined with the violence, is in effect changing the way that children feel about themselves in some very damaging ways," she says. The First Lady apparently saw no irony in making this declaration on *Oprah*.

Even as these programs have taken wretched excess to new heights, a few hosts have vowed to cut back on the sleaze. "I'm not going to be able to spend from now until the year 2000 talking to people about their dysfunction," Oprah Winfrey says. "I won't have people yelling and screaming and trying to humiliate one another." Winfrey now says she wants "to use the show for raising consciousness, for doing good."

Donahue, for his part, never forgets the arena in which he operates. In 1988 he declared: "We are dangerously close to being referred to as an intelligent talk show . . . I'd rather be called sleazy than to be identified as intelligent."

Fine, Phil, have it your way.

Phil Donahue has always been at home in front of a mike.

In his senior year at Notre Dame, this son of a furniture salesman became an announcer at the campus television station, South Bend's Channel 46. Upon graduating in 1958, the only job Donahue could get was at a 250-watt radio station in Adrian, Michigan, covering murders and fatal auto accidents for $500 a month. Then it was on to WHIO radio in Dayton, Ohio, where he read the livestock reports at 5:00 A.M.

Donahue moved up from pork bellies to TV reporting for WHIO, interviewing the likes of Jumping Joe Kissinger, who leapt from hot-air balloons. In 1960 he chatted with Richard and Pat Nixon on a whistle-stop tour through Ohio.

By 1967 Donahue was co-anchoring the TV news and moderating a radio call-in show called *Conversation Piece*. Talk radio was heating up around the country, and Donahue freely borrowed ideas from his favorite host in Boston. "There was energy, passion, sometimes people would get angry," he says. "We had on Bobby Kennedy, Martin Luther King. The people in Dayton could actually call up these people. The damn show went through the roof."

Some days, though, the fare was more prosaic. "People called about the Pill, water retention, spotting, itches. They could get free advice. If I was stuck, all I had to do was call a gynecologist."

But Donahue longed to work for a bigger station, and he finally quit to join the business world. After a brief interlude, he was lured to Dayton's other station, WLW-D, when the general manager offered to put *Conversation Piece* on television.

The first show, on November 6, 1967, featured Madalyn Murray O'Hair, the atheist who brought the suit that outlawed prayer in public schools. The second show—scandalously tame by today's standards—was about single men and what they looked for in women. Rounding out the week were an interview with an obstetrician (and a film of a baby's birth), a session with a funeral director, and the brandishing of an anatomically correct male doll. A call-in poll on the doll's suitability tied up all the switchboards in downtown Dayton. A new kind of talk show was taking shape.

"We were forced to get by with issues," Donahue says. "Issues are what saved us. We discovered women were out there in the daytime and dying for this kind of program. There was tremendous sexism among the decision makers. They thought women cared only about covered dishes and needlepoint.

"I knew if we were going to survive with a visually dull format, with people sitting on folding chairs and two cameras and no budget, we had to do issues that made people sad, mad, glad."

While the critics scoffed at his occasionally freaky guests, Donahue was unperturbed. "Somebody's 'freaky' is another person's real personal problem," he says. "We put a gay guy on in 1968 and they called us weird."

On one level, of course, Donahue was simply making a virtue of necessity. An obscure program in Dayton, Ohio, couldn't land the big celebrities who worked the New York–Hollywood circuit. Stuck with third-tier guests, Donahue had to make his audience the star.

At a time when Merv Griffin, Dinah Shore, and Mike Douglas were hosting popular afternoon variety shows, Donahue was breaking all the rules. He had no band, no sidekick, and just one guest per hour-long show. Still, the program was picked up in Columbus, Cincinnati, Cleveland, Detroit. Success brought the usual growing pains—Donahue's first marriage, which had produced five kids, broke up—and, in 1974, a move to Chicago. Donahue began interviewing such A-list guests as Bella Abzug, Hubert Humphrey, Ted Kennedy, Jesse Jackson, and a former California governor, Ronald Reagan—along with Farrah Fawcett-Majors, Burt Reynolds, John Wayne, Dolly Parton, and Linda Lovelace. His stature was such that in 1979, First Lady Rosalynn Carter appeared on *Donahue*. He struck a deal with the *Today* show to provide three segments a week. And Phil fell in love as only a talk show host can, interviewing his future wife, Marlo Thomas, on the air.

Even as the world began to take him more seriously, Donahue

still reveled in his bad-boy approach. He paired feminist Susan Brownmiller, author of a book on rape, with Eldridge Cleaver, an admitted rapist; Brownmiller wound up in tears. He brought together an American Nazi (who favored deporting blacks to Africa and Jews to Israel) and the national director of the Ku Klux Klan, a fellow named David Duke. And he never flinched from defending his anything-goes approach. "I'm convinced you don't solve problems by repressing inflammatory ideas," he declared.

Donahue did shows on parents of homosexuals, victims of incest, abortion, vasectomy, mistresses, lesbian mothers, breast implants, penile implants. New York stations canceled the program three times, but he kept bouncing back, bigger and gaudier than ever, and finally moved the show to 30 Rockefeller Plaza in Manhattan.

By 1984 Donahue was sufficiently established that he and Ted Koppel were chosen to moderate a New Hampshire debate among the Democratic presidential candidates. "I don't know anyone better as an interlocutor between a studio audience and a guest," Koppel said. Soon Donahue, an unabashed liberal, was being asked about his ambition of running for the Senate.

Donahue had a knack for turning serious issues into televised drama. After Washington Mayor Marion Barry made some controversial remarks about poor women having too many babies, Donahue had the mayor confront a fourteen-year-old welfare mother. Donahue declared that Barry's comments would "get a standing ovation from the all-white Rotary Club."

"I'd get a standing ovation from the all-black Rotary Club, too," Barry shot back as the audience applauded.

When the Reverend Al Sharpton was perpetrating a national hoax in which a black teenager, Tawana Brawley, claimed she had been abducted and raped by a group of whites, Donahue got into the act. He went to the Bedford-Stuyvesant church where Brawley's mother, Glenda, was holed up in defiance of a grand jury subpoena. The show added nothing to the racially inflammatory situation, but Donahue said he was "proud to make a contribution to the dialogue."

And then there was the program on dwarf tossing. Not even Donahue could argue that it had much socially redeeming value.

The respectability that Phil Donahue craved continued to elude

him. Presidential candidates shied away from his show. He tried
and failed to land an interview with Walter Mondale in 1984, and
with Michael Dukakis in 1988. No one from Ronald Reagan's cabinet would appear on the program.

"Being on the *Donahue* show was not presidential," he says.
"You didn't want to have your man on a stage where there were
male strippers. I'm not sure there wasn't a little anxiety about the
audience. You never knew what those people were going to ask."

All that abruptly changed in 1992, when presidential contenders
realized that talk shows provided a safe and appealing way to connect with a broader audience than the kind of folks who watch *Face
the Nation*. Larry King, Arsenio Hall, Don Imus, and MTV became
high-profile stops on the campaign circuit. And, during the bitterly
contested New York primary, Bill Clinton decided to spend an hour
on *Donahue*.

He immediately regretted it as Donahue took on the role of
grand inquisitor. "Now, Governor," he began, "may I just charac-
terize what I think may be some of the suspicions or the concerns
of some Americans? . . . Part of the Slick Willie problem is caused
by what some analysts see as your ability to deflect questions and
give answers which don't really speak . . ."

Clinton interrupted, but Donahue pressed on about Gennifer
Flowers. He interrogated the Arkansas governor about various allegations by the woman who claimed to have been his longtime mistress. He fired questions about Clinton's youthful experimentation
with marijuana. Finally, Clinton had had enough.

"We're going to sit here a long time in silence, Phil," Clinton
said. "I'm not going to answer any more of these questions. I've
answered them until I'm blue in the face. You are responsible for
the cynicism in this country. You don't want to talk about the real
issues."

Clinton won the face-off when Donahue's audience, the source
of his strength over the years, abandoned him. The first woman
Donahue approached with the mike said: "I can't believe you spent
half an hour of airtime attacking this man's character. I'm not even
a Bill Clinton supporter, but I think this is ridiculous." The crowd
burst into applause.

Donahue's questions were certainly not the kind that David

Brinkley or Robert MacNeil would ask politicians. On one program, Donahue quizzed former California governor Jerry Brown about his bachelor status and seemed to question his sexual orientation. "If you want to know, do I go out with girls? Yes, I do," Brown said. "You want their names and phone numbers?"

Donahue's visibility was still growing. He launched a second talk show on CNBC with former Soviet spokesman Vladimir Pozner, applying his confrontational, lecturing, arm-waving techniques to political issues. I got a firsthand taste of the man's delight at putting his guests on the defensive when I appeared on *Donahue,* with Dan Rather and others, in 1994. The topic was tabloid-style news. I made the unremarkable observation that local TV news ought to cut back on body-bag journalism, the explicit and gratuitous footage night after night of homicide victims and bloodstained streets and grieving relatives.

This gave Donahue a chance to cry censorship and wrap himself in the First Amendment. "You want the *blood* and the *reality* of the news out of there?" he demanded from several steps up the aisle. "You want to *sanitize* the bombing of the barracks in Lebanon? Howard, I am struck by your suggestion that we don't need to see the body bags at all."

I tried to interrupt—all I had said was that local crime coverage was overdone—but Phil was in his rhythm. "*You* probably wouldn't have shown Morley Safer's report on My Lai! Or the thatched huts and the Zippo lighter! *You* probably wouldn't show the arriving bodies at Dover Air Force Base after military skirmishes in faraway lands! Don't show people these *terrible* things!"

It's hard to argue with a talk show host when he controls the microphone.

Once Donahue was racking up ratings with colorful histrionics and bizarre guests, the imitators began to push the format to new heights of tackiness, anger, and violence. Soon it was as if all the barriers had melted away and a television personality had to be outlandish just to break through the static.

In 1986 Oprah Winfrey burst upon the national scene. A year later Geraldo Rivera invaded the daytime turf. During the same period, Sally Jessy Raphael, a onetime food-stamp recipient turned St. Louis radio host, was taking her act from radio to television.

Oprah, an emotional and energetic performer who liked to hug her guests, never thought an overweight black woman could make it big. But the former Miss Black Tennessee enjoyed a meteoric rise, from Nashville reporter and anchor to Baltimore talk show host to Chicago talk show host to national sensation. She quickly became the daytime ratings queen, eclipsing Donahue and all other challengers.

"There wouldn't have been an Oprah without a Phil," she says. "Phil was the first to understand that the woman at home was an intelligent, sensitive, knowledgeable person who wanted to know more than how to bake Toll House cookies."

Winfrey specialized in plumbing the darkest depths of the human condition. A typical show began: "Could you still love a husband, a wife, a lover, if they attempted to kill you? My guests today have been shot, strangled, paralyzed, set on fire, stabbed, drugged, badly battered—all in the name of love."

Moments later Winfrey was interviewing a woman named Frances.

Winfrey: "Why did you want your husband dead?"

Frances: "I was unhappy, frustrated."

Ah, that explains it!

On another program, a guest stunned his wife by saying that he was still sleeping with an old girlfriend and that she was pregnant. But Winfrey gradually grew embarrassed by such episodes.

"Maybe five, six, seven years ago, when we started," she says, "a lot of the subjects that were taboo—bringing up child abuse, people's affairs, alcoholism, codependency—I think it was necessary to bring some of those things out of the closet." But, she says, "It's unfortunate it has gone to this extreme . . . In the early days of our talk show, I was probably not as sensitive, certainly not as evolved . . . I never in my life wanted to exploit or sensationalize or use people." That, of course, is often what she did.

But Winfrey's escapades were high-road sermons compared to the raucous new breed that emerged in Donahue's wake. One of the loudest and most obnoxious was Morton Downey Jr., a former radio talk show host who called his guests "jerk" and "sleazeball." When things got dull, Downey would physically throw guests off the set.

"Shut up, you old hag!" Downey shouted at one woman.

"I'm going to sit on your face in a moment," he told a man.

He called a third guest "slime" and declared: "I'd puke on you!"

A onetime Right to Life candidate for president, Downey styled himself in the tradition of Joe Pyne, a right-wing '60s loudmouth who denounced what he called "peace creeps" and once brandished a handgun while interviewing a black militant. *The Morton Downey Jr. Show* was always about Morton Downey; the guests were mere props. He once assembled a Ku Klux Klan delegation just so he could berate and humiliate them.

It was fitting, perhaps, that Morton Downey was also a guest on *Donahue*.

The heated, confrontational nature of these shows occasionally sparked real violence. During a *Morton Downey* taping in 1988, black activist Roy Innis got into an argument with Sharpton and pushed the rotund Reverend Al onto the floor.

That was kid stuff compared to the melee on *Geraldo* a few months later. During a show on "Teen Hatemongers," Innis began choking a member of the White Aryan Resistance Youth who had hurled a racial epithet at him. In the ensuing brawl, a flying chair broke Geraldo's nose, bloodying his face.

"At least I got a couple of real good shots in," he boasted.

Rivera later taped a show called "Has TV Gone Too Far?"

Geraldo Rivera is a fascinating case study because of his journey down the slippery slope from serious reporter to circus act. While he always displayed a disregard for traditional journalistic ethics— as a New York television reporter in 1972, he was reprimanded for making speeches for George McGovern—the former Puerto Rican activist also did some fine exposés of an unsafe mental hospital and filthy welfare hotels. He soon became a million-dollar-a-year star on *20/20*.

By 1985, however, Rivera's flamboyant behavior had become a public relations headache for ABC News President Roone Arledge. When Arledge killed another reporter's segment linking the Kennedys, the mob, and Marilyn Monroe's death, Rivera called it a "fucking outrage" and urged Arledge to resign. But Rivera had his own problems. He had made a $200 contribution to a political campaign, and his girlfriend had reportedly used an ABC messenger to pick

up a small amount of marijuana from a friend. Arledge seized on
these incidents to cut him loose. Rivera promptly took his act into
the gutter.

On one widely hyped special, he opened Al Capone's vault,
only to find a few dusty bottles. He chatted with Charles Manson,
declaring for the cameras: "You're a mass-murderin' dog, Charlie!"
He did programs on female boxers and battered lesbians and a
topless doughnut shop. And then there was the two-hour NBC
special on devil worship, complete with blood-soaked orgies, dis-
membered corpses, and ritualistic child abuse. ("Coming up next, a
look into the dark soul of Satanism. Stay with us.") Critics were
appalled. NBC apologized. But it was the highest-rated two-hour
documentary ever shown on network television.

"I have every ratings record there is on documentaries and
nothing but scathing reviews," Rivera declared. "When you get
fifty million viewers, that is not a cult, that's not a fringe audience,
that's the people. So are these handful of critics from a relatively
narrow slice of American society right and all those fifty million
people wrong?"

As the press cast its spotlight on his increasingly bizarre journalism, his sexual exploits, and his four marriages, even Rivera began
to sense he had crossed some kind of line. He blamed the fact that
he was up against *Oprah* in one hundred twenty-five markets. "I
went too far . . . I used up my quota on deviant behavior," he said.
"I'm out of the freak-show business."

But Geraldo and the freaks seemed to have a magnetic attraction. In 1992 Rivera was charged with battery in Janesville,
Wisconsin, while taping a KKK rally. He said that a Klansman had
called him a "spic" and a "dirty Jew," kicked him and bit his
thumb. Rivera's nose was bloodied in the process. (The charges
were later dropped.) Again in 1995, Rivera's nose was injured during a show on domestic violence when a fight broke out among
three men who had been involved with the same woman. "I feel
embarrassed and a bit silly," Rivera said.

No stunt seemed too far-fetched for Rivera. He had on-air lipo-
suction performed on his butt. He took his cameras into a hospital
to televise a man undergoing a sex-change operation, then interviewed the rechristened "Lisa." He chatted with John Wayne

Bobbitt and his latest girlfriend, a buxom actress named Tiffany, who announced that she was carrying Bobbitt's child. ("I guess the plumbing is working in John's case," Rivera observed.) Rivera brought on a man named Brent, his ex-wife Rachelle (whom he dropped after three weeks), and his new girlfriend Amber, then watched the two women get into a punching, hair-pulling brawl. "I'm glad you dumped the bum," Rivera later told Rachelle.

To no one's surprise, he devoted program after program to O. J. Simpson. Rivera interviewed a man who claimed to have sold Simpson cocaine, although Rivera's spokesman conceded they had no way of knowing whether the guest was telling the truth. On the talk show of the '90s, anyone could hurl an unsubstantiated charge as long as it was good television. Still, Rivera says, "If you compare my show to three or four years ago, we're doing *Masterpiece Theater* now . . . I didn't feel like having to shower every time I hosted a daytime show."

The wilder daytime programs came to resemble soap operas, stranger-than-fiction dramas that packed the added punch of reality. One *Geraldo* show featured a woman named Christine; her husband, Duane, who was serving time for manslaughter; her mother, Wanda, whose young lover, Kevin, was killed by Duane after hitting Christine; and Christine's half-brother, Eddie, whom Kevin once set on fire.

Each program seemed to provide fresh evidence of what Donahue calls "a culture in decay." Confrontation was valued above all. Jerry Springer presided over a literal food fight among a feuding family at a dinner table. He also hosted a strange-looking young woman who barked at her mother: "She doesn't even know who my father is!" The mother promptly collapsed, and the cameras rolled backstage as Springer tried to revive her. "For a few moments there I thought we were losing her. I couldn't feel a pulse at all," he said. Springer later boasted about providing people with "access to the airwaves," as if embarrassing them before millions were some kind of public service.

What drives this sort of dreck? Burt Dubrow, executive producer of *Sally*, says the audience simply grew bored with the same celebrities pushing their books and movies. "We've been accused of

showing women who used to be men, of focusing on nudists and
terrorists, and wives who shot their husbands. We've been accused
of outfreaking each other." But, he says, "we just do subjects we
feel will compel people to watch." *Compel* is the key word here; like
an awful car wreck, the spectacle had to be too gruesome for viewers
to avert their eyes.

Soon, it seemed, the daytime talk shows were multiplying like
rabbits. And they all needed guests, guests with suitably strange or
nauseating tales to tell. A national talk show registry was established, with twenty-four hundred wannabe guests at last count.
Since the relevant gene pool was necessarily limited, the same folks
popped up on show after show. *Geraldo* and *Donahue* both booked
a former Los Angeles police officer who became a prostitute. (Geraldo called his "Men Who Marry Prostitutes"; Phil went with
"Prostitutes and Gigolos.") Sherrol Miller, a self-described
transsexual lesbian from Kentucky, was on *Donahue* three times,
Sally twice, and *Geraldo, Joan Rivers,* and *Montel Williams* once
each. And then there was four-hundred-pound Susan Mason, origi-
nally with the National Association to Advance Fat Acceptance. She
did *Donahue, Geraldo, Joan Rivers, Sally,* and *Morton Downey Jr.*
Great television minds apparently think alike.

Donahue, not surprisingly, rejects suggestions that the daytime
talk industry has slid into the sewer. With practiced ease, he deflects
the question by making the critics the issue. "We've got an awful
lot of posturing, people who want to believe that on one side you've
got *The Washington Post, The New York Times, The Wall Street
Journal,* and all the wonderful, serious, mainstream journalists, and
on the other side you have all these journalists looking up dresses.
And it isn't that simple. Anyone can be a journalist, even me. You
don't have to pee in a bottle. You don't have to pass a test.

"Do we do silly things? Do we throw spaghetti at each other?
Do we wrestle with women in the mud? Yes. So what? Don't watch
that day! Please spare me this 'ain't it awful, we're all going to
hell.' "

For the audience, watching the cavalcade of deviant and dysfunctional types may serve as a kind of group therapy, a communal
exercise in national voyeurism. Perhaps the sight of so many people
with revolting problems makes some folks feel better about their
own rather humdrum lives.

But this is more than just a harmless diversion. It is, all too often, a televised exercise in defining deviancy down. By parading the sickest, the weirdest, the most painfully afflicted before an audience of millions, these shows bombard us with sleaze to the point of numbness. The abnormal becomes ordinary, the pathetic merely another pause in our daily channel surfing. Husbands and wives and mothers and daughters and mistresses and in-laws stage their angst-ridden screaming matches as if in a Roman coliseum. It is addictive, like watching too much pornography. We become desensitized by the endless freak show. Even the most serious human problems are trivialized by the quest for ratings. There is something sad and depressing about this kind of mass exploitation, even if the participants are eager to be exploited for their brief moment of electronic fame and we are all too willing to share in their talk show degradation.

Inevitably, these daily spectacles add to the sense that there is something terribly wrong with the country. They skew our national self-image, just as the nightly news parade of blacks being led away in handcuffs unfairly conveys the impression that most blacks are criminals. The medium becomes the message; after all, middle-class folks who work hard and raise their children in reasonable fashion don't get invited on *Donahue* or *Geraldo*. They do not exist on daytime television. Instead, we are bombarded with negative images of the sort of losers most of us would avoid at the local supermarket.

To fill the endless programming void, the daytime shows have been forced to expand the definition of problems that need therapeutic, and talk show, intervention. Thus we have Oprah looking on as a man named Dr. Ron advises a woman who is self-conscious about her small breasts to get implants. Her "problem" has thus been "solved" within the required sixty minutes. The notion that women shouldn't worry about the size of their breasts is beyond the scope of the show (not to mention the idea that feuding families should work out their problems in private). On television, people don't merely have weight problems; they are "addicted" to food, as Oprah describes her well-publicized dieting struggle. Every human foible thus becomes a self-esteem crisis that must be "fixed" by the sensitive talk show host, often with the help of psychobabble from medical "experts."

In the can-you-top-this environment, one practical problem

looms. There are, at bottom, a finite number of sensational topics. And it shows: Jerry Springer talks to white supremacists.
Montel Williams talks to white supremacists. Geraldo talks to
white supremacists. In some ways not much has changed since
Phil Donahue was chatting up David Duke in the late '70s.

When all else fails, there is always sex, the stranger the better.
PAUL SAYS ERICKA WANTS SEX TEN TIMES A DAY was the caption
on one *Jenny Jones* show, featuring a ditzy-looking eighteen-year-
old girl.

"Do you consider yourself a nymphomaniac?" asked Jones, a
former standup comic.

"I don't mind. You can call me that if you want," Ericka replied.

Edward Jeffords of Elkton, Maryland, went on *The Jerry
Springer Show* to brag about having sex with minors and "keeping
score." Months later, he was sentenced to five years in prison for
having sex with a fifteen-year-old girl.

If a guest's tale wasn't salacious enough, some talk show staffers
tried to embellish it. A seventeen-year-old girl at Michigan State
University responded to a *Jenny Jones* query about women who
enjoy watching X-rated movies. In exchange for a free trip to Chicago with her twenty-one-year-old boyfriend, she improved her
story just a bit. She says the show's producers talked her into saying
she not only liked porno movies but also wanted to perform in them.

As the new breed of talk shows—hosted by Montel Williams, Ricki
Lake, Jenny Jones, Jerry Springer—surged in the ratings, the fabric
of the programs changed. Confessional talk became confrontational
talk. It was no longer enough to haul willing victims onstage and
put them through their humilitating paces. Now there had to be an
element of surprise. The guests had to be presented with some dark
or unsettling secret while the cameras rolled. That created a more
combustible atmosphere that occasionally led to violence.

Inevitably, some of the stunned guests took the programs to
court. Miriam Booher, a domestic worker from Arkansas, went on
Donahue in 1989 to charge that her ex-husband, William, had
raped and impregnated her daughter by a previous marriage.

DAUGHTER HAD HUSBAND'S BABY, her onscreen caption read. Booher's daughter, Nancy, and two family members sued *Donahue,* and Booher, for invasion of privacy and emotional distress (a Texas court dismissed the case on free speech grounds).

Soap opera star Brent Jasmer, who was adopted as an infant, filed a suit charging that Geraldo had tricked him into an on-air reunion with his biological mother. Rivera, apparently immune to irony, accused him of trying to get "cheap publicity."

Yvonne Porter, a San Jose woman, went on *The Montel Williams Show* believing, she says, that she was going to be reunited with an old boyfriend. Her older sister, Kimberly Willis, had arranged the booking by responding to an 800 number aired by the show. Porter, who says she was kept in seclusion until her portion of the program, looked embarrassed as Willis told the world that her sister had allegedly been abused by the man she is living with. But that was just a warmup for the astonishing degradation to follow.

"I had sex with him to get him off of her back," Willis announced. Yvonne Porter's mouth fell open. She was barely able to speak. After an appearance by an on-air psychologist, Montel Williams—whose staff had scripted the entire episode—chided Willis for embarrassing her sister "here on national television."

"I slept with my sister's boyfriend to try to stop him from abusing her—great daytime drama stuff," says Ricardo Amor, Porter's attorney. "It was clearly a setup from beginning to end. These talk shows have been pushing and pushing people's emotions and have gotten violent reactions on the air. That's extremely exciting to them if they can capture it on camera." Yvonne Porter, saying her life had been "destroyed," filed a $10-million lawsuit against the *Williams* show. An out-of-court settlement was later reached.

Ricki Lake also likes the low-blow surprise. She once brought on a young woman and her boyfriend, who announced for the first time that he had fathered children with other women. "We're rooting for you," Lake told the woman after the prearranged sucker punch was delivered.

Corporate advertisers, who might be expected to shy away from this sort of fare, have been eagerly underwriting it instead. A thirty-second spot on the highest rated daytime shows sells for as much as $20,000, and top-drawer advertisers, like Procter & Gamble or American Home Products, were willing to pay it. "Trashy stuff sells," says Marty Blackman, head of a corporate consulting firm. "The American public likes it. There's a market for it."

Ricki Lake credits her producer, Gail Steinberg, for the rise of the confrontational format. "The idea of having somebody onstage telling their side of the story, and having the other person behind the stage . . . so that you can see the reaction as the other person is, like, dissing them, or doing something to them . . . does so much for the energy of the show," Lake says.

But that energy was fueling some ugly scenes. On *Jerry Springer,* a prostitute's boyfriend was surprised by one of her johns. The boyfriend took a swing at the man, prompting an onstage brawl. On another *Jerry Springer* show, a woman revealed to her husband, on the air, that she was having an affair with another woman. On a *Geraldo* episode about criminals who videotape their crimes, a man wound up in a brawl with two girls who bragged of kidnapping and shooting him.

Jenny Jones started out with lighter topics, like exercise and fashion, and nearly went off the air. Then she turned confrontational with a vengeance. She liked to bring people together with their secret admirers, preferably of the same sex. "We originated same-sex secret crushes," she boasted in early 1995. Another innovation, she announced, was "reuniting one-night stands." The concept caught on. Maury Povich did a show on secret crushes. Jerry Springer did a program reuniting a man with a woman with whom he had once had oral sex—revealing for the first time that the woman used to be a man. The gimmick was obvious: the deeper the degradation, the angrier the victim, the more dramatic the television show. Then the host—Jerry, Jenny, whoever—could sympathize on camera with the person the program had just ambushed.

This volatile formula was bound to explode, and it did. In March 1995 Jenny Jones staged another get-together for secret admirers, just as she had done a few weeks earlier. This time, however, events took a tragic turn. John Schmitz, a twenty-four-year-old waiter from Lake Orion, Michigan, was brought on to meet his unknown admirer. He saw a woman he knew and assumed it was her. But that would have been far too tame for daytime talk; the show was about "Secret Crushes on People of the Same Sex."

Schmitz's clandestine admirer turned out to be a neighbor, a bartender named Scott Amedure. "You have to be flattered," Jones said. But Schmitz was mortified. Schmitz later told police he felt "humiliated" and that Amedure had "fucked me on national television." Three days after the show, he found a sexually suggestive note at his door. Police say Schmitz bought a 12-gauge shotgun at Gary's Guns, went to Amedure's house, and killed him with two blasts to the chest.

Richard Thompson, the prosecutor in Oakland County, Michigan, said the televised stunt was partially responsible for the murder. "The *Jenny Jones* show ambushed this defendant with humiliation," he declared. "And in retaliation the defendant ambushed the victim with a shotgun." John Schmitz was arraigned on first-degree-murder charges. And the *Jones* show, owned by Time Warner, retreated behind a wall of official silence. Amedure's family sued the program for $25 million.

"I was devastated," Jenny Jones says. But she insists the tragedy "had nothing to do with the show. We have no responsibility whatsoever because [Schmitz] was not misled. All the guests knew that it could be a man or a woman." Indeed, it is probably unfair to blame the program for a senseless act of violence by an apparent homophobe. But the degree of prior warning does not let the staff off the ethical hook. Jenny Jones had poured the kerosene; all that was needed was a match.

"Ambushes, when it's for malevolent reasons, are almost never justifiable," says Geraldo Rivera, an obvious authority.

But Phil Donahue says it is wrong to blame the *Jones* staff. "This was a homophobic murder, and we are essentially excusing it," he says. "We look the other way when it comes to gay bashing or gay murder."

Still, the editorial condemnation was thunderous. The tabloids, which had relentlessly celebrated the practitioners of daytime talk, now decried what was dubbed "The Jenny Jones Murder." Linda Stasi, a New York *Daily News* columnist, says the daytime shows have become "a vast, scary wasteland where the dregs of society— sociopaths, perverts, uneducated lazy scum who abuse their children and sleep with anyone who'll have them—become stars for fifteen minutes."

Even Howard Stern, no stranger to low-rent entertainment, believes the daytime programs have gone too far. "The basic premise of the shows is to get as many retards as possible onstage and fighting," he says.

There was talk of changing the shows, but it was empty talk. Too many people were making too much money off daytime television.

The relentless parade of grotesque guests inevitably raises the question: Why in the world do these people bare their souls on national television? And why does a sizable chunk of America faithfully watch?

Patricia Priest, a doctoral student at the University of Georgia, has interviewed a number of people who have appeared on *Donahue* and similar shows, including a transsexual lesbian, a "former homosexual," a child abuse victim, and a man whose wife recently decided she is a lesbian. Priest says they are not particular fans of *Donahue* but are seeking a forum with national impact.

"They sought to spread counter-stereotypical information about their lifestyles on the medium they felt often represented them negatively, if it depicted them at all," Priest says.

In that light, simply appearing on a talk show constituted success. "Even those who had discredited themselves on national television reported friendly and excited responses from strangers and neighbors," Priest says. "Most often, they said, people exclaimed, 'I saw you on television!' and seemed thrilled to meet them . . . The deviant label that many *Donahue* guests have lived with for much of their lives is engulfed by the more prestigious 'as seen on TV.' "

Even Phil Donahue wonders about the psychodramas being played out on some programs. "I notice increasing numbers of what look to me to be semi-educated Americans who occasionally make you wince with shouting matches that have to do with very personal conflicts within the family," he says. "There are some folks out there who will do anything to get on TV. We have to wonder what responsibility we have for protecting people from themselves. But we can't be paternalistic. They're all twenty-one and over."

The daytime shows seem unfamiliar with such basic concepts as doctor-patient confidentiality. A New York psychotherapist I know was invited by *Oprah*'s staff to appear on a program on child suicide —provided she could bring along a couple of kids who had unsuccessfully tried to kill themselves. The therapist, who had never seen *Oprah,* found the request, well, crazy.

Still, such programs have their defenders. Christopher Guest, a professor at Bowling Green University, sees the shows as a public service. "It really is a sort of town meeting where things are thrown on the table," he says. "Phil and Oprah and all of them have raised our consciousness about some pretty difficult issues in American life."

But Vicki Abt, a Penn State University researcher, co-authored a study concluding that the daytime shows do more harm than good. Donahue, Winfrey, and company, she writes, are "simply mouthing mantras of pop-therapy . . . Strangers get to give advice without being responsible for its effect. The central distortion that these shows propound is that they give useful therapy to guests and useful advice to the audience."

In this view, the hosts are mimicking the procedure of twelve-step healing programs, bringing together abuser and abused, victimizers and victims, as if their awful, deep-seated problems can be resolved before the cameras in mere minutes.

Winfrey: "You're not a bad person. But maybe you shouldn't work as a psychiatrist if you've taken sexual liberties with your female patients."

Donahue: "Do I understand, Lisa, that intercourse began with your dad at age twelve . . . Do I understand that you were beaten before and after the sexual encounters?"

"It certainly seems that these 'victims' are now allowing themselves to be further victimized by the talk shows," Abt says. "Similarly, perpetrators justify their behavior by adopting the appropriate jargon. They tell us they were abused by their parents, teachers, girlfriends, anybody at all . . . Society's conventions are flouted with impunity, and the hidden message is that the way to get on television is to be as outrageous and antisocial as possible."

After the study was released, Vicki Abt was invited to be on *Oprah*. And, to her surprise, she loved it. "She's the most charming woman I've ever met," Abt says. Then *Donahue* called, and *Rolonda,* and *NBC Nightly News*. These days Abt is guest-hosting at a Philadelphia radio station. For all her criticism, she has become part of the talk culture.

As more than twenty daytime shows increasingly began competing for guests, the price of admission grew more expensive. Phil Donahue began paying selected people to appear, something he had never done before. He paid two jurors in the Rodney King beating case to lure them onto his show. No one could blame people with marketable stories for wanting to be compensated, but Donahue had never bought into the cash-for-trash mentality. The obvious drawback is a loss of credibility, for some people embellish their stories to command higher fees. But the tabloid shows were offering big bucks for the hottest guests, and Donahue felt he had to compete.

"Self-important journalists strut about talking about how horrible it is that some people are paying for guests," he says. "If you're sequestered on a jury for four months, and *Hard Copy* or the *Donahue* show wants you, why should you give what you have—something of value—to a company that's already making a billion dollars a year, for free? So they can, by their own rules, retain their virginity?" Donahue was proud to no longer be a virgin.

On some level, confession—even televised confession—must be good for the soul. Oprah Winfrey acknowledged in the first years of her show that she was a victim of childhood sexual abuse. Winfrey told her audience she was raped by a cousin at age nine, and molested by an uncle and a family friend. More recently, her boyfriend, Stedman Graham, has appeared on the show to discuss the pitfalls of dating a celebrity. And Winfrey, who once confessed to eating a twelve-pack of hot dog buns drenched with Log Cabin syrup, became a symbol of yo-yo dieting. Millions watched her lose sixty-seven pounds, gain it all back, and then swear off drastic diets.

That wasn't all. In 1995 Winfrey confessed on her show that she had smoked cocaine during her days in Baltimore in the '70s. In an emotional segment prompted by a guest's tale, Winfrey described how the man she was "addicted to"—there's that phrase again—had pushed her into drug use. "It is my life's great big secret," she said, choking up. In a talk show nation, it is not only the guests who must reveal the most intimate details of their personal lives.

Such programs invariably employ the language of the self-help movement, yet the words can sound awfully trite when matched against the magnitude of real-world difficulties. "What we are trying to change in this one hour is what I think is the root of all the problems in the world—lack of self-esteem," Winfrey says.

Whatever her grand philosophy, Winfrey grew savvier in the ways of politics as her success—as Hollywood actress, producer, investor—propelled her forward. She became a national advocate for poor and abused children, testifying before the Senate Judiciary Committee and hiring a Chicago law firm to draft a National Child Protection Act. She endowed ten scholarships each year at Tennessee State University, her alma mater. She paid to move some poor families out of the Chicago housing projects. Just as Donahue had become closely identified with women's rights and gay rights, Winfrey tried to stand for something larger than a woman who urged pitiful individuals to pour out their problems before the cameras. The mass audience listened to her views, not because she was more insightful or more noble than other activists, but because she had achieved the pinnacle of talk show wealth and fame.

Yet all these hosts, even the youngest and hippest, owed their existence to Phil, the aging granddaddy of daytime talk. In 1992, when Donahue had his twenty-fifth-anniversary special, they gathered in the Ed Sullivan Theater on Broadway to pay tribute: Geraldo, Oprah, Maury Povich, Sally Jessy Raphael, Montel Williams, Faith Daniels, Jenny Jones, and Jerry Springer, along with Mike Wallace, Larry King, David Letterman, Connie Chung, and Diane Sawyer. "When I think of sex," Dr. Ruth Westheimer announced, "I think of Donahue."

Phil Donahue is laughing and leering, mugging for the cameras, as he chats with the four giggling middle-aged women on the stage. Two have heavily teased hair. All four are married. And all are here to talk about a theme as old as *Donahue* itself.

MARRIED HOUSEWIVES FULFILL THEIR SECRET DESIRE TO STRIP IN A CLUB, says the on-screen caption.

"You think this is easy," Donahue tells his audience. "It isn't. It's an art form." He says knowingly that stripping can "put a little tingle in the ol' twosome."

Lest anyone be tempted to change the channel, Donahue

quickly introduces four professional strippers, who run into the audience, bumping and grinding to music and shedding everything but their bras, panties, and stockings.

Then it's back to the four amateurs, who have been taking lessons. Donahue chats with Geri Iaconi, a heavily made-up woman in her fifties, then introduces her husband, Bob, a balding man in a purple shirt. Bob watches, wide-eyed, as Donahue rolls a tape of Geri stripping in a Manhattan club. The other three husbands are introduced, and the ritual is repeated: Each watches a tape of his wife ripping off her clothes before a room full of strangers. The husbands are grinning like schoolboys.

"You ladies got it, you flaunt it!" a gravel-voiced woman in the audience tells Phil.

But that isn't all. The plot has to build. One of the housewives, Lori Davis, who had stripped down to a skimpy red cowgirl outfit, tells Donahue that she has only six months to live unless she can get a heart-lung transplant.

"This is a dream of my life, being on a talk show, being able to strip," Davis, holding back tears, tells the consoling host. "You have fulfilled the biggest dream."

In the final segment, the husbands return the favor by running into the audience and disrobing down to colorful boxer shorts and bowties. One is bony and scrawny, another has an immense pot belly, a third is covered with tattoos. They are joined by two professional male strippers, their biceps bulging as the women squeal with delight.

What is the point of the program? "It's entertainment," Donahue says matter-of-factly.

A C-SPAN junkie who cares about public issues, Phil Donahue has clearly changed his style to keep up with the '90s brat pack.

"In the '70s we had Bob Dole on the show alone for an hour," he says. "We had Dick Gephardt on alone for an hour. We had a mix: 'My husband doesn't kiss me anymore' on Monday and Watergate another day. Today, Bob Dole is not going to carry his time period. You try to retain a certain image for yourself that you are interested in more than male strippers, without being so guilt-ridden and conscientious that you wind up a dead hero. It doesn't do any good to write if nobody's reading, and it certainly doesn't do any good to talk if nobody's watching."

Donahue is acutely conscious of what the market will bear. When he did a program on the tragic war in Bosnia, he got a letter from the general manager of a Boston station. Bosnia is surely important, the puzzled executive wrote, but why would you do it during sweeps week?

Now, instead of Bob Dole, Donahue devoted a program to raunchmeister Howard Stern, who chased him across the stage in order to kiss him. The ABC affiliate in Dallas refused to air the Stern episode and, after losing some sponsors, dropped *Donahue* for good. The NBC flagship station in New York also abandoned Donahue, leaving him without an outlet in the nation's biggest market. NBC's Washington station dumped the show in favor of Montel Williams, leaving Donahue high and dry until the local CBS affiliate picked him up. He was shut out of the San Francisco market. (His CNBC show was also canceled.) The reasons were obvious: By the middle of 1995, *Donahue* had dropped from third to ninth among the daytime talk shows, a 15 percent decline in ratings. There was growing talk that he might pack it in after twenty-nine years when his contract with Multimedia, the distributor that also handled Sally Jessy Raphael and Rush Limbaugh, expired in the summer of 1996. Still, Donahue was not alone; most of the older daytime programs, including *Oprah, Geraldo,* and *Sally,* were also losing part of their audience. Oprah came close to quitting.

"How many talk shows can survive in the economic reality of this marketplace remains to be seen," Donahue says. "Talk shows that go too far too often are going to fall of their own weight."

That descent may be beginning. "These shows are starting to age," says veteran producer Randy Douthit, a consultant to various daytime programs. "The extremely dysfunctional guest has peaked. It's overdone. People are sick of it. Oprah, in her wisdom, has taken the high road, and she's ahead of the curve. Sally, Geraldo, and Maury are fading. Phil is fading. He should go into politics."

But Donahue was not ready to fade away just yet. The genre he had invented in Dayton a quarter century ago was still thriving. The problem was that what was once considered shocking television was no longer very shocking. The daytime talkers had to descend further into depravity each year just to hold the audience. Sooner or later, that approach had to burn itself out. America was finally becoming inured to the serial killers and the nymphomaniacs and

the housewives who strip in nightclubs. Television had made devi-
ance seem passé.

But Donahue had proven one thing: A man with a microphone
who could connect with the viewers, who valued their opinions,
could turn that into stardom. You didn't have to be able to sing or
dance or play a mean guitar. You didn't have to live inside the
Beltway and hang out with political big shots. All you had to do
was talk about things that interested ordinary people, and even
presidential candidates would have to take you seriously.

While Donahue was transforming the boundaries of television,
another man was trying to talk his way to success on the radio. He,
too, built a career around chatting with ordinary Americans. He,
too, spent years in the minor leagues of broadcasting, far from the
bright lights of Broadway or glittering monuments on the Potomac.
He never went to college, never did any research for his show, but
eventually world leaders would line up to sit at his elbow. His name
was Larry Zeiger.

CHAPTER FOUR

THE KING
OF SCHMOOZE

On June 3, 1985, Larry King made his debut on CNN after nearly three decades as a radio talk show host. His first guest was Mario Cuomo.

"What is it like to be nationally famous?" King asked.

"Who knows better than you, Larry?" Cuomo replied.

The choice of the New York governor was no accident. Cuomo had been on King's late-night radio show years earlier, and the two had become friends. They spoke by phone and exchanged letters. They made joint appearances before paying audiences on the lecture circuit. King spent a few weekends at the governor's mansion in Albany.

The previous summer, five days before Cuomo delivered his spellbinding speech to the Democratic convention, he read it to King over the phone.

"It sounds fine to me," King said. They were both confident that it would be a hit. Cuomo agreed to stop by King's Mutual radio show after the speech.

So the CNN premiere was clearly in both men's interest. King needed a high-profile guest to help him make a televised splash, and Cuomo, who harbored presidential ambitions, received national exposure. The governor could be reasonably certain that King would throw him no curveballs on the air. It would be strictly slow-pitch softball.

Larry King Live, which replaced the long-forgotten *Sandi Free-*

man Reports, was not an overnight success. "King may need to develop a tougher stance unless he wants his program to be a mere pleasantry . . . a congenial chat just doesn't cut it on TV," wrote Tom Shales, *The Washington Post*'s television critic. As it turned out, he was wrong.

King would become a huge celebrity, his suspendered slouch and raspy Brooklyn voice instantly recognizable around the world. He would help launch an eccentric billionaire, Ross Perot, on the most successful third-party presidential candidacy in eighty years. He would be invited to the East Sitting Room of the White House to interview President George Bush and, a few months later, return for the first of four interviews with President Bill Clinton. His program would become the forum of choice for big-name politicians and celebrities—from Mikhail Gorbachev and Margaret Thatcher to Marlon Brando and Barbra Streisand—to pitch their messages to a global audience.

Their reasoning wasn't hard to fathom. In an adversarial media climate in which reporters frequently badger public figures and try to force them into embarrassing admissions, King offered a friendly, low-stress environment in which unpleasant subjects could easily be finessed. He offered direct access to a nationwide audience, unfiltered and unhurried, just Larry and the callers having a chat. For any working journalist, of course, King's personal relationship with someone like Mario Cuomo would have been a blatant conflict of interest. But King does not accept that definition or play by those rules.

"I'm not a journalist," he says. "I'm a feature interviewer. I'm not Mary Poppins, but I'm not Sam Donaldson. I'm the Style section of CNN.

"I listen, I leave myself out of questions, I never use the word *I*. The first thing Mike Wallace wants to know from an FAA inspector is, Is that plane safe? The first question I would ask is, Why do you want to inspect airplanes? To Ted Koppel, the event is the story. To me, the person is the story."

In the hotly competitive world of television booking, King's staff would use his amiable approach as a major selling point. "We used to say to candidates, 'You can go around the national press,' " says Tammy Haddad, King's legendarily feisty producer for the first eight years of the CNN show. "We're not pretending to be journalists. You don't have to go through the producer's view of your story, or the talent's view of your story. You can tell your story."

King transformed the media landscape. His show was built around the callers, as it had been for all those years on the radio; like Phil Donahue, he had a way of connecting with the masses. King was a commoner, a conduit, a means for ordinary folks to talk to the high and mighty. Larry Zeiger from Bensonhurst, who used to practice announcing with rolled-up comic books, had reached the pinnacle of television by perfecting the art of the schmooze.

The benefits of a softer talk show are obvious. If guests don't have to stay in a defensive crouch, sparring with the host and fending off hostile queries, they can reveal more of themselves as real people.

The downside is that they don't have to entertain tough questions—indeed, any uncomfortable question—that might make the program more than a publicity tool for whatever policy or product they are pushing at the moment.

King's second guest during his debut week on CNN was Pat Buchanan, then a Reagan spinmeister serving as White House communications director. Buchanan, like Cuomo, harbored presidential ambitions but also hoped to rejoin CNN after leaving Reagan's employ.

Once again, there were no curveballs. A caller from Georgia asked whether Buchanan was responsible for revving up the helicopter engines on the White House lawn when reporters tried to ask the president a question. Buchanan feigned ignorance.

"I don't know anything about it," he said, suppressing a smile.

"You deny the helicopter blade accusation?" King asked.

"I deny it," Buchanan said. King smiled, too.

There was little hard-boiled skepticism on *Larry King Live*. It was, as always, on to the next topic: Rochester, New York, hello. Columbus, Ohio, hello. Bakersfield, California, hello.

In 1991, shortly after he was forced to resign as White House chief of staff, John Sununu was King's guest. King made no mention of the fact that President Bush's son, George W., had told

Sununu he had to go, or of his frequent use of military jets for personal travel, which had caused an uproar in the press. Instead, he asked: "Take me to the decision. When did you make it? How did it happen?"

"No regrets?"

"Have you left a job before? It never gets easy, right?"

"Where did you go wrong?"

"Do you think the town didn't understand—wasn't prepared for someone who is used to combat and then forgive and forget?"

"Do you think *The Washington Post* was out to get you?"

"Are you going to miss power?"

"How supportive was the staff today with you?"

In 1992 Richard Nixon appeared on *Larry King Live*. There was only brief mention of the scandal that drove Nixon from office.

"Is it hard to drive by the Watergate?" King asked.

"Well, I've never been in the Watergate," Nixon replied.

"Never been in?"

"No."

When Michael Jordan came on to promote a book in 1993, King would not ask about the recent death of Jordan's father, arguably the most important event in Jordan's adult life and one that within months would help persuade him to retire temporarily from basketball. "I don't want to get into that," King told his staff.

On the day that Time Warner announced it was buying CNN and the rest of the Turner Broadcasting empire, King brought on Ted Turner and Time Chairman Gerald Levin for a friendly chat. After praising the "sensational executives on both sides," King asked: "Who do I work for, Ted?"

"We work together," Turner assured him.

King was a bit more aggressive with Mel Reynolds when the Illinois congressman appeared in the summer of 1995 to announce his resignation, days after being convicted of sexual assault and child pornography charges involving a teenage girl. He pressed Reynolds on whether he had let his supporters down and why he didn't appear more contrite, yet still managed to ask sympathetic questions of Reynolds's wife.

King was even polite to mass murderers. In 1995 he did a jailhouse interview with Colin Ferguson, the crazed black gunman who opened fire on a Long Island Rail Road train, killing six people.

Ferguson, who had scrawled notes about his hatred for white people, was conducting a bizarre defense of himself at the trial. He got cold feet just before the taping began, but King talked him into proceeding. He called the killer by his first name.

"What's it been like?"

"How about your family? Have they been in touch with you?"

"Are you sad, Colin, about those people who were the victims?"

"Do you know who the killer was?"

Ferguson was convicted days later, but not before seizing his moment of talk show fame.

People accused of heinous crimes seemed drawn to Larry King. One day after O. J. Simpson was released from prison after fifteen months, he called King on the air. No sooner had he beaten the murder rap in court than he set about trying to reverse the verdict of the talk shows, where so many analysts had pronounced him guilty. Acting like any other caller, Simpson took issue with a previous caller over disputed testimony in his case and blamed it on misrepresentations by prosecutor Marcia Clark.

"Would you describe yourself as relieved, angry, what?" King asked. Simpson said his "basic anger" was at the television "experts" and "what they were reporting on these various shows." King, whose staff arranged the call in advance, tried to ask a question about Simpson's kids, but the onetime football star quickly signed off. He had utilized King's national forum without having to subject himself to any messy cross-examination about the double murder. "Obviously he wanted to get a point across, and we're the place he used," King says. (Days later, when Simpson backed out of a hugely publicized interview with Tom Brokaw and Katie Couric, NBC News President Andrew Lach called King to defend his network's role.)

King makes no apologies for his nonconfrontational style. "I'm as nice to Dan Quayle as I am to Al Gore," he says. "Critics might say I'm too soft on both of them. So be it. I like putting people at ease."

Celebrities love King's royal treatment. Lee Iacocca, another old friend, says he has appeared on the show several times because "I always get a good reaction. On Koppel's show I don't get a good reaction because he never lets you talk much. And Donahue sort of ambushes you."

Nancy Reagan enjoyed her interview so much she invited King for lunch. "He doesn't try to embarrass anybody or put anybody on the spot . . . I was glad I'd found a new friend," she says.

"It's like dancing with Fred Astaire," says Newt Gingrich.

"He's a master," Mario Cuomo says. "He knows what you would ask if you had this guy in your living room. He's where the people are. He'll make a trillion dollars, he'll be married thirty-seven times."

King boasts that he does no research about his guests. If he is interviewing an author, he never reads the book in advance. "I want to start even with the listener," he says.

"I'll try to brief him, but he really doesn't have any interest," says Wendy Walker Whitworth, King's CNN producer. "His theory is that if he's not surprised, he won't ask the right questions." The night that attorney F. Lee Bailey, before coming on the show, called King to say he was joining the O. J. Simpson defense team, King put his hand over his ear and said, "I don't want to hear it. Don't tell me any more."

This tendency to let the guest control the agenda frustrates some CNN staffers. "He will not follow up on a question where you could have gotten a news bite out of the guy," one producer says. "You'd write all these questions for him on blue cards, but you couldn't write the follow-ups."

Tammy Haddad says the image of King as a know-nothing is false. "I've often told Larry, I don't think it's wise he tells people he doesn't do research. The truth is, he's a very well-read guy.

"He's a gut-level interviewer. Whenever anyone goes on a talk show, there are three things they want to get across: the movie's great, the book's great, or whatever. Larry makes the opportunity for you to say what you really want to say, and then gets you to say things you hadn't really planned to say. He knows how to take people to the next level."

King's laissez-faire approach has occasionally turned his show into a vehicle for disseminating rumors. The day that Gennifer Flowers held a news conference to promote the story she had sold to the *Star* supermarket tabloid, King's guests included Cindy Adams, the *New York Post* gossip columnist. Adams said, without offering any evidence, that there were other women who claimed to have had affairs with Bill Clinton. "There's a whole pack of them out there that are sending in information," she said. "I simply haven't used it because until now, until he started to run, I didn't care a hoot in hell for Clinton of Arkansas." King made no attempt to challenge her or to press for substantiation. Conservative columnist Cal Thomas later repeated Adams's comments on *Nightline,* thus ensuring that they remained in play. King later admitted he had mishandled the situation.

King also concedes that he helped spread "completely unsubstantiated rumors" when he asked Clinton weeks before Election Day if as a young man he had ever considered renouncing his American citizenship. The Republicans had been peddling this line without success for weeks.

"Never," Clinton told King.

"Where did that start from?" King asked.

"You tell me," Clinton said.

But King staunchly defends his practice of allowing people to make controversial charges on his show. On January 21, 1993, David Reynard of Florida went on *Larry King Live* and charged, with no medical evidence whatsoever, that using a cellular phone had caused his wife's death from brain cancer. "Some say cellular phones can kill you," King declared in his introduction.

The cellular industry declined to provide a spokesman for the show. The other guests were Eleanor Adair, a Yale University scientist, who said the charges were hogwash, and the publisher of a newsletter about the industry, who said more study was needed. Adair said that "the power output from a cellular telephone is just too low. It can't do that kind of damage to tissue. They have been tested." Still, the callers helped fuel the sense that something must be wrong. One, from Annandale, Virginia, said he felt "kind of dizzy" after using cellular phones. Another, from Kansas City, said AT&T had recently bought part of a cellular company and "I know that they would not be beyond creating a story like this."

Public reaction was immediate. Cellular company stocks plummeted overnight. A poll showed that half of those surveyed believed the allegation. Reassurances from industry and government officials were brushed aside. Ron Nessen, a former White House press secretary turned spokesman for the cellular phone industry, wound up

on the *Faith Daniels Show,* arguing with an audience member carrying what he said was a magnetic resonance image of spots on his
brain. It was, said one industry official, like "fighting a ghost."
Attempts at rational discourse were simply drowned out by uninformed talk. A federal judge later threw out Reynard's lawsuit on
the issue for lack of scientific evidence.

"The man making the accusation was very bright, he wasn't
crazy," King says. The problem, he argues, is that the other guests
were too laid back.

"I know the industry took an awful hit that night," King says.
"The secret in television is you have to be a good guest, be forceful.
The guy [Reynard] was great. The next day all the papers covered
it. That's because we have credibility as a show. If Geraldo ran it,
they wouldn't have covered it."

But King seems to miss the larger point: Television news is
about more than who puts on the best show for the cameras. David
Reynard may have been a dramatic guest, but he had no evidence to back up his explosive charge. The fact that the other
guests turned in tepid performances doesn't let the program off
the hook. On that night, *Larry King Live* helped touch off a
public panic without having the slightest idea whether the charges
were true.

King broke into radio by sweeping the floors at WAHR, a 250-watt
station in Miami. It was 1957. He was twenty-three years old, with
little more than a diploma from Brooklyn's Lafayette High School.
He had grown up listening to Red Barber call the Dodgers games
and dreaming of a radio career. His father, an Eastern European
immigrant who owned a neighborhood bar and grill, had died when
he was ten, and the family had been on welfare for a while. They
lived in a third-floor walkup, and his mother made some extra
money as a seamstress. King had married his high school sweetheart
but the union lasted only a few weeks. All that King had going for
him was his gift of gab. When the morning deejay quit, Larry Zeiger
got to fill in, but not before the station manager told him he needed
a new name. Zeiger sounded too Jewish. The boss suggested King.

Within three years King had landed a mid-morning talk show

at WIOD, which he conducted from Pumpernick's restaurant. The first people he interviewed were the waitresses. One day Bobby Darin walked in and came on the air; another day it was Jimmy Hoffa. King couldn't prepare for these interviews, so he winged it.

Over time, King chatted with the likes of Don Rickles, Ella Fitzgerald, Danny Thomas, Lenny Bruce. He served as the emcee for Jackie Gleason's birthday party. He cohosted Arthur Godfrey's popular radio show. He became a Miami fixture, writing a local newspaper column and providing the color at Dolphins football games.

Politicians were very much part of the King radio mix. In 1964, in a harbinger of things to come, King moderated and took phone calls in a debate for mayor of Miami Beach.

He also received figures of national stature. When Adlai Stevenson, whom King had twice supported for president, appeared on his show, the host was in awe. "To be in your presence is a singular honor," he told Stevenson. King interviewed Eleanor Roosevelt, Bobby Kennedy, Martin Luther King Jr., and Hubert Humphrey, with whom he became particularly close.

There were no national radio talk shows, so even candidates for the highest office had to work the local circuit. In 1968 the three presidential candidates, Nixon, Humphrey, and George Wallace, all appeared on King's Miami show.

Despite his success, King's personal life kept intruding. He married a Playboy bunny and got divorced a few years later. He began spending three times as much as he was making. In 1971 he was arrested for misusing $5,000 from a business associate. Although the charges were dropped, King's station fired him, and he lost his newspaper and television jobs as well. It took him four years to land another steady job in radio.

By 1978 King had been through three marriages, two of them to the same woman. His penchant for playing the horses had him drowning in debt. He declared bankruptcy, listing $352,246 in debts, including $14,000 to the Hialeah racetrack.

It was during this difficult period that a Mutual radio executive named Ed Little decided that Larry King was the man to launch the first national radio talk show. He installed King in a twelfth-floor studio in Crystal City, Virginia, and put him on from midnight to 5:30 A.M. For the insomniacs and graveyard-shift workers of

America, King would corral a guest for the first three hours, then throw open the phones and talk, talk, talk.

"Most people predicted failure," King says. "AM radio was in trouble. The feeling was that national talk could never work because what people in Arizona want to hear is not want people in Miami want to hear." Mutual officials were so uncertain of King's prospects that they wouldn't spring for an 800 number. Anyone dialing King's show had to pay for the call.

And yet it caught on. There were feature stories in *People, Us, The Washington Post, The Wall Street Journal*. Guests ranging from Danny Kaye and Marvin Hamlisch to Al Gore and Ross Perot would talk into the wee hours. The callers spanned the spectrum; one would ask for the name of a good surgeon, another would talk about men from Mars. Between cigarettes, King would dispense advice, reel off sports trivia, recite poems, sing off-key.

"It was wild to sit there in the middle of the night and talk to Philadelphia, Baltimore, Chicago, L.A.," he says. "There was no subject, no soapbox. You could call and talk about politics, and the next guy would talk about the Boston Red Sox."

Unlike today's opinion-mongers, King was there to schmooze. He listened to his callers, seemed to care about them. He did not go out of his way to take partisan positions. "I gave you an opinion if you asked me. If you said, Where do you stand on abortion, I'd say I'm for choice. If you'd say, Where do you stand on school prayer, I'd say there's no place for it in public schools. You can't duck questions. It would be a namby-pamby show."

As a prognosticator, King's record was less than perfect. In 1979, a caller asked about Ted Kennedy's presidential prospects.

"He'll run and win," King declared.

King began with twenty-eight stations and eventually was carried by more than three hundred fifty. One night his guest was Atlanta businessman Ted Turner, who talked about his effort to launch an all-news network on cable television. During a commercial, Turner asked King if he could simulcast the radio show on his new network. King, naturally, was interested. But Mutual demanded a huge sum of money for the rights, and the deal never materialized.

On one evening, a shirtsleeved King, alternately yawning,

stretching and chain-smoking More Lights, took calls on subjects ranging from media bias to the Vietnam War to the Super Bowl. "It's a lock this year: Washington against either the Raiders or Miami," he told a listener in Phoenix.

A caller from Shreveport, Louisiana, complaining about "the power of the media," said Sam Donaldson had made a snide remark in one of his White House reports. King defended it as fair comment.

"If pornography makes people rape people, how come the people who watched it to declare it pornography didn't go out and rape people?" he asked. "Or do they think they're superior to other people? How come, if the media can influence people, it didn't influence you? . . . He changes other people's minds and not yours? You're smarter?"

A San Diego caller asked about King's relationship with the late boxer Rocky Marciano.

"Rocky was a super guy," King says. "Did a lot for me. When I was first starting, Rocky would come on my show and he liked me and we got along."

By 4:00 A.M., all fourteen phone lines were still lit up. King looked punchy but remained in control.

"Sir! I assume you're intelligent," he scolded a Pine Bluff, Arkansas, man who refused to accept King's contention that Vietnam was no longer holding American prisoners of war.

"Of course we're closer to nuclear war today than we were four years ago."

"I have never seen a man so dominate a sport as Gretzky does the sport of hockey."

King even wondered why only 1 percent of the audience utilized the "remarkable privilege" of calling talk radio shows. "Unfortunately, in my opinion, there aren't a lot of really good hosts," he said. "I've never screened a call in my life. Don't believe in it. If a host can't handle calls without them being prescreened, he doesn't deserve to be a host."

Talk had always existed on the fringes of television. There was Joe Pyne's late-night ravings. There was William F. Buckley and his

erudite expositions on public television's *Firing Line*. There was
Tom Snyder, chortling his way through interviews, framed by
plumes of cigarette smoke, after Johnny Carson had signed off.
There was Dick Cavett, the intelligentsia's interviewer of choice.
There were the stilted cabinet officers droning on Sunday mornings. But almost no one, with the exception of Phil Donahue, took
calls, and for Donahue the calls were a minor element in a show
built around a studio audience.

When Ted Turner offered Larry King a $200,000 contract in
1985, matching what he was receiving from Mutual, the question
was whether King's shtick would work on television. Radio, after
all, was a medium that relied on the imagination. You would hear
King's voice, and the callers' voices, and imagine what they looked
like. But TV was a visual medium, and the prospect of the camera
lingering on King while he conversed with disembodied callers
didn't sound very exciting. On radio, King had all the time in the
world. Television viewers expected things to move quickly.

King was reluctant. He hardly ever watched CNN. If he tried
to do both television and radio, he would have no social life, would
never be able to go to a baseball game. Besides, he had already had
one televised flop, a fast-paced affair on the Post-Newsweek stations
that rushed him through five- and six-minute guest segments before
a studio audience. Larry King, it turned out, was no Phil Donahue.

But King had nothing to lose. If the new show failed, at least he
would double his salary for the year. He signed the contract, and
CNN had one week to get the show on the air.

One producer described the approach this way: "Larry's been
on the radio for thirty years. That's what Larry knows. He knows
how to talk to people, how to take calls. He doesn't read books, he's
not that smart, he didn't know squat about politics. He liked talking
to people who were famous. His thing was sitting there smoking,
talking about the track, talking about the old days, philosophizing
about life. We were going to televise his radio show."

Randy Douthit, then CNN's top talk show producer, had another problem: King insisted on asking questions off the top of his
head. He refused to be briefed about the guests, even though CNN
had a well-informed audience that expected a certain level of sophis-
tication. So Douthit had to be subtle. "I'd prepare bullet points of

information on blue cards and put them on Larry's desk," he says. "Then I'd talk to the staff and bring up little tidbits of information in front of him, so he would absorb it."

While King prided himself on the fact that his radio show never screened calls, CNN couldn't afford that luxury. The callers were a crucial part of the program, and they had to be good.

"What Larry King brought to television was a real respect for the caller," says Tammy Haddad, who came with him from Mutual. "Most people used callers as props. For Donahue, Sally, it was a gimmick. For Larry, the calls were just as important as Larry's questions. We took that to the bank. We screened the calls very carefully. We would go through one hundred fifty calls a night to get four or five callers. Now everyone screens calls very carefully."

For Randy Douthit, the callers also filled the interrogatory vacuum left by King. "Larry is Mr. Softball," he says. "The only tough questions were the ones that came from the callers. He would defend the guest, even if the person was a serial killer."

Larry King Live, by design, had the look and feel of a radio show. The set was spare. King began in a suit and tie but later switched to shirtsleeves and suspenders, his tie loosened, his microphone visible. Extreme close-ups fostered a sense of intimacy. But many politicians, businessmen, and celebrities initially refused to appear because they didn't want to field questions from viewers. It was too unscripted, the potential for embarrassment too great. Still, with each guest usually allotted thirty minutes, the lure of such prime-time exposure, even on cable, began to melt the resistance.

King's television guests ranged from Tip O'Neill to baseball great Jim Palmer, from O. J. Simpson to Roseanne to Seka, a porn star. But the producers were careful not to book too many political types. At the time, Haddad says, "the audience would not tolerate talking heads from Washington." That was considered a snore.

King, for his part, still loved to chat up celebrities. "I couldn't stand doing a Rush Limbaugh or Gordon Liddy kind of show," he says. "Politics every day would bore me to death. I'd go out of my mind. I need my Oliver Stone, my William Buckley, my O. J. Simpson, my Demi Moore, also William Kunstler and George Steinbrenner. I need the mix."

King was stretching himself quite thin—television host, radio host, *USA Today* columnist, Baltimore Orioles color man, lecturer, best-selling author—and the workload took its toll. In 1987 he had a heart attack and underwent quintuple-bypass surgery. He quit smoking, put himself on a strict diet, got married again, and bounced back bigger than ever.

As more American homes were wired for cable, CNN was becoming more prominent, and King was well positioned to ride this wave of popularity. The show was becoming more news-driven, and the staff learned how to milk a hot story for all it was worth. *Larry King Live* jumped on the Jim and Tammy Faye Bakker scandal, booking guests to yak about it night after night after night. The idea was to promote the program as the place to turn when news was happening. "The Berlin Wall went down, we couldn't have Connie Stevens on," a staffer says. "CNN was molding Larry's image to be more politically oriented and did a damn good job."

The network did such a good job that ABC tried to lure him away. King had lunch with David Burke, the network president, and Roone Arledge, the president of ABC News, who offered him the chance to follow *Nightline*. They were particularly amazed at the quality of King's calls, not fully understanding how hard the producers worked at screening them. But King decided to stick with CNN, the only network that could broadcast his show to 120 countries.

For all the kudos, however, something was missing. The King show still had a slightly frivolous air, a showbiz sensibility. During the 1988 presidential campaign, King couldn't get George Bush or Michael Dukakis to appear on the program. It might have seemed the ideal forum for the vice president, at least after his highly publicized faceoff with Dan Rather over the Iran-contra affair on the *CBS Evening News*. After all, King wasn't about to press Bush on whether he was in the loop on discussions to ship arms to the Ayatollah Khomeini. But Bush felt a call-in show was too undignified for someone of his stature. Dukakis changed his mind after botching the second presidential debate, the one where he gave a cold, unemotional response when CNN's Bernard Shaw asked how he would react if his wife were raped and killed. In an attempt to repair his image, the Massachusetts governor decided to submit to interviews with King and with Ted Koppel on *Nightline*. On the

King show, Dukakis appeared with his wife, Kitty, and described how his seventy-seven-year-old father had been bound and gagged by an intruder. "My family has felt the pain of crime," he said. It was moving television, although far too late for Dukakis.

Larry King was becoming more than just an entertainer. The show's ratings were the highest on CNN. In 1990 he signed a five-year contract with the network worth a reported $8.7 million, more than forty times the original deal with Ted Turner. Occasionally, though, King's personal life would come back to haunt him, just as it had in the early days in Miami.

When King was in the process of divorcing his fifth wife, Julie Alexander, after just six months, he had a speaking engagement at a Philadelphia synagogue. Seven hundred people showed up to hear him. So did a dozen reporters. One magazine had dubbed him Larry the Lothario.

King told the news conference he would be happy to answer any questions but, on the advice of his attorney, he could not discuss his marital situation. A *Philadelphia Daily News* reporter asked about it anyway.

"It's very personal," King said.

"I don't want to be confrontational," the reporter said, "but you've gotten into this subject matter yourself on many occasions, in broadcast and in print, talking about your personal life . . ."

Larry King, who would never dream of pressing a guest about a sensitive matter, was suddenly being reminded that not everyone in the press played by such gentle rules. "My lawyer said not to . . . Why is this of interest?"

"Because it's gossip," declared a man from the *National Enquirer*. "And because you're a personality, and people like it."

"I have never liked it," King said. "If I were doing an interview with someone, it would be of no interest to me. None. Zip. Zero."

It was, says Larry King, "the beginning of a beautiful friendship."

Ross Perot first appeared on King's show in January 1991 to argue that the United States should not take military action against Iraq. The two men bonded when King broke a cufflink on the air and Perot handed him one of his initialed cufflinks during a break.

It turned out to be a beautiful friendship from Perot's point of view as well. The Dallas businessman would appear nine times on *Larry King Live* during 1991 and 1992, commanding the airwaves virtually at will. Perot used the program as a vehicle to launch his unorthodox bid for the White House, forever altering the relationship between television and presidential candidates. The Talk Show Campaign had been born.

As the '92 season first got under way, the most important media players were the usual Beltway suspects: David Broder and Jack Germond, Tim Russert and Johnny Apple, Ted Koppel and David Brinkley. Larry King wasn't even on the political radar screen.

But there was a growing public anger at Washington insiders, and big-shot journalists were considered charter members of this exclusive club. Many people resented the attack-dog nature of the establishment press, its obsession with polls and punditry, its tendency to harass and harangue public figures in search of a hot headline. At a time when much of the American public was deeply troubled by the sagging economy and insecurities about health care, the talking heads seemed more concerned with Gennifer Flowers, Clinton's draft record, and whether he had inhaled. There was a sense that scandal-mongering journalists were as disconnected from the public as the politicians they loved to ridicule.

Candidates began exploring ways to go around the national press. Jerry Brown courted volunteers with an 800 number that he repeated ad nauseam. Bill Clinton held televised town meetings and mailed copies of his campaign manifesto to any voter who requested one. President Bush did satellite interviews with local anchors from the White House.

On February 20, 1992, Ross Perot told Larry King that if volunteers got his name on all fifty state ballots, he would be willing to mount a "world class" campaign for president. This was not quite as unscripted a moment as it appeared. Perot had said virtually the same thing at a public appearance in Nashville two weeks earlier, warranting only a small item in the Nashville *Tennessean*. He had been discussing a possible candidacy for eight months with two political activists, John Jay Hooker and Jack Gargan. But it was Larry King who provided the electronic megaphone for Perot. King says Hooker "gave me an indication he'd say yes, or I'd never have led with the question."

Tens of thousands of people called Perot's Dallas headquarters after his appearance on *Larry King Live*. The same thing happened after Perot did *Donahue*. A revolutionary method of campaigning was taking hold. The satellite technology of call-in television allowed the candidates to bypass the mainstream press and take their case directly to the viewing audience.

Politicians, of course, had always used entertainment shows to lighten their image. Bobby Kennedy appeared with Jack Paar on the *Tonight* show. Richard Nixon said "sock it to me" on *Laugh-In*. Gary Hart did *Saturday Night Live*. But this was radically different. Talk shows were suddenly moving from political sideshow to main event. And it was Perot who provided the impetus by proving that politics didn't have to be boring, that programs could host presidential contenders and still put big Nielsen numbers on the board. Perot appeared on *Today* four times in two weeks, ridiculing "pompous" and "blow-dried" anchors while doing his "it's that simple" routine with Katie Couric and Bryant Gumbel. When other talk show producers saw the ratings, they quickly jumped on the political bandwagon. They could strike a high-minded pose about serving the public and pull in viewers at the same time.

Larry King's ingratiating approach perfectly suited the needs of a billionaire determined to avoid press conferences and policy specifics. With King lobbing the most general questions, Perot could finesse difficult issues with down-home sloganeering. And the call-in format provided the illusion that he was communing directly with the audience. Only six or seven callers might get through on a given evening, but there was a sense that any ordinary American —Donahue's Louise-from-Omaha—could question a presidential candidate on national television. Average voters could now play Sam Donaldson, and they were asking questions that mattered to them, not the media insiders.

Bill Clinton, who loved to talk, quickly got in the game. He gave the "sooey pig" call on the Nashville Network. He played the sax on *Arsenio Hall*. He fielded questions on MTV, where young people wanted to know his early rock influences (Elvis), favorite musician (Kenny G), astrological sign (Leo), and whether he would inhale if he replayed his pot-smoking experience ("Sure, if I could"). And he sat at Larry King's elbow for the first of three campaign appearances.

King always made the interview pleasant, just as he had for Adlai Stevenson back in the '50s. When Clinton and his running mate, Al Gore, appeared with King, Bill's mother called in to say hi. When Gore did the show some time later, Tipper, his wife, called in anonymously and propositioned him on the air. It wasn't exactly *Meet the Press,* and, not surprisingly, the candidates liked it that way.

Even George Bush, who had solemnly declared that he wouldn't be popping up on any "weird talk shows," made three appearances on *Larry King Live.* Given the mild nature of King's queries— "When was the last time you drove?" "You like campaigning?" "Do you think you're getting a bad rap?" "Is Millie going to do another book?"—Bush felt at ease, even whipping out his wallet to show King his driver's license.

Since King was not in the business of asking tough questions, political strategists tried to exploit the format to put the opposing candidate on the spot. When Perot appeared in June, Republican national chairman Rich Bond called in to challenge his claims about GOP dirty tricks. When Bush appeared in October, Clinton aide George Stephanopoulos called the control room and insisted that he be pressed on Iran-contra. Tammy Haddad talked him into going on the air and questioning the president himself.

"I didn't come here to debate Stephanopoulos," Bush replied. "I'm ready to debate you, Larry. Come on." Bush campaign officials later complained that they had been sandbagged.

By Election Day, six presidential candidates had fielded 122 viewers' questions on *Larry King Live,* and millions more had watched their answers. King had established his program as the preeminent political forum on television. It was a forum that Clinton continued to utilize as president, making three appearances with King in the first two years of his term. He was blunt in telling the mainstream press that talk shows had eliminated the need for him to hold many formal press conferences.

"Larry King liberated me by giving me to the American people directly," the president said.

A week after Bill Clinton took office, an era ended for Larry King.

He threw himself a party at his favorite Washington restaurant,

Duke Zeibert's, where the best lunch table and a plate of matzos was reserved for him each day. King was ending his late-night Mutual radio program, the first national talk show in the country, the one that launched him to prominence back in 1978. He was switching to afternoon drive time.

King rolled up his sleeves and donned a yellow headset as one celebrity after another paid tribute. Don Shula, the Miami Dolphins coach, King's first guest along with Jackie Gleason, called in. So did Don Rickles. Ronald Reagan and Donald Trump sent telegrams. So did Frank Sinatra. Pat Buchanan, Jim Lehrer, and Senate Majority Leader George Mitchell stopped in. Ted Koppel came by after *Nightline*. Phil Donahue did a telephone interview. "You're a long way from hotel lobbies in Miami Beach," he said.

As it turned out, King's afternoon radio show lasted only sixteen months. The ratings were not great. Most of the callers were strident and fiercely conservative, nothing like the eclectic mix that listened to radio after midnight. "These were people who weren't sure the Revolutionary War was a good idea," King says. "Everyone was into conspiracies: Did you hear what Rush Limbaugh said this morning, and Bob Grant yesterday?" He hated the time period and dropped the show, even though Mutual was paying him $1.2 million a year. Larry King was a worldwide TV star. He had finally outgrown radio.

There were other setbacks. The television show, despite such top-drawer guests as Margaret Thatcher and Marlon Brando, went into a ratings slump. King, like CNN itself, was dependent on the news. While he had averaged as many as 2.6 million households during the '92 campaign, now he sometimes drew just 600,000.

King sued a former girlfriend, Rama Fox, for allegedly making slanderous remarks about their relationship. He would later announce his engagement to actress Deanna Lund after just five weeks. But true to form, the relationship dissolved a few weeks after that. King had married Julie Alexander after a couple of months, and that marriage had lasted little more than a year. Just as King craved the variety of different guests every night, he seemed unable to sustain a long-term romantic relationship, and the breakups often led to legal hostilities. King blamed his brief relationships on a "short attention span," but something deeper than that seemed to be at work. It was as if no real-life woman, and the inevitable real-life problems, could compete with the staged thrills of the talk show life and the lecture circuit.

Some colleagues believe King developed a swelled head after the avalanche of publicity he received during the '92 campaign. "If you took his ego away, you'd have the same 250-watt radio station hustler who just spent his last buck on a horse that went backwards," a friend says. "He is exactly the same man he was ten years ago."

But events had a way of continually thrusting King back into the limelight. A year after the election, Ross Perot made one more fateful appearance on King's program. He agreed to debate Vice President Gore about the North American Free Trade Agreement, which was then floundering in Congress. It was a major gamble for the Clinton administration, since Perot was considered a skilled television performer and Gore rather wooden. But with King playing referee, the well-prepared Gore trounced the Texan and gave NAFTA a major boost that helped propel its passage. *Larry King Live* had helped create Ross Perot and, in the space of ninety minutes, had proved his undoing. (Not that Perot simply faded away; he returned to King's side two years later to announce his scheme for a third political party. This time he seemed annoyed as King asked the obvious questions. "Larry, you're missing the point," he snapped.)

King was not shy about taking credit for his role. "Bill Clinton told me, 'I owe you one. You passed NAFTA,' " he boasts. But the novelty of King quizzing the highest officials in the land gradually wore off. Perhaps King began to take himself more seriously, focusing more on policy than personality. In the summer of 1995, he interviewed Clinton for the fourth time as president, with Al Gore at Clinton's side. King asked about Bosnia. He asked about the Middle East. He asked about trade with Japan. He asked about anti-terrorism legislation. It was like a humdrum *Meet the Press* interview, only with little follow-up. Clinton and Gore were flat, reeling off their standard responses, and the session was deadly dull. Only in the final seconds, when Clinton did a bad Brando impersonation, was there the slightest spark of life. The session lacked the magic of the campaign interviews, and viewers went surfing in other directions. Three percent of the cable television audience tuned in.

It is 8:17 P.M., and Skip Smith, the CNN makeup man, is applying a coat of powder to Larry King's face.

King is relaxed, telling stories about his favorite old movies. He is wearing a pink shirt with white collar under pink suspenders, which, he reminds Skip, were given to him by Sharon Stone. King is waiting for Senator Bob Dole, who is making his twenty-seventh appearance on the show. King has already glanced at the blue cards with suggested questions from the staff. Now he just wants to stay loose. He talks about his recent visit to the O. J. Simpson courtroom, where Marcia Clark hugged him and Judge Lance Ito ushered him into his private chambers for a recess that wound up lasting forty minutes. He was treated like a visiting dignitary. He recalls how he approached Simpson, who thanked him for being fair. He wonders if he might be asked to host Simpson's rumored pay-per-view special after the trial.

Dole is the front-runner for the Republican presidential nomination, but he has been booked for only half the show. He will be followed by King's regular panel of Simpson-watchers, analyzing the day's events at the trial. "You gotta do O.J.," King says. "We're the O.J. show of record. The O.J. panel will double Dole's ratings."

At 8:28 Dole walks into the makeup room. "Mister President," King says. They greet each other like old friends.

"I like Larry," Dole says after King leaves. "He knows how to keep it moving. He never tries to embarrass anybody, never tries to nail anybody." Dole has become a fixture on the show. "It's Bob Dole Live," he says.

At 8:55 the two men are wedged into the table on the set, earpieces in place. "Look at me, and at camera six when we take calls," King says.

In the control room down the hall, producer Mary Gregory sits behind an instrument panel, facing a wall of forty-one monitors. Michael Kinsley and Bob Novak are finishing up *Crossfire*. In a small glass-enclosed room to her left, two women are screening calls for the show. All eight lines—six domestic, two international—have been lit up for half an hour. The screeners take the callers' names and numbers, and a second producer calls them back, in an effort to discourage crank callers. Then the most promising calls are relayed to Carrie Stephenson, who is wearing a headset, on Gregory's right. She scribbles their towns and subject matter on a legal pad.

Baileyville, Kansas, line one. Wants to talk about Clinton's weak foreign policy.

Tuscumbia, Alabama, line five. Wonders if Dole is too old to run.

Stockholm, Sweden, line eight. Has a question about Dole's economic policy.

At nine o'oclock, the music comes up and the show begins. "What's it like to be lengths ahead?" King asks.

The interview starts slowly, with Dole sounding uncharacteristically vague. Will he name a running mate early? That's "just an option." What about rumors that retired general Colin Powell would like to run with him? "Well, I don't think that will happen. I'm not trying to duck the question," Dole says, ducking the question. What about the House Republican proposal to end the federal school-lunch program? "We're not talking about taking away school lunches," Dole says, but a moment later admits he is "hedging a little bit" on the proposal.

"Bob . . . I call you Bob because you are the most frequent guest in the history of this program," King says.

"It's Bob Dole Live," Dole says.

What about the balanced budget amendment? "Will the president sign off?" King asks. Small gaffe. "It doesn't have to go to the president," Dole reminds him.

In the control room, Mary Gregory is looking for callers who will touch on recent news stories and propel the discussion forward. "Let's start with Tuscumbia," she says. "How do you pronounce that?" The font operator, a young man on Gregory's left, types Tuscumbia into a machine that will superimpose the words on the screen.

"Larry, line five, Tuscumbia, Alabama," Gregory says softly into a microphone wired to King's earpiece. Button number five blinks silently on a small black console on King's table.

Time for a commercial break. King gives Dole a little political advice. "If Colin wants you, grab it!" he says. "You and Colin—it's over! Race is over!"

At 9:15 Gregory decides to drop Tuscumbia. The issue of Dole's age has already come up. "Larry, let's drop line five. We've already talked about that." She looks at Carrie Stephenson's pad. Charlotte, North Carolina, and Logansport, Indiana, have joined the list. Logansport wants to talk about Democratic demands for a House ethics probe of Newt Gingrich. That could make news.

At 9:17 King takes his first call. "Logansport, Indiana, hello."

It turns out the Logansport man has another agenda. "I understand that the Democrats have launched an ethics committee investigation on some of Newt's speeches," he begins. "And my question is, do you really believe that this dope-smoking, draft-dodging, non-taxpaying, philandering, socialist liar, like Clinton, is going to be reelected?"

"There's no meanness in America," King says sarcastically.

Gregory likes to put some foreign callers on the air because they appeal to the international audience. "Line eight, Maastricht, the Netherlands," she says into the mike. "I'm sorry, Larry, it's MAH-stricht."

The Dutch man asks about Bosnia. Dole gives his standard reply.

Another break. "You're doing great as always, Bob," King says. "One of the great guests." He returns to the subject of the vice presidency. "If you get Powell . . ." He lets out a low whistle.

The screeners keep relaying the calls: Caruthersville, Missouri. Porto Alegre, Brazil. Gregory gives King two more callers. A Detroit man asks how Dole would distinguish himself from the other Republican leaders. A Saudi Arabia man wants to know his interpretation of the New World Order. Gregory says the foreign audience loves New World Order questions.

At 9:28 Dole is through. "Terrific job, Larry," Gregory says into the mike.

At 9:31 it's O.J. time. King introduces his Los Angeles lawyers, Gerry Spence, Milton Grimes, and Burton Katz. Gregory cues a fourteen-second sound bite of Judge Lance Ito admonishing Spence for muttering something in the courtroom that day. It was "Jesus

Christ," but Spence, to Gregory's frustration, won't repeat it on the air.

Small problem: Katz's herringbone suit is "bleeding" on the screen. Gregory picks up a black phone and calls the CNN producer in Atlanta. "Can you tell L.A. never to let Katz wear that kind of suit again?" she says.

Atlanta wants to go to Wolf Blitzer, traveling with Clinton, for a report on Secretary of State Warren Christopher, who has been hospitalized with a bleeding ulcer. Gregory wants to keep it short. "Larry, we're gonna have you out of the commercial throw to Wolf Blitzer in Ottawa," she says. "It's a thirty-second update. No questions, Larry."

"Give me some calls," King says.

The calls are coming in, but Gregory doesn't like them. They are too obscure. Most deal with people's own theories about the case. These are the O.J. addicts who watch the trial all day on CNN. Stephenson writes down the summaries. Indianapolis: Evidence shows Ron Goldman got page at 10:47, no recall. Liverpool, New York: Menu found in Nicole's shower. Gallatin, Tennessee: Discovery of O.J.'s blood was too convenient.

"What else you got?" Gregory asks.

Finally, at 9:47 Gregory gives King the first Simpson question, from Oakville, Ontario. "If the defense feels that there is so much mishandling of evidence, why wouldn't they ask for a mistrial?" the caller says.

"Well, there isn't grounds for a mistrial," Gerry Spence says.

Another break. "Tomorrow night, Tom Clancy joins us," King says. An Austin, Texas, caller tells the screener that Simpson lawyer F. Lee Bailey appeared to be consulting with prosecutor Christopher Darden. Gregory asks King if it looked that way to him. "No," he says. She dumps the call.

"Any more to give me?" King asks. He is itchy for calls.

At 9:54 Gregory puts on a caller from Gainesville, Florida, who asks a question that's already been answered about why prosecutor Darden had to apologize to Ito that day. Two calls were all the producers could scrounge up for the half hour. That's the way it goes some nights.

King thanks his guests, teases an upcoming appearance by

F. Lee Bailey. "Have a great evening," he says. "Who loves ya, baby? We do. Good night."

King is pleased with the program, but he doesn't like to hang around after the show. His work is done. He emerges from the studio, slips on a brown leather jacket and heads for the lobby, where a driver is waiting to take him to his Arlington high-rise.

The contrast could hardly be greater. Journalists try to grill their subjects, to extract nuggets of news at all costs; King is a soothing, reassuring presence. Journalists view politicians as adversaries; King often sees them as friends. Journalists believe they are uniquely qualified to interrogate public figures; King lets his audience ask questions. Many journalists privately scoff at King's gentle style, but he has found his niche. The public has grown tired of the prosecutorial media culture. And if King goes a bit too easy on his guests, most viewers don't seem to care.

It is five weeks after the 1994 elections. King's guest is Mario Cuomo. They still see each other from time to time, most recently at a joint speaking engagement at the Washington Convention Center. King never tires of having his famous pals on the program, and Cuomo, who helped him launch the CNN program a decade earlier, is no exception. This time, however, Cuomo is appearing not as rising national star but as defeated local candidate, having failed to win a fourth term against a little-known state senator, George Pataki. Still, King is suitably upbeat, joshing with Cuomo, reminding him they have the same lecture agent, and telling him he could have been president. Cuomo returns the compliment.

"There are very few people who can do what you do," Cuomo says.

"How true," King says.

"You've been a great friend," Cuomo says.

"And you're a great friend," King says.

CHAPTER FIVE

CAUGHT IN
THE CROSSFIRE

I n the fall of 1979, Michael Kinsley made his reluctant debut on national television.

Kinsley was the editor of *The New Republic,* perhaps the favorite magazine of the chattering classes, and was starting to draw attention as a brilliant young journalist. He was a Rhodes scholar, a Harvard Law School graduate, a former editor at *The Washington Monthly,* and an unabashed liberal with a stunningly analytical mind. A bit nerdy-looking, with short hair and glasses and a slightly perplexed expression, Kinsley was, above all, a man of letters. He was openly disdainful of what he described as "televised journalistic gasbaggery."

The hot political story of the season was an accusation that Hamilton Jordan, Jimmy Carter's chief of staff, had snorted cocaine. Kinsley wrote an editorial in *The New Republic* ridiculing the "giant web of hypocrisy" among journalists and other critics, who barely bothered to hide their own marijuana and cocaine use, trumpeting such charges in the drug-soaked culture of the '70s. A producer for the *Today* show called to ask if he would discuss the piece the next morning. Kinsley protested that he was hardly an expert on the Washington drug scene.

"In those days," he says, "knowing nothing about a subject made me hesitant to talk about it on TV."

The producer persisted, and Kinsley agreed to speak generally about the hypocrisy issue as long as he was not asked to expound on the use of drugs in Washington. He was clearly nervous as he arrived at the NBC studio on Nebraska Avenue, where he discovered that the station's interns knew more about the subject than he did.

Tom Brokaw was anchoring from New York, and his first question was about the use of drugs in Washington: "Tell me, Mike, how widespread is it?" Kinsley mumbled an unintelligible reply, which Brokaw asked him to repeat. Kinsley was furious. "They violated their promise from the word go," he says.

Welcome to the world of television, Mike.

The journey of Michael Kinsley from cloistered magazine intellectual to televised shouting head in many ways mirrors the rise of the talk show culture itself. The growth of these programs depends on a steady supply of print journalists who lend their knowledge and prestige to an entertainment format sorely lacking in both. The talk shows need guests with the little chyron captions identifying them as representing *The New Republic* or *Time* or *The Washington Post*. And the journalists need television for the unmatched visibility and celebrity it bestows.

It is a Faustian bargain, and one that Kinsley's friends never thought he would make. As a writer and editor, Kinsley dealt in subtlety and nuance. He was often eccentric, always cutting against the grain of conventional wisdom. He could expose the weakness in a liberal argument with the same coldhearted efficiency with which he skewered the right wing. The notion that he would wind up as the cohost of *Crossfire,* engaging in verbal wrestling matches night after night, squeezed into an artificial position "from the left," seemed unimaginable to his friends and colleagues.

Mort Kondracke, who was then working with Kinsley at *The New Republic,* drew barbs from the boss each Friday as he went off to tape *The McLaughlin Group.* Someone would ring a bell, and Kinsley would lead the catcalls.

"He thought this was beneath the dignity of a serious journalist," Kondracke says. "His exact words were, 'There goes Mort, off to make a fool of himself again.' I told him, Michael, you will do this one day. He said, No no no no no."

On those occasions when Kinsley dabbled in television, he seemed to feel slightly soiled. After one such experience in the mid-'80s, Kinsley penned this apologia: "I've served as a summer replacement on the Cable News Network show *Crossfire,* which makes *McLaughlin* look like tea with Nancy Reagan. On *Crossfire,* two journalist 'hosts' snarl and scream inhospitably at two bewildered 'guests' and each other for half an hour every weekday . . . By the end of my two-week stint I was a trained killer, unfit for human society and in need of plastic surgery to remove the permanent sneer from my face."

It was just the beginning.

Years before *Crossfire,* when CNN was just a gleam in Ted Turner's eye, there was Braden and Buchanan.

They were a seemingly mismatched pair of antagonists. Tom Braden, a liberal newspaper columnist, was a patrician former CIA agent in a rumpled trench coat who chain-smoked Marlboros. Pat Buchanan, the conservative columnist, was an Irish street brawler and former Nixon operative who favored pinstriped Brooks Brothers suits. The two men didn't like each other much. For a time, they wouldn't even appear on the same program. In the early '70s, Braden wrote a column assailing Buchanan, who fired off a blistering letter to the editor. A morning talk show asked them to debate. Braden refused, saying it wouldn't be good television because he couldn't stand Buchanan.

Tom Braden grew up in a journalistic culture in which ethics were far more relaxed than they are today. In 1975 he strongly supported Nelson Rockefeller's appointment as vice president and defended Rockefeller's practice of making sizable loans to his friends. He neglected to mention that Rockefeller had been his own secret benefactor as well. During the 1950s, Rockefeller had loaned Braden $100,000 to buy a newspaper in Oceanside, California. The New York governor later loaned Braden's wife, Joan, $10,000 to make an unsuccessful television pilot. Rockefeller also helped the Bradens buy their $200,000 home in Chevy Chase, Maryland. When this financial assistance was disclosed during congressional hearings, Braden dismissed it as just "a loan to a friend."

Braden was also a close friend of Henry Kissinger, who, as secretary of state, appointed Joan Braden to a senior department post. The Bradens even threw a book party for Kissinger. Yet Braden saw nothing untoward in writing a column urging Kissinger to run for the Senate.

Pat Buchanan, meanwhile, had emerged from the rubble of Watergate as a high-powered commentator. As a Nixon aide he had demanded an end to the networks' "instant analysis" of presidential speeches, but he now made his living analyzing everything that presidents and other politicians did. Among his outlets was a daily three-minute radio debate with Frank Mankiewicz, a former Bobby Kennedy aide. When Mankiewicz was named the president of National Public Radio in 1977, Tom Braden was tapped as his replacement. Two years later, Washington's WRC gave them a three-hour radio show in afternoon drive time.

The new political odd couple knew how to mix it up. Buchanan called Braden a "pointy-headed liberal" and member of the "Volvo, white-wine and cheese set." Braden called Buchanan an "ideological bedfellow of George Wallace" and "narrow-minded New Rightist." They were developing a pugilistic style that contrasted sharply with the chin-pulling politeness of Beltway programs like *Washington Week in Review.*

"I've always liked radio," Buchanan says. "I like the back-and-forth format. You sharpen your arguments, and you're not just pulpiteering. It takes a tremendous amount of energy to maintain it for three hours of talking," especially when pitted against the "cantankerous" Braden.

"We fought like hell," Braden says. "Pat's a fascist, no doubt about it." Still, they went on the road giving speeches together, went out to dinner, visited each other's homes.

For all their feistiness, the duo sometimes echoed the conventional wisdom. A year before the 1980 elections, Buchanan said: "With the possible exception of Kennedy and, of course, Carter, there are no political candidates out there that strike sparks."

"No one cares about Ronald Reagan," Braden said.

"Don't say that," Buchanan replied.

"Well, it's true."

Braden didn't think much more of Reagan after he became president. "I don't think he understands the difference between announcing a foreign policy and shooting off at the mouth, and you know, Pat, I don't think you do either," he told Buchanan.

Although it was just a local radio show, Braden and Buchanan developed a loyal following among political insiders. Veteran diplomat Ellsworth Bunker once called the show from a gas station. "We had a high-level audience, and we got high-level calls, people who really knew what they were talking about," Braden says. "Senator Gaylord Nelson told me when he walked into the Senate gym, the guys who were doing the rubdowns always said, 'Do you want to listen to the boys?' "

They took turns throwing temper tantrums; that was part of the attraction. Buchanan once walked out twenty-five minutes before the show began because a *Washington Post* reporter had been allowed to sit in. The station called John McLaughlin, who rushed in, red-faced, to fill in.

Another time, Buchanan told Braden to shut up. Braden got so mad that he didn't say a word for the next two hours. "It was an outrageous thing to do, and I shouldn't have done it," Braden says. "But if you get to that level on a talk show, you might as well quit."

Inevitably, the television world took note. Braden and Buchanan were invited to join a late-night syndicated show on Washington's Channel 9. The histrionics grew more animated before the cameras.

One guest was Ken Wollack, then a Middle East policy analyst. He was interrupted so often that he realized he was merely a foil for Braden and Buchanan's high-decibel act. "I felt like I was in a barroom brawl," he said. "The only thing missing was the beer bottle over my head."

Victor Gold, a former Spiro Agnew speechwriter, dismissed the pairing as "a form of ideological masturbation. You get your jerk liberal versus your jerk conservative."

For all the caustic reviews, Braden and Buchanan were getting noticed, and in television terms, that is what mattered. CNN, then a two-year-old venture struggling for attention, needed that kind of star power. Widely ridiculed as the Chicken Noodle Network, it had a largely interchangeable cast of young journalists and plenty of airtime to fill. The producers were drawn to the notion of a high-energy, left-right faceoff as a kind of signature program. They offered Braden and Buchanan a show at 11:30 each night. It would be called *Crossfire*.

• • •

Tom Braden was stunned when he found a Ku Klux Klansman on the set. "I remember walking in and seeing this guy with his goddamn robe on," he says. "Holy Jesus! I was just struck dumb."

When the program began, Braden told the Klansman: "You should be ashamed! You look like you're going to a Halloween party. Why are you wearing this stupid garb?"

"Because your producer asked me to," the KKK man said.

The producer was Randy Douthit, a hard-charging impresario with a somewhat tabloid approach to the news. Since the new show was up against *Nightline,* Douthit knew Ted Koppel would land all the best guests. He needed a gimmick.

"I initially pumped it up to get the excitement going," Douthit says. "I was feeding both guys ammunition. These Washington shows were a bit stuffy. Most shows start out with an explanation of the issue; I didn't want to bother with that. It was 'let's go for this guy's throat, here's the soft spot, just hit him!' I figured after a year, no guest would ever appear on the show again."

Crossfire was the only program on television where the hosts were not supposed to like each other. And few programs could match it in the oversimplification department. The very notion that there was one liberal and one conservative view of each issue was ludicrous, but on a twenty-two-minute show it helped to have the battle lines clearly drawn. There was little room for the "yes, but" argument, for caveat and complexity, but that suited the producers just fine. Braden was the left-winger, Buchanan the right-winger, and the guests would have to fend for themselves.

Crossfire was launched on June 25, 1982, from a makeshift studio near Georgetown, across from a topless bar. It looked like a public access cable show. The set consisted of three chairs: Braden and Buchanan faced each other, with the guest, Senator Charles Mathias, sitting with arms crossed in the middle. The tape holding Buchanan's earpiece peeled off within seconds, and the cohosts asked rambling questions. The topic was the resignation of Secretary of State Alexander Haig, and they began with a telephone hookup to Richard Allen, the former national security adviser, in Tokyo. Allen spoke over what sounded like the roar of the ocean.

"I don't have much background on it, and I'm halfway around the world," Allen said, raising the question of why he was on the show at all. The question was rendered moot when the faint connection was lost.

Braden then posed the query to Mathias, who said: "It's as much a mystery to me as to the rest of the world."

Improvement did not come swiftly. During a show about an execution taking place that night, Douthit had to be talked out of dimming the lights at the moment of death. "They used to have *Geraldo*-type bookings," a CNN producer says. "It was a horrible show in the beginning."

One night, *Crossfire* hosted members of the extremist group Posse Comitatus. Another night, it was Louise James Africa and Laverne Sims Africa, members of the radical group MOVE, whose home had been firebombed by Philadelphia police in a fatal tragedy six months earlier. Representative Robert Dornan was in the conservative chair.

The women, seething with anger, started yelling as soon as the show began. When Dornan called their group "bizarre," Louise Africa said: "You're either gonna be serious or we will walk off this television set."

When Braden said there was no doubt they had antagonized their neighbors by throwing garbage in the street, Louise Africa exploded. "How often have you been to Philadelphia?" she demanded.

"Five or six times," Braden said.

"How much time have you spent on Osage Avenue in the past five years?"

"None," Braden said.

"How much time in the past four years?"

"None."

"How about the last three years? Two years? One? Six months?"

"What's your point?"

"I will make it in my own time in my own way."

When Braden said the garbage incidents had been widely reported, Africa snapped: "I'm asking you a question!"

"Are you saying every newspaper in the country is a liar?" Braden said.

"Yes or no? Simple question!" Africa said. "Yes or no? Then explain to me how you can sit there with your pompous arrogant ass and say, 'There is no doubt'? You take back your statement!"

Braden tried to move on. "No, I'm not going to the next question!" Africa said.

Laverne Africa had been sitting there glowering; now it was her turn to unload.

"Why did you drive your neighbors crazy?" Dornan asked.

"You know what? I do not even want to continue with this show," she declared. "It's obvious that you and you are here to play games. You are here to *browbeat!* You are here out of your *prejudice* and your *racism!*"

When the show ended, Louise Africa called upon Dornan to "die."

It was a stunning demonstration of what can happen when guests refuse to play by the conventional rules. "That was the most vacuous, most outrageous half hour that was ever on television," Braden says.

Douthit, for his part, makes no apologies for the confrontational format. "You have to get them in the tent first," he says.

The program was soon moved to 7:30, and Braden and Buchanan would race down Wisconsin Avenue after finishing their radio show, arriving moments before airtime. Braden much preferred the radio venture, where he and Buchanan thought up the topics and booked many of the guests themselves. "Television was too programmed," he says. "You had too many guys who were interested only in what's going to make raw meat for the audience. Occasionally I'd make a suggestion or two, but in general it was all taken away from us.

"I didn't think it was as good," Braden says. "It got to be a matter of one-liners rather than serious discussion. It was two guys who came pretty close to swearing at each other. It became just a game, more theater than rational argument. The directives came down from Atlanta: Here's the subject. Lots of times the subject would be something you're not particularly interested in. You become an actor rather than yourself. I got so goddamn sick of terrorism that I couldn't get worked up about it at all. You'd always have the same list of characters, and plastered under their pictures would be 'terrorism expert.' It would be some guy from a PR firm. You were doing bullshit. I said to myself, I wouldn't watch this."

Buchanan, by contrast, enjoyed the two-fisted approach. "*Crossfire* has its limitations, but if the show's well done you can hear, aggressively presented, both sides, maybe three or four sides, on major issues of the day," he says. "We don't want the old *Meet the Press,* where someone rattles off his cassette for two minutes. You push and poke and get people to say what they really think. You can punch through the political rote, the patter, that all those politicians develop in Washington. It's sort of a no-B.S. show."

More important, Buchanan's mere presence on the show was, in his view, an ideological triumph. Here he was, a former White House aide who had helped pen the Nixon-Agnew attacks on the press, coming into America's living rooms each week on both *Crossfire* and *The McLaughlin Group*. He had infiltrated the liberal media in a way that would have seemed far-fetched a decade earlier.

"*Crossfire* is one place where people who are conservative can hear their own views represented and argued," Buchanan says. "These folks are desperate to hear they're not alone. The problem conservatives have always had is a sense of isolation. They pick up the paper and don't see their views on the front page . . . The democratization of the media has been of enormous benefit to conservatives."

Buchanan was a true believer, and he abandoned *Crossfire* in 1985 when President Reagan dangled the job of White House communications director. Bob Novak hailed the selection of his friend in the column he wrote with Rowland Evans. "This single staff selection can profoundly affect the second term of the Reagan presidency," they declared, calling Buchanan "the first legitimate conservative activist . . . on Reagan's senior staff."

But Buchanan quickly dropped out of sight, prompting complaints in the press about a communications director who didn't communicate with reporters. Journalists deemed unfriendly to Reagan, such as David Broder, were excluded from White House background briefings. Conservative writers, by contrast, were treated well. "Pat was a good source," Fred Barnes says.

As the criticism grew louder, Buchanan went on *Larry King Live*—back at what King called the "friendly confines" of CNN—to talk about it.

"I am a heretic to the conventional wisdom of most journalists in Washington, D.C.," Buchanan said. "I disagree with their point of view. That doesn't mean you hate the press. That's silly."

"We miss you on *Crossfire*," a caller from Honolulu said.

"Thanks very much. I miss doing *Crossfire*."

CNN did not replace Buchanan, turning instead to Bob Novak as a frequent substitute. Novak didn't particularly enjoy the nightly clashes, and his snarling style had a way of ticking off the guests.

When Christopher Hitchens appeared on *Crossfire,* he got so mad he called Novak a "polecat" and "McCarthyite bum." Novak had Hitchens barred from the program.

A scowling Novak was merciless when the guest was Christopher Matthews of the *San Francisco Examiner.* Novak called Matthews "one of the leading sharks of the news media," said his comments were "silly" and "superficial" and finally declared: "When I first met you, you were a paid flack for Tip O'Neill."

"The reason you keep bringing up Tip O'Neill's name is because he would never give you an interview and he threw you out of his office and you can't get over it," Matthews said. He was referring to a charge by the former House speaker that he had given Evans and Novak the boot in the early '70s after they offered to provide favorable coverage in exchange for regular access, which the columnists denied.

"That is a lie, like a lot of other things that come from you, Mr. Matthews," Novak snapped.

"Bob, for years, for years, you tried to get into his office. I was there."

"That's a flat lie that he threw me out of his office," Novak said. Matthews was banned from *Crossfire*.

Matthews says he knew nothing of the original incident but that O'Neill repeatedly cited it to him in refusing to appear on Novak's CNN show. "I was always a great source for Bob," he says. "I liked the guy. But he decided he doesn't like me. Tip O'Neill was too big for them to take on, so I guess he's decided to focus on me. I was playing defense for my old boss, who I'm loyal to."

A veteran CNN staffer described the program's switch to Novak this way: "Buchanan could be awful to someone, but with that Irish charm they'd want to shake his hand. When Novak did it, they wanted to punch his lights out."

"Novak is a shameless player of the game," Mike Kinsley says. "He's created this persona of a Bob Novak who growls. He's got that sharklike smile. He'll say anything, no matter how outrageous, and work himself into a lather."

The raucous tone of the show often worked against it. While it dealt with substantive issues, some members of Congress, particularly those in leadership positions, shied away from *Crossfire*. The program often had to settle for second-tier guests because many Washington officials simply refused to come on. Others, like Republican congressman Newt Gingrich, enjoyed doing *Crossfire*.

Rick Davis, CNN's senior talk show producer, says the program's shouting-match reputation is overstated. "*Crossfire* is one of the best shows on television, because the whole point is not to allow the guests to get away with having their spin go unchallenged," he says. "Prominent senators and congressmen have told me it's their favorite show because many of these guys are debaters. There are some other people who don't like doing the show and don't come back. They feel they're interrupted too much. There's a real fine line from it being an exciting show to sometimes going over the line. All of us behind the camera don't like that. We get in the host's ear and try to get them to stop."

Pat Buchanan returned to *Crossfire* in 1987. CNN executives did not hesitate to put the man who had just been Ronald Reagan's paid spokesman back on the air, talking about Reagan administration policies. Buchanan was a star, and in the end that was what television cared about. He was soon said to be earning more than $500,000 as a pol-turned-pundit.

Tom Braden, worn down by the nightly grind and nearing retirement age, began to weary of Buchanan's assaults. "It's easier to be a conservative," he says. "As a liberal, you're not absolutely sure of where you stand or what in the world you ought to do about each particular problem. I'd be a little bit unsure of whether I was right, and Pat was never uncertain about whether he was right. Pat knew where he stood."

Others had a less charitable view. "Braden was like a punching bag," Mort Kondracke says. "Braden would say 'this is ridiculous' or 'this is outrageous,' and Buchanan would cut him to ribbons. It was a complete mismatch."

CNN officials soon grew dissatisfied with the second act of Braden and Buchanan. They decided to dump Tom Braden. All that remained was to find a suitable replacement. They sounded out Mark Shields, but he wasn't interested.

"I can't pretend to support whatever is the crazy liberal issue du jour," he says.

Mike Kinsley could not face going on the air.

Each time he was asked to appear on *The McLaughlin Group,* it was a harrowing experience. He did vast amounts of research. He would print out four or five pages of notes from his computer, complete with contingency plans if the conversation took an unexpected turn. One day McLaughlin looked at him and thundered: "Put that away! Don't you know this is a completely spontaneous and unrehearsed program?!" Kinsley couldn't help but observe that McLaughlin had his own set of notes.

One Friday morning there was a last-minute change of topics before the *McLaughlin* taping. "I actually chickened out," Kinsley says. "I freaked out and got stage fright and begged Fred to substitute for me about an hour before the show." Fred Barnes was the perfect choice, Kinsley says, because "Fred's never let talking about something he knows nothing about bother him."

Over time, Kinsley grew more inured to the stresses of television. When he was editor of *Harper's* magazine, he began appearing with William Buckley on *Firing Line.* Soon he was filling in more regularly on *Crossfire,* although he was still embarrassed when the show would book guests like the Amazing Randi to discuss paranormal psychology. "We'd have someone in favor of flying saucers and someone against them," Kinsley says.

On one program, Kinsley was calmly interviewing a member of Congress when the voice of a *Crossfire* producer exploded in his earpiece: "Get mad! Get mad!" Thoughtfulness, it seemed, was not a quality the show valued highly. It was television as temper tantrum.

Still, Kinsley's growing visibility hardly prepared his friends for his next move. In the summer of 1989, as Kondracke was giving Kinsley a ride to work, "he said he was thinking of leaving the editorship of *The New Republic* to do *Crossfire* every night," Kondracke says. "I damn near drove into a tree." He told Kinsley the idea was "crazy."

But Kinsley had tired of a decade of magazine editing and of his constant arguments with Martin Peretz, *The New Republic*'s owner. He convinced himself that a television job would give him more time for his syndicated "TRB" column and other writing. The six-figure salary was also a major attraction.

"I like the fame and fortune," Kinsley admits. "I didn't go on *Crossfire* for self-sacrificing reasons. The pay is great compared to *The New Republic*." He further rationalized the move by insisting that writing for an opinion magazine, no matter how erudite or insightful, was no way to reach the masses. "The real world is that people make up their minds watching TV," he says.

Kinsley was nervous every day he was on, poring over the newspapers and anticipating the "catfight" that awaited him at 7:30. "Someone is trying to make an ass of you, and you're trying to make an ass of them," he says.

Painfully awkward at first, Kinsley gradually learned the rituals of television warfare. He began to make "certain intellectual compromises that you hope aren't corrupting." And then there were Buchanan's attacks and insults. Kinsley never socialized with Buchanan—unlike Braden, they have never been to each other's homes —and the relationship sometimes grew tense.

"Buchanan has this very bad habit of patronizing you, and it's taken me awhile to figure out how not to let him dominate the agenda and frame the issues," he says. "If he brings up some total red herring, you've got to have a sense of how much time you have and whether you're gonna take on the red herring or let it go by. I'm always tempted to play defense. Pat never fears to oversimplify."

An equally challenging adjustment for Kinsley, who enjoyed the theoretical twists and turns of column writing, was the black-and-white nature of the format. A *Crossfire* producer would call in the morning to ascertain his position on some topic, and if it wasn't the usual liberal stance, there would be a long sigh.

"When I first got to the show, it was a big problem for them that I was a free trader," Kinsley says. "Their lock on the issue was, right wing/free trade, left wing/protectionist. Time has solved that problem because Pat Buchanan is the world's biggest protectionist. We now have a new cliché." Still, he says, "I can ask ten skeptical questions on any issue, even if I disagree with it. That way I can have my intellectual honesty."

CNN staffers welcomed this approach. "Michael is easier because he's more intellectually versatile than Pat," one says. "He has legal training, and he can argue an issue very efficiently on television that he doesn't really believe in. It's sort of the dirty little secret of *Crossfire*."

Sometimes the secret got out. On one show Kinsley told attorney Floyd Abrams, his designated sparring partner: "I'm actually on your side tonight, but of course, like any good lawyer, I can argue it round or argue it flat. So look, the case for the other side is this . . ."

Kinsley's friends have trouble hiding their disappointment with his second career. "Being on *Crossfire* is a fate you'd only wish on your enemies, but he's wished it on himself," Marty Peretz says.

"Michael has been polarized," Mort Kondracke says. "He is a much more subtle thinker than you could ever be on *Crossfire*. If you only do combat television all the time, it does scramble your brain."

Disaffected liberals began to grumble that Kinsley was no match for Buchanan's conservative fervor. Writer David Shenk even complained about Kinsley's "croaky voice," saying that "his civility, his affection for the finer points of policy and his lawyerly interrogative style are the antithesis of compelling television."

"Mike looks absurd saying 'from the left' every night," says Christopher Hitchens. "It's hypocritical on the part of both him and the network."

Kinsley concedes that he does not uphold the liberal banner the way Buchanan champions conservatism. In fact, he calls himself "a wishy-washy moderate." But he insists it's not necessarily bad for liberalism that he is less ideological than his right-wing counterpart.

"Certainly real hard-core, left-wing opinions don't get on *Crossfire*, just as they don't get on other shows," he says. "This is partly a reflection of the range of American political debate, from extreme right to moderate left. And it's partly a knee-jerk reaction by television producers."

Kinsley felt hamstrung in other ways. At *The New Republic,* the whole point of publishing the magazine was to spot an intellectual trend before it made its way into *The New York Times* or *The Washington Post.* But at CNN, Kinsley found there was little enthusiasm for getting out in front of the news. The staff seemed wedded to utterly conventional thinking. They were more interested in the Beltway flap of the day, no matter how trivial, than exploring new ideas. "I've actually heard producers at *Crossfire* use the phrase 'ahead of the curve' as a pejorative," Kinsley says.

A basic fact of talk show life is that the politician is always in the hot seat. Journalists sit on one side, asking questions. The senator or governor or cabinet secretary sits on the other side and answers them. The politician bobs and weaves, the reporters press for specifics, and the session often produces something that passes for "news": Senator Jones acknowledged today that he didn't have the votes to pass his legislation. Governor Smith today refused to rule out a tax increase. Congressman White said today he would be willing to negotiate with the president. The two sides might go out for drinks, frequent the same Georgetown parties, send their kids to the same private schools, but on television, the appearance of an adversarial relationship was preserved.

Bob Novak had a different idea.

When Novak quit *The McLaughlin Group* in the fall of 1988, he envisioned a program in which a politician would sit with the pundits each week, just one of the gang, and kick around the week's news. The journalists would not call the guest "Congressman" or "Senator," but Charlie or Trent or Newt. They would pal around and treat each other as peers.

It is a spectacularly bad idea because it conveys the impression that journalists and political figures are all charter members of the same club, the Washington insiders' club. It also makes for boring television, since many of the politicians are rather stiff in the punditry role, and rather predictable. One week the Republican guest talks up the GOP, the next week the Democrat takes the Democratic side of every issue. But Novak believed in the format, and the folks at CNN went along. The new show was called *The Capital Gang.*

"It's interesting to have them work on their own, not be asked questions or deferred to," Novak says of the politicians. "Some people do it well and some really badly. Lee Atwater, and he was a really good friend of mine, was just horrible."

Novak's plan was for a good-natured version of *McLaughlin,* a program that would be live each Saturday night to give it more energy. Randy Douthit, who had launched *Crossfire* and *Larry King Live,* became the producer, and Novak functioned behind the scenes as a sort of coproducer. He picked his panelists—columnist Mark Shields, Al Hunt of *The Wall Street Journal,* and Margaret Warner of *Newsweek*—and made a point of consulting them about each week's show.

Novak served as moderator in the pilot episode, and everyone, including Novak, agreed he was less than stellar. Running the program detracted from his attack-dog role. Novak decided he needed another moderator, one whose conservative outlook matched his own. He decided on his friend Pat Buchanan.

Buchanan jumped at the offer, but the two had a crucial misunderstanding. Novak thought Buchanan would be leaving *The McLaughlin Group* to help him launch the new show. Buchanan thought he would be doing both programs. And so Buchanan wound up on *Capital Gang* without giving up his coveted seat on *McLaughlin.* He was on television six nights a week, twice on Saturdays. Pat Buchanan was by far the most visible conservative in the media world.

As the 1988 campaign unfolded, Buchanan became a tireless cheerleader for Vice President George Bush. This was only fair, Buchanan believed, because most of the liberal media was on Michael Dukakis's side. Still, some of the liberal commentators occasionally criticized Dukakis. Buchanan, who months earlier had been working with Bush in the Reagan White House, saw his role as one of unabashed advocacy.

"I was on *Crossfire,* I hosted *Capital Gang,* I was the lead panelist on *McLaughlin* and a regular on *Good Morning America,*" he says. "As a surrogate, a spokesman for the Bush side, the conservative side, I probably got far more television time than any other Bush surrogate. After one debate, the liberal pundits were beating his brains out, and I said I thought he had eaten Dukakis's lunch."

After Bush won the presidency, Buchanan became a valued ally. Bush cultivated the relationship, even writing Buchanan an admiring note. "The president and I were big friends," Buchanan says. "He was inviting me up to the White House for lunches and those neat little dinners. Bush clearly felt he had a friend in the media."

The friendship did not last. Three years later, disturbed by Bush's domestic policies, Pat Buchanan announced his campaign to wrest the Republican nomination from the incumbent president. He was leaving *Crossfire,* and *Capital Gang,* and *McLaughlin,* for yet another spin through the revolving door, this time as a candidate for the highest office in the land.

As the talk show candidate for president, Buchanan was at home on the television circuit, making stops at *Crossfire* and *Larry King Live* and a spate of other shows. He had transformed himself from host to political aspirant, but the difference, he says, isn't that great. "People mock *The McLaughlin Group* and *Crossfire,* but the training I got there, and on the radio, it is extraordinary for a candidate. Extraordinary!" he says. "Almost nothing catches you off-guard. You are able to articulate your views clearly, sharply, and briefly. You learn to limit the wonk stuff and try to get some humor and wit into it."

Crossfire, meanwhile, needed a conservative to warm the Buchanan chair. Fortunately for the program, John Sununu, Bush's chief of staff, had been forced to resign weeks earlier after his lavish travel expenses and bullheaded style combined to render him a political liability. Sununu, who treated reporters with open disdain, now had a chance to become part of the media world. In December 1991 CNN announced that the former New Hampshire governor would become Mike Kinsley's new cohost, commenting on the campaign of the president he had faithfully served for three years. Big-name conservatives seemed to be popping up everywhere; Buchanan's replacement for three nights was a former Reagan aide named Oliver North.

While Pat Buchanan stormed New Hampshire, his former colleagues watched with bemusement. "It was hard for me to take him seriously as a presidential candidate because he wasn't a serious presidential candidate," Kinsley says. "He met a need for the media and the political system in opposing Bush from the right."

Buchanan captured 37 percent of the New Hampshire vote against Bush, the high-water mark of his campaign. But his candidacy was also a polarizing one. He was widely criticized during the primaries for past insensitive comments about Jews (such as calling Capitol Hill "Israeli-occupied territory") and his defense of some accused Nazi war criminals. Some critics accused him of anti-Semitism. Buchanan strongly denied any such prejudice, and nearly all his talk show colleagues—Mike Kinsley, Bob Novak, Al Hunt, Fred Barnes, Jack Germond—rallied to his defense, saying he was perhaps insensitive but no anti-Semite. They were, in a real sense, his business associates. They had become character witnesses for a presidential candidate who used to work alongside them and, in a few months, would undoubtedly do so again.

Buchanan's last moment in the political spotlight came when he addressed the Republican convention in Houston. He assailed Bill Clinton as a draft dodger who favored "abortion on demand" and "homosexual rights." He ridiculed Hillary Clinton as a champion of "radical feminism" who "believes that twelve-year-olds should have the right to sue their parents." The crowd loved it.

Six weeks after the election, CNN announced that Pat Buchanan was rejoining *Crossfire,* which had been paying him $438,000 a year. He would rotate with John Sununu. The man who had passionately denounced the Clintons before the cheering Republican delegates would now be commenting on President Clinton's performance night after night. John McLaughlin welcomed him back as an occasional panelist. Mutual gave him a nationally syndicated radio show, *Pat Buchanan & Company,* with a rotating roster of liberal cohosts and 170 stations.

"What did they expect me to do, become a brain surgeon?" Buchanan says. "Journalism is what I do for a living. My cards are on the table. Nobody's ignorant of the fact that I worked for Richard Nixon and Spiro Agnew."

Only Bob Novak wouldn't bring back his old friend, who attended his daughter's wedding, as a regular. He had Buchanan on *Capital Gang* twice—in the politician's chair. On another occasion Buchanan substituted for him, but Novak says that wasn't his decision. "Although the rest of us are pretty highly opinionated, we're not activists, we don't give contributions to people, we don't lobby," Novak says. In Novak's view, Buchanan was now more of a politician than a journalist. The rest of the television world didn't seem to care.

The Reverend Jerry Falwell was in the crossfire, and Kinsley was determined to score a direct hit.

Falwell had been peddling videotapes on television that touted all kinds of wild conspiracy theories about Bill Clinton, including an accusation that he had been an accessory to a murder in Arkansas. Kinsley thought the program was the perfect opportunity to expose Falwell, and things quickly heated up.

"The trouble with people like you, Mr. Falwell, is you can dish it out, but you can't take it," Kinsley declared.

Falwell pressed on, calling Surgeon General Joycelyn Elders "a first-class wacko, saying that all Christians are a menace to the children of America."

"She didn't say that. She said that you were a menace," Kinsley replied.

Falwell insisted that Elders is "in favor of sniffing cocaine."

"That's a lie . . . That's a lot of crap," Kinsley said.

Buchanan stepped in to referee. "We're going to try to get my cohost under control," he said.

The wrangling continued, with Kinsley accusing Falwell of spewing "garbage."

"You're going to get ulcers if you don't slow down a little, Michael," Falwell said.

Buchanan intervened again. "Michael, you shut up for a minute," he said. And a moment later: "Michael, stop making a fool of yourself."

Kinsley was seething. When they closed the show, Buchanan said, "You didn't sound very gracious in those thank-yous, Michael."

"I don't feel very gracious, especially toward you," Kinsley replied. He later demanded and received an apology from Buchanan.

"When he gets mad, it's self-righteous anger," Kinsley fumes. "When I get mad, it's 'Michael, you're being childish.' "

Kinsley also chafed at the nasty exchanges he was having with combative guests like Falwell. What television wants, he says, is "jovial disagreement: 'We're all pals here, just joshing around in the locker room,' when I think they're fucking liars."

Political figures quickly learned that hectoring the host was a way to avoid answering questions. When New York Senator Alfonse D'Amato appeared on *Crossfire* to bash Clinton over the Whitewater affair, he kept parrying Kinsley's attempts to press him about his own ethical missteps. "Michael, you asked me a question, give me a chance to answer. Don't be rude and embarrass yourself by interrupting me," he snapped. Kinsley kept breaking in, but to no avail. He got letters from nuns accusing him of being disrespectful to D'Amato.

A number of *Crossfire* guests came away shaking their heads, vowing never to return. They saw no point in the high-volume theatrics. Steven Roberts of *U.S. News* says he "hated" his only appearance, to talk about press coverage of Gennifer Flowers, and refuses to go back. "They spent the whole time yelling," he says. "They just wanted to pick a fight. They had no interest in a calm discussion of the issue. I don't like to do any show where they put you into a partisan or ideological point of view. I've been asked to do *McLaughlin,* and I won't do it."

Norman Ornstein, the political analyst, recalls the frustration of appearing with former Tennessee governor Lamar Alexander. "It was clear that as we disagreed with each other in a civil way, that wasn't what the players in the show wanted," he says. "They both tried to rile things up. They want to goose it to a higher level. That show is geared toward fireworks. There's more entertainment value if it's 'Jane, you ignorant slut!' "

In his writing, Kinsley was far more than a mere entertainer. He would devise clever concepts—a gaffe is when a politician inadvertently tells the truth—that others would recycle for years. He could change the Beltway conversation with a single column that stripped away political pretensions. When the press was filled with hand-wringing over the toll the Iran-contra affair was taking on President Reagan, Kinsley made the case for liberal glee. "Simple honesty requires any Washington type to admit that this is the kind of episode we all live for . . . Repeat after me: Ha. Ha. Ha." He

lectured his readers for getting exercised about congressional over-
drafts at the House Bank, saying: "Get serious. Grow up."

More important, Kinsley was one of the few columnists who
actually pored over the fine print of public documents. He ridiculed
Attorney General Ed Meese's pornography commission by quoting
its bizarre inventory ("Big Boobs, Big Boobs #1 and #2, Big Boobs
Bonanza, Big Boys and their Buddies, Big Bust Bondage, Big
Busted Ball Buster . . .") He showed that President Bush's civil
rights bill was nearly as supportive of racial quotas as the Democratic version Bush kept denouncing. He single-handedly demol-
ished Bush's charge that candidate Clinton had raised taxes in
Arkansas 128 times, showing that the list including such absurdities
as extending the dog-racing season. He deflated one of the more
overheated Whitewater charges by dismissing as "ridiculous" the
notion that a phone call by George Stephanopoulos to the Treasury
Department amounted to some kind of scandal. Other commentators followed suit.

As Kinsley's television fame grew, he became the liberal pundit
most reviled by conservative activists. There was something about
his demeanor, his intellectual style, that drove them up the wall. He
would criticize Rush Limbaugh or Mary Matalin, the former Bush
campaign operative, and they would bad-mouth him with a vengeance. The self-styled man of ideas, who disdained the very notion
of doctrinaire liberalism, became a lightning rod in the ideological
wars.

"Kinsley is symbolic of everything we loathe and despise," Matalin says. "He's a hypocrite, and he's a fraud. He criticizes other
people for 'spin' and then he become Mr. Showbiz, Mr. Sound
Bite. When you speak to a conservative audience, you can get the
same applause trashing Kinsley as trashing Saddam Hussein."

Kinsley shrugs off the animosity. "It's because there aren't too
many liberals out there," he says. "If I'm their idea of an evil
left-winger, they have no idea what one is like."

At times Kinsley seemed to openly yearn for the quieter sanctuary of print journalism. Once, while defending affirmative action
programs, he wrote in *The New Yorker:* "In our sound-bite-and-
spin political culture, it is hard for logic to prevail over emotion.
You cannot trump a simple and ringing principle like color-blind

equal opportunity with 'Wait a minute—it's more complicated than that.' "

Such subtle arguments were lost amid the shouting at CNN. Kinsley was bothered by the way *Crossfire* kept getting overheated. "I hate it," he says. "It's unpleasant. At the same time, we don't want to be *MacNeil/Lehrer:* 'Congressman X, what do you have to say about what Congressman Y just said?' "

The larger problem for Kinsley was that he could not function on television as a Clinton "surrogate," the way Buchanan had been a Bush surrogate. In his writing, Kinsley did not turn a blind eye to the president's flaws. A week before the inauguration, Kinsley wrote that Clinton, like Bush, had known all along that official statistics were underestimating the budget deficit but had been "playing along with the hoax." He found himself unable to argue that Congress shouldn't hold hearings on Whitewater, even though such hearings would clearly damage Clinton. And when Paula Jones accused Clinton of sexual harassment, Kinsley wrote that "it is very hard to believe that Paula Jones is making the whole thing up," and that even if she was exaggerating it did not "justify more lies by the president of the United States."

On *Crossfire,* however, Kinsley could not equivocate in such fashion, or Buchanan would tear him apart. "I'm Clinton's defense lawyer," he says. "Whatever Clinton does, I'm expected to come on and defend it." Kinsley, who had relinquished his editing job for *Crossfire,* finally gave up his syndicated column, the source of his greatest intellectual influence. He still wrote occasionally for *The New Republic, Time,* and *The New Yorker,* displaying the kind of mixed feelings about Clinton that simply wouldn't wash on television.

Buchanan, by contrast, was liberated by the Clinton presidency, free to bash the Democrats night after night with the same passion he had shown at the Republican convention. He knew how to play to the crowd.

One night, when *Crossfire* was staged before a live audience at George Washington University, the hosts were arguing over the faltering prospects of the Clinton health reform plan. Kinsley, who hated all the hooting and hollering, acknowledged at the start that "Clinton has done a bad political job" in selling the plan, thereby eroding his debating position. But he added that "the campaign by Republicans and special interests has been very dishonest."

"Michael, stop this incessant whining!" Buchanan shot back. "You lost the country, Michael. Face it!"

Buchanan accused the Clintonites of writing their health plan in secret. Kinsley replied that Buchanan's former boss, Ronald Reagan, often did the same thing when drafting legislation. "That is a perfect example of the phony-baloney campaign you guys are running," Kinsley said.

"We had a leader, and *you don't have one!*" Buchanan exclaimed as the crowd burst into applause. It was no contest.

If Buchanan seemed like the school bully and Kinsley the student who had crammed all night for the exam, John Sununu had a smartest-kid-in-the-class approach. He would show up late, slip onto the set with little preparation, and breeze his way through. Sununu was still smarting over the way reporters had treated him during the Bush administration, and he sometimes used his cohost's perch to settle scores.

When Bob Woodward, the *Washington Post* sleuth, was on *Crossfire* to promote his book *The Agenda,* Sununu lit into him, saying he had forced top Clinton aides to cooperate through intimidation. "You are probably one of the best practitioners of the art of blackmail in Washington," Sununu said.

"It's called journalism," Woodward replied.

Sununu assailed Woodward's work as "distorted and slanted," saying, "I may be the only one in the city that refuses to talk to you." Finally Sununu got to his real beef: He didn't like the portrait of the Bush administration that Woodward had painted in his previous book, *The Commanders*. Woodward insisted the account was accurate and that no one else had challenged it.

Crossfire was only a part-time gig for Sununu. He was also a paid corporate lobbyist for such clients as Westinghouse Electric Corporation, once meeting with Philippine President Fidel Ramos in Manila to try to win government contracts for the company. CNN officials seemed untroubled by Sununu's other career, saying only that he would not discuss a topic in which a client was involved.

Buchanan remained a prominent political activist while plying the talk show trade. During the 1993 debate over the North Ameri-

can Free Trade Agreement, he campaigned vigorously against the
pact, using *Crossfire* as a forum for his advocacy. During the 1994
battle over the GATT world trade agreement, Buchanan again
emerged as a high-profile opponent, not only on *Crossfire* but on
Donahue and other programs. Buchanan even taped some anti-
GATT commercials, working with the lobbying group American
Cause, headed by Bay Buchanan, his sister and former campaign
manager. In short, Buchanan alternated between political player
and CNN commentator, a dual role that many news organizations
would have deemed a blatant conflict.

Rick Davis says this is not a problem for CNN because Buchanan's partisan views are always challenged and he never set the
Crossfire agenda. "There are no secrets here," Davis says. "The guy
was on the cover of *Time* magazine when he ran for president.
People know who he is and where he's coming from."

But Tom Braden sees a blurring of the lines. "I think Pat re-
gards television and politics as much the same," he says. "*Crossfire*
fits in with his political ambitions."

Those ambitions remained undiminished. Everyone in Washington knew that Buchanan was pursuing another campaign for the
presidency. In late 1994, while he was regularly assailing Clinton
on *Crossfire,* Buchanan was actively testing the waters for a '96
challenge to Clinton. By early 1995, Buchanan was openly campaigning in New Hampshire and courting party members at presidential straw polls in Louisiana and Arizona. "Go, Pat, go!" callers
to his radio show chanted. Even his old friends at *McLaughlin* were
debating his viability as a likely contender. Yet CNN had to cling to
the transparent fiction that he was not a candidate until he officially
announced. And Buchanan wanted to hang on as long as he could.
The show had become a key asset, a vehicle to keep him on the
public stage while he plotted his return to the campaign trail.

Finally, on February 16, 1995, the charade ended. Buchanan
announced his presidential exploratory committee. It was back to
the Sunday shows and *Capital Gang* and *Larry King Live,* once
again as a White House contender. Bob Novak would again praise
his old colleague in print, hailing his "masterful" performance as a
candidate on *Meet the Press* and calling him "the leading conservative alternative" to Bob Dole. "That's a remarkable transformation

of a man who used to sit where we are," Rowland Evans told his partner after they had interviewed Buchanan on *Evans and Novak*. Al Hunt said on CNBC that his former *Capital Gang* colleague was the "early surprise" of the Republican field. Buchanan had, in the space of a decade, gone from *Crossfire* to Reagan aide to *Crossfire* to '92 presidential candidate to *Crossfire* to '96 presidential candidate.

CNN officials didn't even think of getting a journalist to fill Buchanan's chair. Instead, they tried out such Republican activists as Arianna Huffington, Bill Kristol, Lynne Cheney, even Marilyn Quayle. An early Huffington appearance, on the activities of the Progress and Freedom Foundation, the think tank closely allied with Newt Gingrich, degenerated into absurdity when Huffington acknowledged that she was a member of the foundation's board and kept interrupting the guests to defend Gingrich.

Buchanan's final *Crossfire* debate with Kinsley—the end-of-show segment known internally as "the yip-yap"—turned into a paid political advertisement. When Kinsley smirkingly doubted that his colleague could be elected president, Buchanan declared: "I'm the only one out there who is an economic nationalist, who thinks NAFTA was wrong, GATT was wrong, the World Trade Organization was wrong, the peso bailout was wrong." Then he unfurled a fundraising banner—1-800-GO-PAT-GO—which Kinsley helped him hold up for the camera. In the control room, one producer put his head in his hands. The staff had not been warned in advance. But it hardly could have been a surprise. There was no longer much difference between the talk show world and the political battlefield. It was all one long permanent campaign.

Next it was time for a Larry King promo. "Good luck, Pat," King said.

In the space of a few months, Mike Kinsley had two tantalizing opportunities to escape the din of *Crossfire*.

The first was in late 1993, when two senior White House aides, David Gergen and George Stephanopoulos, approached him about becoming a Clinton speechwriter. They talked it over three times. Kinsley thought it would be an awkward fit. He had never written a political speech and believed his style was too idiosyncratic for a

White House operation. But he told Gergen that if the president offered him the job, he would probably feel compelled to accept.

"I've argued again and again that President Clinton is good for the country," Kinsley says. "If they come and say we need your help for Clinton to succeed, then your bluff has been called." To Kinsley's relief, the presidential phone call never came.

In the spring of 1994, the owners of *New York* magazine offered Kinsley the editor's job. He had been itching for another chance to run a magazine but was racked by indecision about whether to move to New York and, more important, whether to leave *Crossfire*. He drove his friends crazy with his neurotic hand-wringing. When Kinsley told CNN President Tom Johnson of the offer, Johnson asked a question that reverberated in his mind: "How can you give up your global visibility?"

It was during a trip to the Middle East that Kinsley realized he had become an international celebrity. "It is a very giddy thing to be recognized on the streets of Jerusalem and Saudi Arabia," he says. "I sort of stumbled into the media of the future and was going to throw it all away for this Gutenberg medium on its way out." Did he really want to put out issues on the ten best pizza places in New York? Kinsley wasn't sure. He tentatively accepted the magazine job, then turned it down, then immediately decided he had made a huge mistake. CNN was indeed a mighty global megaphone, Kinsley concluded, but it was a megaphone he didn't control, one in which he just played the loudmouth's role.

In the end, it came down to a choice between the power of the written word and the reach of the televised shout. Michael Kinsley felt like a tragic character in a Eugene O'Neill play, reciting the same lines night after night. He told friends for months he was dying to leave television. In the last weeks of 1995, after six and a half long years, Kinsley abandoned *Crossfire* and made plans to move to Seattle to launch an online magazine for Microsoft. The man who had ridiculed television gasbaggery and then joined the hot air club had finally had enough of talk show life.

CHAPTER SIX

TOE TO
TOE WITH TED

After a few warmup tosses, Ted Koppel is ready to uncork his best fastball.

He is facing a man who rarely does television interviews, a battle-scarred politician who has a tendency to get tangled up in his own syntax. Senator Edward Kennedy has begun to pull away from his Republican challenger, Mitt Romney, but appearing on *Nightline* is always a high-risk proposition. Koppel, not the guest, is in control.

"Let me put it bluntly," Koppel begins. "You're overweight. Your back is killing you. I can see the pain in your face . . . You've been in the Senate for thirty-two years. No one would take it amiss if at this point you said, 'It's time to step down.' Why not?" It is an unusually personal question, and Kennedy, who had been carefully framing his answers in terms of government programs, insists he can still make a difference.

Koppel's staff loved the exchange. "Ted asks the toughest questions, but he says it in such a gentle way that people take it," says Tom Bettag, executive producer of *Nightline*. "You don't get people to think until you jolt them a little bit. If you throw a hard and unsettling question at someone, they will come back with their best stuff."

For fifteen years, Koppel had proven himself the best interviewer on live television. It was a high-wire act far more demanding than most people realized. On *60 Minutes,* on *PrimeTime Live,* on

Oprah, on *World News Tonight,* the pieces were taped, polished, painstakingly edited. Dumb questions, awkward answers, and boring stretches could easily be excised. Larry King did his program live, but he was engaged in the art of conversation, shooting the breeze with a guest at ease. Koppel had no such luxury. He was, on most evenings, doing verbal battle with wary adversaries whose only means of hearing him was through a small device wedged in their ear. Koppel would sit in his basement studio at ABC, across from the Mayflower Hotel, facing the giant chroma-key monitor on which would be projected the faces of as many as three guests. If they rambled, if they evaded, if they lied, if they attacked each other, if they denounced Koppel himself, he had to press on, trying to balance the competing demands of fair play and compelling television. The only editing he could do was on the air, in front of millions of viewers.

"If you just have people screaming at each other," Koppel says, "there is a tendency to walk away from that program and say, 'Great!' But what did anybody say? It's like eating Fritos or Cheetos. It's a terrific experience while you're doing it, but there's not a whole lot of nutritional value."

The question, in the beginning, was whether a high-fiber diet could work at 11:35 at night. It was a time slot owned by Johnny Carson, and the other networks, with second-string comedians and old movies, had never mounted a serious challenge. No one had dreamed of airing a regular news program so late in the evening.

No one, that is, except Roone Arledge. In his first two and a half years as president of ABC News, Arledge was looking to make his mark at a network whose news shows were mired in third place. He put on forty news specials in the 11:30 P.M. time slot, seizing on such fleeting events as the death of John Wayne or the defection of a Russian ballerina.

When fifty-two Americans were taken hostage in Teheran, Arledge saw his chance. It was November 1979, and C-SPAN's four-person operation was just a few months old. CNN was not yet on the air. News was not a twenty-four-hour affair. Arledge launched a late-night program, *America Held Hostage,* anchored by Frank Reynolds. But Reynolds also had to anchor the nightly news, and he soon relinquished his duties to Koppel, handing him the reins of what was becoming a national obsession.

Ted Koppel was not widely known at the time. Born in England, he had decided to become a broadcaster while listening to Edward R. Murrow's stirring radio reports during World War II. Koppel moved with his family to New York when he was thirteen, and after graduating from Syracuse University and Stanford graduate school, he landed an ABC radio job in 1963. He soon moved into television. The news division at the time consisted of a fifteen-minute nightly newscast and a Sunday morning show, both of which were lowly rated. ABC was the also-ran network.

Koppel did a tour in Vietnam and, in 1971, was assigned to the State Department. Five years later, he was anchoring the Saturday evening news. But Arledge, less than pleased that Koppel was taking a year off so his wife could go to law school, shipped him back to the State Department. His career had stalled.

When the hostage crisis erupted, it was a chance for Koppel to redeem himself. His interviewing skills were immediately apparent. Still, when Arledge decided to turn the hostage specials into a regular nightly program, he felt he needed a big-name anchor such as Dan Rather or Roger Mudd. That effort fizzled, and Koppel, the backup quarterback, was given the starting job.

The logic of turning *America Held Hostage* into a permanent show was inescapable. Since the specials were not rated, ABC could not sell commercials for them. The network had lost more than a million dollars on the programs in less than five months. A regular program would fix that problem, but no one had grand illusions about its ratings potential. Richard Wald, an ABC executive, told Koppel the network wasn't expecting miracles. "Come in a respectable third," he said.

Nightline made its debut on March 24, 1980. The first show brought together by satellite Ali Agah, the Iranian charge d'affaires, and Dorothea Morefield, the wife of an American hostage. At Koppel's prodding, Morefield asked Agah why the hostages were not allowed to receive mail or phone calls, and he was flustered in response, raising the possibility of CIA monitoring. *Nightline* had made an initial foray into what would become one of its signature strengths, pairing people from different locales and different cultures. It would become what TV critic Marc Gunther called "the most significant addition to television news since *60 Minutes*."

The program evolved over the years, but the basic format—opening tease, setup piece, and live interview segment—largely remained the same. There was investigative reporting. There were town meetings around the country. There were breaking-news reports on earthquakes and plane crashes, and campaign strategists chewing the fat about politics. Koppel anchored the show from South Africa, from the Philippines, from Israel, from Somalia, and from a North Carolina prison. He interviewed Carl Sagan, Nelson Mandela, Ted Turner, Muhammad Ali, Gary Hart, Jim and Tammy Faye Bakker, John McLaughlin, Vladimir Zhirinovsky, Oliver North, Phil Donahue, Yasser Arafat.

In what became a national ritual, senior government officials and prominent activists would explain themselves to Koppel at their moment of maximum crisis. Attorney General Janet Reno showed up after the fiery disaster at Waco. Lani Guinier went on *Nightline* the night before she was forced to withdraw her nomination as the nation's top civil rights enforcer—even after Justice Department spokesman Carl Stern called Koppel and tried to block her appearance. Nearly two years later, it was the White House that urged Henry Foster to go on *Nightline* after his nomination as surgeon general ran into stiff opposition. The Tennessee obstetrician had erroneously claimed to have done fewer than a dozen abortions, and he explained himself to Koppel, saying he had answered too hurriedly and the actual number was thirty-nine. On another evening, Michael Eisner, the chairman of Disney, appeared to talk up his company's surprise acquisition of ABC, including Koppel and company, that very day.

While for some, *Nightline* was the television equivalent of a Senate confirmation hearing, for others it amounted to an exit interview, a last chance to speak to the nation. Retired admiral Bobby Ray Inman appeared hours after withdrawing as Bill Clinton's nominee for secretary of defense in a bizarre news conference at which he attacked the press. Joycelyn Elders came on after being fired as surgeon general, Philip Heymann after quitting as deputy attorney general, David Gergen just before leaving as White House counselor, Benjamin Chavis after being fired as executive director of the NAACP.

For all the journalistic kudos, Koppel had to make his living in

an entertainment culture. He was startled to learn that when pollster
Lou Harris asked people to name their favorite talk show host, he
had placed fourth. It wasn't the ranking that bothered him as much
as the nature of the competition. Oprah Winfrey had led the field,
followed by David Letterman and Regis Philbin and Kathie Lee
Gifford. Koppel was tied with Phil Donahue and Jay Leno, and
followed by Geraldo Rivera. The comparisons rankled, for Ted
Koppel, who once traveled the globe with Henry Kissinger, did not
see himself as an entertainer. He may have been up against Letterman and Leno each night, even beating them on occasion, but
that did not mean they were in the same business.

"There seems to be absolutely no difference in the public perception between what I do and what MacNeil and Lehrer do and
what Geraldo Rivera does," Koppel says. "We're all talk show
hosts. I thought I was still a news person, and here I am with Oprah
and Phil and Geraldo and the rest of the guys. I don't think of
myself as a talk show host. It's not what I do for a living. If there is
no discrimination in the public mind between what I do and what
Geraldo Rivera does, then I think we're in trouble."

Perhaps the confusion was understandable. Koppel, after all,
earns his keep by talking to guests. He has a certain theatrical flair.
He's up against Letterman and Leno. He has to get ratings. "Certainly those of us who appear on commercial television are obliged
to draw the audience into the tent, and if we can't do that we are
doomed to fail," Koppel says. "We are not in the business of seeing
if we can find the most boring people on the face of the planet."

But he was also careful not to allow the program to become
frivolous. Once, word reached *Nightline* that Madonna had decided
she was ready to be interviewed by Ted Koppel. Absolutely not,
said Koppel. It was during the buildup to the Persian Gulf War,
and he did not want to waste precious airtime on a pop star, even a
world-famous one. ABC simply waited until he took a night off and
had Forrest Sawyer chat up Madonna instead.

For talking-head television, *Nightline* had more than its share of
drama, and part of that had to do with the way Koppel choreo-
graphed the action. *Nightline* was the first show to regularly interview three guests simultaneously from remote locations, rather than
quizzing and dismissing them one at a time. And Koppel was the

maestro. He could watch the guests on the monitor and gauge their body language and facial expressions, but the guests could not see him. They were alone in a room, staring at a camera lens, connected to the program only by the sound of his voice in their ear. Even the Washington guests were placed in a separate studio down the hall, to preserve the Koppel edge. In the early years, Arledge felt that was what set the program apart. Some politicians, considering a *Nightline* appearance, would negotiate over whether they would be granted the rare privilege of a face-to-face sitdown with Koppel.

Koppel did plenty of research but never drafted questions in advance, feeling that would destroy the spontaneity. Sometimes he did little more than take a nap before a big show. "You don't script for Ted," Bettag says. "You don't write down sample questions. Ted never talks about what he's going to ask and never writes notes. He is just so goddamn confident, to the point of arrogance, although it doesn't come across that way."

Koppel quickly became a huge star, but unlike many other journalistic celebrities, he did not traffic promiscuously in opinion. His prominence came from his uncanny ability to interrogate others, much as an all-star pitcher can excel only by striking out the mightiest sluggers.

"Over the years, I think I've developed a sense of the acceptable and unacceptable conventions of the live interview," Koppel says. "A television audience begins by identifying with the interviewer, not the interviewee. You have certain questions they wish you would ask. You are their representative. They're with you. How can you lose them? Either by asking totally dumb questions, total softballs, or by being too aggressive too early in the interview.

"The classic example—Lord knows I've been guilty of it myself —is Dan Rather's interview with George Bush [on Iran-contra]. You ask the vice president of the United States a question, you have to let him answer it. You actually have to let him over-answer it. If he wants to burble on for a minute and a half, even though you know that costs you a quarter of your whole interview time, you've got to let him do it. The audience at home has got to arrive at the point where they are saying, '*Come on,* Dan, get in there!' If you interrupt before that moment, you're the one being rude. At that point they begin to identify with the person being interviewed."

Koppel is often up against people whose instinct and training is to duck, to finesse, to hedge, to avoid answering the question that *Nightline* wants answered. And his job, simply put, is not to let them get away with it. It is the opposite of Larry King's conversational approach, and it ratchets up the tension level, which also happens to make for good television.

"You cannot force people to answer questions," Koppel says, "but you can make sure the audience doesn't miss what's going on: 'In all fairness, Mr. Kurtz, I do have to point out that I have now asked you the same question four times, and four times you've given me an evasive answer. Let's not waste any more time.' That is a way of saying to the audience, 'It's been bullshit for the last five minutes. You know it, I know it. Let's not let him get away with it, and let's make sure he realizes he has just been portrayed as a bullshitter.'"

Sometimes Koppel knew he had crossed the line. During the 1984 campaign, when Geraldine Ferraro was the Democratic nominee for vice president and was under fire about her personal finances, Koppel chose a different tack. He decided to press her on the nuclear arms race, conventional forces in Europe, tensions in El Salvador and the Middle East.

When Ferraro said she could not talk about classified nuclear surveillance, Koppel said: "Well, I'll tell you what. I just spent some time talking with some folks over at the State Department this afternoon. They don't have quite the same compunctions about not talking about those means as you do." At another point he said, "Yeah, but we're talking facts here, Ms. Ferraro."

"I went into the interview feeling she didn't know a helluva lot about foreign policy, and I was going to reveal how little she knew," Koppel says. "I was patronizing and pompous and rude. It was legitimate to ask her questions on that subject, but it was not legitimate to make it sound as though I was the examiner giving her her doctoral oral exam."

If *Nightline* had a weakness, it was a tendency to reach for the usual New York and Washington suspects, the politicians and pundits, most of them white men, who regularly worked the talk show circuit. There was, in Koppel's view, a perfectly rational reason for this. "When you're doing a live television show, you're running a colossal risk when you put untested people on," he says.

"The risk is they're gonna freak out. The risk is they'll be so nervous they'll end up spouting drivel, or repeating certain things they've hammered into their heads no matter what I ask."

Koppel once invited on the program one of his oldest friends, Ray Foster, a "gun nut," in Koppel's words, who was both eloquent and passionate about his hostility toward gun control. That changed when the program began and Foster had to debate Treasury Secretary Lloyd Bentsen. "God, he was awful," Koppel says. "I mean, he was a real dud. It was a disaster. It's amazing how few people are good their first or second time on live television."

Even when Koppel took a softer tack, people had a way of self-destructing on *Nightline*. In 1987 Al Campanis, vice president of the Los Angeles Dodgers, appeared for what was billed as a tribute to Jackie Robinson. In response to a routine question, Campanis declared that blacks in professional sports "may not have some of the necessities" to be managers or front-office executives. "I gotta tell you, that really sounds like garbage, if you'll forgive me for saying so," Koppel said. Campanis resigned within days.

Koppel had no illusions as to why he was able to attract a steady parade of big-name guests. It wasn't that they thought he was a great guy or felt some moral obligation to submit to his questioning. *Nightline* was a precious chunk of network airtime, and almost every guest wanted to use the program to advance his or her agenda. That was why Gary Hart came on in late 1987 to announce that he was getting back in the presidential race, months after the uproar over the Donna Rice episode. Even *America Held Hostage* could not have stayed on the air if the Carter administration had not decided to play up the crisis for political reasons.

In the fall of 1988, Vice President Bush refused to appear on *Nightline*. He was far ahead in his race for the White House and had too much to lose. His opponent, Michael Dukakis, had also been resisting an invitation. But thirteen days before the election, Dukakis was so far behind he decided he had nothing to lose.

A few minutes into the show, Koppel asked the Massachusetts governor about the Bush campaign's effort to paint him as soft on crime. Dukakis had been hammered over Willie Horton, the convicted murderer who had raped a woman after receiving a weekend pass under Dukakis's prison furlough program. Dukakis launched into his standard, unemotional response, much as he had during the presidential debate when asked about the hypothetical rape and murder of his wife.

"With all due respect, let me suggest to you, I still don't think you get it," Koppel snapped. Dukakis simply repeated his refrain about how a human tragedy was being exploited for political gain.

"It was a glorious opportunity, and he missed it," Koppel says. "Had he, figuratively speaking, grabbed me by the ears and said, 'No, Mr. Koppel, *you* don't get it,' if he had really come after me and showed a little fire in the belly . . . America would have been cheering, 'Yeah, get Koppel!' It was clear that he was a beaten man. He looked beaten on that program."

That was almost always the outcome: Koppel on the attack, the guest furiously backpedaling. But four years later, the tables were suddenly turned. When Gennifer Flowers sold her story to the tabloid *Star, Nightline* producers asked Bill Clinton to discuss her allegations of infidelity. He agreed to come on if his wife could be with him and they could sit in the studio with Koppel. *Nightline* cut the deal, but bad weather made the travel impossible. The Clintons would wind up going on *60 Minutes* instead. In the meantime, *Nightline,* trying to get in the game on a subject the networks had steered away from, booked a program on whether the media should scrutinize a politician's private life.

A *Nightline* producer had seen Mandy Grunwald on *Crossfire* the week before and invited her to join the panel. Grunwald, a partner in the Clinton campaign's media firm, quickly seized the offensive. She accused Koppel of "making this program about some unsubstantiated charges that . . . started with a trashy supermarket tabloid. You're telling people that you think this is important . . . You're setting the agenda, and you're letting the *Star* set it for you."

This time it was Koppel who retreated, gamely insisting that "I tried to put it in the proper context when I began the program" and "we're not devoting a half hour to the story itself." As Grunwald continued to assail him, Koppel acknowledged: "You've done a very effective job of putting me on the defensive."

When it was over, a stunned cameraman exclaimed: "Nobody does that to Ted!"

His error, Koppel believes, was in framing the debate around the media's behavior rather than the topic everyone was really interested in: Did Bill Clinton have a twelve-year affair with a former Arkansas lounge singer? "Mandy kicked my butt that night," he says. "Mandy beat me rhetorically, and she was quick off the mark and handled herself and the subject brilliantly . . . but she was wrong and I was right. We were right to do that program." Still, he admits that "we were couching it in a silly fashion." The media angle was "baloney. The story was, Hey, guess what, he's about to go public [about Flowers] and if he doesn't address this issue head on, he's dog meat."

As the '92 campaign wore on, it became fashionable to say that it was being emceed by Larry King and Phil Donahue and Arsenio Hall. Even Koppel regarded King as a master of the "anecdotal approach" to interviewing. But *Nightline* was driven by reporting, and it had a way of taking center stage at campaign time. Ten days before the New Hampshire primary, a *Nightline* staffer obtained a twenty-two-year-old letter that Clinton had written to the ROTC supervisor at the University of Arkansas, thanking him for "saving me from the draft." Ironically, Jim Wooten of ABC's *World News Tonight* had obtained the same letter but was still wrestling with whether it was a story.

When Koppel called Clinton in New Hampshire and told him he had the letter, the governor agreed to appear on *Nightline* that night. Koppel promised him he would have a chance to raise other issues. Koppel also did him the enormous favor of reading the entire letter on the air—Clinton had declined to read it himself—so that his anguish as a young student torn over Vietnam came through. Once again, Clinton rode out the storm.

"There are times—if you happen to be a presidential candidate, and a letter has just been released indicating you may have dodged the draft and you said some nasty things about the military—that you don't want to go on MTV that night," Koppel says. "And you may not want to go on the *Larry King* show that night. You want to go on a program where the public perception is, 'Okay, Bill Clinton is stepping up to the plate and he's gonna take some tough questions.' That was a night when he needed us."

There came a time, more than a year into Clinton's presidency, when he needed *Nightline* again. The Whitewater affair was dominating the news and threatening to overshadow Clinton's trip to Russia and several European countries. Koppel called his old friend David Gergen and pitched the idea of his accompanying Clinton for a series of programs on how foreign policy is made. The deal hinged on the president agreeing to an on-camera interview each day. Gergen immediately understood that this would help shift the media spotlight away from Whitewater. "If they come to you, they have a vested interest and they think it's legitimate journalism," Gergen says.

Indeed, Koppel was mostly laudatory. "This is a man with enormous energy," he said of Clinton one day. "It is a tough job. The burdens are enough to break an ordinary man," he said the next. Some found his discourses on foreign policy a bit on the pompous side. "Koppel may mistake himself for secretary of state on occasion," Tom Shales wrote in *The Washington Post*.

But things went awry when Clinton lost his temper and abruptly terminated an interview with NBC's Jim Miklaszewski, who was pressing him about Whitewater. Clinton refused to see Koppel that day. The following day, Koppel told Gergen that *Nightline* would pack up and leave unless the president kept his end of the bargain. When Clinton reluctantly agreed to resume the interviews, Koppel was ready.

"Yesterday you lost it," he said. "You lost your touch. You didn't handle the Miklaszewski interview very well. . . . Was it fatigue, was it just the frustration of having [Whitewater] come up?"

Not many interviewers would have lectured the president of the United States in that fashion. But Ted Koppel's stature was such that he could, and did, get away with it.

It was an indisputable fact: When *Nightline* did O. J. Simpson, its ratings jumped by 15 percent.

For all its focus on foreign policy and other sober subjects, *Nightline* was part of the entertainment culture. In an era of tabloid news, Koppel could not afford to ignore some of the cheesier stories out there. *Nightline* did three shows on Tonya Harding, two on Paula Jones, and one on allegations of child molestation against Michael Jackson. And, by the summer of 1995, *Nightline* had done more than fifty-five programs on O.J., devoting nearly half its airtime to the case during one seven-week stretch. Once *Nightline* threw out an already reported piece on the Mexican peso crisis, the top economic story in the world, for yet another talkathon on the Simpson case. Another time, after a heated debate, the program blew off the scandal-driven resignation of Senator Bob Packwood for more O.J. On another night, Koppel visited the *National Enquirer* to praise its coverage of the O.J. case. ABC executives didn't want too many viewers surfing over to Letterman and Leno.

The competition took note. In the first four months of 1995, boosted by the Simpson case and other major news stories, *Nightline* consistently beat *Late Show with David Letterman* and *The Tonight Show*. In the first week in May, for example, Koppel averaged a 6.5 rating, compared to 4.4 for Letterman and 4.3 for Jay Leno. It was a triumph that once would have been unthinkable. Leno even sent Koppel a joking telegram: "Stop the O.J. stuff, you're killing us!"

To hold on to that audience—more than five million homes—Koppel felt he had to offer a mix. The more sensational programs, he believed, gave him the breathing room to do the serious investigative work and the reports from Jerusalem and Johannesburg. But some staffers were frustrated that the program was devoting so much attention to the celebrity trial of the century. *Nightline,* after all, was supposed to be different. Koppel hadn't interviewed Kato Kaelin, like Barbara Walters, or Paula Barbieri, like Diane Sawyer, but there was nothing particularly creative about the show's coverage. There was a piece with taped highlights of the day's developments in court, followed by a Koppel chat with attorneys Leslie Abramson, who had represented one of the murderous Menendez brothers, and Robert Philibosian. They chewed the fat with Koppel like the other lawyers on the other talk shows—just like *Larry King Live,* just like *Crossfire,* just like *Rivera Live,* Geraldo's somewhat tamer CNBC show that was all O.J. all the time. Koppel told viewers the trial was "America's obsession," and increasingly it was *Nightline*'s obsession as well.

"It's funny to watch the whole journalistic establishment decorously trying to ignore the story," Koppel says. "You can't ignore it. There is a point in journalism where you have to accede to the voracious appetite of the consumer. The consumer is saying, 'I don't give a damn what you elitist journalists think, I'm ravenous to know what has happened in the case.' If we were doing O.J. every night, I think our ratings would be soaring. It's tempting. But we'd be giving up our moral high ground.''

Many at *Nightline* strongly disagreed with Koppel's rationale. "The staff really doesn't want to do O. J. Simpson at all," a ranking *Nightline* journalist says. Other important subjects were being ignored as well. While Koppel was keenly interested in politics and diplomacy, he tended to dismiss financial stories or pieces about the environment.

"Ted doesn't like economic stories," the *Nightline* staffer says. "It's the eyes-glaze-over effect." When Britain's oldest bank collapsed because of high-risk trading by a twenty-eight-year-old whiz kid, "a lot of us here were pushing to do that story, and we couldn't get it on. They didn't think it was interesting. *Nightline* can do those stories well."

There didn't have to be big news at the trial; even a dull hearing about DNA testing could prompt another *Nightline* rehash. "It should tell you something about the pace of the proceedings that one member of the audience was expelled for falling asleep," Koppel began one evening. That didn't stop *Nightline* from flogging the story.

If the moral ground was not quite as high during the O.J. period, Koppel still relished his 11:35 time slot for the relative freedom it provided. ABC was making money on the show at that hour. He knew that if he were on at nine, the pressure to do more O.J.-type stories would be far greater. When ABC was launching *Turning Point,* yet another prime-time newsmagazine, Koppel was asked if he would anchor it, or at least be one of the rotating anchors. He refused. He wanted to devote his energy to his late-night franchise.

But even Koppel's time period didn't insulate him from certain commercial realities. In 1992 only 60 percent of ABC's affiliate stations were carrying his program live. The rest were delaying it by a half hour, an hour, even an hour and a half. In its place, these stations were airing syndicated shows and sitcom reruns. It wasn't that they didn't like *Nightline;* it was a matter of dollars and cents. By buying a show like *Hard Copy,* which could be purchased for a few thousand dollars a week, a local station manager would get six and a half minutes of commercial time to sell each night. ABC provided *Nightline* for free, but kept three and a half minutes of commercials for the network, leaving the station manager three minutes to sell. Over the course of a year, some local stations said, carrying *Nightline* live would cost them as much as a million dollars.

Koppel felt he could not compete in the ratings when so many stations were running him after midnight, not when *The Tonight Show,* had a clearance rate of well over 90 percent. In the summer of '92, at an ABC affiliates' meeting in Los Angeles, Koppel delivered a stern warning. "You are making this job increasingly difficult for us," he said. "We are trying to do this with one hand tied behind our back. If this continues, we will reach a point that I decide you don't care enough about keeping the program alive, and I will reach the appropriate conclusion." Roone Arledge, recovering from a prostate cancer operation, sent a similar message by videotape.

Two years later, Koppel, Arledge, Robert Iger, the network president, and Tom Murphy, the chairman of Capital Cities/ABC, flew around the country to meet with executives from the local affiliates. They struck a compromise with some of the recalcitrant stations. In exchange for carrying *Nightline* live, they would be allowed to sell seven more thirty-second spots on other ABC programs, including such news shows as *20/20*.

By 1995, with the pot appropriately sweetened, 78 percent of the local affiliates were carrying *Nightline* live. There were, to be sure, some significant holdouts. Cincinnati delayed *Nightline* for *Cheers* reruns. Minneapolis for *Roseanne* and *A Current Affair*. Denver for *Cheers* and *M*A*S*H*. Kansas City delayed the show ninety minutes, for *Roseanne, Golden Girls,* and *M*A*S*H*. San Antonio also pushed it back ninety minutes for *Coach* and the *Best of Sally*. Still, *Nightline* had made progress in the late-night ratings wars.

Would Koppel really have walked away from *Nightline,* the program to which he had devoted fifteen years of his life? Koppel knows full well he can strike a major syndication deal at any time in the lucrative talk show market.

"I am software," he says. "All these hardware people really need software. What's more, I'm an identifiable piece of software. It was not an empty threat."

• • •

Ted Koppel's day begins with a bit of bad news.

It is 9:00 A.M. on Wednesday, the day that Koppel had hoped to conduct an exclusive interview with Winnie Mandela. She has just been dismissed from the South African government by her estranged husband, President Nelson Mandela, and has not talked to the press. Koppel knows Winnie Mandela from the specials that *Nightline* did in South Africa when her husband was released from prison five years earlier, and he thinks she may be persuaded to tell her side. Negotiations have been proceeding for days.

Koppel is just getting up in his lavish home in Potomac, Maryland, when Tom Bettag calls to say that Winnie Mandela has nixed the interview. They now need a subject for that night's program.

Bettag mentions that the House is scheduled to vote on term limits for members of Congress, one of the major items in the Republicans' much-publicized Contract with America. The proposed constitutional amendment has been a staple of talk radio for years and is tremendously popular with the public. Of course, everyone in Washington knows the amendment will lose by a wide margin. But the final vote is expected to take place around 10:00 P.M., meaning it is "breaking on our clock," as Bettag puts it. *Nightline* thrives on late-breaking stories.

It is, at bottom, a classic talk show topic: a day full of Washington speechifying on a hot-button issue with a foregone conclusion in which nothing happens. Koppel is unenthusiastic, but he is also busy with investigative pieces for the Thursday and Friday shows. No decision is made.

An hour later, at the program's third-floor offices on DeSales Street, Bettag is musing about which congressmen he might book on term limits. There are, he says, the "usual suspects": Henry Hyde, the Judiciary Committee chairman who has broken with the Republicans by opposing term limits, and Bill McCollum, the chief Republican sponsor of a twelve-year term limits bill. Or, to give the debate a partisan flavor, he could have McCollum face off against Democratic firebrand Barney Frank. Bettag also wants to get some "real people" so the program won't be purely about Beltway politics.

Looming in the background is the everpresent specter of the O. J. Simpson trial, which could preempt his plans. Bettag hopes there is no O.J. story. "If something happens, we'll wince and do it," he says. "We're pleased any day you don't have to do Simpson."

At 11 A.M., Bettag and thirteen staff members file into a large room, taking their seats around a long table for the morning conference call. "NIGHTLINE KICKS BUTT," says a huge banner on the wall. Koppel is on the line from home, two producers are in New York, and Judy Muller, who is covering the Simpson trial, is in Los Angeles.

Muller runs down the day's scheduled witnesses: the limousine driver who took Simpson to the airport on the night of the murders and the skycap who checked his bags. "I don't think it's going to be a blockbuster day," she says.

The discussion turns to term limits. "There's enormous public support for this, and the Republicans know they're going to be accused of taking care of themselves," Bettag says.

Koppel's measured cadence emanates crisply from the squawk box. "I think this is one of the world's great nonissues," he says. "I truly don't think this is high in the consciousness of most people. They don't go around saying, 'God, if they could only limit congressmen to three terms, everything would be better.' "

"It's a rhetoric festival," says correspondent Dave Marash.

One producer says that an aide to Bob Inglis, a freshman Republican and strong term-limits advocate, has already called and offered the congressman as a guest.

But Koppel is on a different wavelength. "It occurs to me to have Henry Hyde, who after all has an absolutely unshakable reputation as one of the conservative rocks on the Hill, speaking thoughtfully on the notion of why he doesn't think this is a great idea," he says. "He is something of a constitutional scholar. I'm not sure we need a debate on this, because it ain't gonna pass. All we're talking about here is the rhetoric. If Henry would do it live—given the mood on the Hill and the Sturm and Drang throughout the day —it could be the cement that holds it all together."

Bettag says it might be useful to have someone like Inglis "saying that the Henry Hydes of the world just don't get it, if they see him as one of the Judases here." But he doesn't press the point.

Koppel is the star, and keeping him happy is important. Sometimes Koppel likes to vary the format just for the sake of doing something different.

"There is a sense of Ted being the eight-hundred-pound gorilla," an ABC staffer says. "What Ted wants, Ted will always get. It's his show. People understand that." And what Koppel wants most, this staffer says, is "to get away from doing the standard piece and three white men."

Bettag, a lanky man with longish graying hair, had joined *Nightline* four years earlier, succeeding Dorrance Smith. Bettag had been executive producer of the *CBS Evening News* but was ousted after a dispute with CBS management. It seemed to him that Koppel had grown bored after a dozen years of the nightly grind. There was talk that the program was past its prime, that Koppel was too distracted by his own production company, Koppel Communications.

The separate unit, and the longer hours, had clearly taken a toll on Koppel. "His attention was divided," says Dorrance Smith. "He'd be dealing with what show were we going to do that night, and at the same time he'd be worried about his prime-time special on sex in the Soviet Union. You'd rather he be committed to your piece than lining up hookers in Moscow."

When he joined *Nightline,* Bettag thought the program would last another two years at most. But the program soon got a second wind. The ratings were up. Koppel finally shut down his private company, and he had increasingly come to rely on Bettag. He no longer came into the office in the morning, leaving his executive producer to get things running.

Bettag's subject at the moment is who should be interviewed for Chris Bury's setup piece on term limits. One producer, Richard Harris, suggests they call Frank Luntz, the young Republican pollster whose research helped shape the Contract with America. Luntz is sure to agree. He was thrilled when he was invited on *Nightline* just before the '94 election. "That's when I knew I had made it," Luntz says.

Another producer suggests recording Rush Limbaugh's radio show, since he is sure to declaim in favor of term limits that afternoon. *Nightline* has used this technique before, and Bettag worries that they are overdoing it. A staffer suggests a Chicago talk show on WLS that broadcasts from the same building as the ABC bureau. Convenience counts when you're racing the clock.

"You've also got that very conservative talk show host in San Francisco," Koppel says.

"He's been fired," Richard Harris says.

"Pat Buchanan has been very pro–term limits," another producer suggests.

The program also needs some MOSs, or Man on the Street interviews. Perhaps a crew can be dispatched to a restaurant where people gather to listen to Limbaugh.

"That's a very good idea," Koppel says.

"How about in Georgia?" Harris says.

"That will add the Gingrich element," Bettag says.

Still, the question of the main guests remains. "Let's see if Henry Hyde will play," Bettag says.

Hyde has been on *Nightline* four times, but he doesn't like to stay up until midnight. "In the past," says producer Sarah Just, "he's often been a problem with live. Do we want him here in the studio?"

"No, Capitol Hill is okay," Bettag says.

"Maybe we ought to be thinking about who we'd get if Hyde won't do it," Koppel says.

Harris notes that Tom DeLay, the Republican whip, and Bill Archer, the House Ways and Means chairman, are also against term limits.

"That sounds like a good backup," Koppel says.

Bettag ends the conference call. "Let's go out and scratch that surface," he announces.

Chris Bury gathers his things for a day of roaming the Hill. Harris stops by Bury's office to say that Lamar Alexander's presidential campaign has offered up their man for an interview on term limits. Bury isn't interested. He wants three or four members of Congress, the advocacy group U.S. Term Limits, and some political analyst—"a Norman Ornstein or Frank Luntz"—to round out the piece.

In the main newsroom, the four television sets mounted near the ceiling provide a reminder of the talk show world outside. Sally

Jessy Raphael flickers from one screen. CAROL SAYS SHE HATES
HER DAUGHTER PAULA'S FIANCÉ KEITH, the caption says. As Chris
Bury heads out the door, Keith is backstage, waiting to confront his
future mother-in-law.

It is 6:30 P.M. Diane Sawyer, anchoring *World News Tonight*, is
talking about the Republicans' impending defeat on term limits.
There is just over five hours to airtime. Chris Bury is in his office,
tapping out the first part of his script.

Bury has had a rough day on the Hill. One Republican after
another—Henry Hyde, Tom DeLay, Susan Molinari—would not
talk on camera about their party's biggest defeat of the year. Hyde
also refused to do the interview with Koppel. So did DeLay and
Bill Archer. Koppel put in a call to Hyde's office, hoping to sway
him with a personal appeal. But Hyde relented after *Nightline* staffers agreed to let him pretape the interview at 8:30. True to his
reputation, Hyde did not want to stay up late. Bettag thought the
arrangement would lack the energy of a live interview, but at that
point he had little leverage.

Lisa Koenig, the lead producer for the evening, is back from an
interview with Frank Luntz. The pollster kept mouthing the party
line on term limits. Koenig tells Bury the tape isn't very good.

"You know what you have to do with Frank?" Bury says. "You
have to slap him around: 'Frank, don't give me any of that Republican shit, talk to me as a pollster. Stop trying to be Newt Gingrich's
spokesman.' "

Koenig says she tried asking Luntz a "when-did-you-stop-
beating-your-wife question. He said, 'I reject the question.' "

Bury hasn't written much, but he doesn't look worried. "It's
early," he says.

Ted Koppel appears in the newsroom and makes his first executive decision of the evening. It is a dilemma he confronts every night
at this time: Chinese or Italian? He opts for the Cafe Luna take-out
menu and orders eggplant parmigiana, peeling a fifty-dollar bill
from his wallet.

Mission accomplished, Koppel retreats to his office to look over
a twenty-page research memo on term limits, which includes some

recent clips, an ABC poll, and a Henry Hyde press release. The office resembles a cave. It is almost completely dark, except for a dim lamp on Koppel's desk, and the temperature is set to freezing. Koppel, in shirtsleeves, looks comfortable.

"It's a predictable program," he says, thumbing through the memo. "The issues are fundamentally phony." His mind is on the Thursday night show, an investigation into the Federal Aviation Administration, and an exclusive story on the Aldrich Ames spy case for Friday. He spent part of the afternoon trying to convince a recalcitrant source to come forward on the FAA story. Unlike talk show hosts who simply show up and read the script, Koppel still functions as *Nightline*'s lead reporter.

At 7:30 the lineup for the show is still unsettled. A spokesman for U.S. Term Limits calls and offers his boss as a guest. There is some talk of having Cokie Roberts come on and discuss the day on the Hill. The House debate is continuing on C-SPAN. Barney Frank's voice booms from a portable speaker. Lisa Koenig and two other producers are sitting at their desks, headsets in place, listening to interview tapes, and logging the best sound bites. The three women will crash on the Chris Bury piece simultaneously, each editing a separate section to save time. People are scurrying around the office. The pace is picking up.

Koenig's monitor is replaying Bury's standup in front of the Capitol. "Republicans knew it would be a day of rhetoric over results, talk over action," he says.

Senior producer Mark Nelson has taken charge. "Lisa," he says, "can I get a page one so Ted can write a page two?" Page one, in *Nightline* jargon, is the opening sound bites used to tease the program. Page two is Koppel's introduction, which he always writes himself.

The talk culture flickers across the overhead sets. On *Entertainment Tonight,* Donald and Ivana Trump are talking about how they reunited to make a commercial for Pizza Hut. On C-SPAN, Kweisi Mfume, chairman of the congressional Black Caucus, is shouting from the floor. "Every member of this body knows that none of these measures are going to pass tonight," he declares.

At 7:45 Bury has finished the first three pages of his script, which must be approved by Nelson and Koppel. Nelson is worried about the Hyde interview. "If it doesn't hold up, we can go to Cokie," he says.

Koppel emerges with a bottle of Snapple peach iced tea. He looks relaxed, betraying not the slightest doubt that the taped interview will go well. "I've done it four thousand times, and Henry's probably done it three thousand times," he says.

The food arrives just after eight, and the staff retires to the conference room. Tom Bettag shows up in a beige sport shirt, jeans, and Nike sneakers. He has been playing tennis with his wife. Koppel eats his eggplant from a plastic container and banters with the staff. Asked about the progress of the Thursday script, he announces that he has done "fuckall." He tries a chocolate-covered tart that was included for dessert and pronounces it a failure. Then he slips on his sports jacket and takes the elevator to the basement studio. Henry Hyde, visible on the famed *Nightline* monitor, is getting hooked up in the Capitol's Statuary Hall. Newt Gingrich walks by and asks an aide, "What show is he doing?"

"Henry, it's Ted," Koppel tells Hyde, who cannot see him. "How are you doing? You are looking uncomfortably comfortable in Statuary Hall. You look as though you belong."

"I'm not the real Henry Hyde. I'm an actor," Hyde says.

"You're nice to do this," Koppel says. An assistant brushes the lint from Koppel's jacket. In the control room, Tom Bettag and Mark Nelson don their headsets and face a vast wall of monitors. The three cameramen are ready. The TelePrompTer is set. It is 8:35.

"Stand by, Tedley," says Tony Barrett, the director.

"This is ABC News *Nightline,*" the announcer intones. "Reporting from Washington, Ted Koppel."

"This is not, you may be surprised to learn, a liberal-versus-conservative issue," Koppel begins. He says that "after a full day of debate and voting in the House of Representatives, each of four different versions of a term limit amendment to the Constitution went down to defeat." Actually, the fourth vote hasn't taken place yet, but it will by the time the program airs. In television's time warp, the future is already past. To the viewer, *Nightline* will appear to be live.

"Mr. Chairman . . . why do you think that so many of your

colleagues, and why are you in particular, ignoring what seems to be the public will?" Koppel asks.

Hyde takes the rhetorical high road. "Edmund Burke said we owe our constituency the highest fidelity, but we also owe them our best judgment, and we don't owe our conscience to anybody," he says.

Koppel rephrases the question, citing an ABC poll from his research memo that more than 70 percent of the public backs term limits. "Why aren't you willing to listen to the people in that regard?"

"But you forget the poll every two years called an election," Hyde says.

It is a curious minuet. Koppel personally agreees with everything Hyde is saying—indeed, that is why he wanted him as a guest—but is playing devil's advocate for the sake of talk show convention. *Crossfire* would never do such an interview, but Koppel doesn't feel he needs dueling viewpoints to succeed.

Hyde rambles a bit, but Koppel does not interrupt. "Let's just take a short break, Congressman," he says. In fact, since there are no commercials, the break lasts just a few seconds.

The interview resumes. "Here you are, one of the pillars of the conservative Republican community up there on Capitol Hill, and you broke with your own party on this one," Koppel says.

Hyde touts the virtues of experience, hails the party's elder statesmen, quotes Edmund Burke again. Koppel asks about talk radio's impact on the debate. Hyde wanders off the point: "I think talk radio is very powerful. It is a phenomenon. Some of these hosts on talk radio are very charismatic." But, he says, "C-SPAN is our ally. People have watched the debates and see two sides."

Koppel thanks Hyde for appearing. The interview has lasted eleven minutes and twenty-one seconds. Koppel turns to the other camera and tapes his signoff. "For all of us here at ABC News, good night."

But the night is still young. It is two hours and forty-five minutes to airtime, and the Bury piece is not done.

Bettag is pleased because Koppel can go home early. He knows that Roone Arledge would prefer that the show be live every night, but these early evenings are a way of saving Koppel from exhaustion. Bettag wants to keep his star well rested for foreign trips and investigative projects. More than a third of the *Nightline* programs are now pretaped.

On the set, a college student with a tape recorder is interviewing Koppel. "Mr. Koppel, what advice would you give young people considering a career in journalism?"

"Get a good makeup man," he says.

Koppel tells Bettag he is pleased with the Hyde interview. "That actually hung together pretty well," he says.

The final House vote is beginning. A *Nightline* producer has been monitoring the debate on C-SPAN. McCollum's version of the amendment gets 227 votes, 61 short of the required two-thirds margin.

Chris Bury is still selecting sound bites for his piece. "You need another younger person to give a sense of generational divide," Lisa Koenig says.

"Do we have someone else of Inglis's generation?" Bury says. "Is Hoekstra absolutely unusable?"

"It's redundant," she says. Representative Peter Hoekstra had said that "Congress just doesn't get it. There's a disconnect between Washington here and what the people want." Hoekstra is dropped.

At 9:24 they are downstairs in Edit Room 11. Bury recites the voice-over into a floor mike in a booming voice. "Such ambivalence was also the order of the day for the lunch crowd at a steak house in New York City," he says.

He doesn't like that transition. "The ambivalence echoing at the Capitol tonight was also the order of the day at this steak house in New York City," he says. Much better.

Koenig's job is to cover the narrative with pictures. When Bury says "echoing at the Capitol tonight," she has the tape editor insert a nighttime shot of the famous dome. In two edit rooms down the hall, her fellow producers are doing the same thing. Koenig nervously checks her watch. "We're really running out of time here," she says. On *Larry King Live,* Senator Trent Lott is discussing term limits with the guest host, Ross Perot.

The editing is painstakingly slow. It takes Koenig half an hour just to finish the first half minute of the piece. The videotape must be played and rewound, played and rewound, the seconds counted off. On *PrimeTime Live,* Diane Sawyer is interviewing the police officer who responded to Nicole Simpson's 911 call. "I've always loved him," Nicole says on the tape. ABC is not without its O.J. fix tonight.

Koenig keeps replaying the day's interviews with a woman and two men at Ruth's Steak House in Manhattan. They complain about congressmen being out of touch. None is concise. The woman pauses too long between thoughts.

At 10:22 Bettag walks into the edit room. He wants to make sure the Bury piece isn't too long. "Guess your length," he says.

"These MOSs are not particularly snappy," Koenig says. "If I took these out, it would save you thirty-eight seconds."

Bettag watches the sound bites. "The woman ain't great," he says. He decides to drop all three interviews. "The goal was to get real people, but real people aren't always very good," he says. Only professional talkers—politicians, a lobbyist, a pollster, and a radio host—will appear on *Nightline* tonight.

Bury grabs his trench coat and heads back to the Hill to tape his closing remarks. The only reason for the trip is to get a nighttime shot in front of the Capitol, to give the piece a sense of immediacy. It will, however, be on tape.

In yet another edit room, Sarah Just is screening the Henry Hyde interview. She must cut it by a minute and fifteen seconds, covering the breaks with a cutaway shot of Koppel looking at Hyde on the monitor. This is slightly deceptive, for viewers will have no way of knowing that some of Hyde's words have been excised. Indeed, he will appear to be live.

Just makes two cuts. She drops the second reference to Edmund Burke and tightens up Hyde's long-winded answer about talk radio. The reference to C-SPAN is dropped. The video incisions are easy to make because of Hyde's practiced cadence. "He speaks nicely and cleanly and in whole sentences," Just says.

Tom Bettag is back in the control room. At 11:08 Lisa Koenig calls. She has the final length of the Bury piece. "Eight even," she says.

The atmosphere is loosening up. One staffer calls his wife and leaves a taped message. "I want to fondle your breasts," he says.

Things are on schedule. Bettag hopes the Roone Phone doesn't ring tonight. The phone, a direct line to Arledge's home in New York, occasionally rings when the ABC News president doesn't like the look or sound of a broadcast. Sometimes he calls and suggests a question for Koppel. Staffers have learned to live with these long-distance intrusions.

An aide walks in with the early edition of *The Washington Post*. Bettag scans the front page. "House Rejects Measure to Require Term Limits," it says. Henry Hyde's picture is in the top right-hand corner. Hyde is quoted extensively, saying the same kind of things he told Koppel.

At 11:24 the three sections of the Bury piece are fed into the control room. Technicians are checking the audio and adding the fonts that identify speakers by name. It is the first time anyone has seen the complete report.

The piece finishes with Bury in his trench coat in front of the dome. "It was also a classic case of congressmen caught between public opinion, party loyalty, and their own personal beliefs . . . This is Chris Bury for *Nightline* in Washington."

"Okay, nice!" Bettag tells the staff. "Good piece!"

It is 11:35. "Five to air," Tony Barrett says. "Four. Three. Two. One." The music comes up. "March twenty-ninth, 1995," the announcer begins. Ted Koppel is home, getting ready for bed. A long day of Washington talk is culminating with a final round of televised talk. *Nightline* is on the air.

CHAPTER SEVEN

VIDEO VÉRITÉ

T he angry caller on the line is from Breckenridge, Texas.
"Most of us are getting sick and tired of the slickers in Washington telling everyone what's good for them," he says.

Brian Lamb, who is hosting a C-SPAN roundtable on this particular Friday morning, stares into the camera, his affable expression unchanged. "Give us one example of something that you personally want changed," he says. "Just one."

"I'd like to change all the politicians in Washington."

"Why?"

"Because I don't trust any of them."

Lamb is politely persistent: "What is it that you don't trust them to do?"

"I'm a retired military man, and they've broken the contract with me over the benefits I was promised for doing twenty years in the navy."

Without raising his voice, badgering the viewer, or calling attention to himself in any way, Lamb has gotten to the heart of the matter by eliciting the man's true grievance. It is a style that has attracted an incredibly loyal and well-informed audience for the nonprofit network that is the very antithesis of flashy television news.

On CBS, NBC, and ABC, high-priced celebrity anchors are the centerpiece of each broadcast; on C-SPAN, the self-effacing hosts never utter their names on the air. On *McLaughlin, Crossfire,* and

Capital Gang, high-decibel opinionators trade barbs and insults; on
C-SPAN, journalists ask gentle questions and never hint at what
they think. On commercial television, complex issues are reduced
to ninety-second reports punctuated by brief sound bites; on
C-SPAN, a four-hour hearing on entitlement reform runs four
hours. The camera even lingers as the lawmakers and witnesses
collect their papers and meander toward the exit. C-SPAN is unvar-
nished reality, delivered without the punditry and pontification that
are defining elements of the rest of the talk show culture.

Across the arid desert of television, a few lush oases have flour-
ished. They assume a certain intelligence on the part of the viewer.
They believe that quiet voices can still be heard. They have proven,
year after year, that it is possible to do serious talk without putting
the audience to sleep.

The placement and timing of these programs are very much
driven by economics. The pressures of prime-time commercial television are such that only shows that can attract a mass audience can
survive. In an age when a thirty-second ad on *Roseanne* can fetch
$400,000, network programmers simply will not tolerate ventures
that are high-minded but low-rated. That's why many of the network newsmagazines—*Eye to Eye, 20/20, Dateline NBC, Prime-
Time Live, 48 Hours*—often traffic in crime, sex, and celebrity
stories. They can never forget that they are up against prime-time
entertainment, chasing an audience conditioned by the likes of *Hard
Copy, Home Improvement,* and *Cops.*

Some of the most thoughtful talk shows appear on public television, which is, after all, subsidized by the federal government. Charlie Rose ranges widely across the political and cultural landscape,
from Spike Lee to Mike Tyson to Henry Kissinger, for conversations that last twenty or thirty minutes, an eternity by TV standards. He relishes public television for the chance to do things
that no commercial station would touch, such as spending an hour
interviewing New York investment banker Felix Rohatyn.

"Every week on this program I find someone we didn't know
much about who turns out to be a scintillating guest," Rose says.
"How is it going to do up against David Letterman? It's not even
close. But it has an audience.

"The best political show I've had this year was thirty minutes with David Broder, a very bright reporter thinking out loud about the politics of the country. I don't need to have people shouting at each other . . . There are a lot of people who don't have access to television because of their subject matter, or at best they get a sound bite."

Yet *Charlie Rose* is on at odd hours in some markets, and PBS estimates that he reaches an average of just 690,000 households a night. Rose knows precisely how to make his show more commercial —shorter segments, flashy use of videotape—and is exploring a weekly syndicated version that might incorporate such elements. But he enjoys having thoughtful guests—a doctor who specializes in treating AIDS patients, for example—who don't fit into the "big name" formula of network television.

Famous personalities are also drawn to the program, despite its small audience, because they know Rose will give them an intelli- gent—some would say ingratiating—hearing. In the polar opposite of Larry King's surprise-me approach, Rose prides himself on ex- haustively researching each guest and his subject, the better to push the conversation to a higher level.

"It amazes me how much talk there is on television that is not informed talk," he says. "It's just talk."

Ben Wattenberg, with his show *Think Tank,* hosts the kind of professors and intellectuals—Robert Bork, Lani Guinier, Milton Friedman, Daniel Boorstin, Nathan Glazer, Glenn Loury—who are not likely to pop up on *Crossfire.* That is by design. Wattenberg spent a month cohosting *Crossfire* in the mid-'80s, and he was not anxious to repeat the experience. "The producers would say in your earpiece, 'Kick him in the ass! He's down! Fight! Scream! Yell!' They were looking for blood," he says. *Think Tank,* by contrast, resembles a college seminar, with Wattenberg standing behind a lectern. While other shows chewed over which welfare reform bill was likely to pass Congress, Wattenberg would ask whether welfare causes illegitimacy.

Wattenberg, who lined up funding from Amgen, a biotechnol- ogy firm, says he had no choice but to peddle his program to PBS. "The networks will buy sitcoms, quiz shows, but they will not buy public affairs," he says. "That shuts out everyone else. PBS is the only a place a liberal or a conservative can put a program on TV."

What's more, a public television program can be successful with a far smaller audience than CBS, NBC, or ABC would tolerate.

Cable networks, which serve audiences that pay for access, also have the luxury of indulging in niche programming. On CNBC's evening lineup, both Phil Donahue and Geraldo Rivera have dealt with serious subjects in far less flamboyant fashion than on their syndicated daytime shows. Dick Cavett, who has bounced in and out of commercial television, has also found a home at CNBC. And Mary Matalin, the cohost of *Equal Time,* employs a wacky interviewing style that wouldn't last three days on network television.

"I don't know if it's a woman thing," Matalin says. "I don't know if it's because we're a little loopy. There's some attraction about watching what looks like real people. Sometimes we just babble. It's stream-of-consciousness. Sometimes I pretend nobody's watching and it's really *Wayne's World.*"

America's Talking, a CNBC spinoff, is slowly building an audience with a lineup of largely anonymous hosts and such offbeat programs as *The Pork Show* (about wasteful government spending), *Alive and Wellness* (an alternative healing show), and *Bugged* (in which callers gripe about their pet peeves). The new network now reaches more than twelve million homes and receives twenty thousand calls and e-mail messages a week. Fox is also considering joining the talk show fray. And more programs are undoubtedly on the way.

This burgeoning kaleidoscope of talk is of relatively recent vintage. Just twenty-five years ago, back when most people had black-and-white sets, the only real national show of journalistic opinion was *Washington Week in Review.* Launched in 1967 with Robert MacNeil as moderator, it was designed as an easy give-and-take among a select group of working reporters and columnists. No one interrupted, no one shouted, no one climbed out on an ideological limb. Paul Duke continued the dignified tradition during his twenty years as moderator.

Once likened to a Washington dinner party without the food or the booze, *Washington Week* always staked out the intellectual high ground. Two years after its debut, Martin Agronsky, a former *Face the Nation* moderator, started a competing program on the Post-

Newsweek stations, *Agronsky & Company,* which would feature such elite journalists as Hugh Sidey, Peter Lisagor, George Will, James Kilpatrick, Carl Rowan, Elizabeth Drew, and Strobe Talbott. For the next dozen years, that was pretty much it for Washington talk shows. There was no C-SPAN, no CNN, no network program where the journalists indulged in opinion. Paul Duke and Martin Agronsky had the field to themselves.

Washington Week was very much a creature of the Public Broadcasting Service. Largely insulated from the pressure to deliver huge numbers, the Friday night program developed a loyal, highly educated, and generally older audience. Many of its viewers in more than two million households were senior citizens. Everyone's mother loved *Washington Week.*

"Our ratings are pretty good for public television," says producer Sue Ducat. "If we were on commercial television on Friday night, we'd probably be long dead."

"It's a particular kind of audience that really gives a damn and gets to know the people who are talking to them and takes them seriously," says Charlie McDowell of the *Richmond Times-Dispatch.* "It's very unsettling to be taken seriously on television at a time when television is skidding toward sensationalism. People don't know whether I'm a liberal or conservative. I sort of like that."

Washington Week was leisurely, talking-head television. There were about twenty regulars, with the most frequent appearances by Steve Roberts and Gloria Borger of *U.S. News,* Howard Fineman of *Newsweek,* Gwen Ifill of NBC, and Jack Nelson of the *Los Angeles Times,* along with the likes of author Haynes Johnson, David Broder of *The Washington Post,* and Thomas Friedman of *The New York Times.* If the program had a weakness, other than being a bit plodding, it was that it tended to reflect an establishment point of view. Most of the older panelists were pillars of the Washington power structure, friendly with the veteran lawmakers they had known for decades and disinclined to criticize the accepted ways of doing business. They rarely challenged one another on the show. It was as if they were debating the shape of the political table, but not whether the table was rotting and should be thrown out.

In the early '80s, as shows like *McLaughlin* began littering the landscape, many thought *Washington Week* was too stodgy, too outdated. "From time to time there would be some pressure from people at PBS: Why don't we jazz things up, put more sparkle in it?" Paul Duke says. "But the tried-and-true format has worked over the years. It's one of a vanishing breed of television programs. We were not in the business of making a lot of crazy predictions or voicing a lot of outrageous opinions. It was just reporters talking about the stories they covered. To me it was always absurd to get people on talking about what's going on in Russia when they have no idea what's going on in Russia."

Duke was a stubborn traditionalist, resisting the use of videotape or graphics. "Paul didn't like to change anything," Sue Ducat says. "I had to beat him over the head. He wasn't interested. We're trying to make inroads among 'younger viewers'—those under forty."

The *Washington Week* pundits were almost all middle-aged men, and sometimes they were Duke's friends. McDowell and Duke had covered Richmond together, occasionally playing golf or tennis. "He was looking for someone who would sound vaguely conservative, and so they got a guy with a Southern drawl and thought that was the same thing," McDowell says. "I'm probably a little more liberal than most people."

Ken Bode succeeded Duke in 1994 and quickly concluded that the program needed to be "a little livelier." He began using videotaped highlights, long a staple of other talk shows. He introduced satellite interviews with guests at remote locations. He shortened the segments and added an end-of-the-show roundtable. And, as the father of two daughters, he was determined to put more women on the program. There was an ancillary benefit as well.

"Gloria Borger is enormously popular," Bode says. "She's very pretty. Television is very kind to Gloria. I got one letter that said, 'I'm an eighty-two-year-old guy and haven't missed a program in twenty-seven years. You should have Gloria on more often. She gets my heart started.' " On *Washington Week*'s bulletin board on America Online, more subscribers downloaded Borger's picture than that of any other panelist. Ken Bode was a distant second.

Bode also phased out a few of the thumbsuckers who never left the office except for lunch. "Georgie Anne Geyer is not a prominent Washington journalist," he says. "But when she comes on and she's just back from Bosnia, you can run your fingers through it. You can feel it. Once she came on after a trip to the Dominican Republic. She rented a plane, flew up to the mountains, and watched kids carrying gasoline cans across the border to Haiti, and she talked about it on the program. It was just riveting."

A former reporter for NBC and *The New Republic*, Bode commutes from Greencastle, Indiana, where he teaches at DePauw University and prides himself on being in touch with the heartland. When he tells audiences that *Washington Week* will not cover Tonya Harding, the Menendez brothers, or O. J. Simpson, he invariably gets a round of applause.

In bringing *Washington Week* into the '90s, Bode has arguably made it more like other talk shows. But he has also kept the emphasis on working beat reporters and steered away from obvious partisans. "We don't have a *Crossfire* or *Capital Gang* mentality about the way we line people up: left-right, Republican-Democrat," he says. "There's no presumption of ideology. Bob Novak is a smart goddamn reporter, but Bob has made it his stock-in-trade to be the voice of conservative Republicanism. That's why we don't use people from *McLaughlin* or *Capital Gang*. It changes the character of the program."

Brian Lamb doesn't deign to take ratings.

Since he does not have to deliver an audience to advertisers, he is largely immune from the traditional numbers game. C-SPAN gets its funding from the other cable networks. Lamb wants people to watch, of course, but he doesn't want to chase after a mass audience. His operation is more like a public library, there when you need it, than a commercial bookstore that must move the product.

C-SPAN is built on a no-frills philosophy that has never changed: Let the viewer decide for himself. By stripping the product to its barest essentials—an austerity dictated by a $20-million budget, or roughly three times what Diane Sawyer makes—C-SPAN serves up news without spin, information without editing. This does not always make for scintillating television, as anyone who has sat through a House subcommittee hearing or National League of Cities conference can attest. But it is a radical concept because it eliminates the journalist as middleman. On C-SPAN, people can see the whole speech, the whole debate, the whole convention, without the compression and analysis and sarcasm of the talk show types.

"C-SPAN is the only form of television that can be accused of raising standards," says Robert Lichter, director of the Center for Media and Public Affairs. "If the mainstream media let the elites talk to each other, and talk radio lets the masses talk to each other, C-SPAN lets the masses see the elites in action. At a time when the media are laden with opinion, C-SPAN shows without telling. It's the medium without the messengers."

The Cable Satellite Public Affairs Network is very much the creation of Lamb, the company chairman, a low-key Hoosier whose evenhanded persona perfectly captures the network's mission. The *Chicago Tribune* calls him "the anti-Geraldo." "A guy so square he's totally hip," says *Mirabella*. "All the charisma of a test pattern," says *The New York Times Magazine*. He has become famous for his unorthodox approach to journalism, even as he disdains the idea of such fame.

Lamb's salary was $195,000 a year, remarkably low for a chief executive officer. He roamed the halls several mornings a week, greeting the lowliest employes by name and asking about their kids. Many viewed him as a sort of priest, an Irish-Catholic who doesn't drink, doesn't smoke, and has no kids, and themselves as devoted members of the congregation.

Lamb relished the notion of a network without stars, of a new media culture that revolves around substance, not glitzy packaging. He even issued a written declaration urging staff members not to talk about their political views in casual hallway conversations. C-SPAN was to be an opinion-free zone. "The driving reason this place exists is for people to be able to see the event in its entirety and make up their minds themselves," Lamb says.

"I grew up being told that journalism is one thing, and now I see it on television often being another, more tabloid. People who love journalism and accuracy and balance are having a hard time accepting people who sell themselves for high salaries to a medium that encourages nothing but sex and violence. It's very painful."

Susan Swain, C-SPAN's senior vice president, puts it this way:

"Every place else, you tune in to see what the star is going to do next. What Larry King is going to say, or how Sam Donaldson is going to approach his interview." At C-SPAN, "we don't want to get in the way."

Here, for example, are some of the first questions that Brian Lamb asked Stanley Greenberg, President Clinton's pollster, in an interview about his book: Have you always been interested in history? How long have you been married? How did you meet? You do a lot of focus groups—how does that work? How do you put together a focus group? Where do you find the people? Do they know there's a one-way mirror? Do you record them? Do you moderate them? Do you keep their names confidential? Are you concerned about the Perot voters in 1996? Where do those Perot voters go? How many of them are there? At no point does Lamb call attention to himself in the slightest.

Lamb's network is having a growing influence on the rest of the media, if only because so many of its big names, from Rush Limbaugh to Don Imus to Tim Russert, tune in. "It's liberating for the networks," Russert says. "I don't think there's a week that goes by where we don't rely on something C-SPAN has shot. When you have ten people running for president, being out there every day with every one of them is something we no longer do, nor could we do."

C-SPAN's unblinking eye provides a check on the version of reality dished out by the big networks. During the gay rights march on Washington in April 1993, most television viewers saw pictures of three hundred thousand well-dressed, well-mannered people peacefully demonstrating for an equal place in American society. But C-SPAN viewers saw another side of the march: Topless lesbians. Gay men in leather harnesses. Drag queens. A woman who told the crowd she wanted to "fuck" Hillary Clinton. Another who spoke of "getting it on" with Anita Hill. These colorful exhibitionists were clearly a minority, but their presence was simply erased from most news accounts. The bawdy footage upset some viewers, but C-SPAN officials say matter-of-factly they do not censor the news. What you see on the screen is what you would see if you were there. And that approach has changed the balance of power between television and the audience. For the first time, the discerning viewer

can look at the *CBS Evening News* or *NBC Nightly News* and say:
Hey, that isn't the way it happened.

Around a sixth-floor conference table at 400 North Capitol Street,
five men and five women are deciding what C-SPAN will cover the
next day.

It is a Monday afternoon in the spring of 1995, and the meeting
is being led by Terry Murphy, the network's vice president, a ge-
nial, balding man who started as a camera technician thirteen years
earlier. In an age when the average network news report runs a
minute and forty-five seconds, what Murphy controls—twenty-
four hours a day of unedited airtime—is more precious than gold.
Politicians, congressional committees, think tanks, and universities
are all angling to get their events on C-SPAN as a way of boosting
their visibility. The most savvy among them schedule their events
on Mondays and Fridays because they know that C-SPAN is
swamped with congressional events during midweek.

Steve Scully, the political editor, has already been called by
the spokesman for Lamar Alexander's presidential campaign. The
campaign wants C-SPAN to carry Alexander's fundraiser that night
at the Marriott Hotel in Washington. There are no other prominent
guests, but Alexander will be playing the piano.

"Sometimes you get a lot of pressure," Scully says. "People call
you constantly about events. They say my job is on the line, or this
is a made-for-C-SPAN event." Within C-SPAN, Haley Barbour,
the Republican Party chairman, is known as the most relentless
lobbyist. He will call five or six times about televising a party event
and isn't shy about taking his case to Brian Lamb. "First he gets
angry, then he starts begging: 'I've got all these executives coming
and I promised them national coverage,' " a C-SPAN staffer says.

In sizing up the day's offerings, Terry Murphy's limitations
have nothing to do with time. Each event C-SPAN covers will be
replayed five or six times. But he has just thirty-five crew members,
enough for perhaps four two-camera crews for longer events, and
three one-camera crews for shorter speeches.

Some events are already set: a Clinton news conference on violence against women, a Phil Gramm speech at the National Press

Club, a conclave of Jimmy Carter aides at the Carter Center in Atlanta, a gathering of political cartoonists at Harvard. Murphy is leaning toward a Senate Foreign Relations Committee hearing, and a Senate Commerce Committee hearing on cable television rates. Everything else must compete for the remaining crews. The staffers solemnly study a three-page listing of twenty-seven speeches, hearings, and seminars that has been culled for the most promising events. They take their job seriously. Nothing will make it on the air simply because it sounds entertaining.

Ellen Schweiger, an assignment editor, begins by announcing that Senate Democratic Leader Tom Daschle will hold a news conference to unveil the party's version of legislation giving the president a line-item veto over the budget. Steve Scully pitches the Alexander fundraiser.

Murphy runs down a list of the action in Congress. Senate confirmation hearings will begin for Dan Glickman's nomination as agriculture secretary. Both parties are having their regular Tuesday policy lunches. All will be covered.

A Senate Aging Committee hearing on programs for the elderly. "Any interest?" Murphy says. Silence. Another Senate hearing on health care fraud. It sounds sexy: a mysterious "Doctor A" will testify from behind a screen. A couple of staffers like it. No decision. A House Appropriations subcommittee hearing on the National Endowment for the Humanities. "Any interest?" There is none.

The House Ethics Committee will be meeting behind closed doors to consider a Democratic complaint against Newt Gingrich. This is potentially a big story, but could also mean a lengthy stake-out with no comment by the panel members afterward. Murphy decides to pass.

After several more hearings, they turn to the day's speechifying. Interfaith Impact, a religious group, is holding a conference. The speakers include Hillary Rodham Clinton. "I have a feeling Hillary is going to talk about religion," Scully says.

"Why is that interesting?" says Regina Hunter, a senior field producer.

"The First Lady talking about religion?" Scully says. "I think it's interesting when you have a public figure talking about faith."

"It's not like we're starving for Hillary," Hunter says. The First

Lady is addressing a political group that C-SPAN plans to cover the following night. C-SPAN worries about tilting too much toward any one speaker. But Murphy decides to cover her anyway.

The Center for Science in the Public Interest is holding a news conference on the fat content of American sandwiches. The group's previous studies on Chinese, Italian, and Mexican food have drawn heavy news coverage.

"What is the public policy in the sandwich?" Murphy asks. Public policy is the criterion by which C-SPAN judges all events.

"It gets down to your health," another staffer says. No one seconds the motion. The food event is nixed.

Next is Education Secretary Richard Riley speaking on "religious conficts in public schools." No takers.

A provocatively titled forum, "Bambi Meets Business," turns out to be a bit more pedestrian. "It's the American University School of Public Affairs forum on regulatory takings," says Caroline West, an assignment editor. "It's pretty balanced." C-SPAN loves events with partisan balance.

Someone has put on the list a speech by Mr. Sulu (actor George Takei) from the starship *Enterprise*. This prompts a round of laughter. C-SPAN doesn't do *Star Trek*.

The pace picks up slightly. Georgetown University has Jeane Kirkpatrick and other speakers on "UN Issues for the Next Half Century." "Any interest?" None.

Commerce Secretary Ron Brown on the Copyright Awareness Campaign? Attorney General Janet Reno on Women's History Month? Clearly B-list speeches.

Murphy goes back over the list, hoping to squeeze in an extra event by dropping something marginal. "Is Foreign Relations a must-do?" he asks.

"We haven't gotten Jesse Helms doing this yet, and there's Madeleine Albright. There's balance," Schweiger says.

"Is cable a must-do?"

"It's A-plus speakers, and it's a topic that affects everybody," Schweiger says.

Steve Scully, who loves politics, makes one more try. "I'd like to see us get Alexander," he says.

"I wouldn't," Hunter says.

"We did Gramm's fund-raiser," Scully says. "This is a time that they're all trying to raise money. It shows you how this process works."

"I just don't like covering dinners," Schweiger says. Alexander is nixed.

The meeting is over. Another day of talk has been successfully negotiated.

For Newt Gingrich, C-SPAN was a perfect way to send a message to the other end of Pennsylvania Avenue.

It was 1981, and the Georgian was a mere second-term backbencher in a party that looked like it would remain in the House minority forever. The Reagan White House wasn't paying much attention to Gingrich's small band of conservative firebrands, who included Robert Walker of Pennsylvania and Vin Weber of Minnesota. Out of frustration, they turned to C-SPAN. They communed with the C-SPAN audience through the use of "special orders," or hourlong speeches delivered after everyone else had left the chamber. The capital elite was barely aware of C-SPAN's existence because the city would not be wired for cable until the end of the decade. But out in the heartland, Gingrich and Walker were bigger celebrities than many senators. People would stop them in airports. They had discovered a way to circumvent the mainstream media and reach a cadre of political activists across the country. "C-SPAN is more real than being there," Gingrich liked to say.

But there were times when Gingrich was consciously aiming at an audience of one, the ultimate in narrowcasting. "Ronald Reagan was a creature of the electronic media," he says. "Reagan would literally, particularly when Nancy was out of town, sit upstairs and watch C-SPAN. Sometimes, when we wanted to get messages to him that the staff didn't want to get through, we'd simply do special orders. And then he'd call us. He'd say, 'That was really good stuff.' We got more time with Reagan on C-SPAN than we did with Reagan in his office. That's a very important reality."

Brian Lamb immediately saw what was happening. "More than anyone else who's ever appeared on C-SPAN," he says, "Gingrich knew what he was doing from the very beginning. He was a history professor who knew how to give a fifty-minute lecture." While many ridiculed this sort of partisan droning, Lamb viewed it as democracy in action. "Even though people make fun of that, it's very important in a society like ours where an elected official can get up for an hour and take their chances with the audience."

No one could foresee it at the time, but something even larger was in an embryonic stage. Since the birth of television news in the 1950s, the camera's eye was always focused most tightly on the president. The cult of personality that has surrounded the postwar presidency is very much a function of the magnifying effects of television. It was far easier for journalism to cover one commander-in-chief—even if he wasn't doing much more than answering a couple of shouted questions or waving from the steps of *Air Force One*—than 535 mostly obscure politicians on Capitol Hill. For television purposes, the president *was* the government.

Congress, quite simply, made for terrible television. There was too much dull speechifying that always seemed to drag on into the night, way past deadline. Dramatic moments were few and far between. Legislation moved at a molasses pace, constantly delayed by partisan maneuvering. There were too many subplots, too many compromises, too many complicated amendments. Even after the subcommittees and the full committees and the House and Senate had finally acted, the debate could be mired for weeks in a conference committee. Television valued simplicity. Viewers simply could not find out much about the legislative process from brief reports on the nightly news.

C-SPAN changed that by allowing people to see the sausage-making close up, for as long as they could bear to watch. It gradually turned the congressional leaders and major committee chairmen into TV personalities. It allowed lawmakers to talk to a mass audience on lengthy call-in shows. In short, C-SPAN brought Congress into the talk show age. It would take sixteen years, but the focus of news coverage would one day shift from the White House to Newt Gingrich's House.

None of that seemed possible when the fledgling network was making its first tentative attempt at talk. The initial foray took place on the afternoon of October 7, 1980, in a back room at the National Press Club, where Brian Lamb was fumbling with an ill-fitting earpiece.

It was nearly five years before the debut of *Larry King Live*. Only five million homes were wired for cable. Television news shows were still an exercise in one-way communication. Yet here was Lamb, with the editors of four trade publications and one phone line, trying to open up the process.

The show got off to a disastrous start. At 2:00 P.M. Charles Ferris, the chairman of the Federal Communications Commission, stopped by for an interview after addressing the press club. Just as Lamb was introducing Ferris, C-SPAN's power failed, knocking the network off the air for several minutes. Ferris patiently waited for the program to resume, then made way for the four editors.

Viewed through the prism of history, the scene looks like something out of the video Stone Age. A tangle of microphone cords is strewn across a bulky round table in front of the guests. Earpiece wires dangle awkwardly from each man's face. One editor puffs absently on a cigarette, another rubs his eyes.

"We're going to open the phones up here for those of you who might have a question, no matter how simple it may seem to you or how technical it may seem to you," Lamb says.

A few moments later: "This is the first time we've tried this . . . I can't even get this thing in my ear." And: "Ask us any question."

Finally, the first call comes in. "Where is that, Gail?" Lamb asks an assistant. "What's the name?" It is Bob from Yankton, South Dakota, who wants to know if it is illegal to put a satellite dish in his backyard.

From that inauspicious start, C-SPAN each year now airs eleven thousand viewer calls, one of the network's most popular features. "We copied it right off the radio," Lamb says. "It wasn't any genius on our part. It's taken off like crazy."

Lamb's determination to provide unedited programming, often to the point of boredom, grew out of his dissatisfaction with the slice-and-dice nature of television news. He recalls watching a half-hour speech by black activist Stokely Carmichael in the 1960s. "Maybe two minutes was incendiary," he says. "The rest of it was thoughtful and intelligent and very well stated . . . What made it on was the fire and brimstone."

The son of a tavern owner in Lafayette, Indiana, Lamb attended Purdue University and created a local TV music show called *Dance Date*. After the navy sent him to Washington as a press officer, he became a radio reporter for United Press International, a press secretary to a Republican senator from Colorado, and an assistant in the Nixon administration's Office of Telecommunications Policy.

It was during the Carter years, when Lamb was Washington bureau chief for *Cablevision* magazine, that he began proselytizing around the idea of televising the House of Representatives. Using $25,000 in seed money from a sympathetic cable operator, he sold the speaker, Tip O'Neill, on the concept of gavel-to-gavel coverage. Lamb and his three employees set up shop in a Rosslyn, Virginia, apartment building. The set consisted of some tables hammered together with plywood from a local hardware store, a blue curtain, and a C-SPAN sign, which fell down during one interview. C-SPAN went on the air in March 1979, and no one much noticed. "You can't imagine how insignificant I was," Lamb says.

But the obscure operation soon gathered momentum. C-SPAN began televising committee hearings, speeches, and campaign events. President Reagan and Vice President Bush appeared on call-in programs. Dozens of big-shot journalists showed up for the morning roundtable show, and many got an earful from angry callers complaining about the liberal media. There was a far wider range of guests than on the other channels. The network even spent an evening at Larry King's radio show. "More people have mentioned the C-SPAN telecast than anything I can remember," King said afterward.

C-SPAN often resembled radio in that it consisted mainly of talking. Holding up a newspaper article was considered an exciting visual. In an MTV era in which everything on television was speeding up, C-SPAN still meandered like a snail. Despite these limitations, Lamb's network soon emerged as an important political tool. Conservative viewers flocked to C-SPAN in the early '80s. One caller, saying he was "ashamed to be an American" when Jimmy Carter was president, complained that "ABC, CBS, and NBC are so biased to the Democratic side."

During an interview with Susan Swain, Gingrich said: "We are to some extent manipulating you. You've provided us a vehicle to reach out to every neighborhood in America . . . There's a chance for any citizen who wants to watch—they don't have to agree with me—to learn what I think."

As Gingrich's televised attacks on the Democrats grew more incendiary, Tip O'Neill decided to retaliate. In 1984 the House speaker ordered the cameras to pan the empty seats to show that the Republicans were speaking to a deserted chamber. The majority party, not C-SPAN, had control of the cameras. But O'Neill's move made Gingrich an even bigger star and did nothing to dim the luster of unlimited exposure. In 1986 the Senate, jealous of the attention being lavished on the other body, voted to televise its proceedings on what became C-SPAN 2.

Lawmakers and candidates regularly trooped to the North Capitol Street studio, grateful for the chance to speak at length in an atmosphere utterly unlike the adversarial posture of *Meet the Press* or *Nightline*. There were practical considerations as well, for 98 percent of C-SPAN viewers voted. They were twice as likely as nonviewers to contact members of Congress, make political donations, or volunteer for campaigns. It was, like talk radio listeners, a plugged-in audience.

With seemingly endless hours of airtime available, C-SPAN soon became a factor in presidential politics. Candidates agreed to wear wireless mikes as they made their rounds in the early primary states. In 1987 C-SPAN cameras caught Senator Joseph Biden making exaggerated boasts about his academic record to a heckling voter in Claremont, New Hampshire, an incident that helped derail Biden's White House candidacy. In 1991 a C-SPAN microphone picked up Senator Bob Kerrey's off-color joke about lesbians and Jerry Brown (the network didn't broadcast it, but Chris Matthews heard about the tape and broke the story in the *San Francisco Examiner*). Savvy strategists turned C-SPAN's need for live events to their advantage. When Bill Clinton was gearing up for the '92 campaign, his aides targeted C-SPAN with a series of speeches they urged the network to carry. These speeches, particularly one at Georgetown University, created a favorable buzz among the small coterie of journalists and Democratic activists the Arkansas governor was trying to impress. Ross Perot, Dan Quayle, and Al Gore all appeared on call-in shows. The network carried 105 debates during the 1994 campaign, events that the other networks routinely dismissed as too "local."

The notion that the viewer is all-important is what sets C-SPAN

apart from a talk show kingdom in which journalists reign supreme.
When President Clinton prepared to make his first televised address
after the Democratic debacle in the 1994 elections, the network
pundits had a field day. "Bill Clinton is trying to get in front of a
parade that is moving without him," Pat Buchanan said on *Good
Morning America*. "The fact is that he can only look reactive and
panicky," Fred Barnes said on *CBS This Morning*. "He's in real
trouble . . . the kind of trouble that one speech cannot possibly fix,"
Jeff Greenfield said on *Nightline*.

After the speech, however, the networks immediately cut back
to the likes of *Seinfeld* and *ER*. CNN switched to its reporters
and analysts for instant reaction. But C-SPAN took calls, allowing
viewers from around the country to sound off on the president's
remarks.

Sarah Trahern, a former manager of the call-in programs, says
C-SPAN refuses to screen calls for content. "We don't get into the
business like some other shows of saying, 'This is a really hot call
and I'm going to put it up first,' or 'This is a really stupid question
and I'm not going to put it on.' "

In the wake of the Republican takeover of Congress, C-SPAN
prepared a three-hour profile of its first star, Newt Gingrich. The
incoming House speaker granted Brian Lamb a long interview at the
Atlanta zoo, where they fed Gingrich's favorite rhino and chatted in
Lamb's easygoing style. "I have loved what you've done for
America," Gingrich said. The new speaker quickly agreed to allow
greater coverage of House activities, including his morning news
conference (although he later decided the cameras were capturing
too many unflattering outbursts and canceled the regular briefings).
The Republican National Committee even took out full-page ads:
"Tune into C-SPAN tomorrow and watch Republicans deliver on
their promise to change the way Congress does business." For the
first time since FDR, the center of journalistic gravity had shifted
from the president to Congress. Gingrich was making more news
than Clinton, and it was all on Lamb's network. C-SPAN had arrived.

As its programming grew increasingly sophisticated—from
Lamb's *Booknotes* to *Inside Congress,* from the British House of
Commons to the nightly translation of the Moscow evening news—

the other networks began to view C-SPAN as a serious rival. A 1995 survey found that its viewing audience had jumped 44 percent in four years, to 68 million people, and that they watched C-SPAN an average of two hours a week. "C-SPAN is on all the time doing things that our viewers who watch talk shows would find interesting," says Rick Davis of CNN. But no one knew just how large the C-SPAN audience was because of Lamb's refusal to take ratings. If he worried about Nielsen numbers, he would hardly have staged the reenactment of the 1858 Lincoln-Douglas debates in seven Illinois towns. Each debate ran at least three hours, and C-SPAN carried every minute.

Serious viewers came to see the network as a godsend. During the debate over the GATT world trade agreement, a caller from Sausalito, California, told Lamb: "I followed the GATT hearings on C-SPAN very carefully. I listened to many talk shows . . . Then I watched NBC, ABC, and CBS's coverage of GATT and I had a terrifying moment of clarity that the networks are totally irrelevant when it comes to issues of substance."

The weakness of C-SPAN is the same as its strength: Live events are often as exciting as watching paint dry. Many people don't have the time or inclination to watch an entire speech or hearing unfold. And since anyone can say anything without being challenged by the hosts, the network can sometimes be a conduit for misinformation. Lamb, for one, doesn't view this as a problem. "We're better off listening to everyone, no matter what they say, rather than us being the gatekeeper," he says. "Politicians say things every day that aren't true. People who write columns say things that aren't necessarily true, make a lot of accusations. This is probably naive, but I have an enormous faith in the system to work over time. There are plenty of checks and balances. Although someone on a call-in show can say things that are unfair, that's one of the prices you pay in public life."

In the end, intelligent talk shows are not unlike small, artsy movie houses in an age of nine-theater cineplexes. They offer a respite from the clamor of commercialism, inspiring fierce loyalty among their fans, but they are relegated to the margins of the marketplace. They will never be big box office.

The Brian Lamb philosophy, that journalists should quietly facilitate the conveyance of information, is simply unthinkable in most of the broadcast universe. Profit-making television, from Phil Donahue and Larry King to Diane Sawyer and Connie Chung and even Ted Koppel, is built upon the marquee value of the host, the star who puts fans in the seats. For more than three decades, only one dusty corner of the network news divisions was insulated from these pressures. The journalists who dwelled in this particular ghetto were content simply to ask questions of important people. And then, inevitably, the talk show culture spread to Sunday morning.

CHAPTER EIGHT

SUNDAY RITUAL

I n the fall of 1985, Ferdinand Marcos, the embattled ruler of the Philippines, appeared by satellite on *This Week with David Brinkley*.

Minutes after the show began, George Will politely inquired "if you would not be willing to move up the election date, the better to renew your mandate soon, say, within the next eight months or so. Is that possible?"

"I am ready to call a snap election . . . perhaps in three months or less than that," Marcos declared. News of the election, which would lead to Marcos's ouster by Corazon Aquino, made front-page headlines around the world. Another coup for the *Brinkley* show.

But it was hardly a spontaneous moment. Nevada Senator Paul Laxalt, the Reagan administration's special envoy to Manila, appeared on the show before Marcos. Laxalt believed after returning from the Philippines that Marcos was ready to call an election. He quietly suggested to Will, a conservative ally, that he pop the question.

"It took absolutely no skill on my part," Will says.

For nearly fifty years, the Sunday morning talk shows have been the preferred vehicle through which members of the Washington establishment communicate with each other and with the public. Administration officials and congressional leaders use their appearances to send signals, proffer compromises, rattle sabers, deflect criticism, and float trial balloons.

The Sunday programs have a small but influential audience, heavily weighted with journalists and power brokers, who believe that watching middle-aged white men chew the policy fat is a perfectly normal way to spend the weekend. Since Sunday is a slow news day, the Monday papers usually pick up the sharpest comments, and that too is part of the exercise. Each week, *Meet the Press, Face the Nation,* and *Brinkley* enable the Beltway establishment and the network establishment to jointly manufacture something that feels and smells like news.

In a television environment in which shouting matches are passed off as thoughtful dialogue, it is difficult to criticize the Sunday shows. They deal with substance. They explore issues in depth. They host important newsmakers. And yet, week after week, as the likes of Bob Dole and Pat Moynihan and Newt Gingrich and Warren Christopher are put through their paces, the programs can be dreadfully dull. They often have the feel of a colloquy among insiders, conducted in an obscure legislative dialect, a television ritual masquerading as real conversation. And that is in part because the politicians stick to platitudes, running in rhetorical circles to avoid answering risky questions.

"It's gotten to be a game," Sam Donaldson says. "They come on with one thing in mind—to put forward their view on a particular topic or two, but make certain they don't give us anything else. The secretary will say, 'Our position is this, that, and the other.' And I will say, 'But sir, your critics contend . . .' '*Our position is this, that, and the other.*' And something else: They'll lie as part of their game plan. I can't immediately disprove what they're saying. I can't pull out a document, like we do on *PrimeTime Live*. They can always get away with not telling us what we want to know. We're just an extension of the PR mechanism."

In a talk show era, the savviest guests are invariably well trained and well briefed. Once, after House Democratic Leader Richard Gephardt appeared on *Meet the Press,* an NBC staffer found a crumpled memo in the men's room. It outlined potential questions and twelve suggested sound bites. When host Tim Russert checked the transcript, he found that Gephardt had managed to use eight of them. "Damn," Russert said, "this has gone too far."

But if the interviews are usually less than scintillating, the balance of power has shifted to the journalists in one important respect. Their opinions are now at least as important as those uttered by the politicians. The media heavies are showcased each week in round-table segments that have become a major drawing card. The under-lying message is simple: Now that Senator Smith is done blathering, we'll give you the real scoop. Network executives who once would have been horrified at the sight of correspondents becoming pon-tificators now see it as a way of creating bankable stars. People tune in to watch Brinkley, Will, Donaldson, and Cokie Roberts shoot the breeze. Same thing with Tim Russert chatting up David Broder and William Safire, or Bob Schieffer with Gloria Borger and Tom Friedman. And they are not shy about slinging opinions.

Thus, on the fourth Sunday of 1995, the *Brinkley* panelists, having disposed of Senator Bob Kerrey and White House chief of staff Leon Panetta, turned their attention to President Clinton:

"The least consequential president since Calvin Coolidge," George Will announced.

"It's over, I think, for President Clinton, no matter how hard he tries," said Sam Donaldson, who flatly declared three weeks earlier that Clinton would not run for reelection.

Only Cokie Roberts sounded a note of caution: "We're living in a period where politics is so volatile that predicting what will hap-pen two years out is not a safe thing to do."

Such prognostication is a way of attracting viewers. "The roundtable is the money part," says Dorrance Smith, the producer of the *Brinkley* show and one of its creators. "Guests have become so easy and attainable that you no longer look up from your Sunday paper to see one congressman arguing with another congressman, whether it's on *Crossfire* or *Newsmaker Saturday* or *Brinkley*. Some of these throwaway guests are just filling air time. It's like *Mc-Laughlin:* You want to hear how the panelists are going to weigh in."

But the atmosphere is quite different from what Donaldson calls "Dr. McLaughlin's Gong Show." This is, after all, network televi-sion, and the tone is serious, high-minded, relentlessly reasonable. The panelists pride themselves on not making inflammatory state-ments or manufacturing disagreements. And after watching the pol-iticians bob and weave, a little straight talk can be refreshing.

"People very rarely see anything on television that isn't

scripted," George Will says. "Jay Leno does his monologue: that's scripted. He sits down with the guest: that's scripted. On *Good Morning America,* a writer calls you in advance and interviews you. There's no risk there. Viewers know they're seeing shtick. The roundtable is spontaneous. There's some danger something un-planned could occur. What television does best is sports, for pre-cisely the same reason. This is four people they're familiar with, who have been coming into their living rooms for thirteen years."

Back in the dark recesses of television history, there dwelled a non-descript show called *Issues and Answers.*

The ABC program had been on the air since 1960. Its panel-interview format was the same as that of its rivals, the same as all the half-hour Sunday shows had been for decades. Bob Clark, the moderator, asked politicians the same kind of policy questions as Bill Monroe at *Meet the Press* and George Herman at *Face the Nation.* And *Issues and Answers* had the particularly unenviable time slot of 1:30 P.M., often up against pro football.

"I thought they were all colossal bores, ABC's worst of all," David Brinkley says. "It was all a matter of pulling in some senator and questioning him for half an hour, usually getting answers we already knew, or that didn't matter whether we knew or not. They were really poorly done, part of the wallpaper."

In nearly forty years at NBC, Brinkley had appeared on *Meet the Press* exactly once. "I hated Larry Spivak, so I never went back," he says.

In truth, all three shows were designed not for the general viewer but for other journalists. They aimed to produce the kind of incremental news that would warrant a Monday-morning headline, thus burnishing the reputations of insecure network executives who yearned for approval from *The New York Times* and *The Washing-ton Post.* That was how they measured success.

Unbeknownst to most of the television industry, David Brinkley in 1981 was quietly planning a new weekend talk show for NBC. He would own the show, but the network had agreed to finance it and air it on some local stations, and was looking for advertisers. Brinkley even taped a couple of pilot episodes. It was certain to be a major event, for Brinkley was something of a television legend.

He had seemingly been around forever. Brinkley started out with the Wilmington, North Carolina, *Morning Star* in 1941 for $11 a week. He spent a couple of years with United Press before moving to NBC radio and then television. Over the next four decades, he won a slew of awards and helped invent modern TV news. The pairing of Chet Huntley and David Brinkley at the 1956 political conventions, and then on *NBC Nightly News,* had ushered in a golden era for the peacock network.

Brinkley was less the curmudgeonly outsider than he seemed. He was quite friendly with Bobby Kennedy. Days after President Kennedy's funeral, Bobby and Ethel and Ted and Joan came to his Chevy Chase, Maryland, home to share their grief. President Johnson named Brinkley to the National Council on the Arts. LBJ occasionally called after midnight and had Brinkley and his wife, Ann, drop by the White House for a drink. One Sunday afternoon in 1966, Johnson sent a helicopter to a Maryland farm where the Brinkleys were picnicking and had the pilot ferry them to Camp David to spend the weekend. Viewers knew nothing of this sort of coziness. (On the other hand, Richard Nixon considered Brinkley his greatest enemy on television, especially after Pat Buchanan turned in a report assailing NBC's coverage. Jeb Stuart Magruder, a Nixon aide later convicted of Watergate crimes, suggested that the White House push advertisers to complain to NBC's owners about Brinkley's coverage.)

In later years Brinkley sometimes dined with Bob Dole, his "good friend," who, like Brinkley, owned an apartment at the Sea View Hotel in Bal Harbour, Florida. And he socialized with "one of my closest friends in the world," Robert Strauss, the former Democratic Party chairman and ambassador to Russia. Strauss also had a place at the Sea View. So did former Tennessee senator Howard Baker, Tip O'Neill, and Dwayne Andreas, chairman of Archer-Daniels-Midland (a major sponsor of *This Week*), who helped arrange Brinkley's purchase of an apartment. "It's a cozy little scene," says Brinkley. He says his friends are "sophisticated" enough to know that he must treat them differently on the air.

Brinkley's spare writing style and wry irreverence gave him a unique television persona in an age of vapid blabbermouths. The soft-spoken Southerner understood politics as well as anyone in the business. He was a man of few words, but those words were invariably well chosen.

During the '70s, despite coanchoring stints with John Chancellor and Frank McGee, Brinkley seemed out of sorts. His first marriage had fallen apart. He was fronting *NBC Magazine with David Brinkley,* which was up against *Dallas* and clearly struggling. The brass didn't quite know what to do with him. "They kept dictating stupid ideas to put on the show," Brinkley says. "I said screw it, and quit." There was more to it than that: Brinkley refused to work for the new NBC News president, Bill Small. The Brinkley talk show was dead; NBC's Washington station would turn to John McLaughlin instead.

Roone Arledge quickly seized the opportunity. The ABC News president, who would propel his news division into first place by luring stars from other networks, offered Brinkley an irresistible challenge: The chance to create a new kind of Sunday talk show. Arledge viewed the Sunday shows as "dinosaurs from prehistoric times." Months earlier he had asked Dorrance Smith to devise a prototype for a faster-paced, hour-long program. Smith's plan was a hybrid of other shows: There would be a little breaking news, a setup piece like on *Nightline,* a talk segment like *Agronsky & Company.*

"We approached it like a Sunday paper," Smith says. "You cobble together the best of the week. It sounds simple in hindsight, but the thinking at the time was 'Get Jim Wright and talk for a half hour and watch TV die on the air.' "

One day Arledge called Smith and told him the show would be built around David Brinkley. This was a coup of stunning proportions, on a par with Barbara Walters's defection to ABC.

Since the three Sunday programs competed for top newsmakers, Smith worried about breaking with the traditional format. "One of the great fears was that guests would rather go on *Face the Nation* or *Meet the Press* for twenty-two minutes, rather than come on *Brinkley* and be interviewed by three guys for a few minutes," he says. "As it turned out, the guests were thrilled. They hated being on for twenty minutes because it meant they were that much more likely to make a mistake. Most guests have five minutes' worth of material they want to get out."

The next task was filling out the roster. George Will was already on board. With his Oxford education, bow-tied demeanor, and scholarly erudition, the conservative columnist was a rising star of the punditocracy. He dined regularly with Nancy Reagan, his wife Madeleine worked for the administration, and he moved easily in the corridors of power.

"No doubt the brief conservative moment in Washington under Ronald Reagan might have helped make them more interested in me," Will says.

The son of an Illinois philosophy professor, Will had moved from academia to Capitol Hill, where he worked for Republican senator Gordon Allott of Colorado and wrote some pieces for the *National Review*. After Allott lost in 1972, William F. Buckley made Will the magazine's Washington correspondent, and *The Washington Post* gave him a column.

"Does this mean I have to stop writing speeches for Jesse Helms?" Will asked Philip Geyelin, then the *Post*'s editorial-page editor. Geyelin, stunned by the question, extracted a promise that Will would do no more political work on the side. Will soon added a *Newsweek* column to his portfolio and became a regular on *Agronsky & Company*.

But he still liked to dabble in politics. Before the 1980 presidential debate, Will privately coached Ronald Reagan, then went on ABC and hailed Reagan's performance, calling him a "thoroughbred." The disclosure of Will's dual role was a serious embarrassment, but it had barely slowed his career trajectory when he got the call from Brinkley.

Brinkley asked two other friends to join the roundtable: Karen Elliott House of *The Wall Street Journal* and Ben Bradlee of *The Washington Post*. Bradlee, the paper's executive editor, had appeared many times on *Meet the Press* and was a big name in the business. He didn't really want to work Sundays but felt he couldn't say no to Brinkley and Arledge, another longtime pal.

The first edition of *This Week* aired on November 15, 1981. Budget Director David Stockman was to be the guest, but he canceled at the last minute after the publication of his controversial interviews about economic policy with William Greider of *The Atlantic Monthly*. Brinkley, setting the tone for the show, said Stockman's indiscretions were "a little more serious, perhaps, than if he had sipped coffee out of a White House saucer and eaten peas with a knife."

The program had too many guests and too many segments, hopscotching from one correspondent to another like ABC's *Wide World of Sports,* which Arledge had once produced. Brinkley, as the sole interviewer, asked gentle questions that did not push the guests very far.

Brinkley introduced the roundtable as "an ad lib free-for-all in our studio about whatever comes to mind." He was joined by Will, Bradlee, House, and Hodding Carter of PBS. Most of the panelists were stiff, and the segment fell flat. Even Brinkley thought the show wasn't much good.

Karen House was the first to leave the program. "She wasn't worth a damn," Brinkley says. "She knew it, I knew it, and she quit." Bradlee quietly resigned after less than a dozen shows.

"It quickly became apparent that what they had in mind was to pit me against Will—the liberal and the conservative—and I didn't want to play that," Bradlee says. "I'm not a knee-jerk liberal. I didn't want to have to whip up a liberal enthusiasm that I didn't have. What they wanted you to do was pick a fight, be outrageous, be vituperative. Dorrance would say, 'If George says something that pisses you off, go after him!' "

But there was someone at ABC who was more than willing to fill that role. Dorrance Smith had been Sam Donaldson's White House producer, and he brought Donaldson on the show as an experiment. Donaldson was still covering the White House and anchoring the Sunday night news. "Sam brought energy," Smith says. "He was in there looking for a sound bite for his six o'clock show, a good fifteen-second bite that he could build a piece around. George and David could care less about that. They're a little more philosophical. Sam brings an edge to anything, even a dinner party."

"Both David and George were horrified," Donaldson recalls. "They thought I was nothing but a loudmouth ignoramus."

Donaldson was famous mainly for his lung power. A former mutual fund salesman and announcer from El Paso, Texas, he had climbed the television ladder with little formal training in journalism, other than *Sam's Show,* the radio program he did as a teenage disc jockey. He began in 1959 at KRLD in Dallas, where he read the noon news, then moved to New York and tried to get a job at one of the networks. No one was interested, and Donaldson, desperate for work, wound up filming a commercial for a chocolate company. But he caught on as a summer announcer with WTOP, the CBS affiliate in Washington, moved up to reporter and weekend anchor and, in 1967, was hired by ABC.

Donaldson was a Capitol Hill reporter when he was dispatched to Jimmy Carter's presidential campaign, and he rode that assignment to the White House. During the Reagan years, Donaldson's bellowed questions, often shouted over the roar of helicopter blades, became fixed in the public consciousness. Alternately engaging and exasperating, he became the country's most famous White House reporter through sheer aggressiveness. The White House beat had long been a prime launching pad for television careers—boosting Dan Rather, Tom Brokaw, Lesley Stahl, Judy Woodruff—and now it was Donaldson's turn.

But Donaldson was wary of joining in the Sunday punditry, for in the early '80s there remained a sharp division between reporting and opining. "I was and still am a hard-news reporter," he says. "I said to Roone, 'Here I am expressing opinions, and you see me on the White House lawn doing a straight news story on these very subjects.' On Sunday people would hear me denounce the idea of building an MX missile—'We don't need it, it's too expensive, there's no place to put it'—and on Monday I'm at the White House reporting on Reagan's effort to build an MX missile." But Arledge told him not to worry, and Donaldson decided he could keep his opinions out of his reporting.

Donaldson loved to mix it up. He asked Defense Secretary Caspar Weinberger whether he was anti-Semitic, Secretary of State George Shultz whether he was anti-Arab, and Illinois Governor James Thompson whether he was "a crook." But sometimes his mouth got the best of him. He once misquoted Reagan about the nuclear arms race and had to apologize on the air the following week; the president called to thank him. Even worse, "on one show I said, 'Ronald Reagan, he can't fire anyone, but Mrs. Reagan is different. She's tough. She's the black mama of the White House.

She'll bite you.' I realized I had called her a snake. I'm not always
the most eloquent person. That's the danger of ad libbing. I wrote
the most abject note to her: 'Dear Mrs. Reagan, I am so embarrassed and ashamed. I grovel.' "

Donaldson's uneasy relationship with the First Couple was
markedly different from that of one *Brinkley* colleague. Each year,
Ronald and Nancy Reagan would go to George Will's home in
Chevy Chase, Maryland, for a private dinner. Donaldson sometimes
stood outside in the cold with the other reporters, waiting to shout
a question at the president as he left.

On the air, Sam Donaldson clearly worked without a net. Years
later, in one of the biggest gaffes in the show's history, he prattled
on at some length about a VAT tax, ignoring anguished looks from
the other panelists, only to discover that they had been talking about
a flat tax. "I made a complete fool of myself," Donaldson says. "I
stammered and stuttered and said I hadn't studied the flat tax. I got
letters saying, 'You silly ass.' 'You pompous fool.' 'We always knew
you were just a big bag of wind.' "

Donaldson shrugs off such episodes as the price of being a talking head. "I can be stupid, have mental lapses, ask questions in
the wrong way. If you're not willing to do that, you can't do live
television."

George Will had very different frustrations with the genre.
"There are just lots of issues you can't do on TV," he says. "It's
extremely hard to talk on the *Brinkley* show about Supreme Court
rulings. You can't lay out the predicate of the case. Television is
a slave to a superficial news-gathering instrument, which is the
camera."

They would meet each Sunday morning at 9:30 to finalize the
topics for the roundtable. Donaldson and Will would make their
pitches, but Brinkley's word was final. Brinkley presided over the
show like a kindly uncle, telling guests, "Thank you for coming.
Nice to have you. Come again. Good luck to you." He was periodically criticized for his laconic style, but as a self-described "old
goat," he didn't much care.

"I'm not vivacious and scintillating off the air," he says. "I am
myself. I have a journalistic personality. I certainly don't have any
idea of changing. I couldn't change if I wanted to."

Somehow, Brinkley's approach worked. "David wants to know things I think are irrelevant, but surprisingly, he gets interesting answers," Donaldson says. "His charm puts guests at ease. He says to the guest, 'You're going to get to say what you want before I deliver you to these two tigers.'"

This Week's formula—a taped piece always explained an issue before the gang debriefed some senator or White House aide—made it more accessible to the general audience. It was the first Sunday show to recognize that congressmen and cabinet officers are rather predictable guests.

"Whatever question you ask, the guest has anticipated it," Brinkley says. "He very often will give you a paragraph out of his last campaign speech, which he has memorized. Sometimes it gets boring, and that's when I cut it off. Our job is to get something else out of them beyond what we've already heard twenty times."

Brinkley was equally aware that the show dwelled on subjects, such as the war in Bosnia, "that nobody gives a damn about. It's in the nature of our kind of program that very often we're going to bore people. It's inescapable. Not everyone cares about every issue. Sometimes we succeed, sometimes we don't. But they stay with us anyway. We've sort of become a habit."

Many people tuned in to watch the clashes between Will and Donaldson, which sometimes led to chilly feelings off the set. "Occasionally," says Donaldson, "George might look at me and sneer and say, 'I wouldn't expect you to understand.' Or I'd look at him and say, 'That is the most heartless thing I ever heard.' But that is rare."

With help from Mort Kondracke, Hodding Carter, Tom Wicker, and Jody Powell in the "rotating" chair, the *Brinkley* show dominated the ratings, drawing an audience of about four million households. By the time of its fifth-anniversary party, the program was so prestigious that twenty senators and Vice President Bush showed up.

There was just one problem: a certain lack of diversity. It was, like most other talk shows, a collection of aging white males. Dorrance Smith tried to fix this by adding Cokie Roberts to the roundtable in 1987.

She was a natural choice. At the age of twenty-one, Roberts was anchoring a Sunday public affairs show on Washington's WRC. She had gained a modicum of fame as a National Public Radio reporter and gotten plenty of television exposure on such shows as *MacNeil/Lehrer*. Roberts had even turned down a chance to be on *McLaughlin*. "It's very difficult to come across on a program like that without screaming," she says.

Mary Martha Corinne Morrison Claiborne Boggs Roberts was born to the Washington establishment. As the daughter of Hale Boggs, a Louisiana Democrat who became House majority leader, and Lindy Boggs, who succeeded her husband in Congress after his death, she learned the social graces at a young age. On her office wall is a White House photo of Cokie as a young woman, with white gloves and an upswept hairdo, being presented to President Johnson and Lady Bird.

Roberts got an early education about the importance of talk shows. "They used to joke about my father that he'd come in snow and sleet to be on *Meet the Press*," she says.

Roberts was hardly an acerbic critic of the capital's go-along, get-along culture. Her brother, Tommy Boggs, was one of the city's most high-powered lobbyists. She covered Congress for a decade while her mother was a member of the House, sometimes reporting on men who had been to her parents' home for dinner. "I just love the institution," Roberts says. That was hardly the majority view in America.

For all her poise and experience, her first appearance on *Brinkley* was a bit daunting. "I was very nervous about the prospect of giving views," she says. "I was a reporter. I said, 'As long as I can analyze instead of giving opinions.' Nobody knew what I was talking about, so I decided I'd just shut up and do it.

"It was a little intimidating, to put it mildly. One of the very interesting things for a woman on the air is you can't just come right in and start talking. The audience has to get used to you. You have to prove to the audience you have something to say and it's okay for you to keep speaking up." Otherwise, "they think you're a bitch."

The Brinkley family was complete: George on the right quoting from Madison or Machiavelli, Sam on the left snarling at guests, and Cokie in the middle as Miss Common Sense, a woman who did her own grocery shopping and went to church after each show.

Brinkley was the aging patriarch in his mid-seventies, not quite as sharp as in the old days and nearing retirement, but beloved by the relatives who tried to compensate for his declining powers.

Sometimes the gang was as predictable as the *McLaughlin* panelists, each seemingly playing an assigned role. When Bill Clinton proposed an increase in the minimum wage, Sam Donaldson was for it because it would help the working poor. George Will was against it because it would mainly help "middle-class children." Cokie Roberts deftly straddled the issue but said an increase would help working wives.

Viewers became hooked on the ensemble cast. They rooted for their favorites and disparaged their rivals, as suggested by comments on an America Online computer bulletin board:

"For too long Sam has thrown around his obnoxious personality and ultraliberal views on ABC. I currently change the channel when I hear his voice or see his face."

"Sam is an attack-dog journalist, but he is not a liberal."

"I was always disappointed when that arrogant liberal Sam Donaldson would cut George off in midsentence and dominate a discussion with his leftist chatter."

"Sunday morning coffee wouldn't be the same if I couldn't watch George and Sam arguing it out, using the old baseball parables."

"As I listen to [Roberts's] recounts of Congress, I get this vision of me nibbling on her ear while she recites the Whitewater affair."

"Thank heavens for Cokie Roberts, the only reasoned voice on the show. Oh, and shut up, Sam."

After just two years in talk show land, Tim Russert landed an Oval Office interview with the president of the United States.

It was the fall of 1993, and Bill Clinton had accepted a longstanding invitation to appear on *Meet the Press,* the first sitting president to do so since Jimmy Carter. Clinton was launching an all-out campaign to salvage the NAFTA trade agreement, which was in deep trouble on Capitol Hill, and he wanted the chance to communicate in more than a couple of sound bites. Union leaders, who bitterly opposed the pact, were threatening to withhold contributions from any lawmaker who supported it. Clinton wanted to blunt these threats and demonstrate that he was willing to take on a key Democratic constituency. Russert, joined by Tom Brokaw, quickly raised the issue, and Clinton accused organized labor of "naked pressure" and "real roughshod, muscle-bound tactics."

Clinton's top aides—David Gergen, George Stephanopoulos, Dee Dee Myers, Mark Gearan, Mack McLarty—were huddled in the Roosevelt Room, watching the boss on TV. About halfway through the show, Colette Rhoney, the producer of *Meet the Press,* walked in with the first wire-service report, which led with the attack on the unions, and handed it to Gergen. Gergen slipped into the Oval Office during a break and whispered to Clinton. As the show was ending, the president tried to soften his comments about labor. "These guys are my friends," he said. "I just don't agree with them on NAFTA."

(Thomas Donahue, secretary-treasurer of the AFL-CIO, retaliated the only way he could—on another talk show. He called the president's comments a "cheap shot" on CNN's *Late Edition.*)

After the program, Clinton autographed a picture for Russert. "I think I enjoyed it," he scribbled. "I know it was good for America." Both men had gotten something out of the encounter. For the president, it was a nationally televised platform to advance his NAFTA strategy. For Russert, the exclusive interview underscored the extent to which he had put *Meet the Press* on the political map.

NBC was determined to make Tim Russert a star. The *Brinkley* show had permanently altered the Sunday environment by making journalists the chief attraction, and both of its rivals were trying to adapt. *Face the Nation* had turned to CBS's high-profile White House reporter, Lesley Stahl. *Meet the Press* had brought in a series of well-known moderators: Marvin Kalb, Roger Mudd, Chris Wallace. Wallace, like Brinkley, had defected to ABC after being bumped from the show, and the program was now in the hands of Garrick Utley, a distinguished but colorless correspondent who had little feel for Beltway politics. *Meet the Press* was in third place and going nowhere.

By 1991 Michael Gartner, the president of NBC News, was ready to make a change. He had been increasingly impressed by

Russert, his Washington bureau chief. During the 9:30 conference call each morning, Russert dazzled the brass in New York with his lucid analysis and delicious gossip about the capital. "He was just so filled with information and lore," Gartner says. "He lives, breathes, and dies politics."

The beefy Russert was nobody's idea of a matinee idol, but he had a gut feeling for politics because he had worked on the inside. The son of a *Buffalo News* truck driver, Russert was a youth coordinator for Bobby Kennedy's 1968 campaign. He was hired by Senator Daniel Patrick Moynihan right out of Cleveland-Marshall law school and, at age twenty-nine, became the youngest chief of staff in the Senate. In 1983 the wily operative became counselor to another prominent New York Democrat, Mario Cuomo, the newly elected governor. When Gary Hart was launching his '84 presidential campaign, *The New Yorker* quoted him as commanding his aides, "Get me a Russert!" (Hart insists he never uttered these words, but it instantly became part of the lore.)

Russert had a hankering for the television business, and in 1985 he left Cuomo's staff to become the assistant to Lawrence Grossman, then the president of NBC News. A skilled practitioner of office politics—and a canny self-promoter—Russert won the coveted bureau chief's job within five years and talked openly about becoming the next NBC News president.

But Gartner saw him as a natural performer. First he made Russert a political analyst on the *Today* show, giving him a chance to strut his stuff. Then he installed him as a panelist on *Meet the Press*. In a bloodless coup two months later, Garrick Utley was out and Tim Russert was in. There was some resentment among Washington reporters that Russert was grabbing so much airtime that might have gone to them, but the network was banking on its newest celebrity. Soon Russert was given his own interview show on CNBC. His youth and energy were an obvious asset; Russert, in his early forties, was more than three decades younger than Brinkley.

Even Russert's detractors had to admit he did his homework. As a Jesuit-trained lawyer, he was meticulous about cramming for interviews, and before long *Meet the Press* was making news. Russert asked politicians who denounced the budget deficit which programs they would cut. He pressed opponents of foreign aid on whether they would end U.S. assistance to Israel. He challenged David Duke, the extremist running for governor of Louisiana, to name the state's top three employers (Duke couldn't). During the 1992 campaign, he asked Sam Skinner, President Bush's chief of staff, whether the White House was guilty of "abysmal staff work, or is there a dramatic decline in the fear and respect of this president?" He asked Paul Tsongas whether his cancer would recur. He asked Bob Kerrey why he had flip-flopped on abortion. He asked Bill Clinton whether "there is nothing in your background that might emerge which would doom your candidacy and the Democratic Party."

Russert's secret weapon was Colette Rhoney, a former *Washington Post* researcher for David Broder. She did what amounted to opposition research, combing through voting records in *Congressional Quarterly* and calling strategists and budget experts in both parties. She had helped Broder prepare for his *Meet the Press* appearances, and she knew the importance of having the facts nailed down. In December 1987, armed with Rhoney's numbers, Broder asked Vice President Bush what percentage of Americans were without health insurance, what percentage of the jobless had no unemployment benefits, and what proportion of infants lived below the poverty line. Bush couldn't answer the questions, underscoring Broder's point that he was out of touch with average folks.

Rhoney was equally dogged as Russert's producer. She discovered during the '92 campaign that Al Gore, as a House member eight years earlier, had voted for a law defining the fetus as a person from the moment of conception. When Russert asked him about it on the air, the vice-presidential nominee, who now backed abortion rights, tried to pass it off as a "misunderstanding." But Russert kept at it, asking whether he would vote for such a law today. "Well, that particular measure is no longer relevant," Gore said. After several more questions, his shift of position was clear.

Russert's most dramatic confrontation was with Ross Perot in the spring of 1992. He read Perot's interviews, looked at tapes of Perot, studied a Perot biography, and called Bush's budget director, Richard Darman, to check some numbers. Perot had been insisting that he could wipe out $180 billion in government waste, fraud, and abuse without breaking a sweat. Accustomed to the gentle queries of Larry King, Perot grew testy when Russert challenged his figures. The host started ticking off programs that a private commission had said would have to be cut: AIDS research. Breast cancer research. Mass transit.

"Now then, this is an interesting game we're playing here today," Perot said. When Russert interrupted, Perot said, "May I finish?"

"May I finish? It was a simple question," Russert replied.

"Well, you've already finished. Go ahead, finish again. It's your program. You can do anything you want to. Go ahead."

"Well, I'm trying to get a specific answer to a proposal you've made. That's fair."

"Well, I am trying to answer it."

"Please do, sir."

"Are you sure you're finished?"

"Absolutely."

"Okay, may I talk?"

"I wish you would."

Perot said afterward he had been given "bad information," and his switchboard lit up with callers who felt he'd been treated unfairly. But *Meet the Press* had clearly knocked his campaign off stride. Russert worried at times about looking overbearing, but the show was winning rave reviews in Washington, where it passed *Brinkley* in the ratings, and nationally its Nielsen numbers were up 68 percent, making it a close second. Russert put out the word that he had eclipsed Sam Donaldson as the most aggressive Sunday-morning interviewer. And he got some help from his friends in the press. William Safire, a frequent panelist on *Meet the Press,* boosted Russert in his *New York Times* column, calling *Meet the Press* "the most tough-minded panel show." Bob Novak, another regular, wrote in his column that Secretary of State Warren Christopher had been reduced to "a thin-smiling punching bag pummeled by Tim Russert's penetrating questions."

Sometimes Russert had help with those questions. It had become increasingly common for both Democratic and GOP operatives to feed the panelists statistics and propaganda in an effort to influence the questioning. At the Clinton White House, Russert trusted Gene Sperling, the economic adviser who was known for calling the Sunday talkers and offering his spin. When *Meet the Press* was slated to discuss the Republicans' Contract with America, Sperling sent some documents assailing the proposals to David Broder. When Broder got his research packet from *Meet the Press,* it had the same Sperling material.

Russert welcomed such help from all sides, for he believed there was no such thing as being overly prepared. "What we have is a rare commodity on television, almost an endangered species," he says. "Most of the guests are used to four-, five-minute interviews where they can pop on and pop off. They do it all the time with local anchors. It's a video press release. It usually takes us a good twenty minutes to get beyond the boilerplate."

Russert now had the time to do that, for NBC had expanded *Meet the Press* to an hour. This enabled him to launch a weekly roundtable with such journalists as Novak (who was a bit more subdued than on *Capital Gang*), Broder, Safire, Jack Germond, Mary McGrory, Gwen Ifill, and Lisa Myers. *Meet the Press* had gone the *Brinkley* route. Russert even added a bit of *McLaughlin*-style theater, predicting one morning that Henry Foster, Clinton's nominee for surgeon general, would be defeated and then challenging the other panelists to make their predictions. Guests mixed it up and were routinely asked to serve up predictions about the 1996 campaign.

"Bob Novak, how will Pete Wilson do?" Russert asked.

"Badly . . . He can't be the nominee," Novak said.

"Bob Woodward, will Bill Clinton be reelected?" Russert asked.

"Who knows?" Woodward replied.

"Bottom line, Gwen Ifill, does Colin Powell run?" Russert asked.

"I don't know. I don't think so," Ifill said.

"I wouldn't bet on his running," said author Kevin Phillips.

"I kind of think he may," said David Broder.

"I kind of thing he may," said Lisa Myers.

"I think he'll run," Russert declared.

One Sunday, Russert interviewed Senator Robert Byrd, Senator Bob Dole, and then Bill Safire. The *Times* columnist fielded questions on the future of China, the strife in Russia, the '96 elections, his views accorded the same weight as those of the congressional leaders. On another Sunday, after interviewing Bob Dole in Russell, Kansas, Russert, David Broder, and Lisa Myers took questions from the audience, serving up their views on the media and politics.

Tim Russert was clearly the biggest star, and he had an uncanny way of provoking politicians into making news. He pressed Newt Gingrich, the incoming House speaker, on why he had called Bill and Hillary Clinton "counterculture McGoverniks," noting that Gingrich had also tried marijuana and avoided the draft. Gingrich promptly uncorked a charge that a quarter of the White House staff had used drugs in the past four or five years. Unfortunately, Russert failed to press him on the unnamed law-enforcement source that Gingrich said had given him the information, or whether it was irresponsible to make such an allegation without detailing the evidence. Still, it was the lead story in the next day's *Washington Post*. Gingrich had made the same charge a year earlier, but no one had noticed. He was still in the minority party, and, more important, he hadn't said it on a Sunday talk show.

While *Brinkley* would occasionally devote an interesting hour to baseball or space exploration or teenage pregnancy, knowing full well these subjects would generate no headlines, Russert almost always focused on inside-the-Beltway politics. *Meet the Press* did not take the time to explain the issues, for it was aimed at the insiders. "If you don't have the background when you turn on these shows, forget it," a staffer says. "You're gonna be dizzy by Tim's third question."

Russert basked in the spotlight as interrogator-in-chief. "We frankly don't have the resources that *Brinkley* has: correspondents, crews, producers, editors," he says. "The red light goes on and the questions start. Whatever people expect from *Larry King Live* or C-SPAN, they should expect something different from *Meet the Press*."

As Russert's show surged in the ratings, occasionally even beating *This Week,* the Brinkley camp grew a bit nervous. Dorrance Smith, who returned as producer in 1995 after a hiatus of several years, wanted to jazz up *This Week* and start preparing for Brinkley's inevitable retirement. There was no reason, he thought, that the roundtable had to be limited to ABC journalists. On Easter

Sunday, while Sam Donaldson was on vacation, Smith tried to book Mario Cuomo for the roundtable. When that fell through, he tried former Texas governor Ann Richards. Finally, he recruited Rush Limbaugh for the coveted seat beside Will, Roberts, and Brinkley.

Many *This Week* staffers, and a number of viewers, were upset. "When we go outside the news field, the risk is people will not take us as seriously," Sam Donaldson says. "They'll say, 'Look, they're just trying to put on entertainers who have a great following.' That's the risk when we put someone like Rush Limbaugh on."

Some *Brinkley* staffers saw a troubling shift in direction. "I'm appalled," one says. "Clearly we did it to hype the ratings, to get press, to pull Tim's tail—all the wrong reasons. Why not get Letterman? This is indicative of the way the whole business is going."

Dorrance Smith dismisses the notion that the move was controversial because Limbaugh is not a journalist. "It's a liberal dislike of Rush Limbaugh," he says. "There was no hue and outcry about having Jody Powell on. We could put Mu'ammar Qadhafi on for an hour and you don't hear a peep. You put Rush Limbaugh on and the place goes crazy."

Smith makes no bones about trying to change the program. "It's a fair criticism to say this show has evolved into a routine that's predictable," he says. "I want to bring in some new and different voices. If people have a problem with that they don't have to watch."

As Brinkley and Russert repackaged their programs, *Face the Nation* was left behind. It was still a half hour, a distant third in the ratings and lacking a clear identity. In 1991 CBS turned the show over to Bob Schieffer, a veteran correspondent who worked out of a closet-sized office in the Capitol and roamed the corridors day after day. The soft-spoken Texan was cut from an old-fashioned mold: He came from a newspaper background. He didn't make flamboyant comments. He didn't argue with guests. He prided himself on being a shoe-leather reporter.

"I don't want our show to be like theirs," Schieffer says. "The star of our show is the guest. I don't like this idea of journalists and newsmakers being equal. This trend in journalism now that the question is more important than the answer is dead wrong, and I'm fighting it. I'm not trying to set myself up as a paragon of journalistic virtue, but I've always thought the point of an interview is to elicit information."

Schieffer got into television by accident. As a reporter for the *Fort Worth Star-Telegram,* he had returned from a tour in Vietnam when WBAP, the local NBC affiliate, had him on a talk show. Station officials liked Schieffer so much they offered him a job, which boosted his salary from $135 to $150 a week. "I got into television for the money," he jokes. Schieffer moved to Washington's Channel 5 in 1969, and months later walked into CBS's Washington office without an appointment and talked to the bureau chief, Bill Small. "We don't hire people with regional accents," Small told him. But Small, who knew Schieffer's old boss in Fort Worth, agreed to take him on as a third-string reporter. Schieffer kept volunteering for night assignments in the hope he might get on the air, which meant a $50 bonus.

After two decades of Washington pavement pounding, Schieffer had built personal relationships with most of the key Hill players. In the Senate, Sam Nunn was a golfing buddy, Warren Rudman was a pal, and Jim Sasser was an old family friend whose son had dated Schieffer's daughter. All had appeared on the show. Other lawmakers would hint, with varying degrees of subtlety, that they would love to be on one Sunday.

Schieffer focused on the issues and had little use for glitz. "I'm such a hard-news junkie, I think we have an obligation to do these things even if they are dull," he says. "Edward R. Murrow said sometimes the news is dull. The ins and outs of the balanced budget amendment is not something people are going to talk about at a cocktail party."

He was right. With Schieffer's gentlemanly style—he was once called the Perry Como of network television—*Face the Nation* produced few fireworks. And official Washington took that into account.

"We send our nervous performers to Schieffer," a Clinton administration official says. "He tends not to question them hard. We don't send them to *Brinkley.* You never know what Will and Donaldson are going to ask."

Schieffer didn't worry about jazzing up the show. "The company gives us that leeway," he says. "They don't expect *Face the Nation* to have the kind of ratings *Murphy Brown* does."

But Schieffer soon came under pressure to make the show more like *Brinkley*. The single-moderator format was phased out in the hope that a rotating guest journalist would ask sharper questions. A new roundtable was designed to produce a left-right face-off. The show would line up ideological opposites for the segment: Fred Barnes and Chris Matthews. David Gergen and Joe Klein. Republican strategist Bill Kristol and Democratic strategist Frank Greer. One week the show used two journalists and Pat Buchanan, who months earlier had been a presidential candidate. Schieffer eventually managed to kill the format.

"You wound up using professional liberals and professional conservatives," he says. "I thought it was becoming hackneyed and predictable. They just turned out to be shills. I wrote a memo saying this is a bunch of crap, let's just go back to a journalists' roundtable. The public is tired of smart alecks on TV."

Every administration has its strategies for dealing with the Sunday shows. There is even a phrase—"going out"—for those officials whom the White House makes available for various shows. What is less well understood is that bureaucratic rivalries and personal agendas also play an important role.

The talk shows had removed the anonymity of White House aides. A George Stephanopoulos or Mack McLarty was no longer a backroom assistant but a public personality, with his own image to worry about. There was jealousy and backbiting about who was going out and who was not. Some thought Stephanopoulos looked too young to be an effective television spokesman. Just about everyone thought that one of McLarty's failings as chief of staff was that he was not good on television. When the more telegenic Leon Panetta succeeded McLarty, he began making nearly all the Sunday appearances himself in an effort to more tightly control the White House message.

"If you didn't put your person on the air, the other side was going to get the airtime," David Gergen says. "The other point of view was going to dominate the programs. You can't afford not to play."

As a Republican newcomer to a Democratic White House, Gergen had been turning down most talk show invitations. He was afraid it would look like he was hogging the spotlight. Many of his new colleagues, he knew, did not trust him.

In the fall of 1993, Gergen went on *Meet the Press* to talk up the president's new health care plan. Privately, Gergen had opposed the plan as big government run amok. For talk show purposes, however, he said the plan was "on the verge of passing" and that "President Clinton deserves a lot of credit for bringing us this far." There was a method to this seeming duplicity. "I strongly disagreed with the program," Gergen says. "I wanted to get out there early and show the flag, to show that I was going to be a team player."

When the Whitewater affair heated up, a number of commentators noted that Gergen seemed to have vanished. "I was in a no-win position," he says. "If I went out and spoke, I was looking for glory. If I didn't speak, I was hiding." Gergen hesitated to accept an invitation from the *Today* show until he got a call from Mark Gearan, the communications director. Gearan said he had to turn in a report on who was defending the president on the talk shows and who wasn't. As a friend, he was urging Gergen to go on *Today*. Gergen saw the light and made the appearance.

Many Clinton aides remained angry that Gergen was seen so rarely on television. "He ostensibly came to the administration to help us with our communications problems, and yet he found himself to be above communicating," a White House official says. "He was a deeply reluctant message carrier for the president."

Such internal jockeying often influenced the Sunday morning lineup. Senior White House officials were determined to position Warren Christopher as the administration's chief foreign policy spokesman. The taciturn secretary of state was repeatedly sent out for Sunday duty, while national security adviser Anthony Lake almost never appeared on television. He told Tim Russert he didn't like to work Sundays.

Sometimes the stakes were quite high. In December 1993, after eighteen American soldiers were killed in Somalia, Defense Secretary Les Aspin was in deep political trouble. He played the talk show card, going on *Meet the Press* in an effort to salvage his job. But Aspin turned in a weak performance as Russert pressed him on whether Clinton's support for him was lukewarm.

"I don't think there's any problem," Aspin said. Four days later, he was fired.

Every White House tries to milk the shows for partisan advantage. The Reagan administration had a rule that senior officials could not appear on the same set with critics, and sometimes insisted that its people have the last word by following the critics. During the Iran-contra furor, the only official who was going out was communications director Pat Buchanan, who assailed Reagan's detractors but had no personal knowledge of the scandal.

On a typical Sunday in 1990, the Bush administration sent Vice President Dan Quayle to *Meet the Press,* Budget Director Richard Darman to *Face the Nation,* and chief of staff John Sununu to *Brinkley.* White House spokesman Marlin Fitzwater usually pulled the strings. "Fitzwater would be on the phone: 'You're gonna get Dick Cheney and the other shows are gonna get Jim Baker and Brent Scowcroft,' " Russert says. "They'd roll out the big guns and roadblock the networks."

The Clinton White House had no such coordinated strategy. The result was that the president made far too many television appearances in his first two years, overexposing himself with Larry King, Ted Koppel, C-SPAN, and MTV and blunting what should have been the administration's most powerful weapon. He answered reporters' questions while jogging, the sweat dripping down his face. He frittered away what remained of the presidential mystique. If people in an airport saw Clinton on television, they kept on walking. White House officials repeatedly urged Clinton to limit his media exposure—one said he had become "the commentator-in-chief"—but to no avail. He was a talk show president, convinced that he could persuade people by pleading his case before the microphones.

Network officials, meanwhile, complained that White House officials routinely ignored invitations from the Sunday programs, despite their combined audience of ten million households. "These guys just don't get it," Russert says. A Sunday producer puts it more bluntly: "We have to beg, push, scream, and yell to get their attention. Their lack of understanding of how they could utilize the Sunday shows is unbelievable."

A senior administration official dismisses such criticism as sel serving: "The idea that we'd be getting better press if we knew how to work the Sunday shows is a crock of shit. They don't stand there with their legs spread."

Indeed, the two sides often had fundamentally different agendas. In early 1995 the White House, trying to emphasize the crime issue, offered Attorney General Janet Reno to the *Brinkley* show. But Dorrance Smith insisted they needed someone to talk about the growing furor over Henry Foster's nomination as surgeon general. The White House refused. Smith sent word that he would simply have his Republican guest, Senator Phil Gramm, discuss the Foster nomination unopposed. The administration relented and put out Donna Shalala, the health and human services secretary.

For the most sought-after guests, there has long been an informal rotation among the three network programs and CNN's *Late Edition*. All the shows insist on exclusive rights to the guest for that weekend. Only when an issue reaches white-hot intensity do the producers waive this rule. In early 1994, when the Whitewater story was dominating the news, White House counsel Lloyd Cutler performed his damage-control duty with Brinkley, Russert, and Schieffer on the same morning.

The programs try to outfox each other by locking up the right newsmaker early in the week. "People try to steal guests," a CBS staffer says. "They promise to give you more time or say their ratings are higher." Once, when it was Christopher's turn to appear on *Face the Nation,* the State Department told the CBS show that he would be out of town that weekend. Days later, when *Face the Nation* producer Carin Pratt learned that Christopher had been promised to *Meet the Press,* she went ballistic. Administration officials agreed to pull Christopher from Russert's show and put him on *Face the Nation* instead.

Sometimes it is the guests who get angry. In the fall of 1994, *Face the Nation* agreed to host Ross Perot just before the United States dispatched tens of thousands of troops to Iraq during a dispute with Saddam Hussein. Carin Pratt decided she couldn't ignore such a huge story, so she booked Defense Secretary William Perry and bumped Perot to the second half of the show. When Perot got to Washington's Four Seasons Hotel and heard the news, he called Pratt at home and started yelling. He said the Clinton administration had cooked up the Iraq crisis and was using it to keep him off the air.

"I just flew up here on my private airplane," Perot said. "Do you have any idea how much that costs?"

Each Thursday and Friday, top administration officials find out which journalists are in the Sunday lineup and make their off-the-record pitches. One Friday, during the battle over Henry Foster's nomination, Donna Shalala called Cokie Roberts and Sam Donaldson. She said that Lamar Alexander, the former Republican governor of Tennessee, was among those backing Foster for surgeon general. Roberts repeated this on *Brinkley,* saying it was too early to write off the nomination.

Among those watching was Paul Begala, a senior Clinton adviser. The next morning at 7:00 A.M., Begala was debating Haley Barbour, the Republican Party chairman, on CNN. He repeated Cokie Roberts's line about Lamar Alexander's support. It turned out the administration had fed Roberts bad information. By noon, Alexander had put out a press release blasting Begala for misrepresenting his position. "I probably should have checked with Alexander before I went with it," Roberts says.

On another occasion, Mickey Kantor, the U.S. trade representative, called Roberts at home on a Saturday. Her husband, Steve Roberts, answered the phone. When Kantor explained why he was calling, Roberts said: "Well, I'm going to be on *Meet the Press* tomorrow." Kantor achieved a double spin for the price of a phone call.

Such talk show lobbying has become routine. Both parties hold regular "message meetings" and, as the weekend approaches, dispatch their best spinners to call the talk show panelists and make the appropriate pitch. When Robert Byrd was Senate majority leader, he used to call Jack Germond every Friday morning, like clockwork, to peddle the Democratic line before he went on *McLaughlin*. Germond could only chuckle when the phone rang.

"I talk to Mort Kondracke two or three times a week," says an administration strategist who deals with the press. "I talk to Eleanor Clift twice a week, Mark Shields once a week, and Margaret Carlson once every two weeks. I talk to Cokie Roberts occasionally. The Schieffer folks are happy to ask for material when a Republican is on. Fred Barnes is willing to listen, although he's more open-minded in his writing than he is on the tube. I used to think these were really smart people who did their own reporting and thought great thoughts. But they don't have an opinion on everything and are willing to be led, as long as it doesn't disturb their belief system. If they don't hear from us at all, they either make up their own shit or believe the other side."

There was a time when presidential aides staged background briefings primarily for newspaper and magazine columnists. But on the Thursday after Clinton's 1995 State of the Union speech, Leon Panetta summoned some of the top talking heads—Cokie Roberts, Gloria Borger, Gwen Ifill, Eleanor Clift, Jack Germond, Mort Kondracke, Gordon Peterson, David Broder—to trumpet the alleged success of the eighty-two-minute speech. The White House knew the print people had already filed their analysis pieces. "They basically didn't give a shit what was written," Broder says. "They care what is said on the weekend talk shows."

If the three Sunday morning shows often seemed similar in tone, that may be because they were populated by the same small cast of Beltway characters. During 1993 and 1994, Bob Dole was on the Sunday shows thirty-five times, Warren Christopher twenty times, Newt Gingrich sixteen times, Al Gore sixteen times, Pat Moynihan sixteen times, Sam Nunn twelve times, Richard Gephardt eleven times. Leon Panetta appeared eleven times just in the last six months of 1994.

Talk show producers kept booking certain politicians for the same reason they like Fred Barnes or Bob Novak: They are entertaining. They give good sound bite. They know how to play. Bob Dole is every show's favorite guest. He is the undisputed lifetime champion, having been on the Sunday shows more than 160 times. Dole knows precisely what the programs want: a bit of wit and a bit of news.

"People kept saying, 'Why is Bob Dole on every week?' " Cokie Roberts says. "The answer was, you had a Democratic Congress and a Democratic president. The problem was getting Republicans of stature. Bob Michel, as much as I love him, and I do love him, was never wonderful on television. It was very hard for him to answer a question succinctly."

Of course, the kind of "news" Dole produces on these shows meets that definition only in the incremental, process-oriented world of Beltway insiders. In the spring of 1995, for example, these Dole comments generated headlines in major newspapers:

Meet the Press, April 15: Dole says he will oppose Henry Foster's nomination as surgeon general.

Face the Nation, May 7: Dole says he wants to sit down with Henry Foster before deciding whether to bring his nomination to a vote.

Meet the Press, June 4: Dole says Henry Foster probably has enough votes to be confirmed if his nomination reaches the floor.

Face the Nation, June 18: Dole says Henry Foster's nomination will come to a vote and that he hopes to meet with Foster this week.

Other guests are viewed as hit or miss. "I like Gore, he's a charming guy," Schieffer says. "But every once in awhile he goes into his elm-tree stance and just doesn't have anything to say. That's a deadly killer, when they go into this government boilerplate."

Still others quickly got scratched from the A-list. *Meet the Press* shied away from using Tom Foley and George Mitchell, even when they were the two top Democrats in Congress. "They were just duds," an NBC staffer says. "It was very difficult to get them to say anything beyond the party line."

For the politicians, the exposure was priceless. Not only would they get their ten or twelve minutes of precious airtime, but there would be the ritual stakeout outside the station, where reporters from other news outlets would ask the same questions so they could get their own footage on the flap of the day.

Bill Kristol was once summoned to Capitol Hill by an influential senator who, once they were alone, demanded to know: "Why are you on TV so much?" "Face time" with Brinkley or Russert had become a principal Washington measure of influence. "These guys lust to be on television," Kristol says. "They would kill, they would run over people." (When Kristol launched the conservative magazine *The Standard* with Rupert Murdoch's money in 1995, his talk show stature was undiminished. He simply moved from being a "Republican activist" guest on *This Week* to part of the journalists' roundtable.)

"It's kind of sad how many members of Congress write to me,

call me, and ask to get on the air with something or other," David Brinkley says. "It's pretty degrading. I'm embarrassed for them."

No one was more determined to get on the air than the men seeking the White House. By the summer of 1995, the Sunday shows had become the prime forum for the '96 Republican presidential primaries. On July 16, to take a typical Sunday, Bob Dole appeared on *Brinkley,* Pat Buchanan and Arlen Specter duked it out on *Meet the Press,* and Pete Wilson fielded questions on *Face the Nation.* Most of the country was not yet tuned into the campaign some seven months before the New Hampshire primary, but Brinkley, Russert, and Schieffer were always eager to offer the combatants a chance to make news.

Phil Gramm, who appeared on *Evans and Novak* the day before, understood the importance of the talk show campaign: "When we announced over an eight-day period, I was on three Sunday talk shows, I was on *60 Minutes,* I did five morning shows, my announcement speech was run nineteen times on C-SPAN, and I jumped in the polls from 5 percent to 15 percent."

A few prominent politicians, such as Ted Kennedy and Jesse Helms, almost never appeared on the Sunday shows. But one of the most elusive guests had to be Richard Nixon. The *Brinkley* producers had courted him for years, and in early 1994 they were convinced they finally had him.

Nixon was heading back from Moscow, where he had made headlines because Boris Yeltsin had refused to meet with him. The *Brinkley* show seemed an unlikely forum, since Sam Donaldson was no Nixon fan and George Will had repeatedly called for his impeachment during the Watergate scandal. But the prestigious program was tempting for a disgraced politician trying to recast his reputation as an elder statesman. During back-channel negotiations with Dimitri Simes, a Russian scholar and close associate of the former president, Nixon laid down one condition: He did not want to talk about Watergate.

Donaldson had never before surrendered his right to ask about a topic. But under pressure from the staff, he gave in. "I said, 'Okay, I'll make the deal. Unless he brings it up, I won't talk about Watergate. It's been done and done and done.' " With that assurance, Nixon agreed to appear the following Sunday.

"He was not a fan of Sunday talk shows," Simes says. "He was particularly concerned about Sam Donaldson. He did not like a format where several people would question him. He prepared for any event as if he was still president of the United States, and of course you have much less control when several people question you at once."

Days before the broadcast, Nixon backed out. Simes says he was simply exhausted from the trip. Nixon died the following month.

For conservatives, Sunday morning was a crucial beachhead in the war of ideas.

As journalists became the dominant presence on the Sunday shows, the way they framed the debate was increasingly important. They were no longer there simply to coax newsworthy comments from politicians. Their thoughts mattered. Their take on the issues was news. And this presented a rare opportunity for conservatives to make their case on network television, just as Pat Buchanan was championing the cause on cable shows. The top conservative commentators—Buchanan, Safire, Will—had come from the world of politics, and for them television was simply another means of waging intellectual battle. Sam Donaldson may have been Brinkley's house liberal, but he was really a career reporter who happened to lean to the left. He did not support Bill Clinton the way George Will had ardently backed Ronald Reagan; in fact, he often joined Will in bashing the Democratic president. Donaldson was, by his own admission, not very interested in the kind of philosophical arguments that energized George Will.

Will believed that most network journalists had a liberal "agenda," but that "they would be genuinely bewildered if you suggested that, because everyone they know thinks that way. Peter Jennings is in serious denial about the course of the twentieth century."

Will fully appreciated the significance of the talk show platform. "The conservative ascendancy in political argument today was preceded by the emergence of conservative columnists, conservative magazines, conservative academics," he says. "If it's true, as Bertrand Russell said, that power is the power to achieve desired results, then it's very hard to measure the power of me or anyone else. But cumulatively, these columns and magazines made it respectable for people to say certain things. Before Ronald Reagan, there was Goldwater. Before there could be Barry Goldwater, there was Bill Buckley with an idea for a magazine. There's no question, without the *National Review,* Goldwater would not have been nominated. Only ideas have large and lasting consequences."

In the talk show culture of the '90s, the role of the *National Review* had been eclipsed by the *Brinkley* show and its brethren. An ideological magazine was still an important incubator for ideas, but those ideas could achieve national resonance only through the power of television. And since so few television shows dealt with political substance, the importance of Sunday morning was paramount.

In a more subtle way, the Sunday shows also communicated a kind of cultural conservatism. By debating who was up and who was down and which legislation was likely to pass Congress, they bought into the status quo in a fundamental way. The existing order might need serious tinkering, one set of hacks might have to be replaced by another, but the fundamental premises of American capitalism were rarely challenged. The range of debate was limited by the constricted range of political reality. Health care or welfare reform or the minimum wage was an "issue" to be dissected and analyzed, but not one that personally affected the well-heeled panelists. The Sunday programs rarely had black journalists, with the notable exception of Gwen Ifill, and even more rarely Hispanic or Asian American or gay journalists. Their tone often resembled that of an upper-middle-class dinner party. "I go to the movies every six months and I'm so disgusted I don't go back again," George Will told viewers, airily dismissing a large slice of American pop culture.

Sometimes the *Brinkley* clan sounded truly insular, clucking over the unruly behavior of the mob beyond the gates.

"The way people communicate on computers is so rude and offensive I can't get over it," Cokie Roberts says.

"The whole country needs to be sent to bed without its dessert," George Will says.

"Listen to some of the radio talk show hosts . . . they think nothing of calling people the worst, uncivil names," Sam Donaldson says.

"Let's go on," Brinkley says. "Should we bail out the Mexican peso?"

It is, in the end, like sitting through a congressional hearing—an important democratic ritual, to be sure, but at times a tedious, posturing, ego-driven enterprise. The networks were bringing together two groups of powerful people—big-name politicians and big-time journalists—who in the public's eyes were simply charter members of the same Washington elite. There was, however, one important difference. The journalists were making a lot more money.

CHAPTER NINE

TALKING
FOR DOLLARS

J ames Kilpatrick has described the practice of lawmakers accepting lucrative speaking fees as nothing less than a "scandal."

"Members of the House and Senate . . . accept invitations to
speak to a trade association or other special-interest group," the
conservative columnist writes. "The member, often accompanied
by his wife, goes to such agreeable spots as Boca Raton or Honolulu,
makes a little talk, and picks up a check for $2,000 plus travel
expenses . . . The practice smells to high heaven."

Soon after that column was published, Kilpatrick, a regular on
Agronsky & Company, was asked about his own practice of giving
twenty to twenty-five paid speeches a year. "I think that's my own
personal business," he declared, apparently failing to detect any
unsavory odor from journalists taking corporate cash.

Kilpatrick is hardly alone in hiding behind such an embarrassing double standard. While Congress has since banned honoraria for its members, the market for reporters and pundits who speak
to business audiences has never been hotter. Some big-name media
people routinely receive $15,000, $30,000, even $50,000 for a single
speech. And the bulk of that money comes from corporations and
lobbying organizations with more than a passing interest in the
issues the journalists write about and yak about for a living.

The talk show culture is built upon a mountain of cash. The
programs themselves, which cost little to produce, are quite profitable for their owners, bringing in plenty of advertising dollars from

the likes of Ford and General Electric and Archer-Daniels-Midland. And they are extraordinarily profitable for the superstars of talk: Rush Limbaugh earns an estimated $25 million a year, Howard Stern a cool $7 million, Ted Koppel $6 million, Larry King $4 million, Don Imus $3 million, Sam Donaldson $2 million. Oprah Winfrey, who owns her syndicated show, could buy and sell her competitors several times over. Her net worth is roughly $340 million.

Yet even below these stratospheric levels, the talk show world bestows all sorts of financial rewards. While the journalists appear either for free or for a few hundred dollars per program, the television exposure is a gateway to the good life. *Newsweek* reporter Howard Fineman, a regular on *Washington Week,* is hired to speak to a group of lawyers on a twelve-day cruise from the Netherlands to Russia. Other *Washington Week* regulars—Paul Duke, Charlie Mc-Dowell, Jack Nelson—take all-expenses-paid luxury cruises to such places as Hong Kong and Singapore, organized by a Florida travel agency. "It's an easy way to visit a lot of places," Duke says.

Margaret Carlson, the *Time* columnist, says her speaking fee doubled (to about $10,000) after she became a weekly member of *The Capital Gang.* "I just got on the gravy train, so I don't want it to end," she says. But her *Time* colleague, Hugh Sidey, who once made up to fifty speeches a year, says his lecture income all but vanished when he stopped appearing regularly on *Agronsky & Company.*

"If you're on one of these shows and then you're off, in six months your lecture money is gone," Jack Germond says.

At the very least, the issue of journalists taking money from interest groups would seem a legitimate subject for public debate. Yet here is how these champions of the First Amendment, who have relentlessly poked and pried their way into other people's business, have responded to questions about their paid speaking engagements:

"We are private citizens," says David Brinkley.

"I'm not an elected official," says Fred Barnes.

"I'm a totally private person," says Robert Novak.

"I'm a private citizen," says Chris Wallace.

"I'm not an elected official," says Gloria Borger.

"I'm not going to disclose it," says Al Hunt.

"I don't exercise the power of the state," says George Will.

"A private matter," says Robert MacNeil.

"That's private," says Hugh Sidey.

"I didn't do it for years, but it became more socially acceptable," says Michael Kinsley.

Indeed it has, at least within the insular and self-serving world of talk show journalism. But many readers and viewers would no doubt be appalled at the web of potential conflicts of interest. And some members of Congress are downright angry that those who piously demand full disclosure from politicians insist that they get to play by a different set of rules.

"Their audience deserves to know if they pick up a fat check from a group they report on," says Wyoming Senator Alan Simpson. "It applies to Congress, and it sure as hell ought to apply to this elite press corps in Washington."

"What I find most offensive lately," says Representative David Obey of Wisconsin, "is that we get the Sanctimonious Sam defense: 'We're different because we don't write the laws.' Well, they have a hell of a lot more power than I do to affect the laws written."

By the summer of 1995, the resentment of journalistic buckrakers had reached new heights. West Virginia Senator Robert Byrd, who had denounced reporters as "vultures" and buzzards" after being ambushed outside his Virginia home by a *Prime Time Live* crew, decided to get even. He introduced a resolution that reporters who receive credentials to cover the Senate should be required to reveal their outside income in financial disclosure forms. After stubbornly resisting voluntary disclosure for years, reporters had left themselves vulnerable to a maneuver that amounted to government licensing of journalists. Not a single senator spoke up on behalf of the press. The nonbinding resolution passed, 60 to 39.

In an age of instant communications, it is disingenuous at best for the nation's most prominent talking heads to claim they have little impact on public policy. Who are they kidding? They eagerly reap the benefits of fame, sell themselves on the lecture circuit, and then claim that they are merely working reporters with no public obligations.

The spectacle of pundits pocketing large sums for little work

raises another, equally insidious problem: They lose touch with the
vast majority of their audience. Many are now in income brackets
that would have been unthinkable a generation ago, before the un-
holy union of journalism and televised entertainment. Although the
pontificators vehemently deny it, this privileged status invariably
skews their view of the world. They are part of the moneyed class,
just like the people they report on.

When President Clinton raised income taxes on the wealthiest 1
percent of taxpayers in 1993, most of the talking heads took a hit.
They were personally affected by a policy that had no affect on most
Americans. This may have contributed to the widespread misim-
pression, confirmed in poll after poll, that Clinton had raised taxes on
the middle class. If taxes have gone up for you and all your friends,
it's easy to get the idea that just about everyone is paying more.

When health care reform was at the top of the national agenda,
many commentators argued that there was no health care crisis—
and indeed, for them and their well-heeled colleagues, there was
not. They did not worry about rising premiums, or preexisting
conditions, or losing health benefits after losing a job. The problems
of the thirty-seven million Americans without insurance were simply alien to their experience.

When the NAFTA trade pact was languishing in Congress,
pundits across the political spectrum, from George Will to Michael
Kinsley, rallied behind it, secure in the knowledge that they would
not be among the factory employees or textile workers who might
lose their jobs. It is easy to be for an abstraction—free trade—when
the pain is inflicted on faraway individuals outside your professional
and social circles. No television network was going to pull up stakes
and move to Mexico for the cheap labor.

Public education is another issue much debated by TV commentators whose kids are safely ensconced in pricey private schools.
When Clinton put his daughter Chelsea in Sidwell Friends, a
$10,000-a-year private school in northwest Washington, rather than
one of the capital's public schools, the punditocracy rushed to his
defense. Mark Shields praised Sidwell on *MacNeil/Lehrer,* but had
to admit that his children went there, as did Jim Lehrer's. Al Hunt
supported Clinton's move on *Capital Gang,* but had to make the
same disclosure. Carl Rowan, whose grandchildren attended the

school, did the same on *Inside Washington*. So much for the voice of
the little guy.

It's not that these journalists have a pressing need to moonlight;
they are already raking in big piles of dough. Those who are ferried
by limousine to five-figure speaking engagements are making themselves even more remote from the working stiffs of America.

"It's hard to imagine being paid $20,000 for a speech," says
Paul Emerson, managing editor of the Lewiston, Idaho, *Tribune*.
"That's more than some of our reporters make in a year."

Sam Donaldson is trying to convince me that he's just a regular
guy.

He has invited me to lunch at Charley's Crab, a fancy eatery
on Washington's Connecticut Avenue, to explain that despite his
millionaire's salary and 27,000-acre New Mexico ranch, his daily
life is pretty much like anyone else's. Unfortunately for Donaldson,
the maître d' walks over at that moment with a complimentary
seafood hors d'oeuvre.

Whatever his tax bracket, Donaldson remains one of the hard-
est-working reporters around. But fairly or unfairly, he has become
a symbol of the wealth of the talk show aristocracy. Through his
television fame, first as a White House correspondent for ABC and
later as coanchor of *PrimeTime Live* and a *Brinkley* panelist, Donaldson is much in demand on the speaking circuit.

In the spring of 1993, *PrimeTime Live* aired a report on a congressional junket to Florida sponsored by the Electronic Industries
Association. ABC executives were rather embarrassed when it
turned out that Donaldson had accepted a speaking fee from the
same group.

In early 1994, the spotlight fell on Donaldson again just as
PrimeTime was gearing up for another of its patented junket stories.
This one involved a trip to Key West, Florida, for thirty congressional staff members, courtesy of the American Insurance Association and other insurance groups. Two days before the report was to
air, insurance officials decided to launch a preemptive strike. They
leaked me a contract showing that Donaldson had accepted an hono-
rarium the previous year from an insurance coalition that included,

yes, the American Insurance Association. He received first-class air fare for the speech at New York's Waldorf-Astoria, along with hotel accommodations and limousine service. His fee: $30,000.

Donaldson found himself in the awkward position of explaining why it was news when the insurance group paid for a trip for some Capitol Hill staffers, but perfectly kosher for him to accept a large check from the same folks.

"I was not beholden to them, and they were not beholden to me," Donaldson told me. "I of course do not make the laws under which the insurance industry operates. I have not spoken about the laws affecting the insurance industry on the *Brinkley* show or in any of my pieces."

Paul Equale, senior vice president of the Independent Insurance Agents of America, pounced on the issue in his taped interview with *PrimeTime* correspondent Chris Wallace. Equale even had his own camera crew tape the interview for protection. "The total cost for the conference, the two-and-a-half-day conference including air fare and hotel, was about the same amount of money for the one-hour speech from Sam Donaldson to the same group last year," he told Wallace.

"What's that?" Wallace asked.

"It was about $30,000," Equale said. Those remarks, for some strange reason, were left on the cutting-room floor. Wallace briefly mentioned Donaldson's speaking engagement in his piece, but not the $30,000 figure.

Donaldson, who was giving a half dozen speeches a year, dismissed such arguments as "a smoke screen. We're going to continue to investigate people and groups whether I've spoken to them or not. Raising my name is not going to deter *PrimeTime* from doing this type of investigation."

The hand-wringing over the issue has gone too far, he says. "Suddenly there's a view that all of us making these high-money speeches are discrediting ourselves, and there's a great wave to reform," Donaldson says. But he concedes that "appearances can be reality. I've covered politics long enough to understand that."

The breathtaking level of Donaldson's compensation took on larger-than-life dimensions as critics began to wonder which other talkers were talking their way into big money. My stories in *The*

Washington Post triggered similar reports in *The New Yorker, American Journalism Review,* and *The Wall Street Journal.* Donaldson, it turns out, has plenty of company. Pat Buchanan earns $10,000 a speech. William Safire, the *New York Times* columnist and frequent *Meet the Press* panelist, takes in $20,000 a speech. Cokie Roberts's fee is at least $20,000; she is said to have earned $300,000 a year from speechifying. Mike Wallace fetches $25,000 a speech. Rush Limbaugh commands a $30,000 fee. Larry King receives $50,000 for each appearance, pulling in at least a million bucks a year.

"Norman Schwarzkopf says it's white-collar crime," King says, referring to the retired general who made it big on the lecture circuit.

"It's amazingly lucrative," agrees Kinsley, who won't reveal his fee.

Booking agencies, which take a commission of 10 to 15 percent, have taken notice. "Once you get one of those regular guest slots, your rates go up dramatically," says Susan Stautberg, whose New York firm, Master Media, has a speaker's bureau. "People want you. You can say 'as seen on *David Brinkley* or *Washington Week.*' It just makes them more credible." Fees can shoot up from $5,000 to $20,000 overnight, she says.

But Stautberg is frustrated by groups that insist on seeing a videotape of the speaker's last TV appearance. "We have some remarkable authors who are brilliant, but because they don't have the same kind of tape as someone on *Oprah,* they're harder to book," she says.

For the kings and queens of talk, television success seemed to confer the stature of world leaders. A glossy brochure touting the Kennedy Center lecture series for the 1995–96 season invited patrons to pony up $195 to hear George and Barbara Bush, Mikhail Gorbachev, Queen Noor of Jordan, and . . . Oprah Winfrey.

For journalists, the financial logic is irresistible. That's why Chris Matthews of the *San Francisco Examiner,* who hosts a nightly show, *Politics with Chris Matthews,* on America's Talking, made more than forty speeches in 1993. He does less speaking now but takes in $5,000 to $6,000 per appearance. "My salary at my newspaper is $71,000," Matthews explains. "I have fifty-three papers carrying my column; that's about $13,000, $15,000. It's prestigious as hell, but that's it. Three speeches matches your syndicated column income."

For some pundits, the lecture circuit can become a constant preoccupation. When David Gergen was a *MacNeil/Lehrer* commentator and *U.S. News* columnist, he was paid $466,625 for 121 speeches in 1992. He pulled in another $239,460 for 50 speeches in the first half of 1993.

The list of Gergen's benefactors reads like a who's who of corporate America: the American Stock Exchange ($12,000), American Trucking Association ($10,000), Cosmetics and Toiletries Association ($7,000), Grocery Manufacturers Association ($6,500), Snack Food Association ($6,500), Edison Electric Institute ($6,500), American Bankers Association ($6,000), Chase Manhattan Bank ($6,000), and Salomon Brothers ($6,000), to name just a few. "It was an important part of my income," Gergen says.

What's more, IBM paid Gergen more than $55,000 over two years for ten separate appearances in places ranging from New York to Albuquerque, New Mexico, to Palm Springs, California. "The attraction in having David Gergen speak is his background in Washington and his expertise in public policy," says IBM spokesman Tom Beermann.

Needless to say, most of these groups have important interests in the political issues that Gergen was regularly discussing on *MacNeil/Lehrer*, on other shows such as *Face the Nation*, and on Mutual radio and Washington's WMAL radio. And yet he must ask the public to believe that taking $55,000 from IBM had absolutely no effect on his public views—an assertion that would be laughable if made by a politician.

The ambitious nature of Gergen's moneymaking travels underscores the paradox of the talk show culture. The journalists who rise to prominence through their writing and reporting gradually find they have less time for the unglamorous work on which they built their reputations. The pursuit of journalism begins to take a backseat to the pursuit of lucrative opportunities.

Gergen sounds a bit guilt-ridden on this point. "Doing too many speeches can have a negative impact on your journalism," he concedes. "You're on a plane a lot. Particularly on television, it's possible to fake it. You can skim right over the surface without doing the legwork. You become an actor, an entertainer. If you get too heavily into the dog show business and the lecture business, you can call yourself a journalist, but in fact you're not. You don't feel good about yourself. I've done it. I know you can fake it.

"There is a corrupting influence. Just the physical demands on your body, to go from here to L.A. or Vegas or Florida on a Tuesday and give a speech Wednesday and then do a show on Friday. You stay at a ritzy hotel. You shut people out. You just talk to these well-groomed, well-heeled business folks. You're traveling in a bubble. It tends to encourage a pro-establishment viewpoint. You're talking to the establishment, you're with them a lot."

During the first two years of the Clinton administration, no issue was higher on the national agenda than health care reform. And the largest health care organizations, which had a huge stake in the outcome, were funneling large amounts of cash to some of the very journalists who were covering and commenting on the debate.

One recipient was Fred Barnes, who gives six to eight speeches a month, most of them for a $5,000 fee. Barnes is a regular on *CBS This Morning* as well as *McLaughlin,* fills in on *Crossfire,* hosts a syndicated radio show and a Voice of America program. "If you do a lot of TV and speeches, you have less time to commit real journalism," he admits.

Here's how the process works. In the spring of 1993, when Washington was abuzz about the need for health reform, Barnes declared on *McLaughlin* that the notion of a health care crisis was overblown. After seeing the McLaughlin segment, Wladyslaw Pleszczynski, managing editor of *The American Spectator,* called to ask Barnes to write a piece on the subject for the conservative magazine. As the idea gained currency in Republican circles, Barnes expanded his indictment, saying in a piece for *Forbes MediaCritic* that the calls for sweeping health reform were based on "media-generated myths." Republican analysts like Bill Kristol and Republican members of Congress began to embrace the argument that there was no crisis. In the fall of 1994, the American Managed Care and Review Association, which represents health maintenance organizations, flew Barnes to Atlanta to deliver a keynote speech to its members. The talk show spiel eventually produced the lecture circuit invitation.

"Maybe I did write something they liked," Barnes says.

"Maybe they want me to come because I'm on television." Barnes sees no problem with undue influence because, he says, "I work for an opinion magazine."

Officials at the managed care association say they don't agree with everything Barnes says on health care but liked his outspoken commentary on *McLaughlin*. "We were also trying to get his perspective on working with the media and how to get the managed-care message out," says Steven Gardner, the group's director of education. "That was part of our discussion. Knowing of his savvy, we wanted to get some pointers."

During the height of the health care battle, George Will went to Washington's Grand Hyatt Hotel to speak to the Health Insurance Association of America, maker of the famed "Harry and Louise" ads attacking the Clinton health plan. Will, too, has argued that complaints about a health care crisis are vastly exaggerated. "No one can seem to think of a better system than ours, and it's hard to define what this crisis is when, I guess, 80 percent of the American people say they're satisfied with their health care," he said on *Brinkley*.

Will says his receipt of industry cash "doesn't make a particle of difference in what I'm saying" and that his speeches are not "tailored" to any group. "Virtually everything I say in my talks has appeared in what I've written."

During the same period, Mike Kinsley and Margaret Carlson flew to San Francisco to address a gathering of the American Medical Association. Kinsley says he donated the fee to charity—not because he thought there was a problem, but because I might "pester" him about it in *The Washington Post*. Kinsley also split $25,000 with Bob Novak and Mona Charen for speaking to the Independent Insurance Agents of America at Disney World's Dolphin Hotel. And, in a *Crossfire* roadshow, Kinsley, John Sununu, and Juan Williams appeared before the Group Health Association of America, arguing about health care.

"It's potentially corrupting, but so is everything," Kinsley says. He abides by "a series of perverse rules," such as refusing to speak to college audiences. "If the corporations want to shell out this kind of money, that's the stockholders' problem," he says. "But I resent the money coming from student fees."

Cokie Roberts joined the long line of journalists appearing before the health care industry when she addressed the Group Health Association. But the health care issue was growing so hot that she decided to donate her fee to a Princeton medical center named for her late sister. "I realized it could be construed as a problem and said, 'Don't even bother sending me the money' . . . I didn't want anybody to question it," Roberts says.

Health care lobbyists have no monopoly on writing checks to moonlighting journalists. Cokie Roberts has spoken to the American Automobile Association, Mortgage Bankers Association of America, National Association of Chain Drug Stores, National Restaurant Association, and Snack Food Association. She and her husband, Steve Roberts of *U.S. News,* were paid a reported $45,000 by Chicago's Northern Trust Bank for appearing at a cocktial party, breakfast, and luncheon.

Roberts says all the publicity about honoraria has clearly created "a perception problem. But I do not know of a living soul who has slanted a story, done a story, or not done a story because of speaking fees.

"It's like when I would sing for a living," she says, recalling her college days in an all-female a cappella group. "You are hired to entertain. You show up, you entertain, you go away. They're looking for celebrity value."

Roberts, whose parents both served in Congress, sees no analogy to congressional honoraria because she reports to ABC executives, not the taxpayers. Still, she says, "If it's going to cause everyone a lot of trouble, it's better not to do it. I don't like being the center of controversy. I didn't run for office. I'm the only one in my family who didn't."

Steve Roberts, for his part, says *U.S. News* has an in-house speech agent who makes such bookings because they are good publicity for the magazine. He says he occasionally gives his fee to charity when he believes he has a conflict of interest, as he did in donating about $2,000 for speaking at an upstate New York forum sponsored by Representative Sherwood Boehlert. And, Roberts says, it puts him in contact with real people outside the Beltway.

"It's a classic free market," says Roberts, whose speaking gigs have included American Express and the Greater Washington Society of Association Executives. "I've often compared giving speeches

to having a little stall in a souk in Damascus. Why do Sam Donaldson and Diane Sawyer and Cokie Roberts make fees five to ten
times what someone like me commands? Because they're on TV.
It's not that they're ten times smarter than me. They're ten times
more famous than I am. And there is the bragging rights factor:
'Gosh, we had Cokie Roberts for dinner.' "

This celebrity factor has clearly boosted Larry King, who gives
thirty-five speeches each year. He has spoken to the restaurant association and the chain drug store group, moderated a panel for IBM
and another for a doctors' group. In one two-week stretch, King
traveled to San Francisco, Baltimore, and Milwaukee for speaking
engagements. A speech in Paris before an international pharmaceu-
tical group brought in $60,000. And King keeps the cash register
ringing without a prepared text. "I just do shtick, tell stories," he
says.

The schedule can be taxing. During the 1992 campaign, King
did his CNN program with President Bush on a Sunday and had an
interview scheduled with Bill Clinton the following night in Ocala,
Florida. In between he picked up some extra cash, stopping in
Michigan for a speech to a women's garden club. He had to rent a
private plane to get to the Clinton interview on time.

One of the most popular forms of entertainment for business
groups is mock debates that mimic those on television. *The
McLaughlin Group, Crossfire,* and *Capital Gang* have all taken their
shows on the road. Margaret Carlson, who has joined Bob Novak
and Mark Shields before paying audiences, says the result is more
outlandish than what people on the air. "These fake wrestling
matches are really phony," she says. "You tend to speak in absolutes
and end up further to one side than you really are." In an unforget-
table metaphor, she declared: "We are like monkeys who get up on
stage." Carlson's act was curtailed in 1995 when *Time* banned its
reporters from accepting corporate speaking fees.

John McLaughlin heatedly rejects any criticism of his moonlighting as "laughable." He has made as many as eighty speeches a
year, although by 1994 he had cut back to a mere seventeen engagements. These include the *McLaughlin Group* road shows and mock
programs, such as one with members of the American Bankers Association, where he quizzed the bankers on financial issues as if

they were panelists on his show. McLaughlin's rationale is rather inventive: He takes so much special-interest cash that it means nothing because he can hardly remember who gave it to him.

"I've talked to hundreds and hundreds of different groups," he says. "I can't remember one from the other. I've got an appearance coming up next week, and I don't know who it is. It becomes a blur. The blurring sets in within six hours of leaving the site. Then it goes into a black hole.

"The underlying reason for the criticism is that we are going to slant, to distort, to trim, or otherwise modify our journalistic reporting by reason of having been paid a fee from an organization whose name, purpose, structure, and membership we can't remember. It's farcical."

The road shows even extend to network shows. Tim Russert has staged a mock session of *Meet the Press* before the American Bankers Association, with Senator Bob Dole and Robert Rubin, then the White House economic adviser, as his guests. Russert, whose reported fee was $20,000, says he turns down one hundred speaking invitations a year from groups because of conflicts of interest and accepts only half a dozen. He doesn't see the banking appearance as a conflict because he didn't ask Dole and Rubin about banking. "Whatever I share is something I've said on the air," he said. "It's an honest reflection of what I do. If they had said, 'Here are the questions we want you to ask,' I wouldn't have done it."

Russert says he cannot avoid all entanglement with corporations because *Meet the Press* sells commercial time. "We have Archer-Daniels-Midland, United Airlines, and General Electric as sponsors," he says. Nevertheless, he says, "We did a story on Archer-Daniels and their political contributions on *NBC Nightly News.*"

Mark Shields, who writes a syndicated column in addition to his television work, makes well over thirty speeches a year. "I don't have an institutional base," he says. "I have to pay for rent at the National Press Building, a secretary, a phone. The economics are such that that can't sustain me. The television leads to speaking, and that enables you to report. I have a speech in San Diego soon, and I'm doing a California piece. I've got a Boston speech, and I'll tie that into two days in New Hampshire."

Shields says he won't take money from political parties and won't accept an engagement "if someone says we want to talk about how this Congress is going to deal with roofing and asphalt contractors. I don't feel I'm singing for my supper. What they're getting for their money is someone who makes them think and maybe even makes them laugh."

While Shields draws the line at political organizations, such groups have found other places to rent journalistic talent. In 1990, Bob Novak and Mort Kondracke made a joint appearance before the Republican Governors Association in Pinehurst, North Carolina. Kondracke was paid $4,000 plus expenses; Novak declined to reveal his fee. After addressing the governors, Novak wrote a column about the conference. He later acknowledged that perhaps he should have told his readers he had been a paid speaker.

(In my own case, I have made a handful of speeches over the years, usually for $500 or $1,000. My current rule, and the rule of my employer, is not to accept invitations from corporations or lobbying groups, which means I speak once or twice a year at universities and turn down many more.)

To be sure, some journalists have always made paid appearances. Walter Cronkite, who took money for speeches when he was anchoring the *CBS Evening News,* says he never thought much about it. Now, he says, "I would have to agree with the critics that it probably is better avoided." It is, says Cronkite, "a perception issue."

The Big Three network anchors—Dan Rather, Peter Jennings, and Tom Brokaw—either accept no honoraria or donate the money to charity. They can, of course, well afford to take the high road. A few other top television journalists, such as Ted Koppel and Jim Lehrer, have abandoned the lecture circuit.

Koppel says his speaking invitations soared after he started doing *Nightline.* To get the biggest bang for the buck, he recalls telling his agent: "Instead of doing speeches for $10,000, let's see what happens when we ask for fifteen. Make it twenty. Make it twenty-five. Make it thirty." Each time, the requests kept pouring in.

Koppel stopped making paid speeches a half dozen years ago after one group offered him a $50,000 fee. "I began to feel uncomfortable about it," he says. "No one who makes $18,000 a year is ever going to believe that someone can get $30,000 for a couple of hours' work and not be influenced in some fashion by the people giving him that much money. It would be superhuman. In truth, it is different. If you're making hundreds of thousands of dollars a year, then your $30,000 fee is more or less equivalent to someone making $18,000 getting a gift of twenty bucks. It's not as big a thing as it seems to be. In all the years that I did speeches for money, I can honestly say that no one ever called up before, or tried during or afterward, to say, 'How about doing a story on the Lumberman's Association of America?' Or, 'I was sort of disappointed, Ted, I thought you and I had become friends down there in Gainesville and I was a little disappointed at your take on the lobbying we're doing.' Not even close. But with the level of public mistrust in us where it is . . . Lord knows I'm well enough paid that I don't need anything from anyone else."

Still, some news executives don't see a problem. Says Ed Turner, the CNN vice president who must approve his employees' speaking engagements: "I don't like to say no. I'm proud when our guys can pick up a few extra bucks, and it's good exposure for CNN."

But that exposure can lead to embarrassment when a journalist lends his professional prestige to the companies he covers. Lou Dobbs, CNN's senior vice president and the host of *Moneyline* and *Moneyweek,* has accepted more than $15,000 for making promotional videos for Paine Webber, Shearson Lehman Brothers, and the Philadelphia Stock Exchange. In the Paine Webber video, he praised the brokerage for its "twin traditions of integrity and client service." Dobbs failed to grasp what was wrong with the arrangement. After *The Wall Street Journal* disclosed the deals, he told me: "It is nonsensical to talk about this as a conflict of interest any more than giving a speech to a corporation, and journalists all over the country do that." (Dobbs had a point: The same *Journal* article had to disclose that the paper's page-one editor at the time, James Stewart, had been paid $6,000 for a speech to Dean Witter Reynolds.) CNN quickly reprimanded Dobbs, who returned the money and apologized for his "arrogance."

In radio, where many hosts court advertisers and read commercials on the air, there is often less sensitivity to questions of financial impropriety. In 1991 ten top radio talkmeisters jetted to Alaska on an all-expenses-paid trip, courtesy of the American Petroleum Institute. The cost of the junket was $20,000. Yet the hosts breezily dismissed suggestions that they might be compromised in any way by two days of industry propaganda on the virtues of Alaskan oil drilling.

"The only problem in my mind would be appearance," said Mike Siegel of KING in Seattle, whose station decided to reimburse the lobbying group. "I've been in this business twenty years. Nobody can buy my opinion."

"I don't see myself as a journalist in the purest sense," said Mary Beal of KNSS in Wichita.

"I don't understand what the big goddamn fuss is . . . I'm a talk show host. I give opinions," said Patrick Murphy of WNIS in Norfolk.

The only network that has belatedly adopted a hard line on the issue of journalists speaking for pay is ABC. In 1995 the network imposed a restrictive policy drawn up by Richard Wald, its senior vice president and ethics czar. In a memo to the staff, Wald said that a few correspondents, "either because of the frequency or the size of their fees, in fact have a second, high-income job . . .

"We don't tilt what we say to please any special interest, we don't sell special access in the guise of fees—and we don't want to risk looking as though we do . . . It isn't just how big a fee is, it is also who gives it and what it might imply. Therefore, rather than get into the details of what reasonable men and women might do, we have decided on a general prohibition against the core of the problem. You may not accept a fee from a trade association or from a for-profit business. Their special interest is obvious and we have to guard against it."

The memo was about as popular as a communicable disease at ABC's Washington bureau, where most of the big-name correspondents work. Sam Donaldson, Cokie Roberts, David Brinkley, Brit Hume, and Jeff Greenfield were among those who signed a letter objecting to the ban.

Greenfield says, with some justification, that drawing a clear ethical line is difficult. "The whole idea of avoiding conflicts of interest is exactly right," he says. "When you start trying to figure out what is and what isn't, it gets really tricky. You can speak to nonprofit groups—they don't have a legislative agenda? They lobby all the time."

At an annual all-star talkathon in Bakersfield, California, the speakers one year included Sam Donaldson, George Will, Larry King, Mike Wallace, and Peter Jennings, along with Henry Kissinger, James Baker, Ross Perot, Colin Powell, Rich Little, and Paul Anka. This is perfectly permissible under ABC rules because the town, which charges guests $125 a ticket, is the sponsor. Yet Bakersfield probably has as much interest in what happens in Congress as the American Banking Association.

And there were ways around the ban. In 1995 Cokie Roberts made a $30,000 speech to the Junior League of Greater Fort Lauderdale, which Wald approved because it is a civic group. But the money was actually put up by JM Family Enterprises, a $4 billion firm that includes the largest independent American distributor of Toyotas. Roberts says she was never told where the money came from and that most nonprofit organizations, including her other employer, National Public Radio, have corporate underwriters.

And there were always exceptions. When *Good Morning America* became part of ABC's news division, cohost Joan Lunden was allowed to continue her lucrative endorsement deal with Vaseline and to peddle her line of exercise videos.

The Wald policy doesn't address other forms of income, such as stock holdings by network executives that could easily run into millions of dollars. "Should I be allowed to own fifty thousand shares of General Motors stock?" Donaldson asks. "The rules say I can. You extend the logic and you'd proscribe everything but Treasury bills. And maybe even those, since I report on government activities."

In fact, as ABC had to report in 1995, Donaldson does more than report on government; he receives help from the government. He has pocketed $97,000 in federal wool and mohair subsidies for the sheep on his New Mexico ranch. While perfectly legal, these payments have taken a bit of the punch out of his reports on government waste. The master of the ambush interview was later ambushed himself by Steve Wilson of *Inside Edition,* who sheared Donaldson over the sheep money. And on *Brinkley* one morning, when Donaldson was sparring with Newt Gingrich about perks for congressmen, Gingrich shot back that the House doesn't have "very many magnates of mohair."

At bottom, the defense of journalists who speak for money goes something like this: I am just a private person who wields no official power. What I do on my own time is my own business. I have no obligation to disclose my outside earnings to anyone. These payments do not influence what I write or say in any way. No one from these interest groups has ever asked me for a favor. I cannot be bought for the price of a speech.

There is little doubt that these renowned journalists really believe this line of argument. And there is no hard evidence that any of them has pulled a punch or slanted a story in exchange for a financial one-night stand. But corruption can be a subtle thing. The more time you spend with lobbyists and corporate officials, the more you come to identify with their worldview. It may be easier not to pursue a complicated story about an industry after you have taken the industry's money, if only to avoid potential criticism. At $10,000 or $20,000 or $30,000 a pop, your lecture schedule becomes as vital as your journalistic duties. And the hypocrisy question is unavoidable, for when it comes to politicians and businessmen, most journalists believe that the appearance of a conflict of interest is as troublesome as an actual one. They ought to hold themselves to precisely the same appearance standard. And the appearance of what many pundits are doing, to borrow a pungent phrase from Jack Kilpatrick, "smells to high heaven."

In a larger sense, the lure of fat lecture fees is quietly altering the fabric of journalism. The dozens of talking heads trying to get more airtime must conform to the demands of the medium for short, snappy, provocative opinions. They must market themselves as colorful personalities. They must strike a pose of negativity and cynicism toward the political system that, as it happens, is shared by many of the business groups looking for speakers. It's little wonder that the airwaves are filled with the sound of bombastic arguments and predictions and outrages of the week. Most of the players are also auditioning for a better-paying audience.

• • •

For many years, *The New York Times* strongly discouraged its reporters from appearing on television. An occasional stint on *Meet the Press* or *Washington Week* was permissible, but anything more was viewed with disdain.

Then the paper joined the video age.

Executive Editor Joseph Lelyveld told the staff in a 1993 memo that the *Times* had hired a public relations firm "to try to place some of our writers on TV and radio interview shows as a means of promoting the paper." The *Times* also launched its own nightly interview program on the New York 1 cable network. Publishing a high-quality newspaper was no longer enough. The triumph of the talk show culture was complete.

Steve Roberts, who left the *Times* in part because he wanted to appear more regularly on television, says the paper "always had a very retrograde view that television was stealing something the *Times* owned . . . It came from an institutional snobbism. The *Times* thought they were better than TV."

No one believes that anymore. The *Chicago Tribune* has hired a TV coach to work with its reporters. *Time* and *Newsweek* pay their writers cash bonuses of $50 to $100 for each television or radio interview. *Newsweek* even boasts in a promotional ad—featuring Eleanor Clift, Howard Fineman, Evan Thomas, Jonathan Alter, and Joe Klein on various shows—that "TV news organizations turn to *Newsweek* for expertise." When Tina Brown moved from *Vanity Fair* to *The New Yorker,* she brought along her publicist, Maurie Perl, to help generate the buzz that Brown considers crucial to the magazine's success. And the way to create buzz is to get *New Yorker* writers on *Good Morning America* or *Larry King Live* or *Charlie Rose.*

"I try to push the writers out there because I want attention for the articles," says Brown, who has herself been profiled on *60 Minutes*. "We can't deny this helps sell magazines."

That is now the accepted wisdom. "This is not just about stuffed-shirt pundits and their own self-aggrandizement," a *Time* official says. "This is becoming a large way in which news organizations market themselves. It's purely about image building. Before we had a PR department, Margaret Carlson sat in a dusty office and did no TV."

Once they get a taste of television fame, some reporters abandon print journalism altogether. Julie Johnson, after occasionally filling in on *Brinkley,* jumped from *Time* to ABC. Margaret Warner, who was a regular on *Capital Gang,* switched from *Newsweek* to *Mac-Neil/Lehrer.* Michel McQueen, a frequent panelist on *Washington Week,* moved from *The Wall Street Journal* to *Day One.* Gwen Ifill, another *Washington Week* regular, quit *The New York Times* for NBC. "You make stars out of these people and they leave you," the *Time* official sniffs.

Fledgling pundits start out on C-SPAN, where they can practice their delivery in a low-pressure environment and the only compensation is a coffee mug emblazoned with the network logo. The talented ones work their way up to midlevel pontification on CNN, CNBC, or PBS. The glibbest of the glib might get a coveted invitation to appear on *Nightline, Meet the Press,* or *Face the Nation.*

Sue Ducat, the *Washington Week* producer, says reporters determined to get on the prestigious program regularly call her or fax her clips. The *Chicago Tribune*'s publicist was constantly calling, at least until Ducat made her displeasure known after booking a reporter who turned out to have a serious speech impediment. "Being on *Washington Week* enhances their credibility within their own bureaus," Ducat says. "Bureau chiefs call me all the time to hawk people, including themselves. If they're on TV, boom! Suddenly their sources will call them back faster. And it's money. The lecture agents monitor shows like ours. Our show is often a recruiting ground for shows like *Meet the Press.*"

Journalistic calculations are affected by the need to keep the publicity machine humming. Clarence Page, the *Chicago Tribune* columnist, says he left Chicago for Washington several years ago to enhance his visibility. "One of the reasons I moved, quite frankly, was to get more exposure on the talk shows," he says. "It's pundit heaven here. It helps me to sell my column. In modern society you only exist if you're on television." As for speeches, for which Page charges $5,000 to $6,000, he says: "Before I started getting a lot of *McLaughlin* exposure, my invitations were primarily from universities and nonprofit organizations. Now I've been getting more corporate invitations—Grumman Aircraft, Met Life, Allstate. I've gotten a new audience."

Bob Beckel, a political analyst on *CBS This Morning* and substitute host on *Larry King,* describes television as "this mystical gateway in Washington that sort of separates you out . . . Since I started to do television on a regular basis, my speaking engagements have gone up dramatically. No question there's a direct relationship. I can write a good solid column about a presidential campaign in the *L.A. Times* and nobody will pay a hell of a lot of attention. I get on *Crossfire* and people seem to think that's more important."

Alongside the crush of journalists trying to elbow their way on television are hordes of academics, consultants, publicists, think-tank types, lawyers, authors, strategists, unemployed politicians, and other talking head wannabes. They collectively comprise what might be termed the guest industry, people trying to promote their organizations, their clients, and, naturally, themselves by sucking up the precious oxygen of airtime.

And it works. The camera performs like a bubbling elixir that with a single gulp can transform the imbiber from policy wonk to Wunderkind. A voluble professor or attorney can ride this sort of self-promotion to national prominence.

"Universities pitch us with their earthquake experts, with their plane crash experts," says Tammy Haddad. During the Persian Gulf War, she and the *Larry King* staff were inundated with "all these faxes from the universities, the PR firms, the book publishers: 'My person spent a week in Iraq.' 'My person flew over Iraq.' "

Neophytes are generally preinterviewed to screen out what Haddad calls "digit heads" and "numbers crunchers." Those who don't make the cut don't get called back. "You can never forget it is television," Haddad says. "They have to be able to explain it in such a way that my mother in Pittsburgh understands what they're talking about . . . If we don't get people interested, they will spin the dial."

It will come as no surprise to regular viewers that most of the talk show experts are white, male, and moderate to conservative. In August 1990, according to the liberal advocacy group Fairness and Accuracy in Reporting, 98 percent of the guests on *Nightline,* and 87 percent of those on *MacNeil/Lehrer,* were white. About nine out of ten were men. Half the American guests were current or former government officials. Such an approach gives a decidedly establishment coloration to these programs, with the likes of Henry Kissinger, Pat Moynihan, and Bob Dole appearing again and again. Producers acknowledge that they lean too heavily on the usual suspects but say that most newsmakers tend to be white men. This is an obvious cop-out, for there is no law requiring that talk show guests be heavyweight officials and ex-officials. It also helps explain why so many of these programs are a snooze and the range of televised debate so frustratingly narrow.

Peter Dykstra, a former spokesman for the environmental group Greenpeace, sees another, more circular reason why some activists have trouble getting on talk shows. "I've been told by several different bookers, by way of suggesting why the person isn't qualified, that they've never seen them on television before," he says.

Stephen Hess exemplifies the modern breed of sound-bite superstar. A political analyst and scholar at the Brookings Institution, an old-line Washington think tank, Hess fields more than a thousand media inquiries a year. I have quoted him many times in *The Washington Post*. He is savvy, concise, centrist, and, best of all for reporters on deadline, returns calls quickly.

A former White House aide in the Eisenhower and Nixon administrations, Hess has come to understand that he is a bit player in the talk show nation. When he first started doing television, "I thought they were really interested in my opinion. I would be very worried—did they use something I had said that was stupid, or controversial, or profound? Then I realized: I was a spear carrier. To have used any of those things would have thrown the story out of kilter. They didn't bring me in to have some profound thought."

Still, the affable Hess makes himself available day after day. "Mostly it's an ego trip . . . it's celebrity," he says. "It's people thinking that somehow you're more worthwhile or significant because you've been on television."

After hundreds of interviews, Hess began to lose patience with producers "who need someone to say 'The sky is blue,' someone else to say 'The sky is green'—and they're sounding you out to see if you think blue or green." He wrote a stinging opinion piece for *The Washington Post* declaring that television news "is increasingly dishonest" because "reporters tend to interview only those who fit a preconceived notion of what the story will be." A few days later, the bookers began calling Hess for interviews again. He had publicly denounced the whole process, and no one cared. Television was still willing to use him, and he was still willing to be used.

When a major story breaks, television experts, like their journalistic counterparts, try to catch the wave. After O. J. Simpson was arrested, lawyers of every persuasion filled the airwaves with analysis and speculation, some on Court TV, some on the networks, many as paid consultants. Former L.A. prosecutor Ira Reiner on NBC. Leslie Abramson (who would later get her own Fox talk show) on ABC. Laurie Levenson on CBS. Greta Van Susteren on CNN. Larry King corraled Gerry Spence (who later got his own CNBC show) and former attorney general Dick Thornburgh. "When I go through the airport, people don't come up to me and say, 'You're the former governor or former attorney general,' but 'I saw you on *Larry King,*'" Thornburgh says. Johnnie Cochran and Alan Dershowitz also worked the TV circuit—before joining Simpson's defense team. (Dershowitz later launched his own radio talk show.) While it's hard to put a price tag on this kind of exposure, some attorneys are convinced that the increased visibility helps them attract high-profile clients.

Victoria Toensing, a former Justice Department official brought in to analyze the Simpson trial on *Rivera Live* and America's Talking, says she enjoys "the adrenaline flow" that comes when "you have to get it up for that half hour." As for the impact on her law practice, she says: "People say they've seen you on TV, but they're never the clients you want. They're the ones who want to talk to you for two hours and then say 'I don't have any money.'"

Greta Van Susteren is the fourth legal commentator—after Gerry Spence, Leslie Abramson, and Alan Dershowitz—to parlay O.J. exposure into her own talk show. She insists her CNN exposure hasn't helped her law firm (although the firm has been accused of improper solicitation for sending brochures with her newly prominent picture to accident victims). And televised fame clearly has its downside: Van Susteren received several threatening phone calls during the Simpson trial. Still, there have been compensations. "I was invited to speak at my Catholic high school," she says with a note of triumph, "where they suspended me in 1971 for buying cigarettes."

Each major news story produces its own talk show stars. After the bombing of the federal building in Oklahoma City, terrorism experts, former FBI officials, disaster consultants, and health specialists flooded the airwaves. Another invasion of high-priced talent occurred during the Persian Gulf War, when a small division of retired military officers stormed the television battlefield. The retirees included General George Crist and General Michael Dugan on CBS, Lieutenant General William Odom on NBC, Admiral William Crowe on ABC, and Major James Blackwell on CNN. Many such experts were wildly off-target with dire predictions that tens of thousands of Americans would be killed or wounded in a ground war against Iraq. But with their ramrod-stiff posture, military jargon, and color-coded war maps, they made for good television.

One of the most aggressive military analysts was retired army colonel William Taylor, vice president of the Center for Strategic and International Studies, a blue-chip, conservative think tank whose advisers include Henry Kissinger and Zbigniew Brzezinski. When Saddam Hussein's tanks rolled into Kuwait, Taylor's phone started ringing. *Today* had him on four mornings in a row, *NBC Nightly News* for three straight nights. He signed consulting contracts with *Good Morning America* and the NBC station in Washington. CNN also tried to enlist Taylor, but he was too busy.

Taylor says he makes the television rounds for the greater glory of CSIS. "There's nothing as important as coming back from *Good Morning America* and, on the elevator, to have a secretary or a vice president say, 'Bill, you were right on. It was terrific.' That's the payoff."

But there is another payoff as well. Taylor gives 175 speeches a year, and while half are for CSIS backers at no cost, he charges up to $10,000 apiece for the rest. Being a television personality doesn't hurt. Steve Hess makes about thirty speeches a year. Many are to academic groups, but he charges trade associations $5,000 a pop.

There is another, lesser-known way to turn routine punditry into positive cash flow. Many American experts charge foreign journalists for TV and radio interviews. "You're talking about private citizens who are selling their time," Hess says. "I don't see any reason why you should do it as a public service."

Walter Laqueur, a foreign policy expert at CSIS, charges fees ranging from $50 for a brief session to $2,000 for a long program. "If I went to the dentist, he wouldn't treat me free of charge," Laqueur says.

For an audience with Norman Ornstein, the oft-quoted analyst at the American Enterprise Institute, the enterprising foreign reporter must pay $300 a session. "If you do an interview with domestic television, there is some mutual value in it," Ornstein says. "You're getting a point of view across, you're getting your name or face out there. It's harder to make that case if you're going on Swiss TV."

Clearly, for journalists and self-appointed experts alike, television is the key to big-bucks success. James Reston was the preeminent reporter and columnist of his generation, but few Americans knew what he looked like. By contrast, the tube has turned John McLaughlin, Larry King, David Brinkley, Cokie Roberts, and Sam Donaldson into bona fide celebrities who can put paying customers in the seats.

But the essence of journalism, even for the fiercest opinion-mongers, is professional detachment. The public has a right to expect that those who pontificate for a living are not in financial cahoots with the industries and lobbies they analyze on the air. Too many reporters and pundits simply have a blind spot on this issue. They have been seduced by the affluence and adulation that comes with television success. They are engaging in drive-by journalism, rushing from television studio to lecture hall with their palms outstretched. Perhaps when they mouth off on television, a caption should appear under their names: PAID $20,000 BY GROUP HEALTH ASSOCIATION OF AMERICA. TOOK $15,000 CHECK FROM AMERICAN MEDICAL ASSOCIATION. The talk show culture has made them rich but, in a very real sense, left them bankrupt.

CHAPTER TEN

THE
RUSH HOUR

Three weeks after the stunning Republican victory in capturing Congress, a triumph in which he had played a key part, Rush Limbaugh found himself in an unaccustomed dilemma.

To be sure, Limbaugh had good reason to celebrate, as he did by playing James Brown's "I Feel Good," turning on his "gloat-o-meter," and describing himself as a "conquering hero." He regaled his audience with tales of how liberals had become the new dinosaurs, fossilized relics of a bygone era. In just six years, Limbaugh had turned himself into the most influential radio personality in the history of the medium, and his message of conservatism had now been dramatically ratified by the 1994 elections. His star had never pulsated more brightly.

But on this particular Wednesday afternoon, as he sat in his corner studio seventeen stories above New York's Penn Station, Limbaugh was getting a bit of flak from some listeners. Most of the self-proclaimed "dittoheads" agreed with him, of course, but some of his conservative fans were upset about the GATT trade agreement. GATT was the hottest issue on talk radio at the moment, with the likes of Pat Buchanan, Ross Perot, and Ralph Nader warning that America would surrender its sovereignty by agreeing that its trade disputes could be resolved by some faraway tribunal.

Limbaugh, a committed free trader, was in favor of GATT, as were his staunch allies, the Republican leaders in Congress. His radio and television shows had refused to sell time to Buchanan and other activists for their anti-GATT ads. He had dismissed Perot's claims about sovereignty as "outrageously untrue." But some callers remained unconvinced. If Congress approved GATT, one woman said, "one hundred and twenty-nine countries will be able to tell us how to conduct our affairs."

This was too much for Limbaugh. "We are predisposed to believe the worst," he said with a touch of exasperation. "We'll believe that without facts. We'll believe there are conspiracies that are at work to destroy the country." A moment later he declared: "I don't want to be in a negative mode."

It was a moment of exquisite irony. Rush Limbaugh, who had spent the previous two years clobbering Clinton and his "Raw Deal," hammering Hillary, dissing Democrats, was now decrying the politics of negativity. He was trying to defuse the kind of half-truths and innuendo that talk radio so often specialized in spreading. He no longer had the luxury of remaining solely on the attack. Now his ideological soul mates, the newly elected conservatives, had to govern.

That Limbaugh had become an appendage of the Republican Party was no longer in dispute. Days later he traveled to a refurbished Baltimore warehouse to address a gathering of seventy-three freshman Republican lawmakers, a partisan pep rally in which praise was heaped upon Limbaugh and he was declared an honorary member. Former representative Vin Weber captured the worshipful tone by announcing: "Rush Limbaugh is really as responsible for what has happened as any individual in America. Talk radio, with you in the lead, is what turned the tide."

There was a time, not so long ago, when Limbaugh scoffed at suggestions that he aspired to some kind of political leadership role. His commentary, he insisted, was nothing more than "shtick."

"I'm not out to save the country," he said in 1989, soon after launching his nationally syndicated radio show. "I'm out to get a large audience. I'm an entertainer first and a conservative second."

"I'm not doing this to reshape America into what I think it should be . . . This is showbiz," he said three years later. "It doesn't influence policy." But the 1992 election, in which he openly embraced President Bush, and his subsequent emergence as a shrill critic of President Clinton, elevated Limbaugh to a loftier platform as talker-in-chief of the opposition party. He began to take himself, and his program, far more seriously. He was no longer merely an entertainer. He began appearing with Ted Koppel on *Nightline,* with Tim Russert on *Meet the Press,* with David Brinkley on *This Week,* with Charlie Rose and Barbara Walters. He had, with his stunning financial success, become part of the dreaded media elite.

Limbaugh's remarkable rise is best understood as a cultural phenomenon. He is above all a satirist, a bombastic speaker with great comic timing, who knows how to rub the raw nerves of American conservative discontent. Again and again, on radio, on television, in his newsletter, and in best-selling books, Limbaugh returns to his central theme: that ordinary, hardworking, God-fearing Americans are being disrespected by the liberal establishment. Ignoring the fact that Republicans controlled the White House, with one four-year interruption, from 1969 through 1992, he depicts a country besieged by left-wing filmmakers, journalists, environmentalists, feminists, gays, vegetarians, spotted-owl lovers, and other assorted wackos. Whether these disparate factions actually wield the kind of power that Limbaugh claims is beside the point. He and millions of dittoheads believe that they do.

Limbaugh filled a previously untapped void for millions of conservatives who felt that the major newspapers, newsmagazines, and networks were speaking a different political language. To be sure, they could watch Pat Buchanan debate Mike Kinsley, or Fred Barnes spar with Eleanor Clift, or Bob Novak needle Mark Shields. But these were quick sound-bite battles in which the liberals generally got equal time. Limbaugh, by contrast, had the microphone to himself for three hours every afternoon. He had time—time to articulate a philosophy, to reassure like-minded listeners, and skewer the left, without contradiction or interruption. He did not bother with guests. He took calls from his loyal listeners and, like Larry King, treated them with respect. He called the men "sir." He was their trusted companion, their friend.

In this politics of cultural resentment, no target loomed larger than the media, which have lavished endless publicity on Limbaugh even as he lambastes them as pillars of the despised liberal order.

Rush, during the '94 campaign: "I predicted the mainstream Beltway press, who are willing accomplices of this administration—

in an effort to resuscitate not just the president but the Democratic Party's fortunes this fall—would do everything they could, pull out all the stops. But I think they shot themselves in the foot when they go around blaming you, blaming the voter. It's just an extension of what liberalism thinks: You are bumbling idiots."

Rush, in a magazine article: "These are the people whose most heartfelt convictions have been dismissed, scorned, and made fun of by the mainstream media."

Rush, on television after the election: "This program has served many purposes. One of them is to sidestep the dominant media elites and to get a version of the news out that may happen to be and in most cases is literally true, but that you never see on mainstream elite newscasts . . . The best way to confront the lies and distortions of the mainstream press is to show you stuff they won't show you."

Rush, on the radio a few days later: "They believe inside the White House that I was cherry-picked by some Republican organization and put on the air. That I have bamboozled you, and gone out there with slick packaging and convinced you of my lies . . . The American people were fed up with the single version of events they were getting from the mainstream elite media. Someone on the air—me—has finally started saying what millions of people have believed all their lives."

Whatever his detractors may say, Limbaugh has reached the pinnacle of success on the strength of his voice and the power of his ideas. And he did it through a medium that many believed had outlived its usefulness. It is not much of an exaggeration to say that Limbaugh single-handedly revived AM radio. He turned many money-losing stations into financial winners and cleared a path for the stampede of conservative hosts that followed in his wake. He is heard on 665 stations, reaching twenty million people over the course of a week. He is more influential than Larry King or John McLaughlin or Dan Rather or Tom Brokaw or Peter Jennings. He defined talk radio in a way that no one ever had before.

On a spring morning in 1994, Rush Limbaugh achieved the singular status of being attacked by the president of the United States.

Bill Clinton had been under assault on talk radio for months, over the Whitewater affair and his faltering health care plan and his wife's commodities trading and a dozen other issues. Limbaugh, as usual, had been leading the charge, opening each show with a refrain about "America held hostage" for whatever the number of days since Clinton had moved into the White House. The president had been boiling over with frustration, and weeks earlier had complained in Atlanta about "Rush Limbaugh and all this right-wing extremist media just pouring venom at us every day."

Now, as he headed for St. Louis on *Air Force One,* Clinton could no longer contain his anger. He told KMOX radio: "Look at how much of talk radio is a constant, unremitting drumbeat of negativism and cynicism . . . After I get off the radio with you today, Rush Limbaugh will have three hours to say whatever he wants, and I won't have any opportunity to respond, and there's no truth detector." It was front-page news everywhere. Limbaugh had truly become "the leader of the opposition," as a *National Review* cover story had dubbed him.

Limbaugh talked about little else for days, and who could blame him? In assailing him by name, Clinton had elevated a noisy critic to the same level as the president. The idea that one guy with a radio show had greater access to the public than the man with the presidential bully pulpit was, of course, absurd, but Clinton obviously felt his message was being drowned out.

In truth, Bill Clinton's election was the best thing that ever happened to Rush Limbaugh. During the Bush years, Limbaugh had become wildly popular for his cultural conservatism, but he did not occupy a central place in the political debate. He would attack the National Organization for Women as a bunch of feminazis. He would assail AIDS activists and homeless advocates. He would denounce abortion as "the modern-day holocaust." He would beat up on such well-worn targets as Ted Kennedy and Jane Fonda. He would say things like "I love the women's movement, especially when I am walking behind it." He was often wickedly funny, although he enraged critics with some of his more tasteless gags. He would attack environmentalists by playing the song "Born Free" to the accompaniment of machine-gun fire, squawks, and squeals. And then there were the "caller abortions," in which Limbaugh would cut short an annoying call by turning on the sound of a vacuum cleaner.

"The shit that hit the fan over that feature was unlike anything I've ever done," Limbaugh says.

Limbaugh was clearly catching on. Restaurants across America were boosting lunchtime business by setting aside special Rush Rooms. But Limbaugh's antics and attacks were not sufficient to make him into a first-rank political player. That would require a presidential campaign.

Like many Republicans, Limbaugh was disenchanted with President Bush, particularly over Bush's abandonment of his no-new-taxes pledge. He found a kindred spirit in Pat Buchanan, who had taken leave from *Crossfire* to challenge the president in the GOP primaries. As Buchanan campaigned in New Hampshire, Limbaugh urged Republicans in the state to vote for him as a protest against Bush. Limbaugh often announced where Buchanan would be appearing, and Buchanan occasionally phoned in to the show. "It was a clear boost for me," says Buchanan, who promised, if elected, to name Limbaugh his communications director.

While Buchanan's candidacy faded after his strong New Hampshire showing, Limbaugh did not immediately gravitate to Bush's corner. Another talk show conservative, Bob Novak, tried to play matchmaker. He wrote in his column with Rowland Evans that Bush "would do well to imitate the style of Rush Limbaugh" and that a top Republican had asked the White House spokesman, Marlin Fitzwater, "to compile a tape of Limbaughisms that the boss might study."

It took another Republican, Roger Ailes, to bring them together. Ailes, a veteran media consultant, had created Bush's harshly negative ad campaign in 1988. He was now easing his way out of politics, although he continued to advise Bush informally, and was planning the launch of Limbaugh's syndicated television show. In June 1992 Bush, Limbaugh, and Ailes had dinner and took in a musical at the Kennedy Center. Limbaugh spent the night in the Lincoln bedroom at the White House—the president insisted on carrying his bags upstairs—and called relatives to brag about where he was sleeping.

This was heady stuff, but Limbaugh seemed worried about the

appearance of being co-opted. He said in a written statement to *The Washington Post* that Bush did "ask me for my views on a few things," but "did not ask me to discuss anything at all on my radio program." And, he added, "I did not ask him to guest on my program." Limbaugh went on the *Today* show, telling Katie Couric that the president was a "genuinely nice guy." And Bush was on the same wavelength, telling a Grand Rapids, Michigan, radio station: "Rush is a very sound man and he's got good, strong conservative principles and, of course, I have a lot of respect for him." Bush later sent him a note, which Limbaugh described as "a thrill."

Limbaugh soon made an exception to his practice of never having guests on the show. He hosted Dan Quayle at his WABC studio in Manhattan. The vice president made a pitch for the boss's reelection, and Limbaugh decried the "malicious" reporting of Quayle's speech attacking television's Murphy Brown for having a baby out of wedlock. Limbaugh increasingly began to ridicule Ross Perot, who was doing well in the polls, calling him "a hand grenade with a bad haircut." When Perot dropped out, Limbaugh took a slap at Larry King for having been "bamboozled" by the Texas billionaire.

The spring courtship turned into a torrid summer romance at the Republican convention. Limbaugh sat in the vice president's box at the Houston Astrodome, at one point arm-in-arm with Marilyn Quayle, as the crowds chanted: "Rush! Rush! Rush!" Limbaugh spent another evening in the Bush family convention box.

Pat Buchanan stopped by Limbaugh's radio show after his controversial convention address. "You are on a high and you should be," Limbaugh said. "That speech was tremendous."

Introduced at a rally by Phyllis Schlafly, Limbaugh told the crowd: "You don't know how you are being savaged. I look at this crowd and see happy, upbeat faces. But according to the media, you are forlorn, you are depressed, you are divided, you are suicidal." When he mentioned Hillary Clinton, a man shouted: "Feminazi!"

The delegates seemed to adore Limbaugh. "He's a gift from God," said a secretary from New York. "When he talks about abortion—I love it when he turns the vacuum cleaner on," said Sarah McDougal, a delegate from Texas.

By the fall, Limbaugh, who had already appeared at several Republican fund-raisers, seemed a full-fledged member of the Bush team. When Mary Matalin, the campaign's political director, caused a stir with an attack fax about Clinton's "bimbo eruptions"—repeating a phrase that had been coined by a Clinton aide—Limbaugh called her. "He was incredibly deferential and respectful . . . I was amazed when he agreed with me," Matalin says. "He understood the hypocrisy immediately."

Limbaugh rushed to Matalin's defense. "The liberal Democrats have been lying about Reagan and Bush in a low-ball, sleazy way for years," he said. "It's about time that stopped and fire was fought with fire." Matalin was so thrilled she made a tape and carried it around with her Walkman.

A few weeks later, Matalin asked Limbaugh if the president could appear on his show, and he again waived his no-guests rule. On September 21 Bush visited Limbaugh at WABC, first stopping by the adjoining studio to greet Bob Grant, a fierce conservative whose program is carried in the New York area. Limbaugh offered Bush a sympathetic ear during the forty-five minute session.

"The first thing I want to bring up is my conviction that people are not rabidly eager for Governor Clinton to be president," Limbaugh said. Under gentle questioning by the host, Bush attacked Clinton's veracity on whether he had dodged the draft, reviving the issue as a front-page story. The partnership was sizzling. On the campaign's final day, Limbaugh appeared with Bush at an election-eve rally in Madison, New Jersey. "I am proud to be able to call him my friend," Limbaugh told the crowd. The president later called Limbaugh from *Air Force One* for an on-air chat. Limbaugh predicted that Bush would win reelection by four to six points.

Despite Limbaugh's enthusiasm, Clinton won the presidency with 43 percent of the vote. Limbaugh was unbowed the following day. Insisting that "there is no mandate," he said: "I was not wrong about anything . . . I did blow the prediction, but let's be honest: I was simply remaining true to my cause."

It was a striking admission for a commentator who likes to describe himself as the source of all truth. Rush Limbaugh was saying that he had predicted a Bush victory, knowing full well it would not happen, simply to be a good Republican soldier. Partisanship, it seemed, was now more important to him than accuracy.

· · ·

For a man who would one day rule radio, Rush Limbaugh sure had trouble holding a job.

The son of a prosperous lawyer in Cape Girardeau, Missouri, Rush Hudson Limbaugh III grew up listening to his father rail against communism and grumble at Walter Cronkite while he delivered the news. A self-described "dork," he spent many nights listening to Harry Caray call the action at St. Louis Cardinals games. Rusty, as he was known, had his own radio show during high school, playing rock music after class at the local station, KGMO. It didn't hurt that the station was partially owned by his father.

Limbaugh dropped out of Southeast Missouri State University in 1970. Like Larry King, he would never earn a college degree. Limbaugh was not drafted for the Vietnam War because he obtained a conditional deferment based on a pilonidal cyst and a football knee injury, circumstances he would later insist were entirely different from the draft avoidance for which he castigated Bill Clinton.

As author Paul Colford has recounted, Limbaugh was fired from a series of rock deejay jobs held under the name "Jeff Christie," when he sported a Fu Manchu mustache. He was canned by WIXZ in McKeesport, Pennsylvania; by KQV in Pittsburgh; by KUDL in Kansas City, and, after just a few weeks, by KFIX in Kansas City. In some cases he had personality conflicts with the station managers. "I was miserable," Limbaugh says. He was, he says, an "abject failure." His radio career seemed over, and in 1979 he became a $12,000-a-year publicist for the Kansas City Royals, hanging out after games with the likes of George Brett.

Five years later, Limbaugh gave radio another shot, signing on with KMBZ, the team's Kansas City outlet. He never registered to vote—even when his hero, Ronald Reagan, was on the ballot—but he was developing a political voice. It was at KMBZ that Limbaugh began to do commentary, stirring controversy by attacking such prominent Democrats as Ted Kennedy and Gary Hart. Management asked him to stifle his political opinions, and he was fired after ten months.

Limbaugh caught a break when Morton Downey Jr. got into trouble at KFBK, a Sacramento talk station. Downey was fired for telling an ethnic joke, and Limbaugh got the job. He gradually built an audience, assailing communism and feminism and honing the mischievious act that would soon carry him to national prominence. He got a brief taste of that prominence in 1986, when he took the show to Washington and chatted with such guests as George Will, Sam Donaldson, and David Brinkley. Things were finally clicking. Even Limbaugh's three hundred-pound frame came in handy as he shed some pounds while serving as a radio spokesman for Nutri/ Systems, the weight-loss program.

In 1988 Limbaugh hooked up with Ed McLaughlin, a former president of ABC radio, who worked out a national syndication deal. Limbaugh would move to New York and be based at all-talk WABC. His salary would be $150,000. McLaughlin told *Newsday*'s Paul Colford that Limbaugh "will be the most-listened-to radio personality in the country—bigger than Larry King, Sally Jessy Raphael, and Tom Snyder." It seemed like a wild boast at the time, for the real action in talk radio was in morning drive time and at night. Midday was a wasteland, filled with canned features and second-rate local acts.

Limbaugh's national show premiered on August 1, 1988, carried by a relative handful of small and medium-sized cities. With his braggadocio about "talent on loan from God" and "the epitome of morality and virtue," Limbaugh quickly got noticed. He was a showman who proved that right-wingers could be funny. Callers began to say "ditto" to signal agreement with his conservative spiel. Limbaugh made no apologies for the careful screening by his assistant, nicknamed Bo Snerdley, that allowed mostly admirers and sycophants on the air. "The purpose of a call is to make me look good . . . There's no right to be boring on my show," he says.

Limbaugh skated along the edges of bad taste, making fun of women with premenstrual syndrome, but on rare occasions he conceded he had crossed the line. He dropped a running bit on AIDS victims after two weeks, saying, "It's the single most regretful thing I've ever done because it ended up making fun of people who were dying . . . It was a totally irresponsible thing to do."

The Rush Limbaugh Show was soon picked up in Washington, Detroit, Chicago, and by 1990 he had two hundred stations. A San Diego station dropped Michael Reagan, the former president's son, in favor of Rush. "Limbaugh was destroying local legends," says Jim Bohannon, the Mutual broadcaster who inherited Larry King's late-night slot. "Many people lost their jobs because Limbaugh came into town by satellite and kicked their butt."

Limbaugh's personal life was in disarray. His second marriage failed after the move to New York. He told a woman he didn't know in an e-mail message on CompuServe that he was "in an interminable funk, no end in sight, listless, uninspired, and self-flagellating." Whatever his mood, his national reputation was growing by leaps and bounds. More than five hundred people paid $1,500 apiece for a weeklong Caribbean cruise on which Limbaugh was the drawing card. Ted Koppel began listening on Washington's WMAL while driving to work, and just before the Persian Gulf War he invited Limbaugh, a proponent of military action against Iraq, to debate Mark Shields on *Nightline*.

"It was clear to me he was going have an enormous impact," Koppel says. "I was one of the first people here to say you've got to pay attention to this guy." Limbaugh later complained that Shields had unfairly alluded to his lack of military service by stressing his own basic training in the Marines.

Tim Russert also became a fan. "I listen to Rush regularly," he says. "He is obviously very smart and has an astute understanding of trends."

But major elements of the media elite remained skeptical. After C-SPAN simulcast Limbaugh's radio show in 1990, Walter Goodman wrote a dismissive review in *The New York Times*. "Mr. Limbaugh is in the business of telling his fans what they want to hear," Goodman said. "There is no conversation worth the word."

The *Times* also ignored Limbaugh's book, *The Way Things Ought to Be,* written with *Wall Street Journal* editorial writer John Fund. The book would sell more than 4.5 million copies in hardcover and paperback, but not until it had spent months on the *Times* bestseller list did the paper deign to publish a review.

"The poor in this country have an average of three television sets in their houses," Limbaugh wrote. "Let's go and get two of them. The poor in this country all have cars. Let's repossess them."

This manifesto struck a chord with certain segments of the country. Of Limbaugh's most loyal listeners, a Times Mirror poll found, 92 percent were white, and 56 percent were men. A third described themselves as evangelicals.

Limbaugh erected yet another pillar of his media empire when he and Roger Ailes launched the nightly television show in 1992. Most critics panned it. The set looked rather cheesy, and the program often featured recycled bits from that day's radio show. But more than two hundred stations picked it up, and in some markets Limbaugh was beating Jay Leno and David Letterman. Other cities, such as Washington, relegated him to 1:00 A.M. oblivion. New York moved him to 2:30 A.M., and Los Angeles bumped the show to 1:00 A.M., giving its previous time slot to reruns of *America's Funniest Home Videos*.

"They call me the most dangerous man in America. Know why? Because I am," Limbaugh announced in his first week on television. Increasingly, his favorite topic was himself. One critic counted Limbaugh making forty-four references to himself in a twenty-two-minute show.

Some of those who admired Limbaugh's radio skills thought he did not come across in front of the camera. "He will not wear well on TV," Ted Koppel says. "He will not be on television five years from now. It doesn't translate."

Even Limbaugh conceded that his television persona was less successful. "I don't think I'll ever like TV as much as radio," he says. "But I enjoy it more than I once did because I feel I've gotten better at it."

By the first year of the Clinton presidency, Limbaugh was basking in the warm embrace of the nation's top Republicans. Ronald Reagan wrote him a note saying: "You have become the number one voice for conservatism in our country." Senate Republican Leader Bob Dole called him "a powerhouse antidote to the liberal cheerleading you hear all the time from the national media." Texas Senator Phil Gramm said the radio host "has had a profound impact on conservative thinking in America." Former education secretary William Bennett, a close friend, declared that Limbaugh "may be the most consequential person in political life at the moment. He is changing the terms of debate."

Just as quickly, Limbaugh became the right-winger that liberals love to hate. Texas columnist Molly Ivins complains that Limbaugh aims his barbs "at powerless people. It's not his humor I object to; it's his targets. Women, children, dead people, the homeless, and animals." *New York Times* columnist Anthony Lewis says Limbaugh's game is "to throw dirt on government and anyone who believes that society needs government . . . He is really trying to destroy public faith in our institutions."

"I listen to Rush," Mort Kondracke says, "and almost every time there's something over the line, that blacks are inferior or Clinton did something truly nefarious . . . There really is something corrosive about some of this stuff."

Some of Limbaugh's radio brethren are equally uncomplimentary. "Talk shows like Limbaugh's appeal to the worst in us—the selfishness, the anger, the fear," Larry King says. And Howard Stern, whose ego rivals Limbaugh's, declared: "This guy is starting to believe his own press, that he's a great political thinker. Rush Limbaugh is a big, fat, uninventive jerk."

Even Sally Jessy Raphael got into the act. When asked to present Limbaugh with a Radio Hall of Fame award at a Chicago convention, she could barely hide her distaste. "He calls women like me feminazis, so I will read this as written for me," Raphael said. "Please note that it does not express my opinion."

But no one could suggest that the former Kansas City deejay was not being taken seriously. David Brinkley, in a Sunday morning interview, asked Limbaugh what he would do as president. When Limbaugh gave a speech in Fort Collins, Colorado, thirty-five thousand people showed up. Limbaugh's line of merchandise was hot, from the $15 golf hat to the $40 sweatshirt to the $79.95 beer stein bearing his likeness. There was grumbling in Democratic circles that perhaps it was time to revive the Fairness Doctrine, the equal-time rule that the Reagan administration had jettisoned in 1987. *The Wall Street Journal* quickly dubbed the idea the Hush Rush Bill.

Limbaugh's political clout had never been greater, but he was losing something as well. He was no longer as funny as in the feminazi days. He was so devoted to bashing Clinton that even liberals who had laughed along with Rush began to find him tedious. Much of the program was now devoted to sober policy analysis of such issues as supply-side economics. Limbaugh admitted as much to the *National Review*. "For the past six months there has been a pretty serious devotion to the Clinton economic plan, and there hasn't been a whole lot of irreverence," he said.

Limbaugh sees another reason for his shift in tone. During the Bush years, he says, "all the liberal groups were panicked and making fools of themselves: the animal rights movement, the homeless, the wacko environmentalists, the feminists." But under Clinton, he says, "they don't make any wild news. They're not funny." Besides, Limbaugh says, he has "a full-time job riding herd" on the Clinton administration.

Few subjects were more serious to Limbaugh than the Whitewater affair, which he believed confirmed his longtime view that the Clintons were conniving liars. The tangled details of the couple's Arkansas finances were obviously fair game for critics. Limbaugh, unfortunately, sometimes strayed beyond the facts. When he got word of the Johnson Smick newsletter account of Vincent Foster's death, he told his listeners: "Brace yourselves. This fax contains information that I have just been told will appear in a newsletter to Morgan Stanley sales personnel this afternoon . . . that claims that Vince Foster was murdered in an apartment owned by Hillary Clinton, and the body was taken to Fort Marcy Park."

Later in the show, Limbaugh refined the account to say "that Vincent Foster committed suicide in an apartment in Washington owned jointly or rented jointly by a number of Arkansas people who came to Washington to serve in the administration, and the body was then moved to Fort Marcy Park . . . The original rumor was that Foster was murdered in this apartment and then moved." Limbaugh said he had talked to a skeptical *New York Post* reporter, "so there are those who disbelieve already the Johnson Smick International report. But that's the big news today."

Limbaugh says he merely passed on the report, "along with a thousand million other people . . . I don't apologize for the way that was handled." He seems to believe he has no personal responsibility if he merely repeats unsubstantiated claims made by others.

On another occasion, Limbaugh picked up on a *New York Post* column about the saga of L. J. Davis, a freelance writer who was investigating Whitewater for *The New Republic*. Davis had said he was rendered unconscious for four hours in a Little Rock hotel room, the clear implication being that he was conked on the head by some nefarious assailant. But Davis, who later admitted downing several martinis before the incident, says he had no evidence he was mugged and that he had "gone on a couple of far-right-wing radio programs to say that this thing was just absolutely out of hand."

But Limbaugh, citing the *Post* piece, declared ominously that "journalists and others working on or involved in Whitewatergate have been mysteriously beaten and harassed in Little Rock. Some have died."

Limbaugh recited the litany: The L. J. Davis incident. A fire on the fourteenth floor of a Little Rock bank that lent money to Clinton's presidential campaign. Vince Foster's "still-mysterious death." The shooting death of Luther Parks, whose Arkansas company provided security for the Clinton campaign. A plane crash that killed an Arkansas lawyer who was a member of Clinton's campaign finance committee. "All this adds up to, of course, is nothing concrete or substantive," Limbaugh allowed, but "there are all kinds of rumors that have popped up in association with these occurrences." And Limbaugh seemed determined to repeat them all.

He got another opportunity when a caller asked about an article in the London *Sunday Telegraph,* a piece so unsubstantiated that almost no American news organization would touch it. The headline, the caller said, was "Clinton Took Cocaine While in Office." The conservative paper quoted anonymous sources as saying that Clinton had used drugs while he was governor of Arkansas.

"Are you upset that I'm not talking about Clinton using drugs in the White House?" Limbaugh asked.

"Yeah," the caller said.

Limbaugh replied that Clinton's policies were far more dangerous than his alleged personal behavior. "I do not know that he is taking drugs in the Oval Office . . . This stuff will all come out in due course," he said. "I don't want to deal here in allegations. I don't want to deal here with those kinds of things that I can't prove and I don't know about criminal behavior." Of course, by repeating the unsubstantiated charges on 665 radio stations, Limbaugh was helping to spread them even as he disclaimed any knowledge of their veracity.

Sometimes Limbaugh seemed carried away with his own importance. "This administration's policies do not, except on programs like mine, receive the kind of scrutiny regularly aimed at me," he said. Did Limbaugh seriously believe that his own utterances were drawing more criticism than, say, the Clinton health plan? Or was this simply more of what he had once termed shtick?

Limbaugh usually seemed confident and in control, but occasionally he would lose his cool. When a caller named Dave complained that Limbaugh was too mean-spirited in his attacks on Clinton, the host shouted: "Dave, shut up! *You shut up!* Take him off the air. It is not mean-spirited, Dave. It is dissent, and done with humor. You are a *bloody fool!* You are an *ass!*"

He had become a fat target, and not just by virtue of his girth. Brian Keliher, a California writer, began to mock him in a publication called the *Flush Rush Quarterly*. Political opponents led a nationwide boycott to protest his hiring as a pitchman for Florida orange juice. Fairness and Accuracy in Reporting compiled a report of Limbaugh errors called "The Way Things Aren't." Some of the items were simply arguments of interpretation or ideology, but in many cases the liberal group had Limbaugh cold.

On the Iran-contra investigation, Limbaugh said: "There is not one indictment. There is not one charge." Fourteen people were indicted in the probe, eleven of whom were convicted or pleaded guilty.

On gas shortages, Limbaugh said: "Those gas lines were a direct result of the foreign oil powers playing tough with us because they didn't fear Jimmy Carter." The first and most serious gas lines occurred in 1973 and 1974, during the Nixon administration.

On the Persian Gulf War, Limbaugh said: "Everybody in the world was aligned with the United States except who? The United States Congress." Both houses of Congress voted to authorize the use of force against Iraq.

On Whitewater, Limbaugh said, "I don't think *The New York Times* has run a story on this yet." The *Times* broke the Whitewater story in 1992 and had run several front-page stories about the case in the weeks before Limbaugh's remark.

That a man who is on the air seventeen and a half hours a week would make occasional misstatements is hardly surprising. But Limbaugh, in a written response weeks later, refused to concede error in most cases and assailed the liberal media for spreading FAIR's propaganda. For example, Limbaugh had said on the air that "banks take the risks in issuing student loans and they are entitled to the profits." In fact, banks take no risks because the loans are federally insured. Rather than admit the mistake, Limbaugh produced a weak statement from an industry representative that banks don't get reimbursed by the feds unless they "have followed a very careful, very detailed, very exacting set of procedures."

Perhaps the most telling example of how half-truths make it onto radio talk shows involved Chelsea Clinton's exclusive private school, Sidwell Friends. Limbaugh had said: "A recent eighth-grade class assignment required students to write a paper on 'Why I Feel Guilty Being White' . . . My source for this story is CBS News. I am not making it up."

He was not. That, however, did not make it true. Limbaugh's source was the *CBS Morning Resource*, a tip sheet for radio hosts that has nothing to do with CBS News, although the confusion was understandable. The tip sheet got the information from *Playboy*. *Playboy* got the information from the *Washington City Paper*, an alternative weekly. The *City Paper* reporter got the information from an unnamed Sidwell Friends parent. After checking back with its source, however, the *City Paper* said it had erred. The essay was titled "Should White People Feel Guilty," and was assigned in the wake of the Los Angeles riots.

Before writing about the FAIR study, I had had two phone conversations with Limbaugh, both friendly. One was an interview for a story on talk radio. The second time, a year later, Limbaugh called me to complain good-naturedly that Ed Koch's ratings in New York were not higher than his, as WABC's general manager had told me for a piece in *The Washington Post*. Limbaugh went on about the ratings formulas for several minutes, so I gather it was important to him.

A few months after the FAIR report, I found myself the object of Limbaugh's wrath. I had written a front-page story about the harsh tone of many of the 1994 campaign ads, quoting Republican consultant Don Sipple as saying that voters "want the meat."

"The meat, in 1994 terms, is rather raw: for the death penalty, longer prison terms, and cutting off welfare benefits; against taxes, immigration, and congressional perks. In devising thirty-second

spots, strategists say, specific issues are far less important than tapping into the electorate's surly mood."

This adjective, for some reason, set Limbaugh off. He talked
about me on the radio. He talked about me on television. And he
talked about me in the *Limbaugh Letter,* his 500,000-circulation
newsletter, in a column appropriately titled "According to Me."
The headline: "ARE YOU SURLY?"

"You in the press . . . let me suggest to you that [people] are
motivated by specific issues," Limbaugh wrote. "They are not surly
because they're uninformed. People are not surly because they're
mean. People are not surly because they don't understand how great
their government is. People are not surly because they're conservative. People are not surly because they listen to the radio . . . It's
real simple. The people of this country are fed up and tired . . . So
you in the press and in politics who think the people in this country
are stupid, realize this: They think you pose the greater threat. They
think it is you in Washington who threaten this country and its
traditions and institutions."

A pretty impressive piece of political rhetoric. It was also a total
straw-man argument. I wasn't "blaming the voters," as the headline
put it. I didn't say that Americans "are stupid." I simply reported
that the blizzard of campaign ads was harshly negative—hardly a
bold or unique observation—and quoted political consultants of
both parties as explaining why. Suddenly I was a threat to American
democracy. Still, I had to chuckle over Rush's tirade. He is, after
all, in the controversy business. He loves a good fight, even if occasionally he has to manufacture one. He will seize any opening that
enables him to beat up on liberals and the press. I guess I should
have been honored to have my article used as talk show fodder.

Two weeks later, I gave Limbaugh one more opportunity to
sound off, but this time I was merely the messenger. I had asked
Paul Begala, the Clinton adviser and Democratic consultant, what
he thought of Limbaugh. His response: "People who listen to the
radio in the morning are normal people. People who listen to Limbaugh in the afternoon are has-been, shut-in malcontents. I don't
pay much attention to right-wing, foam-at-the-mouth radio because
they just talk to each other. It's twenty million people telling each
other how they hate Hillary."

Limbaugh gleefully recited the quotes on the radio that day.

This, he chortled, is what the Democrats think of you. Begala later admitted it had been a dumb thing to say.

Gradually, almost imperceptibly, Rush Limbaugh began to crave a different kind of acceptance. He wanted to be respected at the highest levels of the news business, the very same mainstream liberal press he so fervently denounced on the radio.

And there were signs he was succeeding. ABC, which helped distribute his radio show, asked him to become a television commentator for the network. A major newsmagazine asked him to write a column. He starred in a commercial for *The New York Times*. He appeared on *Donahue*. Ted Koppel had him on *Nightline* for the third time, and David Brinkley allowed him to join his celebrated roundtable. Limbaugh toned down his act on these occasions, acting as polite and well mannered as the other network pundits.

He came to value his relationship with these high priests of talk. When Simon and Schuster put a blurb on his second book quoting "no less a liberal than Ted Koppel" praising Limbaugh as a conservative "icon," the radio host quickly called Koppel to apologize for the ideological description.

Soon the shoe was on the other foot. In the summer of 1994, Limbaugh complained on the radio that he had been quoted out of context in a *Nightline* story. He had a legitimate beef. In a taped piece about the Whitewater probe, correspondent John Martin said that "in the background was a darker charge, fed by radio talk show hosts and televangelists. There were rumors of possible criminal activities." The program used a clip of Limbaugh saying: "People are dropping like flies." But Limbaugh was referring to all the administration officials who had been hit with subpoenas. *Nightline* made it sound as if he were referring to the series of deaths that Jerry Falwell and some fringe characters were trying to link to the Clintons. Limbaugh had raised that issue once or twice, but he clearly had not embraced it.

When Koppel heard of Limbaugh's complaint, he called to apologize. A producer, he explained, had added the sound bite at the last minute. There seemed to be no hard feelings.

But Limbaugh soon decided that ABC had it in for him. Two

other incidents had gotten under his rather thin skin. On the radio one Thursday afternoon, he exploded. He said there had been "three blatant assaults on the integrity of this program, and of you, your honesty, your integrity, your character." He said he had even called Tom Murphy, the chairman of Capital Cities/ABC, to complain.

First Limbaugh recounted the *Nightline* incident. "Ted Koppel said to me on the phone, 'I knew the minute we played it that it was wrong . . . and you have my personal apology, you have my utmost, profound apology for doing this . . . If you want to rip me a new one, feel free to go ahead and do it.' Which I didn't do. I just accepted his apology and that's that." Still, Limbaugh said, "It was as big an error as one can make."

The second complaint was laughably thin. ABC's *World News Tonight* had run an "American Agenda" segment on talk radio and its impact on the debate over health care reform. Limbaugh had refused to cooperate, and now he was outraged at the result. He called the report a "hit piece" that "attempted to position me as the symbol, the champion, the essence of talk show misinformation. This was an entire effort to discredit talk radio with me as the monster head of it . . . The reporter, Tom Foreman, got several important things wrong. If you're ever watching ABC News, any ABC News program where a report is done by Tom Foreman, you should be immediately suspect, or suspicious of the facts purportedly contained in it."

And what were Foreman's sins? First, he said that Limbaugh was on "more than 500" stations, when the figure was 660, and that "listeners tune in every day," when Limbaugh is only on Monday through Friday. Second, Limbaugh was quoted as saying that the Medicare program is "running ten times the cost of projections," while a health policy expert said the actual figure is seven times projections. There are studies backing up Limbaugh's estimate, but the gap was hardly so wide as to warrant such a fierce denunciation.

Foreman also reported that "liberal talk shows . . . play fast and loose with the facts," but Limbaugh was not mollified. He turned the report into a scathing indictment of the media—which had grown quite critical of the ailing Clinton health plan—and, in his favorite formulation, an attack on Limbaugh's listeners.

"Isn't it true for the most part that what *World News Tonight* is upset about is that there is opposition to this plan, and they have sought to cast aspersions on those who oppose it, but they do not seem to cast the same aspersions on those who support it? . . . Talk radio itself was being castigated, and you, its listeners, as being negative, uninformed, willing to accept falsehood, lie, and untruth unquestioningly . . . They have to discredit you because of your increasing numbers . . . ABC News set themselves up as the arbiter of truth . . . Have any of you at ABC ever heard of the First Amendment? . . . . What is it you people are so afraid of? The administration you love so much is in trouble? . . . . You call yourself a reporter . . . How do you expect to have any credibility, Mr. Foreman?"

Rush was just warming up. The final insult had come from a new ABC comedy program, *She-TV*. In a scathing parody of Limbaugh, actor Nick Bakay lumbered onto a mock TV set filled with Limbaugh books. While he had mellowed, the faux Limbaugh announced, "I still hate the Clintons and black people." This was irrefutable evidence of ABC's vendetta against him.

"I'm not standing for it any longer . . . What we are in the process of doing is attempting to find out if this statement in this parody is the official position of the ABC network . . . or if it is simply just a statement made by a left-wing writer on the show which happened to get past the network censors. I have instructed my legal team to get a copy of the show for review and to demand an apology and/or a retraction . . .

"I would consider [my] program to be one of the most beneficial things a black American could be exposed to . . . The producers of this show should apologize . . . ABC is a publicly held company. They have many stockholders, and it is not wise of them to anger such a large segment of the population on these kinds of grounds. Twenty million people not watching ABC. Twenty million people not watching ABC *World News Tonight*. *Good Morning America*. *Nightline*. That makes a difference. I'm not telling you what to do. I'm telling you what I'm going to do. And that is, I'm going to choose some other venue when I seek information or entertainment until such time as somebody comes forth and apologizes and sees to it it doesn't happen again."

Whew. Over the course of an hour, Limbaugh had worked himself into a lather and managed to suggest that his listeners might want to consider a boycott of ABC. He was perfectly justified in complaining that *She-TV* had unfairly ridiculed him as a racist; there is no evidence that he has ever uttered racist remarks. But it was a parody, a piece of broad satire that, while it undoubtedly crossed the boundary of fair play, was intended as humor. This, after all, was the same man who had done the vacuum-cleaner abortions, who had made fun of feminazis, who had mocked the Clintons, who had even spoken of speculation of a possible link between the White House and a series of murders. What's more, he was lumping Ted Koppel's news program in with the Hollywood writers at *She-TV*.

Koppel was not pleased. Colleagues say he wrote Limbaugh a stinging personal note, saying it was simply unfair for him to accept Koppel's regrets for an inadvertent error and then denounce him on the air as part of some network conspiracy. Limbaugh backed down immediately, *Nightline* staffers say, writing Koppel a long, effusive letter of apology.

Friends concede that Limbaugh is supersensitive about the way he is portrayed in the media, that he feels he has not gotten his due. "He is not Howard Stern," says Mary Matalin, who talks to Limbaugh regularly. "He is not a shock jock. He saved AM radio. He's studied the issues in a very serious, very methodical way. His is a legitimate conservative voice. He's more influential than other conservative voices, and yet he's the one most regularly maligned. He thinks he is more often treated with scorn and categorized with the nutcakes like Gordon Liddy."

But Larry King sees Limbaugh's attacks on media figures as "contrived." The CNN host laughed it off when Limbaugh falsely accused King of having called him a "racist," when all King had done was tell Colin Powell on the air that everyone seemed to love him except Rush Limbaugh. "He comes to the broadcast with an agenda," King says. "Agenda broadcasters will do anything. They'll lie, they'll fabricate, to keep an agenda going."

Limbaugh's ambivalent relationship with the nation's media heavies soon became a pattern. When *Time* was preparing a cover story on him, Limbaugh, who had stopped doing interviews, reluctantly agreed to have dinner at Patsy's, one of his favorite New

York restaurants, with Margaret Carlson. They had a desultory conversation over shrimp and wine. Then Limbaugh went on the air before the piece was published and criticized Carlson, saying she was soft on the Democrats and had actually had the audacity to try to get him to criticize Newt Gingrich. He had gotten it both ways: a *Time* cover piece and the chance to assail the *Time* columnist, on his own terms, behind the mike, where he felt most comfortable.

Limbaugh had it both ways in other realms as well. He could position himself as an avatar of Christian virtues, and no one questioned the fact that he didn't go to church. He could chastise Bill Clinton as a draft dodger and counterculture figure, and few questioned his own military deferment or his own youthful experimentation with marijuana. He could wax eloquently about the sanctity of the family—"Marriage has been devalued in this country," he said —and hardly anyone raised the fact that he had been divorced twice.

In 1994 Limbaugh got married for the third time, to a former aerobics instructor from Florida who had sent him a message on the CompuServe network. The wedding took place at the home of Supreme Court Justice Clarence Thomas, who officiated. Despite Limbaugh's paeans to family values, his wife's children did not come to live with them, and he remained uncertain about having kids of his own.

Still, Limbaugh had all the trappings of success. He and his new bride bought a $5 million apartment on Fifth Avenue (and got into the inevitable spat with the decorator). There were weekends in Florida and golfing vacations in Hawaii and out-of-town football games. For the most part, though, Limbaugh tried to stick to the daily regimen he had followed when he first launched the national show on WABC. He still got by on five hours' sleep, rising at 7:30 to read *The New York Times, The Washington Post*, the *New York Post*, the *Daily News, Newsday, USA Today*, and *The Wall Street Journal*. While he now had a staff to help with his research, he did not want to tamper with the formula that had propelled him to the top. Still, even for a man in love with the sound of his resonant voice, there was the fatigue factor, the relentlessness of being Rush.

"The days where it's not as much fun has to do with the routine," he says. "You've got to be there every day at the same time. You have to be imbued with the desire to shout at the world what you think. There are some days I don't care. But you've got to do it anyway. I try to make sure that I don't get too distorted a view of who I am. I'm just a radio and television talk show host who has the freedom to be myself and say the things I believe."

Inevitably, some listeners wondered whether Limbaugh was losing touch, whether he now identified more with the Ted Koppels and David Brinkleys of the world. One day it was a caller from Texas. "The guy said, 'Rush, you used to be one of us, pal, but you don't know America anymore. You've had a lot of success. You have a lot of money.' . . . I said, I think you're dead wrong. I think I'm the epitome of what this country is about. I've seen life from every financial angle. I've been out of work seven or eight times. What happened to me is an example of what can happen in America."

But Limbaugh could not shake all the old insecurities. Perhaps he would not be on top forever. "You think it could end every day," he says. "This could all be over tomorrow, and it will be someday."

In the wake of the '94 elections, Rush Limbaugh was clearly relishing the Republican sweep. "This is good stuff, folks," he said. "Every day brings us more pleasure."

No one brought Limbaugh as much pleasure as Newt Gingrich, the conservative firebrand who was now the House speaker. They had been friendly for several years, chatting by phone and hanging out together at the '92 convention. Limbaugh's Washington researcher, Joel Rosenberg, had done lunch with Gingrich's press secretary, Tony Blankley, who would call every few days when an issue was hot. Gingrich sent Limbaugh faxes on his legislative strategy, and Limbaugh often took up the cause. Now, at the moment of Republican victory, they had formed a mutual admiration society.

Limbaugh called Gingrich "rock solid, decisive, committed, unwavering," one of the "great leaders" in history. And Gingrich acknowledged "a very close symbiotic relationship" between Limbaugh and the Republican leaders.

"Rush has made it significantly more expensive to be liberal and significantly easier to be conservative . . . He does for conservatives what NPR does for liberals," Gingrich says.

If the press dared to criticize "Mr. Newt," as Limbaugh called him, he would set the record straight. On one show, Limbaugh said: "Some media research people have done a definitive study and they found out that the negative coverage that Newt Gingrich has received in the dominant media is 100 percent. There has not been one favorable or even neutral story about Newt Gingrich. Every story has been negative, every story has been slash and burn."

Limbaugh was again overstating the case. The study, done by the Center for Media and Public Affairs, indeed found that 100 percent of the comments made about Gingrich had been negative—a truly horrendous record—but it examined only the Big Three network evening newscasts for a seven-week period during the campaign. It did not include newspapers, newsmagazines, other networks, or even other shows on CBS, NBC, and ABC.

But Limbaugh was just warming up. He showed a clip of Gingrich recounting how he had been driving with his wife in South Carolina, listening to Rush talk about him and then calling into the show to chat. Gingrich then learned that two fellow GOP lawmakers, Robert Michel and Connie Mack, had been listening to the same show. Mack promptly called Gingrich with some words of advice: "Be bold and be decisive."

"And he is!" Limbaugh declared as the videotape ended.

Soon Limbaugh was complaining about press attacks on Gingrich. He even defended the $4.5 million book deal that Gingrich signed before becoming speaker, which the congressman himself later acknowledged was a mistake. "You know, all this stuff they're hitting him with is personal . . . It's being done with a vindictiveness and a meanness to discredit Newt on the issues," Limbaugh said. "I'm just saying the same bunch did not ever engage in this same sort of stuff with Clinton." This assertion was nothing short of remarkable, since the press had been filled with stories about Clinton's love life, draft record, and marijuana use since the 1992 campaign, and Limbaugh had not been shy about mentioning Gennifer Flowers and Paula Jones.

In the spring of 1995 Limbaugh and Gingrich spent a weekend together in Florida at the estate of a wealthy Gingrich supporter. A few months later Limbaugh told his listeners: "I just had an hour and a half meeting with Mr. Newt in my office. They're on track, and he's very confident about the future." The friendship was growing closer.

On rare occasions Limbaugh found himself out of step with the new leadership. He repeatedly argued that a balanced budget amendment to the Constitution would be "worthless" unless it contained a provision requiring a three-fifths vote to raise taxes. The morning after the House passed the amendment without such a provision, Limbaugh changed his tune. "Mr. Newt" had called him shortly before the program, Limbaugh said, and explained that he had promised the Republican freshmen a vote on the three-fifths rule the following year. It was a garden-variety political fig leaf, but Limbaugh now pronounced himself satisfied.

By the time the amendment reached the Senate, Limbaugh was openly serving as a mouthpiece for the GOP leadership. He was fed the line of the day as if he were a press secretary. When Bob Dole, the majority leader, had to delay a scheduled vote because he could not muster the required two-thirds majority, he gave Limbaugh the proper spin. "I got a phone call this morning from Senator Dole," Limbaugh told his listeners. "He said, I have delayed the vote so the American people can be heard . . . You know what that means." Limbaugh dismissed Senate Democratic Leader Tom Daschle as "a babbling five-year-old." Despite the implicit invitation to flood the Capitol with angry calls, the amendment was defeated two days later by a single vote. The Democrats had clouded the issue by charging that the amendment posed a threat to Social Security. Talk radio seemed to have lost a bit of its resonance in the new Republican era.

During this period, Limbaugh also grew close to Bill Bennett, the former education secretary and conservative author. Limbaugh joined a secret strategy session with Bennett, Bill Kristol, and others at Washington's Four Seasons Hotel in an effort to persuade Bennett to run for president in 1996. Limbaugh was no longer just commenting on Republican affairs; he was at the table.

Should anyone suggest that he is carrying the party's water, Limbaugh offers a simple explanation: "It has never been the express purpose of this program to criticize Republicans, and I have never hidden this fact . . . I am on their side. I am a Republican . . . I clearly come to you each day and tell you what my bias is, and I admit that I have one."

Limbaugh deserves full credit for this kind of honesty. But by declaring himself an unofficial spokesman for one political party, he has narrowed his range as a social commentator. Among the true believers, the millions who tune in each day, this matters little. But for those who are merely open to persuasion, Limbaugh has placed himself in a position where a partisan agenda seems to matter more than an unflinching social and political critique.

However biased the mainstream media might be—and even Newt Gingrich agrees that the press has given Bill Clinton a hard time—it pales in comparison to Limbaugh's acknowledged role as a party propagandist. Did Republicans never screw up, never do anything dumb? In Rush's world, they were as protected a species as the spotted owl, virtually immune from jest or criticism. It was as if Jack Germond or Michael Kinsley had resolved never to utter a negative word about any Democrat.

Rush Limbaugh remains a cultural phenomenon. He is a celebrity with the first-name fame of Cher or Madonna and inspires an even greater degree of passion in his fans. By early 1995, a Harris poll showed that 5 percent of Republicans supported Limbaugh for president, placing him ahead of Newt Gingrich, James Baker, Lamar Alexander, and Dick Cheney. Limbaugh dismissed any talk of running for office, but some of his admirers clearly saw him as far more than just an entertainer. He was, in their eyes, a moral leader.

"Liberals fear me," Limbaugh says, "because I threaten their control of the debate . . . I have not attracted and kept my audience by being a blowhard, a racist, a sexist, a hatemonger . . . If I were truly what my critics claim, I would have long ago, deservedly, gone into oblivion." On that score, he is right. Limbaugh had the intellectual firepower and the marketing genius to build a massive following from scratch, tapping into the disdain that conservatives feel toward the major media outlets. There can be no liberal Limbaugh because there is no comparable hunger on the left for alternative sources of information. Limbaugh fills a need that most of the press didn't even realize existed. In his larger-than-life way he personifies the potential, and the pitfalls, of talk radio.

But it is also clear that the Republican takeover of Congress has been a mixed blessing for Limbaugh. It is simply more fun to be on the offense, to skewer the opposition, than to defend incumbents and deal with the messy realities of governing. And Limbaugh's personal situation had changed in ways that could no longer be ignored. When one of his callers took a swipe at David Brinkley, Limbaugh quickly insisted that Brinkley was not such a bad fellow. Left unspoken was that the veteran newsman had hosted Limbaugh on his prestigious program. Rush Limbaugh's extraordinary success was making it harder to maintain the pose of angry outsider.

"All of these rich guys," Limbaugh declared on the radio, "like the Kennedy family and Perot, pretending to live just like we do and pretending to understand our trials and tribulations and pretending to represent us, and they get away with this." It was a line that would have had a bit more resonance from a man who wasn't making $25 million a year.

CHAPTER ELEVEN

RADIO REBELS

I n March 1992 a dozen of Bill Clinton's strategists gathered in a Chicago hotel room to figure out how their candidate could deal with the voracious New York press that was certain to carve him up in the next major primary.

The answer, they decided, was Imus.

A craggy-faced curmudgeon who had been insulting people on the radio for twenty-five years, Don Imus was little known outside the New York area. But his sharp-edged satire had a strong following at home, and local politicians regularly vied for the privilege of being abused by him.

"I knew people listened to Imus in the morning and talked about it at lunch and around the water cooler," says Mandy Grunwald, the Manhattan native who was part of Clinton's media team. "Since Imus was mocking Clinton and calling him Bubba, to go on and prove you could dish it out and take it would be the kind of thing New Yorkers would admire."

In a strange initiation rite into talk show politics, the Arkansas governor traded barbs with Imus—who admitted the "redneck bozo" had a sense of humor—and went on to win the New York primary, essentially clinching the presidential nomination.

Three years later, Alfonse D'Amato, the brash New York senator with a gift for blabbing his way into trouble, made one of his regular appearances on *Imus in the Morning*. He was one of the program's favorite guests because, as Imus put it, "he'll say anything." Caught up in the show's freewheeling spirit, D'Amato launched into a joking tirade against "little Judge Ito . . . making a disgrace of the judicial system," delivered in a mocking Japanese accent.

"Senator, let me stop you before you wind up on the front page of the *Daily News* again," Imus warned. It was too late. Asian Americans were furious. What had sounded merely silly on the radio was a jarring ethnic insult in the real world. "NO JOKE," declared the *Daily News* banner headline. "EVEN TOO MUCH FOR IMUS," *Newsday* blared, as if that defined some new standard of outrageousness. *The New York Times* and *The Washington Post* denounced D'Amato in stinging editorials. A terse apology failed to quiet the storm. Imus reveled in the controversy but felt compelled to defend the senator as "a good person," even if he was "a wack job."

The two incidents underscored the promise and the shortcomings of talk radio as it became hardwired into the culture of American politics. The most valued currency on the airwaves seemed to be sheer outrageousness, a talent for pushing the acceptable boundaries of humor or anger or personal diatribe. The strange and sudden importance of Imus, a former freight-train brakeman on the Southern Pacific, paralleled the explosive growth of the medium itself.

Imus makes light of the notion that he wields any great influence, that he is engaged in anything more than making people laugh. "The whole purpose of the show is to goad people into saying hideously inappropriate things that they regret as soon as they hang up," he says. In D'Amato's case, at least, he had succeeded.

But many other hosts are deadly serious about using the airwaves for personal and political ends, and their success has been nothing short of remarkable. The rise of talk radio—from three hundred news/talk stations in the late '80s to more than a thousand in the mid-'90s—has revolutionized the way millions of Americans get information and opinions about public issues. Talk is now the most popular format after country music, drawing about 15 percent of the radio audience. From Boston to Butte, commentators, shock jocks, morning-zoo zanies, interviewers, ideologues, ex-pols, ex-felons, satirists, and schmoozers are spewing all manner of data and diatribe. They have broken the monopoly of the major media in ways that, at bottom, are healthy for public debate.

But with all this chat has come a litany of questions about the rights and responsibilities of those who control the airwaves. Do they have a duty to correct misinformation, to air dissenting views, to give those who are attacked a chance to respond? I strongly believe they do, but that is not the prevailing view. Many programs have settled on an anything-goes approach, leaving it to listeners to separate the rhetorical wheat from the chaff. The notion that obvious untruths or unproven gossip should not be disseminated over the airwaves is derided as an attempt at censorship. Talk radio, it seems, does not play by the everyday rules of journalism.

Even worse, the fringes of the radio spectrum have become a common carrier for hate and invective. Unlike television, which must seek mass acceptability, radio can indulge hosts who spew racist or anti-Semitic or simply mean sentiments, in part because "narrowcasting"—reaching, say, 10 percent of the audience—is a successful radio strategy. Many station managers and advertisers simply look the other way when certain hosts, and their listeners, give voice to the rawest kind of prejudice. And no group has a monopoly: There are white hosts who denounce blacks as criminals, while some black commentators heap abuse on whites as oppressors.

Despite these excesses, diversity remains radio's greatest strength. It is a medium that encourages the offbeat and the eccentric. Satire of the most politically incorrect ilk thrives on the airwaves. The range of opinion is immensely more varied than on television, where most commentary comes with the rough edges sanded away. Politically, talk jocks run the gamut from Jim Hightower, the left-wing Texas populist, to Beverly LaHaye, the pro-life Christian conservative. Stylistically, they range from Michael Jackson, the gentlemanly Brit in Los Angeles, to Howard Stern, Long Island's king of raunch. Even National Public Radio, where some officials balked at turning over the precious airwaves to unknown listeners, fields a daily *Talk of the Nation,* with Ray Suarez fielding calls from a mostly upscale audience. Within the thriving subculture of black radio, the offerings range from the anti-white invective sometimes served up on New York's WLIB to such staunch black conservatives as Washington's Armstrong Williams, a former aide

to Senator Strom Thurmond, and Denver's Ken Hamblin, sometimes known as the "black Rush Limbaugh." In between are such
colorful characters as G. Gordon Liddy, the onetime Watergate
burglar, and Curtis Sliwa, the former Guardian Angel.

In a world of e-mail, fax attacks, and pay-per-view, radio seems
rather low-tech, a quaint throwback to the days of transistor tubes.
But it has become the perfect medium for an on-the-go audience,
allowing folks to tune in while driving the carpool or sitting at their
desks or skimming a magazine. The power of words, unadorned by
flashy videotape or computer graphics, retains a surprising hold on
the imagination. One survey found that more than half of Americans
listen to at least one hour of talk radio each week.

Radio is at once a form of entertainment, an educational vehicle
and a political organizing tool. But it functions especially well as a
megaphone for conservatives who feel shut out by the likes of ABC,
CBS, and NBC. It is no accident that 70 percent of talk radio hosts
dwell on the right side of the spectrum. Nor is it a coincidence that
80 percent of the hosts, and most of the callers, are men. Many
women feel less comfortable holding forth on the air, and that has
made the medium fertile ground for the stereotypical angry white
male.

Once relegated to the fringes of the media world, talk radio in
the Age of Rush is a vibrant force of considerable potency. While it
amplifies the grievances of the disaffected in quadrophonic sound,
its crackling airwaves also serve as an early-warning radar for public
discontent. Now that talk radio is believed capable of sinking legislation and toppling public officials, its influence has been chronicled
on the covers of *Time* and *Newsweek,* surveyed by the *Los Angeles
Times* and certified on the front page of *The New York Times.*

"Talk radio has allowed the rest of America to penetrate inside
the Beltway," says Bill Kristol, who often makes use of the medium.
"It's thrown open the mores of Washington to national public in-
spection."

Given the medium's range from savagery to silliness, it's not
surprising that some radio folks don't think much of their brethren.
Michael Jackson says much of the medium has become "cheap"
and "utterly trite." David Brudnoy, a gay conservative in Boston,
derides many hosts as "opportunistic twits."

Others say the media hype has gone too far. "The idea that a few talk show hosts have led a revolution, storming the gates of power, is beyond an exaggeration," says Jim Bohannon, whose late-night show is carried on four hundred stations. "It's just not true. The only thing it did is crystallize the discontent. To be perfectly honest and elitist about it, if you listen to a talk station, you're probably better educated, higher income. Most people don't know about this stuff like GATT. They listen to music."

Those who listen to talk are, almost by definition, more passionate about issues, more activist, more likely to call their congressman about a hot controversy. Like the C-SPAN audience, talk radio fans are on the front lines of public debate, giving them a level of clout that exceeds their raw numbers. What is less clear is whether professional radio loudmouths are whipping them into a frenzy or simply tapping into existing public frustration.

"The only influence the host has is if you're an effective communicator, you say things in a way that draws people to you," says Mike Siegel, the high-profile host in Seattle. Siegel rarely talks about the fact that he is pro-choice, for example, because much of his audience is strongly opposed to abortion. "I don't want to spend three hours a day defending myself," he says.

Michael Harrison, who edits the industry magazine *Talkers,* likens the question to whether a disc jockey can turn a lousy song into a hit simply by playing it over and over.

"If a talk show host goes on the radio and begins to bang the table and tries to drum up cynicism on any particular issue, if it isn't real, if it doesn't resonate with a significant amount of public opinion, people will turn that talk show host off," he says. "I see all the Rush Limbaugh wannabes go down the drain. I see all the Howard Stern and Don Imus and G. Gordon Liddy wannabes who don't have it . . . Even the biggest of them, even Rush Limbaugh can evolve in the next year or two into one of the biggest buffoons this nation has ever seen if he doesn't get control over the change in the wind out there."

To be sure, radio talk shows are hardly a new phenomenon. But, like Imus, they are resonating with a growing audience. When Diane Rehm began her program on Washington's WAMU, a National Public Radio station, in 1979, she talked mainly about investments, personal health, vegetarianism, books, movies, life in outer space, and how to find a good doctor. Now she spends much of her time dissecting political issues with the help of journalists, political analysts, White House officials, and members of Congress. Rehm's audience has grown tenfold, to well over one hundred thousand, in the process, and counts Hillary Clinton among her fans.

A platinum-blonde moderator with a whispery voice, Rehm is an outspoken critic of radio hosts who allow the airing of unsubstantiated allegations. When a caller from Richmond, Virginia, told Rehm he had some information on Vince Foster's death, she quickly asked: "Are you giving me fact or are you giving me one more rumor to add to the mill?"

"I don't have any proof for this, but I think your listeners ought to know it," the caller replied.

Rehm objected again. "I think I have a right to say this on the air," the man insisted.

"Not on my program you don't," she said, dumping the call.

In an era when people make all kinds of outrageous comments on the radio, it is rather unusual for a listener to be denied the opportunity to vent. So unusual, in fact, that when Rehm recounted the tale at a media forum, Michael Harrison took umbrage.

"You set yourself up as the judge and jury of which rumors people can hear," Harrison declared.

"I have the obligation not to further air unsubstantiated rumors," Rehm shot back.

Harrison was not persuaded. "There's nothing wrong with people having access," he argued. "There's nothing wrong with the potential for misinformation and inaccuracy to be part of that message. The mainstream press has been doing that for years."

Even by the increasingly coarse standards of modern politics, talk radio has more than its share of nastiness.

In Los Angeles, Emiliano Limon of KFI says: "If homeless people cannot survive on their own, why shouldn't they be put to sleep?" He calls the homeless "a burden" and "a waste of space" and says they should be shipped to desert camps.

In New York, Bob Grant of WABC says: "We have in our city,

we have in our state of New York, we have in our nation, not hundreds of thousands but millions of sub-humanoids, savages, who really would feel more at home careening along the sands of the Kalahari or the dry deserts of eastern Kenya—people who, for whatever reason, have not become civilized."

In Washington, Julianne Malveaux of Pacifica says of Supreme Court Justice Clarence Thomas: "I hope his wife feeds him lots of eggs and butter and he dies early like many black men do, of heart disease . . . He is an absolutely reprehensible person."

In Colorado Springs, Chuck Baker of KVOR says of the attorney general: "We ought to slap Janet Reno across the face . . . [and] send her back to Florida where she can live with her relatives, the gators."

In Atlanta, Neal Boortz of WSB says: "The most dangerous humans on the face of the earth are young urban black males . . . If you should shoot one in your pawnshop, you should be able to use white fear as a legitimate defense."

In Fairfax, Virginia, G. Gordon Liddy of WJFK says: "I and my family and friends were out firing away at a properly constructed rifle range with what the newspeople insist on calling assault weapons . . . I drew some stick-figure targets and I thought we ought to give them names, so I named them Bill and Hillary. I thought it would improve my aim."

In Phoenix, Bob Mohan of KFYI says that gun-control advocate Sarah Brady "ought to be put down. A humane shot at a veterinarian's would be an easy way to do it . . . I wish she would just keep wheeling her husband around to go to speaking engagements—wiping the saliva off his mouth once in a while—and leave the rest of us damn well alone."

In San Francisco, J. Paul Emerson of KSFO says: "Everybody in California who's a taxpayer and an American can be a bounty hunter, can go out there and shoot illegal immigrants who come across the border."

Under the First Amendment, all of this ranting is constitutionally protected opinion. But it is also exceedingly ugly. And it is clear that station owners and managers have tolerated it because vicious personal attacks and extremist views help attract an audience. That's why Morton Downey Jr., having failed on daytime television, was able to revive himself as a talk radio host in Washington and Dallas, referring to one caller as an "ugly bitch," another as a "piece of dreck" and once using the word "asshole" on the air.

Chuck Baker, who sometimes broadcasts from a gun shop, defends the right of citizens to mount an "armed revolution." He punctuated his show with the sound of a gun being cocked, at least until his boss ordered him to tone things down.

"The problem we have right now is who do we shoot," a caller told Baker. ". . . You've got to get your ammo . . . We cannot do it as individuals, we have got to do it as an orchestrated militia." Chuck Baker did not utter a word of disapproval.

Baker briefly took himself off the air in 1994 after newspaper reports suggested a link between his program and a Colorado Springs man, Francisco Duran, who fired several rounds of ammunition at the White House. Baker said he could not be held responsible for violence committed by "the jerk, the wacko, the creep, this piece of crap that shot the White House."

It would not be the first time that radio has incited violence. Alan Berg, a liberal Jewish radio host in Denver, was shot to death in 1984 by a neo-Nazi.

On shows like Baker's, it is often the callers and guests who spread the vitriol. On KPFK, a left-wing Pacifica station in Los Angeles where Jews have occasionally been blamed for slavery, a caller said: "The Jews haven't seen anything yet. What is going to happen to them is going to make what Hitler did seem like a party." On another show, Steve Cokely, who once worked for former Chicago mayor Harold Washington, said that Jewish doctors had invented the AIDS virus to kill black babies.

On Boston's WRKO, one caller told liberal host Marjorie Clapprood: "You would vote for Hitler if he were a Democrat!"

"You Republicans have cornered the market on all the Hitlers," Clapprood responded.

Clearly, some listeners do not place a premium on tolerance. When Joann Rossall of Snohomish, Washington, sent a letter to *USA Today* criticizing talk radio for stirring up hatred, she was assailed by Michael Reagan, the former president's son, on his Los Angeles show. "I was swamped by hate calls, including six that were actual, violent threats," she says.

Larry Elder, a black conserative in Los Angeles, says that when he first launched his show, "I was called Uncle Tom, ass-kisser, Jew-lover, boot-licker, and house Negro, although the word *Negro* wasn't used."

For better and for worse, radio provides an outlet for those who feel shut out of the mainstream. In 1994, on a day when most of Washington was in mourning for a police officer and two FBI agents who had been gunned down at police headquarters, the tone was very different on WOL, the city's black station ("where information is power"). Despite the tragic deaths, the callers had little sympathy for police.

"The average person on the street gets treated badly by police officers because they have an us-and-them mentality . . . It's happened to me personally," one said.

Another caller wondered what all the fuss was about: "There are people being killed out on the street every day. They're law-abiding citizens . . . Law enforcement is not an occupation you can seriously be proud of."

On another day, Cathy Hughes, the station's owner and most popular host, complained that Hispanics have "taken over" parts of Washington. She said that in some buildings "Hispanic families . . . are sleeping four to five to an apartment, families to an apartment, and putting the mattresses in the hallways . . . The housing inspectors are looking the other way . . . There have been several terrible car accidents involving Hispanics who have been drinking and driving . . . They're letting Hispanics bring ten and twelve folks over, without green cards, stay in the buildings, open up businesses, get jobs, get on the welfare system, and there seems to be a tolerance."

Hughes insists she was not trying to insult Hispanics. But, she concedes, "I listen to my tapes and see I was sometimes offensive to white people."

On WLIB in Manhattan, which often provides a forum for the Reverend Al Sharpton and his allies, one caller has said there's nothing wrong with "actually killing these cops and killing the white man."

Even as some stations channel the rage of black listeners who feel abused by white society, others offer a rallying cry for bigoted whites who are furious at blacks. And no radio host captures these emotions more starkly than Bob Grant, who routinely pushes the envelope on race baiting and immigrant bashing.

One day, Paul from Holtsville, Long Island, declared: "I say to white people who are listening, it's time to oil your guns." Grant voiced only mild disapproval.

After the bombing of the federal building in Oklahoma City, a caller named David refused to apologize for unfounded speculation that it had been the work of Middle Eastern terrorists. "If it were up to me, I would take a lot of these people from the Middle East back," he said. "They do not belong here. They don't think the way we do, they don't like us and don't belong here."

On another show, Frank from Queens had this to say about a speech by Nation of Islam spokesman Khalid Muhammad: "Bob, I saw that pile of human garbage screaming out his vile hatred up at Howard University to that snarling pack of savages and rabid dogs."

Grant is the leader of this particular pack. He has called the Reverend Martin Luther King Jr. a "scumbag." He has called former mayor David Dinkins "the men's room attendant." He has called Haitian boat people "swine" and said that "the ideal situation would be if they drowned." He has said after a gay pride parade: "Ideally, it would have been nice to have a few phalanxes of policemen with machine guns and mow them down." He has called Patricia Ireland of the National Organization for Women "that ugly dyke." He has called welfare mothers "maggots" who should be subjected to "the Bob Grant Mandatory Sterilization Plan." Little wonder that *New York* magazine dubbed his tirades "the white equivalent of gangster rap."

Grant begs to differ. "Except for a call to violence, free speech should be uncensored," he says. "I plead guilty to allowing free speech."

Grant has provided a forum for such neo-Nazi groups as the National Alliance and National Association for the Advancement of White People. But he dismisses the charges of racism, saying he has lauded such black conservatives as Clarence Thomas and Thomas Sowell. Since he doesn't balance his denunciations of blacks with similar criticism of whites, he says, "I pay the price in that some people jump on it as a racist thing." Besides, he says, the station's black mailroom attendant has assured him that "you ain't no racist."

Bob Grant got his start at KABC in Los Angeles after John Kennedy was assassinated. The station thought it best to take Joe Pyne, a rabid Kennedy hater, off the air for a few days, and Grant was given the chance to fill in. He has been on the air in New York since 1970.

Grant argues that black racists aren't held to a similar standard: "As long as they're black, they can say anything they want. There's a double standard. If they've got a white bigot, a white hater . . . first of all, they wouldn't allow it. And secondly, if they did allow it, the thugs, the savages, the refugees from the Kalahari would be tearing the place apart."

The *New York* piece triggered a furor in which Al Sharpton and other black activists picketed the station and a few of Grant's sponsors pulled their ads. But WABC stood by the popular afternoon host. "He is extremely angry with rioters and criminals, period," says John Mainelli, then the station's general manager. "If critics want to say that means blacks, that's their problem."

To suggest that Grant's insults are not aimed at blacks seems a transparent fiction. Still, Grant's agent, George Hiltzik, sees his client as the voice of the common man. "Bob has a unique skill of saying what people really think but would never say at a cocktail party, lest they be ostracized," he says.

With Grant and other hosts lighting fuses around the country, talk radio was hot and getting hotter. So hot, in fact, that Phil Donahue got into the act. The onetime Dayton radio host had a half dozen talkers on his television show and got into a shouting match with some of the conservatives.

While radio is "much more aggressive" and "less reverent" than television, Donahue said, there is also "a little bit of superficiality."

This brought an angry retort from Neal Boortz. "We're superficial?" he demanded. "I have never once in twenty-five years ever done a talk radio show on blind transvestite lesbians having an affair with their plumbers' wives! We're superficial? Hey, Phil, I've never dressed up as a woman to do a radio show. I'm superficial?"

"We're doing it again next week," Donahue said sarcastically. "I hope you'll be watching."

Boortz later told Donahue they had once met and chatted about talk radio—a meeting Donahue had apparently forgotten. Boortz thanked him "for teaching me how to do this twenty-five years ago."

The boundaries of what is acceptable on radio have changed radically in that time. A quarter century ago, G. Gordon Liddy was a Nixon White House aide who had moved to the president's reelection campaign, where he masterminded the Watergate break-in. An eccentric former FBI agent, he hatched other preposterous schemes—such as a secret plan to kill columnist Jack Anderson—that proved too much even for the lawless Nixon gang. Liddy refused to talk to prosecutors and served nearly five years in prison, longer than any other Watergate conspirator.

That résumé turned out to be perfectly suited to a '90s talk culture that thrives on criminal celebrity. The convicted felon who would not talk to the authorities was soon talking to a radio audience four hours a day. Liddy's shaved head, deadpan wit, and hand-over-the-flame intensity quickly won him a cult following. Since going into syndication in 1992 from a nondescript Virginia office building, the G-man has been picked up by two hundred sixty stations.

Liddy's "Radio Free D.C." program, which he bills as "jamming the signal of the liberal establishment," focuses on guns, law enforcement, and personal safety. Liddy tells listeners he can "cut the heart and sever the spine" with one thrust of his two-edged stiletto.

"Mr. Liddy . . . how many techniques do you have to kill a person with your bare hands?" asks Dave from Fairfax.

"How do I kill thee? Let me count the ways," Liddy says. "Let me see. I have never gone through my martial arts repertoire for lethality and counted, but I can assure you they are numerous." Asked about concealed weapons, he exults: "I like a revolver. A semiautomatic takes much longer to get into operation than does a revolver. A .44 special. Rossi makes a nice five-round one."

Liddy's number-one target is the Bureau of Alcohol, Tobacco and Firearms, which he says has "run amok" and is conducting a "terror campaign" against gun dealers. Day after day, he repeats the same alleged horror stories about bureau agents: Slamming a pregnant woman against the wall and causing her to lose her baby.

Stealing the medicine of a cancer patient and stomping his cat to death. Federal officials flatly deny these allegations, but no matter. Liddy tells his listeners what to do if attacked by these agents. "Head shots, head shots—kill the sons of bitches!" he says. And if one has insufficient marksmanship to hit the head, "shoot them in the groin."

This sort of ugliness is way beyond the pale of civil discourse. Yet Liddy insists he is only counseling people in self-defense and does not actually advocate "hunting down" federal gun agents. While he speaks of using pictures of the president and First Lady for target practice, "I accept no responsibility for somebody shooting up the White House," he says. Liddy seems to willfully disregard the notion that his violent fantasies might encourage crazed listeners to take the law into their own hands. It's little wonder that Clinton has denounced him by name, or that Al D'Amato, having chosen to honor Liddy at a Republican fundraising dinner, abruptly disinvited him after a storm of criticism.

Much of the public has been turned off by such on-air fulminations. In a *Washington Post* poll taken after the Oklahoma City bombing, 58 percent agreed that some talk show hosts "spread hateful ideas and give the impression that violence is acceptable." And, in a troubling sign for those who believe in the First Amendment, four in ten called for greater restrictions on what people may say on the radio.

Beyond the fringes of the mainstream are a band of right-wing extremists who make Gordon Liddy and Bob Grant look like mild-mannered moderates. These radio warriors rail about one-world government, give voice to wild conspiracy theories, and foment talk of violence. They are obsessed with the deadly federal assault on the Branch Davidian compound in Waco, Texas, in 1993. Some are nationally syndicated, while others rely on shortwave radio to carry their message. The media spotlight briefly illuminated them after the Oklahoma City bombing spurred criticism of those who preach bigotry and insurrection on the airwaves. They range from William Cooper, a white supremacist who addresses militia groups on the Nashville-based World Wide Christian Network, to Ernst Zundell, a self-proclaimed Nazi on WRNO Worldwide in New Orleans, who argues that the Holocaust never happened. Bo Gritz, the former army lieutenant colonel, hailed the Oklahoma explosion as "a Rembrandt—a masterpiece of science and art put together." Mark Koernke, a leader of the Michigan Militia and host of *The Intelligence Report,* warned on his shortwave program of "the Nazification of America" and insisted the government had planted the Oklahoma City bomb. "There is no doubt in my mind that this . . . is yet another foot stomp on the part of the New World Order crowd to manipulate the population," he said. World Wide Christian Radio dropped Koernke days after the explosion, saying his program was too inflammatory.

No plot, no matter how bizarre, is too far-fetched for such paranoid pontificators. They plant their irrational ideas in the fertile soil of popular discontent with government, international bankers and other real and imagined targets, stirring up listeners who believe they are under siege and their way of life threatened. The talk is often replete with violent imagery and apocalyptic visions, stoking fears of federal authorities as the root of all evil.

Dave Emory, host of *One Step Beyond* in Los Altos Hills, California, says that "the real responsibility for the World Trade Center bombing, in all likelihood, lay with elements of our own national security establishment . . . in combination with their German masters . . . There are very serious elements of our national security establishment that have been engaged in some of the very terrorism they profess to be opposed to."

On KDNO in Delano, California, general manager Richard Palmquist denounces "a renegade government" run by "a bunch of outlaws." He calls federal agents "terrorists" and argues that top government officials have become the puppet of "master controllers." Other KDNO hosts insist that federal authorities caused the Oklahoma City bombing, or allowed it to happen so they could persecute militia members. And some of their callers agree.

"I would bet my last cent that the government is behind this," says Pamela from Visalia.

Talk radio has been around for decades. Jerry Williams says he invented it in 1950.

Williams was working at WKDN, an obscure station in Camden, New Jersey, when he launched a show called *What's on Your Mind?* There was just one problem: Federal rules required that phone calls be delayed for a few seconds to prevent any obscenities from being uttered on the air, and no such technology existed. "There was no way to broadcast phone calls without a delay," Williams says. "I had to repeat what people were saying on the air: 'You mean to tell me that . . . ?' "

Still, Williams persisted. "Everyone thought I was crazy," he says. "People would call up and talk about how dirty the streets were in Boston. It was so unusual, so different." He also used the show to assail a man he depicted as an anti-Catholic religious leader, who took out full-page ads denouncing him.

Williams may have been the first radio host to take calls, but he was hardly the first talker. Walter Winchell, the famed gossip columnist, drew a huge audience for his Sunday night broadcasts in the 1930s. Over the next decade, Arthur Godfrey began doing three shows a day from New York. Jack Eigen often broadcast from restaurants in New York, Chicago, and St. Louis. Don McNeill hosted his popular *Breakfast Club* show from Chicago.

The longest-running survivor of that era is Barry Gray, who began as a New York celebrity interviewer in the mid-1940s and was still going strong a half century later. A newspaper writer sniffed in 1951 that Gray had amassed "a following of drowsy worshippers who consider him the closest thing to the Oracle. His brashly inchoate and adolescent declamations are considered gospel by these, or 'provocative' by others."

Gray's career has had its ups and downs. He has twice been beaten up after completing his show. He was dropped by WMCA after failing to disclose that an airline had provided him with two free trips to Europe. But he has always bounced back.

When Jerry Williams moved to Boston in 1957, technology had improved to the point where he could actually put callers on the air. It was an awkward setup, involving the simultaneous use of two tape recorders, but it provided the necessary delay. "The show was an immediate sensation," he says. "We had unbelievable, phenomenal ratings. We did all the controversial things that had never been talked about.

"I had Malcolm X on at least a dozen times. Nobody would

give an interview to Malcolm—certainly not *The Boston Globe* or the TV people. It was very hot. Malcolm was leading a revolution among blacks. During one broadcast, our transmitter was bombed."

Over the next couple of years, all manner of local dignitaries, from Cardinal Cushing to Jack Kennedy to Tip O'Neill, stopped by the studio for the 10:00 P.M. show. "I was kind of discovered by the politicians in town," Williams says. Not everyone was a fan: A Republican state committeeman took a swing at Williams one night while he was on the air.

Despite his success, Williams was frustrated. "We were never taken very seriously, although half the town was listening," he says. "Television and the newspapers treated us with such disdain. We were all looked upon as being some sort of wackos."

Talk was beginning to catch on in other major markets. KABC in Los Angeles switched to all-talk in 1960, an ideal format in a city of freeways. New York's WNBC followed suit in 1964. That year, while Larry King was still mired in Miami, Bobby Kennedy and Kenneth Keating held a Senate debate on Barry Gray's show. In 1965 Jerry Williams moved to WBBM in Chicago, where he sometimes put blacks and whites on the air together during those racially tense years. It was, he says, an attempt to start a dialogue.

Williams returned to Boston in 1972 as one of the nation's greatest political dramas was getting under way. "I talked about Watergate every night for two years," he says. One of his regular guests was Father John McLaughlin, who came on to defend the Nixon White House.

By the late '70s, the talk radio terrain was populated largely by self-help gurus and advice programs. With a few exceptions, such as Paul Harvey's syndicated commentaries and Braden and Buchanan's daily sparring in Washington, political analysts took a backseat to clinical psychologists, real estate experts, sex therapists, auto mechanics, sports fanatics, and marriage counselors. The most celebrated radio personality in New York was "Uncle Bernie" Meltzer, who dispensed financial advice on his *What's Your Problem?* show. Detroit's WXYZ had an on-air psychic named Jacqui. Allan Prell ran a matchmaking service on a Virginia station. Joan Hamburg hosted *How to Cope* on New York's WOR.

Radio was, in short, a service-oriented business. And the man who did more than anyone to change that, oddly enough, was a gangly, shaggy-haired rock deejay who loved to talk about masturbation.

Howard Stern never thought much of his chosen profession.

"Radio is a scuzzy, bastard industry that's filled with deviants, circus clown rejects, the lowest of the low," he says.

Stern brought talk radio to the rock generation. He pioneered the idea of a four-hour program built around one person's ramblings. Sure, he played records, did comedy bits, and took phone calls, but the attraction of the program was Stern. The show was about him—his neuroses, his sexual fantasies, his marriage, his unhappy childhood, his pet peeves, his penis size, his arguments with his staff. Although the material was often crude, he leavened it with musings about politics, movie stars, music, television, and, always, sex. It was stream-of-consciousness radio that defied the notion that a jock had to stick to a predictable format. In a strange twist of fate, Stern's bad-boy success paved the way for the more serious monologues of Rush Limbaugh and his legion of imitators.

After graduating from Boston University in the late '70s, Howard Stern began with little fanfare at WRNW, a 3,000-watt rock station in Briarcliff Manor, New York, where it was clear he cared little about the music. Stern gave away albums and interviewed moviegoers and read commercials for two dollars a spot. From there it was on to a $12,000-a-year job at WCCC in Hartford, and then to WWWW in Detroit, where he honed some of the skits that would make him famous. There was a Leather Weather Lady who said things like, "Bitch, this is the weather, and if you don't like it I'm gonna come over and beat the crap outta you." Stern wrestled women as a promotional stunt, interviewed biker gangs, and staged a "Burn your B-R-A for ERA" event.

In 1980, while Limbaugh was still flacking for the Kansas City Royals, Stern was hired by WWDC, Washington's top AM rock station, where he hooked up with sidekick Robin Quivers, a former air force nurse. "You have to train this audience because they've never had talk radio geared to them," Stern said. "Rock and roll audiences have never been exposed to talk radio; it's never been mixed with music . . . For young people, it's much better than hearing some old bag, a sixty-year-old housewife who obviously doesn't have an orgasm."

And train them he did. Stern did Beaver Breaks, mocking the old sitcom by imagining Wally Cleaver with an inflatable doll or Ward after a sex-change operation. He played Lesbian Dial-a-Date and Gay Dial-a-Date and Guess Who's the Jew. He chatted with callers, mostly for the purpose of insulting them, sometimes signing off with "ah, your mother!" He even made fun of his wife's miscarriage. In a particularly tasteless gag, he called Air Florida after its plane had crashed near the Potomac River and asked the one-way fare from National Airport to the Fourteenth Street Bridge. And he quadrupled the size of his audience.

Stern could also be serious. He had an on-air discussion with a battered wife and took calls after Ronald Reagan was shot. *Washington Post* critic Richard Harrington wrote that "Stern's show is like being caught in a lunatic party line . . . [he] has a lot to say and much of it infuriates, irritates, irks, and provokes his listeners." WWDC management tried to rein him in, saying its surveys showed that Top 40 listeners didn't want to hear phone calls between records. "They didn't explain in the survey that the disc jockey . . . is going to take these phone calls and talk about women's tits," Stern says.

The station dumped Stern in 1982, but he had already cut a deal with New York's WNBC. He took the AM station from number eleven to number one in afternoon drive time, but he clashed bitterly with management, which tried to impose such rigid rules as one comedy bit per break. "No jokes or sketches relating to personal tragedies," an executive's memo warned. "No slander, defamation, or personal attacks on private individuals or organizations unless they have consented or are part of the act . . . No jokes dealing with sexual topics in a lascivious manner." No point in trying to be funny, apparently. Stern ridiculed his general manager on the air and garnered all kinds of publicity, including an appearance with other so-called shock jocks on *Donahue*. Perhaps inevitably, he was fired in 1985.

Stern was snatched up by WXRK, an FM station known as K-Rock, and this time he was allowed to go wild. He dispensed with records and just rapped. Like Limbaugh, he needed a station that would give him the freedom to find his voice. While Stern still did low-rent bits, like playing "butt bongo" on female backsides, he became more overtly political. He talked about how Social Security was a "big scam," being ripped off by retirees who were secretly working, and how his generation was "never gonna see it anyway." He denounced George Bush for being anti-abortion, saying any woman who voted for him might as well mail her vagina to the White House. He chatted with Gennifer Flowers. He said the L.A. police were right to beat Rodney King. He played the taped messages of a Ku Klux Klan organizer, ridiculing him at every turn. He pronounced O. J. Simpson guilty and wondered if a black jury would let him off the hook. He was anti-government, anti-drugs, anti-welfare, anti-immigrant. He made fun of blacks, Jews, homosexuals, and the handicapped, and while he could be mean-spirited, his message resonated with working-class men in the demographically crucial 18-to-34 range. It mattered little that Stern's sex-obsessed persona contrasted sharply with his placid private life as a dutiful husband and father of three daughters. On the air, he served up sleaze with humor.

After a talk show pilot for Fox fizzled, Stern launched a raunchy late-night TV show on New York's WOR, with half-naked women hanging all over him. He wrote a book, *Private Parts,* that became the fastest-selling in Simon and Schuster history, with more than one million copies in print. Despite the steadfast belief of general managers that only local jocks could make it in morning radio, Stern's show was syndicated, first to Philadelphia and Washington and then to more than a dozen other cities. Although skeptical reporters would insist that this or that city was "too conservative" for Stern, he became number one in many of the markets. Big-city stations paid as much as $750,000 a year to carry the program. Advertisers gladly paid $10,000 for five spots a week if Stern would read the copy. The program was earning his employer, Infinity Broadcasting, an estimated $15 million a year. Soon the E! network was taping the radio show for nightly rebroadcast.

There were limits to Stern's self-exposure. While asking guests the most personal questions on the air, Stern kept tight control over his own image, almost never granting interviews to reporters, except

when he was promoting his book. "All journalists are lying skunks,"
he says. Still, he was showered with publicity each time he said
something outrageous. The relentless narcissism worked, particularly when contrasted with the tired formats of all news, all sports,
and classic rock. As Stern belched and farted his way to the top of
the radio heap, legions of Howard imitators materialized, seemingly
one in every city. But the Stern shtick soon ran afoul of the Reagan
revolution. In 1986, when the administration was mounting a con-
certed campaign against obscenity and pornography, Donald Wild-
mon, president of the National Federation for Decency, filed a
complaint against Stern with the Federal Communications Commission. The FCC soon announced it was expanding the definition
of "indecent" speech to include "patently offensive" talk about
"sexual or excretory activities and organs," as judged by the ever-
amorphous "contemporary community standards."

Led by its Republican chairman, Alfred Sikes, the FCC seemed
to single out Stern in applying the new standard. Others with anti-
Stern agendas jumped on the censorship bandwagon. Americans
for Responsible Television, a conservative group led by Michigan
activist Terry Rakolta, and the African-American Business Association, a Washington organization upset with Stern's attitude toward
blacks, filed new complaints with the FCC. Al Westcott, a Las
Vegas resident who hated the show, bombarded the commission
with tapes and transcripts.

In one offending monologue, Stern said, "The closest I came to
making love to a black woman was masturbating to a picture of
Aunt Jemima." He described a rape scene in a Madonna movie
and suggested that Pee-Wee Herman, who had been charged with
exposure in a Florida porn theater, ejaculate on his audience. He
talked about his wife's panties. He asked his wife if she had had an
orgasm the night before ("Not really"). He joked about having sex
with the puppet Lamb Chop. He did an utterly tasteless parody
of Woody Allen talking about his twenty-one-year-old girlfriend:
"Soon-Yi enjoys my old Jewish penis . . . I love to eat chow mein
off of Soon-Yi's bare ass."

The FCC fined Stern's employer again and again. By the end of
the Bush administration, the commission had hit Infinity with $1.7
million in fines for allegedly obscene broadcasts. Even more

troubling, the FCC delayed Infinity's $170-million purchase of three radio stations, raising the stakes even higher. But the company appealed the fines and bought the new stations, and Stern refused to back down. He wished on the air that Sikes would develop cancer. He supported Bill Clinton in the vain hope that a Democratic president would get the commission off his back. He insisted, with some justification, that his material was milder than what was broadcast every day on *Donahue* or *Oprah*.

"Penis out of my mouth is bad," Stern says. "But penis out of Donahue's mouth is good. Donahue can say he's talking about penis because he wants to help people and I'm talking about penis because I want ratings. Bullshit! Donahue talks about penis in November because he wants big sweeps."

Stern became a First Amendment cause célèbre, championed by such unlikely allies as Al D'Amato and the American Civil Liberties Union. He accused the FCC of "kowtowing to the religious right." His message to those who were offended by his show was simple: Turn it off. Stern was so exercised about the FCC that he endorsed Kyle McSlarrow, a pro-life, pro-gun Republican in Virginia, after hearing that his Democratic opponent, Representative James Moran, was supporting the FCC fines. Stern's informant was none other than G. Gordon Liddy. McSlarrow called Stern "a little bit of a nut" but said he was happy to have his support. (He lost anyway.)

Whatever one thinks of Howard Stern, it was truly disturbing to see the full weight of the federal government brought to bear against one person for off-color material that would barely raise an eyebrow on daytime television. It had the look and feel of a vendetta, an attempt at official intimidation. Infinity finally caved in September 1995, paying the $1.7 million—sixty-eight times larger than any previous FCC fine—to clear the way for the company to acquire more radio stations as federal ownership limits were relaxed. Stern called it "the biggest shakedown in history" and said the government was "out of control."

The FCC's moral crusade had the paradoxical effect of making Stern a martyr in the eyes of his fans. "I don't think you can go too far on the radio," Stern says. While some listeners are "shocked by the honesty . . . I am not on the air as a raving lunatic, but as someone who is opening up the microphone. Every time I feel myself thinking, maybe I shouldn't say that, I consciously say it . . . That's the point of the show."

Stern does something else that separates him from most of the talk show pack: He denounces the celebrity culture of which he is a part. His listeners are understandably suspicious of the phony camaraderie with which entertainers always praise other entertainers as wonderful and talented friends. Stern gleefully flouts these conventions.

Among his favorite targets are Johnny Carson ("a goofball . . . another Hollywood phony"), Chevy Chase ("a really sad case"), Kathie Lee Gifford (a "mediocrity"), Larry King ("should be evaluated psychiatrically"), Phil Donahue (a "hypocrite"), Oprah Winfrey ("a big dolt with an empty, oversized head and $250 million"), Arsenio Hall (a "moron . . . with that phony back-slapping, kiss-ass sucking up to anybody who comes on the show"), and Roseanne (a "fat slob" who makes "wild, unsubstantiated charges" and "dumps her husband"). Roseanne, in return, minces no words, calling Stern "a racist, sexist, homophobic fucking pig."

Stern's attacks are replete with cheap shots, and he builds himself up by trashing others. But he also illuminates the hypocrisy and backscratching of Hollywood.

What Stern's detractors fail to see is that he has touched a nerve among a significant chunk of the population, including college-educated yuppies who would never admit to laughing along in their Volvos. Millions of people who never watch the evening news or the Sunday morning shows essentially share Stern's cynical view of politicians as greedy hacks whose droning rhetoric has little to do with their daily lives.

Sure, he can be gross and tasteless on occasion. Stern's endless prodding of women to describe their lesbian experiences can grow tiresome. After the Spanish singer Selena was murdered, he utterly failed to grasp what was offensive about his producer playing the sound of a gunshot over one of her records while Stern criticized her music. He eventually apologized, reading a statement in Spanish.

Like Imus, Stern insists that his opinions should not be taken too seriously. "I'm just another asshole with a view . . . In fact, most of my views are quite absurd," he says. "I'm not here to educate anyone."

Still, Stern's joking monologues about race and crime and politics often have the kind of passion that is all too often missing from the mainstream media. His hold on his audience is so strong that congressmen and governors come courting in the hope of winning a few favorable words. Howard Stern strips away the polite veneer of social discourse and presents himself, neuroses and all, to his audience. He pushed the boundaries of talk radio in a way that made room for a new generation of egomaniacs.

It must be a law of the talk show world that the most successful jocks despise one another. A staple of Stern's on-air routine was to trash Imus, his former WNBC colleague, as "Anus," the "most despicable human being on the planet." When Imus was hospitalized with a collapsed lung, Stern said he hoped he would die. Imus returned the favor, ridiculing Stern as a foul-mouthed adolescent and his listeners as high-school dropouts. And both men routinely denounced Rush Limbaugh as a pompous windbag.

Imus's transformation from sophomoric jock to political sage was nothing short of remarkable. John Donald Imus Jr. grew up on an Arizona cattle ranch, enlisted in the Marines, and attended college only briefly. He worked at a variety of odd jobs, from gas pumper to mannequin dresser. He broke his leg in a uranium mine and hurt his neck in a freight train accident. He was homeless for a while. He started a music act with his brother, Fred, in hopes of becoming a rock singer.

After a stint at the Don Martin School of Broadcasting, Imus broke into radio in Palmdale, California, in 1968. He called himself "Captain Don" and was earning $80 a week. While Stern was still in high school, Imus was asking women callers if they were naked. He ran for Congress, as a joke, against Barry Goldwater Jr. He claims that some of his early stunts, like ordering twelve hundred McDonald's burgers, led to the FCC rule requiring deejays to identify themselves when making on-air calls.

From that inauspicious start, Imus moved to Stockton, California (where he was fired for staging an Eldridge Cleaver lookalike contest), then Sacramento, then to WGAR in Clevelead, and finally the big time: New York's WNBC. With his stable of bizarre characters— Crazy Bob, Judge Hangin', the Reverend Billy Sol Hargis—Imus became an overnight sensation. He started doing standup comedy at local clubs. He bought a Lincoln Continental. He was written up in *Life* magazine as the country's most outrageous disc jockey. And he reveled in his bad behavior, hanging up on callers whenever he wanted. WNBC lost the Irish Airlines account when Imus, reading a commercial, announced that Protestants had to fly coach.

Imus's twisted humor played well in the Apple, but he had a debilitating habit of not showing up for work. He was spending as much as $4,000 a week on cocaine. "Everybody knew I was a drunk and a coke addict," he says. Imus was fired by WNBC in 1977 and, after being banished to Cleveland, rehired a year and a half later. But his problems were far from over. His marriage broke up. While he garnered some publicity by working as an MTV announcer, his radio popularity was slipping. As Howard Stern moved to K-Rock and began to dominate the morning market, *Imus in the Morning* slipped to fourteenth in the New York ratings. In 1987 Imus checked into an alcohol rehab clinic.

Just as he was getting himself clean, fate intervened. NBC sold its AM station to Infinity Broadcasting, which turned it into all-sports WFAN. Freed from the need to spin rock records, Imus launched an all-talk show in 1988. The program, which dwelled heavily on political news, was picked up in Washington, Boston, and other cities. Imus's reputation as a radio version of Lenny Bruce grew by leaps and bounds. National politicians began appearing on the show, particularly after seeing the boost that Bill Clinton got.

But Imus's embrace was hardly an unmixed blessing. Unlike Limbaugh, who never said an unkind word about President Bush after his night at the White House, Imus continued to ridicule President Clinton as an Arkansas hick who couldn't keep his zipper zipped. He called him a "fat pantload" and did bits like "Beavis and Bubba." Yet Clinton continued to call the show, even after Imus played this song parody about Hillary Clinton:

> *She always takes top when she fornicates,*
> *Gets really cranky when she menstruates,*
> *Prefers to stand up when she urinates.*
> *That's why the First Lady is a tramp.*

Nevertheless, Imus got a VIP tour of the White House and had lunch with Mark Gearan, Clinton's communications director. The logic was clear to Imus. The president, he declared, "needs to be on this show a lot more than we need him."

The politicians understood that Imus was a way to reach a broad, highly educated audience. "It's not some tribal ritual of Washington that only insiders watch, or the media elite . . . like *Crossfire*," says Paul Begala. "You go on Imus and reach everybody. In Washington, people know me as Bill Clinton's adviser. In New Jersey, where the entire state listens to his show, I'm the guy who goes on Imus."

"I'm not Ted Koppel," Imus says, "but I know enough about politics to get by." In fact, as a member of the cut-the-crap school of interviewing, Imus could do things that the more dignified Koppel could not. If Begala insisted, as he did on one show, that Bill Clinton was "the best president of my lifetime," Imus would simply deride him as a "Clinton butt boy." Like many in the raw arena of talk radio, Imus did not have to play by the gentlemanly rules of political discourse. He used ridicule as a weapon. He pushed the medium in a far different fashion than Howard Stern.

Mainstream reporters learned to monitor the *Imus* show for news. Sober-minded politicians like Senator Bill Bradley would call in, join in the banter about Clinton, and be surprised to learn that their remarks had made the papers. The president found himself talking about how he used to put Astroturf in the back seat of his truck (or, as Imus later put it, "humping babes in the back of the pickup").

Not that Imus's prognostications were always on the mark. When Christine Todd Whitman, a candidate for governor of New Jersey, appeared on the show after admitting she had hired illegal immigrant help, Imus told her: "You're not going to be governor, so get over that." He offered to chauffeur her limousine for a year if he was wrong. Governor Whitman is not known to have taken him up on the offer.

For all his on-air savvy, Imus has no discernible political philosophy. He voted for Ronald Reagan in 1984, George Bush in 1988, and Bill Clinton in 1992. He initially endorsed Jerry Brown in '92 before concluding that the former California governor was a head case. He is one of the few radio hosts to defend Clinton—at least until deciding that the president and his wife were "lying weasels" on Whitewater—yet he is equally enamored of Bob Dole, a regular guest, and says he would gladly vote for Dole in '96. He loves both Bradley and D'Amato and gets on well enough with Lowell Weicker that Weicker let him be governor of Connecticut for a day.

Imus relishes public figures who will come on the show and tease and banter; those who can't, or won't, are duds. They are "not happening." And, increasingly, politicians want to be happening with Imus's audience. His high-tech basement studio in the Astoria section of Queens has become a hot ticket for those who want to plug into the talk show culture. It is hardly a coincidence that Connecticut Senator Joseph Lieberman announced his reelection bid on *Imus,* or that Clinton's lawyer, Bob Bennett, gave Imus his only interview on the Paula Jones lawsuit. Bob Dole knows that cracking jokes around on *Imus in the Morning* is as important as discussing legislative strategy on *Meet the Press.*

The I-man is equally popular among the media elite. Dan Rather, Tim Russert, Connie Chung, Cokie Roberts, Frank Rich, Jeff Greenfield, and Anna Quindlen have become regular call-in guests. Imus shares their cultural zeitgeist; he watches *MacNeil/Lehrer* and C-SPAN and reads *The New York Times* and *The Washington Post.* Yet he can also host Geraldo Rivera, who in one appearance attacked Bryant Gumbel for supposedly knocking him off the *Today* show. The program's fast pace, with Imus constantly signaling the producers for this tape or that piece of music, has a '90s sensibility.

"Like Letterman, he's really quick," Rather says. "If you're not alert with Imus, you'll wind up like an armadillo hit by a truck. He's become a must-listen in New York because when you get to the office, people are talking about him."

"If you're interested in politicians and pundits," Russert says, "they are more refreshingly candid on that program than where you normally see and hear them." While some bits are "distasteful," he says, "anyone who dismisses it is being a little aloof and arrogant."

Not that Imus spares the press from his tirades. He assailed *The New York Times* for naming the accuser in the William Kennedy Smith rape case (in a phony "Jeane Kirkpatrick" commentary) and chided Connie Chung for misleading Newt Gingrich's mother (in a "Walter Cronkite" routine). He regularly discusses Peter Jennings's love life and trumpets the extramarital affairs of prominent journalists. He once announced that when he sees NBC newswoman Giselle Fernandez, he thinks of going to the studio and tying her up.

And that is the essence of his appeal, for Imus can say whatever hideous thing pops into his head. He acts like a mean sonuvagun and gets away with it. Media types find him fascinating because he breaks all their rules. Imus's sexist, homophobic, and politically incorrect routines echo what many journalists joke about in private. Imus, newsman Charles McCord, producer Bernard McGuirk, and the gang reproduce the typical newsroom banter, only live and on the air. McCord calls Imus "a weird, manic-depressive genius." Imus is just sinful enough for those who can't relate to Howard Stern's lesbian fantasies but relish the naughtiness of someone who can *dis* the president of the United States and still get him on the program.

In a single show, Imus called Newt Gingrich "a man who would eat road kill," O. J. Simpson a "moron," Alice Rivlin a "little dwarf," Bob Novak the man with "the worst hair on the planet," and Ted Kennedy "a fat slob with a head the size of a Dumpster." He has called O.J.'s lawyers "cheap, sleazy, low-rent, scummy weasels." And then there were the inevitable penis jokes.

Not everyone is amused. Mort Kondracke criticized Imus as a "scuzzball" on *McLaughlin*. Imus returned fire by calling him "a tight-ass wussy" and a "loudmouth yuppie jerk on some hideous, unwatchable show."

For others, the program is a dark obsession. "I listen. And I cringe . . . I hate myself," wrote *Washington Post* sports columnist Leonard Shapiro. Imus dismissed him as a "homo" and a "Jew."

Outrageousness sells, and by 1995 Imus was red hot. He married a woman twenty-five years his junior after she auditioned for a skit on his show. He bought a million-dollar house in Southport, Connecticut. The program was picked up in seventy cities. He was invited on the *Brinkley* show. *The New York Times* took him to the White House Correspondents' Dinner. C-SPAN simulcast his radio show. Imus returned the favor by interviewing Brian Lamb and calling him a "dork." The buzz from his program was incredible, as I learned when I went on to discuss "why journalists can't suck enough," as Imus so elegantly put it.

Don Imus had created a new kind of radio show, one that meshed eighth-grade locker-room jokes with fairly serious talk from pundits and politicians. He talked like most people talked in the privacy of their living rooms. He understood what the long-winded pontificators did not, that the average person's mind flitted from sports to sex to politics and back again. He would serve up hilarious parodies of Cronkite or Limbaugh or Nixon before quizzing Bob Dole about Bosnia. He would insult Tim Russert or Dan Rather and they'd come back begging for more. He did what most journalists could only dream of doing, ridiculing the high and mighty while exploiting them for ratings. He made politics fun without the pretentiousness of public television or the staged combat of *McLaughlin*.

Journalists and politicians alike learned that going on *Imus* could be a form of damage control, a way to defuse a controversy with some laughs. When Dan Rather and Connie Chung got embroiled in a public feud over CBS's decision to drop Chung as the network coanchor, Rather tried to smooth things over on *Imus*. When Sam Donaldson was being kicked around for accepting $97,000 in federal mohair subsidies, he called Imus and mocked his detractors for portraying him as a "scumbag." "My critics think I'm worse than O.J.," Donaldson said.

After I wrote a story about how Mike Wallace had secretly videotaped another journalist without her knowledge, prompting a reprimand from the CBS brass, the *60 Minutes* veteran turned up on *Imus*. Wallace talked about the "great hoo-hah" and admitted he had made "a big mistake."

"We're not talking about Geraldo Rivera or some bozo," Imus scolded him. "We're talking about Mike Wallace, American icon."

A few minutes later, Imus was kicking around Wallace's transgression with brother Fred in Santa Fe.

"He should have his nuts cut off," Fred decreed.

"You crude white trash!" the I-man said.

A recurring theme on talk radio is the distrust of the press.

Harry, a caller to WRC in Washington, says: "We would not

get the straight poop, we would not know what was going on, if we had to get it through the filter of the liberal media. Don't call them mainstream. They're far left."

A listener tells Jim Bohannon he is upset about negotiations over North Korea and wonders why "the press is covering up for the president."

"The press doesn't have any agenda to cover up for the president," Bohannon says. "I mean, that is just blatant paranoia. Good Lord, the press certainly hasn't been cutting Clinton a lot of slack."

A caller to Rush Limbaugh demands "congressional hearings on the outrageous media bias."

"You can't," Limbaugh says. "There's a First Amendment."

Hostility toward the media takes many forms. Some liberal callers voice the opposite complaint, saying reporters are too harsh on Bill Clinton and refuse to recognize his accomplishments. Others argue that the press is too sensational, too caught up in sex and scandal stories about public figures. And on black stations, the press is routinely disparaged as part of the white power structure.

Walter, a black caller to WOL, assails *Washington Post* columnist Richard Cohen for daring to criticize Mayor Marion Barry. "Richard Cohen, I know he's Jewish. I believe he's racist . . . It's just the overall denigration of the black man," Walter says. "The systematic racism that is inborn in all white media is ridiculous, man."

"There are a lot of African Americans working at the *Post*," host Bill Christian says.

"Yeah, a lot of sellouts . . . Nobody wants to talk about the low, underhanded moves of Israel or the Jewish Defense League."

Not all black hosts buy into the charges of racism. When Philip calls KABC in Los Angeles, complaining that a bank wouldn't give him the opportunity to start a business, Larry Elder takes vigorous exception. "I know that a lot of people believe that banks discriminate against black people, and I think that's bull," Elder says. "To suggest that implies that bankers are so stupid that they're willing to leave profits on the table because they're racist. If there's anything I trust, Philip, it's green greed."

Armstrong Williams, who left Washington's WOL to launch a syndicated program, says: "I got tired of hearing all the racism spewing out of that station. There's more to life than conspiracy and hating white people and hating Jews."

Some programs are infused with a streak of jingoism. On New York's WOR, Jay Severin calls the North Koreans who shot down an American plane "Stalinist pig terrorists who have illegally killed one of our soldiers. We need to remind them that while their nuclear weapons may not work yet, ours do. This is the American flag they're screwing around with."

Uncorroborated gossip is retailed as if it were fact. On G. Gordon Liddy's show, Ruth from Silver Spring, Maryland, recounts rumors about Clinton's "dalliances with various Hollywood starlets." She says there is a sealed underground tunnel to the White House that has secretly been reopened "to allow young ladies to pass between the Treasury and the White House unperceived." Liddy doesn't challenge a word.

In other corners of the radio world, questions of morality loom large. On WAVA, a Christian station in Arlington, Virginia, one host complains about the widespread availability of condoms. "It seems we're trying to say to youngsters it's all right to be promiscuous, but do it right," he says.

"The problem with getting involved in a sexual relationship is it destroys a teenager's self-image," a guest agrees. "God's plan was that one man and one woman would be committed to each other for life."

And then there is the garden-variety weirdness. When Jimmy Carter appeared on Diane Rehm's show, recounting his diplomatic efforts in Haiti, Somalia, and North Korea, a caller named Elaine demanded to know about "information indicating the U.S. Air Force recovered a crashed flying saucer in 1947 in Roswell, New Mexico. Do you deny that the U.S. government has in its possession physical proof of the reality and the extraterrestrial nature of UFOs? Do you deny that, President Carter?"

"I don't have the slightest idea what information the U.S. government has," Carter said.

In purely political terms, the medium obviously tilts to the right. This is probably a matter of market economics, for no left-leaner has been able to attract a fraction of the audience of Rush Limbaugh. KSFO in San Francisco tried out some liberal hosts for a few months, then dropped them in favor of a conservative "Hot Talk" lineup that included Pat Buchanan and Michael Reagan, along with J. Paul Emerson, who had been fired by another local station for railing about the "stinking Japanese." KSFO dumped Emerson six weeks later after he called gays "sick" and "pathetic" and declared that AIDS victims should be quarantined. This talk, apparently, was a little too hot.

"It's easier to get a conservative show on," says Alan Colmes, a pro-Clinton liberal who broadcasts from New York. His program is carried on more than one hundred stations, but not in any of the top twenty markets. "Everyone wants to be the next Rush," he says. "Every programmer wants to put on the next Rush."

Jim Hightower, the prairie populist, is critical of both parties. "The way I see it, the Democrats get leased from time to time by the global corporations, and the Republicans are wholly owned by the global corporations," he says. But he reserves his special ire for the GOP: "What a hoot to watch Newt Gingrich and . . . some of Newt's right-wing nutballs," he says. Hightower's Texas twang, backed by AFL-CIO advertising, is heard weekends on 156 stations. But he failed to crack half the top hundred markets, including Washington, Boston, and Los Angeles, and in the fall of 1995 ABC radio dropped its syndication deal with Hightower.

"What happened is the progressive side forgot radio," Hightower says. "My generation looked to television and mass demonstrations and other ways of communicating, whereas the conservatives—Ronald Reagan, Paul Harvey—hung in there and continued to build an audience. Now it's just follow the leader. People look across the street and say, 'If that sucker is doing well with a conservative, that's what I need, too.' "

While some women host popular local shows—Lynn Samuels in New York, Diane Rehm in Washington, Gloria Allred in Los Angeles—talk radio is male-dominated at the national level. Judy Jarvis, a former *Time* and *Boston Globe* reporter based in Hartford, Connecticut, calls herself "one of the few nationally syndicated females who's not a shrink. Most general managers think women can't do talk radio and think people don't want to talk to women. It's a prejudice, a longstanding bias."

While Jarvis voted for Bill Clinton, she refuses to be pigeonholed by ideology. "I piss on people I think are doing a terrible job, and I don't care whether they're liberal or conservative," she says.

David Brudnoy is a conservative, but he is also a gay man with AIDS. When he revealed to *The Boston Globe* that he had the disease, there was a tremendous outpouring of affection from listeners. A dozen people even told Brudnoy they had been moved to tell their own families they had the AIDS virus. "Talk radio is the last neighborhood in town," Brudnoy says. "People know their talk hosts better than they know the person who lives next to them."

It's no accident that television has almost no openly gay commentators. John Mainelli, the general manager who helped build WABC into a talk powerhouse, says radio can be more daring because it's primarily a local medium with local sponsors. Network television must rely on national advertisers, who often get spooked by opinion and controversy.

"Talk radio is much less politically correct than television is," Mainelli says. "It's more scrappy. It's also more intimate, because it's radio. Ultimately you'll hear the most outrageous things said. The sheer volume of calls guarantees that."

That, in the end, may explain its magnetic appeal. In an age of mass-produced sitcoms and cookie-cutter Hollywood sequels, talk radio is unpredictable. In an era of eight-second sound bites, radio programs last three or four hours. In a world of blow-dried commentators with carefully modulated opinions, radio talkmeisters still have rough edges and fiercely ideological views.

The most successful hosts—Limbaugh, Stern, Imus, Liddy—are raging egotists who dominate their programs in a way that television could never tolerate. And, of course, most shows are built around the callers, who provide the rest of the audience with an authentic sense of being plugged in. Ridiculous statements and unproven assertions alternate with savvy observations and factual commentary. Talk radio serves a web of overlapping subcultures, each speaking a different dialect. No formal training, advanced degree, or lengthy apprenticeship is required. It is a tower of babble, the rawest form of media democracy. Once talk radio achieved critical mass, it was only a matter of time before the reverberations would reach the world of politics.

CHAPTER TWELVE

THE
INFLUENCE GAME

I n the final week of the 1994 campaign, Tom Foley, the embattled
speaker of the House, made a crucial error: He showed up in
Richard Clear's studio.

Foley had been hammered on talk radio for months as he struggled to hang onto his seat. In Spokane, Todd Herman called him
"the most corrupt man in the United States of America" and "the
current sphincter of the House." In Seattle, Mike Siegel derided
him as "Aristocrat Foley" and gave plenty of free air time to his
Republican opponent, George Nethercutt.

But no one was denouncing Foley as fiercely as Richard Clear,
the most popular host in Spokane. Clear, who had been fired from
his last radio job, had signed on four months earlier with KGA.
The station had just switched from country music to an all-
conservative talk format that included Rush Limbaugh and G. Gordon Liddy. Clear's political philosophy was evident from his phone
number: 448-RUSH. He was a man with a mission, spending 90
percent of his time excoriating Foley. Clear endorsed George Nethercutt, showed up at Nethercutt rallies, even attended meetings of a
group called De-Foley-Ate.

Strangely enough, Clear had been fond of the Democratic congressman in the late '80s. He had even suggested on the air that Tom
Foley run for president. But after Foley voted for a congressional
pay raise and against term limits, Clear concluded he had grown
arrogant and out of touch with the fifth district of Washington state.

Richard Clear loved controversy. In one of his wilder forays, he embraced the cause of Larry Nichols, an overzealous Clinton hater from Little Rock who was peddling a bizarre book and videotape purporting to link the president to a series of murders and a cocaine-smuggling ring. "People called me nuts," Clear says. That didn't bother him a bit.

Clear's afternoon program became a clearinghouse for a daily barrage of anti-Foley attacks and rumors. A neighbor in D.C. even faxed him information on Foley's house, saying it was worth twice as much as the $600,000 assessed value. Things took a nastier turn when several people called the show to say that Foley was a homosexual. Clear replied that while he had no evidence of that, the rumor had been around for years.

"We allow everything on the air," Clear says. "My opinion is information's not gonna kill people."

Foley had turned down several requests for an interview, but now, as Election Day approached, he finally agreed to appear on Clear's program. Clear pressed his bosses for permission to ask "whether Tom Foley is a fag," as he put it, and they reluctantly granted it. When Foley got to the studio, he pounced.

"I've gotta tell you, the rumor mill is at it again," Clear began. "It's been around for years, and I thought maybe you'd want to take the opportunity to address it. People have stated, even on this program, that you are a homosexual. Would you like to address that?"

"That's ridiculous!" Foley said angrily. "I mean, I think that's really bringing the campaign down to a pretty low level. I mean, the fact of the matter is there is absolutely no truth to any of those terrible and slanderous suggestions."

Some local news organizations refused to carry the exchange, but the damage had been done. Talk radio had put in play a completely unsubstantiated allegation against Foley. The communications director of the Republican National Committee had been ousted five years earlier for spreading the same sleazy rumor, a tactic that President Bush had branded "disgusting." No responsible newspaper or television station would have suggested the married congressman was gay without a smidgen of proof. But a radio host determined to defeat the speaker had allowed his listeners to spread garbage on the air and then used that as an excuse to ask Foley about it.

"It was pertinent to the campaign because it had already been brought up on the air," Clear says. "He ought to know that and have a chance to respond. I think constituents have a right to know, if there's suspicion, whether or not a person is gay, particularly if they're trying to hide it."

Foley undoubtedly would have lost his reelection bid in any case. There was, after all, widespread popular disgust with the Democratic Congress of which he was the most visible symbol. But the incident underscores the extent to which talk radio has been turned into a crudely partisan tool.

To be sure, not all talk radio folks openly campaign for political candidates. Many offer a fair discussion of issues and a welcome forum for politicians of both parties. But a striking number of high-profile hosts have been functioning as a propaganda arm for Republican candidates, giving them a significant boost toward capturing control of Congress. In 1994, according to network exit polls, 71 percent of talk radio listeners voted for Fred Thompson in Tennessee, 69 percent for George W. Bush in Texas, 66 percent for Bill Frist in Tennessee, 66 percent for Jeb Bush in Florida, 62 percent for Spencer Abraham in Michigan, and 58 percent for Mitt Romney in Massachusetts—a far higher level of support than they received from the electorate as a whole.

"Without C-SPAN, without talk radio shows, without all the alternative media, I don't think we'd have won," Newt Gingrich said on Rush Limbaugh's show the day he was sworn in as House speaker. "The classic elite media would have distorted our message. Talk radio and C-SPAN have literally changed for millions of activists the way they get information."

Not all Republicans are big fans of the medium. The outgoing House GOP leader, Bob Michel, told his wife as they tuned into radio talk shows: "Listen to those people's venom. Ye gods, that's what people are listening to."

Politicians, of course, have been utilizing radio for more than sixty years. Franklin Roosevelt exploited the new medium with his fireside chats and fed material to Walter Winchell, who used it on his weekly radio show. Days after their first meeting in 1933, Winchell praised FDR on the air as "the nation's new hero." Jimmy Carter took calls from listeners with Walter Cronkite at his side. Ronald Reagan, after stepping down as governor of California, did regular radio commentaries to keep himself in the public eye. Reagan deliberately turned down television offers, telling friends that "people will tire of me," says longtime aide Michael Deaver. Reagan understood that radio could pack an intellectual punch without the risk of overexposure.

In recent years, the dramatic growth of talk radio has been accompanied by an increasingly elaborate and sophisticated apparatus aimed at influencing what is said on the air. Political parties, think tanks, and advocacy groups use so-called burst fax technology to inundate radio hosts with their talking points. Savvy publicists steer prominent guests to the most sympathetic shows. And all sides agree that the conservatives have a far more effective communications network.

"We send out a weekly newsletter to our list of several hundred radio talk shows," says Chuck Greener, spokesman for the Republican National Committee. "It's done in radio vernacular, to cut through all the other stuff these guys get every day." The RNC faxes include supportive quotes culled from various newspapers so the hosts can appear well read.

"You create a wave," says Craig Shirley, a veteran conservative publicist. "You get an op-ed piece in *The Wall Street Journal* and you fax that out. That stimulates the radio talk shows to call, and that stimulates people to call their member of Congress. There's still an ideological resistance on the part of NBC, CBS, ABC, and CNN to taking too many conservatives."

Newt Gingrich has been courting talk radio hosts since the days when he was a young GOP lawmaker scrambling for media attention. "They predominantly tend to be in line with our views and give us what in the business is called repetition," says Tony Blankley, Gingrich's press secretary. "Rush Limbaugh repeats a concept dozens of times in a show. We from time to time let his producers know when something is happening on the floor that might be of interest. When they use it, it has a dramatic impact. Rush Limbaugh doesn't give out congressional phone numbers, but when he talks about an issue, the switchboards light up."

Bill Kristol, former head of the Project for the Republican Future, was giving a speech in Minneapolis when he stopped for an interview with a local radio host named Wes Minter. "He was getting our faxes," Kristol says. "He knew a lot about me and the Project for the Republican Future. He was very plugged into politics in Washington in a way I don't believe, ten years ago, a local radio personality in Minneapolis would have been."

Talk radio has become a potent conservative marketing tool. When Wayne LaPierre, executive vice president of the National Rifle Association, wrote a book called *Guns, Crime and Freedom*, he pushed it onto *The New York Times* best-seller list without a single national television interview. Radio was part of the secret. "He's been on Liddy's show four times," Shirley says. "He's been on Michael Reagan. He's been on Bob Grant in New York, Gary Nolan in Dallas, Jerry Williams in Boston, Michael Jackson in L.A. Liddy even taped an ad, which we placed on his show and on other conservative talk shows in markets where Wayne was going to be."

Limbaugh alone could help push an author toward best-sellerdom, as he did by praising David Brock's *The Real Anita Hill*. "If Rush puts his imprimatur on a book or newsletter, it's worth its weight in gold—or his weight in gold," Shirley says.

And what of the Democratic opposition? "The Republicans have a whole machinery," says Ellen Ratner, a liberal host based in Washington. "The Democrats have zilch."

At the Democratic National Committee, spokesman Jim Whitney says that "we certainly make every effort to reach out to talk radio and provide friendly hosts with information." But Whitney has only a hundred sympathetic shows on his list. "It's very hard for Democrats to drive a message because of the sheer volume of conservative hosts," a party strategist says.

That is starting to change. House Democratic Leader Richard Gephardt recently hired a New York radio producer, Fred Clarke, to act as chief booker in placing Democratic lawmakers on talk shows. Gephardt himself does up to a dozen radio shows a week. "We have to overcome our fear of not being effective on these shows," says Laura Nichols, Gephardt's spokeswoman. "We have to be willing to walk into the lion's den."

President Clinton did eighty-two radio interviews in his first two years in office, granting access to such liberal voices as Jim Hightower and Alan Colmes, while Hillary Clinton did eighty. "We do more than punching the Imus button every three months," a White House official says. "The president does a lot of radio. The cabinet does a lot of radio. But we have not built up a constituency. I don't know if there are more than a half dozen people pitching for us on a daily basis."

Administration officials are acutely aware that the president is regularly pummeled on the radio, and the situation is not without irony. During the 1992 campaign, Bill Clinton skillfully used local radio interviews, along with television talk shows, to articulate the resentments and frustrations felt by much of the audience. "He played talk radio like a piano," Michael Harrison says. And there were grand plans to keep the instrument vibrating after the election.

In the fall of 1993, the administration invited two hundred talk radio hosts to Washington. They received special briefings from the president, vice president, and First Lady, who proclaimed herself a "talk show junkie." They were allowed to set up shop on the White House lawn. It looked like a giant flea market, a tangle of long wooden tables, microphones, and wires as top officials such as Mark Gearan, Ira Magaziner, and Roy Neel moved from one interview to the next. They were trying to sell the Clintons' new health care reform plan.

Many of the hosts, such as Tom Sebastian, the longhaired morning jock at Tampa's 98 Rock, knew little about health care and were simply milking the publicity value of broadcasting from the White House. A wacky Minneapolis host, Barbara Carlson, asked a red-faced Mark Gearan if he would continue the interview in her hot tub (he politely declined). Beneath the circus atmosphere, there were plenty of snide and hostile comments toward what was depicted as a government takeover of health care. The fledgling romance between the new president and talk radio was already fading.

This was far more important than it seemed at first, for the radio personalities were starting to wield an unprecedented degree of clout. According to a Kaiser Foundation survey of members of Congress and their staffs, 46 percent found talk radio the most influential media source during the health care debate, with many naming Rush Limbaugh in particular. By contrast, only 15 percent cited *The New York Times,* 11 percent said *The Wall Street Journal,* 9 percent said television, and 4 percent each said *The Washington Post,* the *Los Angeles Times* or *The Washington Times.* On health care, at least, talk radio had eclipsed the establishment press.

By the time the midterm elections were under way, the health care plan had wilted, the Whitewater affair was in full bloom, and Bill Clinton had become an object of vitriol and derision on many radio programs. One caller to Sean Hannity's show in Atlanta called Clinton "a liar, a faker, an impostor." Another listener crudely raised the possibility of violence: "Lee Harvey Oswald, where are you? I don't know how else to say it."

The conservative hosts pulled out all the rhetorical stops. Bob Grant called Clinton "that sleazebag in the White House." G. Gordon Liddy called him "dreadful, disastrous, venal, corrupt, sleazy" and "the coward-in-chief." Rush Limbaugh called Clinton "pathological," said he had perpetrated a "scam" on the American people and that Hillary Clinton was "dishonest" to boot. Bo Gritz called the president "Hillary's vegetable." Bill Cunningham, a rabid right-winger in Cincinnati, told his listeners: "They wake up every day in the Clinton White House and say, How can we screw the American people today? How can we trick them? They lie, cheat, steal, and do whatever is necessary to win."

Talk radio had found its biggest target in many years.

In the beginning, Ralph Nader turned to local radio shows out of desperation.

It was 1965, and Nader was a little-known consumer advocate trying to get some attention for his budding crusade against unsafe cars. He was struggling for publicity and found he could not get on television. "The media did not like to discuss defects in cars by make and model, so it was very difficult to get any attention when it involved cars like Corvair or Pontiac," Nader says.

On a trip to Chicago, Nader was invited on Jerry Williams's show on WBBM, one of CBS's flagship stations. The popular radio host allowed Nader to deliver his indictment in full, and the resulting publicity led to other radio appearances. "That was the first breakthrough," Nader says.

Williams's bosses were not pleased. "I was called on the carpet by CBS: Why did I do that? They were afraid we were going to lose our GM billing," he says.

Williams continued to stir things up when he returned to Boston. He mounted a campaign that forced Massachusetts lawmakers to rescind a mandatory seat-belt law. He led a crusade against a new prison for suburban New Braintree, forcing the governor to cancel the project. "I can generate five thousand calls to the state house in one afternoon if it strikes the right chord," Williams boasts.

Jerry Williams was hardly the first to use the radio for political causes. In the early 1950s, Arthur Godfrey pressed Lyndon Johnson, then the Senate Democratic leader, to secure more funding for B-52 bombers. Johnson told him to urge his listeners to write Congress. As Godfrey later recalled, "Johnson used to call me up and say, 'Arthur, cut out the letters! There's no more room in my office. I know I asked for mail, but I never thought it would be like this!' "

By the '60s and '70s, radio activism was beginning to spread. Mike Siegel, a lawyer with a doctorate in communications, took his Seattle program to the state capital in Olympia each year to blow the whistle on government waste. In one case, Siegel helped torpedo a million-dollar day-care center for state workers. "The audience was livid about it," he says.

Even Howard Stern, before he hit it big, got into the act. When he was in Hartford during the gas crunch of the '70s, he launched a "The Hell with Shell" boycott that drew some local notoriety. "That was my first taste of the power of radio," Stern says.

But radio remained a regional medium. The first great national test of talk power took place in 1988, when members of the House moved to raise their salaries by 51 percent, from $89,500 to $135,000.

The issue was a bit more complicated than the outraged voices on the radio would allow. In exchange for higher pay, the lawmakers were proposing to ban the acceptance of nearly $10 million a year in speaking fees that had allowed so many corporations and trade associations to buy congressional influence. But such distinctions were drowned out in the roar of radio-generated anger.

On December 14, 1988, Roy Fox, the host of a popular show on

Detroit's WXYT, took a call from Tony in Roseville, Michigan. Tony suggested that voters send tea bags to Washington "and attach a little message to the end of the string that says 'no pay increase.'"

"I thought it was a moronic idea," Fox says. But the next day, after realizing that the anniversary of the Boston Tea Party was approaching, he urged listeners to join a tea-bag protest. Mary Fox, his wife and producer, lined up a dozen other talk show hosts around the country. Fax machines were just coming into widespread use, which simplified the task. Jerry Williams in Boston and Mike Siegel in Seattle joined the effort, as did deejays in Washington, Los Angeles, Cleveland, San Antonio, Des Moines, and West Palm Beach. They interviewed each other on the air and trumpeted the protest. They joined forces with Ralph Nader and the National Taxpayers Union, which established a Washington post office box for the tea bags. When congressional Democrats held their annual retreat at the Greenbriar in West Virginia, Roy Fox gave out the hotel's fax number over the air. Greenbriar officials were so inundated with faxed protests that they had to shut down their machines.

"What really surprised me was how little it took to turn the tide," Fox says. "It just shows how little impact there is from the public."

Within weeks, organizers were dumping one hundred sixty thousand tea bags in front of the White House. The tea-bag revolt sparked so much adverse publicity that Congress withdrew the pay raise. "The talk show hosts and Ralph Nader won this round at the expense of the long-term interests of the country," fumed Tony Coelho, the House Democratic whip.

Nader says most members of Congress refused to appear on the radio shows, ceding the turf to critics. "A lot of the rap against these shows comes from people who aren't willing to go on," he says. "I've done shows with some pretty yahoo, right-wing types because I want to get my message out." In radio, says Nader, "everyone's manipulating everyone."

WXYT ran ads touting itself as "the radio station that moved a nation." But privately, Roy Fox says, station executives told him to cool it. John Dingell, the powerful House committee chairman who held sway over the communications industry, represented the Detroit area, and "our manager was scared to death he was going to come down on broadcasters." Fox left the station soon afterward.

A few months later, Mike Siegel had his turn in the media spotlight. Outraged over the massive Exxon Valdez oil spill that fouled the pristine waters off Alaska, Siegel called for a consumer boycott of Exxon. "It really started from the grassroots," Siegel says. "Large numbers of people were fed up." The movement caught fire locally, and Siegel was at the center of a publicity bonanza. He appeared on *Donahue*, was written up in *Time*, and delivered seventy-five thousand letters of protest to Exxon's president in New York. Nearly forty thousand people turned in their Exxon credit cards. The company ended up selling some of its gas stations in the Seattle area.

"What I'm really trying to do is empower people to have an impact on the system," Siegel says.

A clear pattern was emerging. On issues where the elites—the nation's top journalists, politicians, and academics—had formed a consensus, talk radio provided a way for Peoria and Birmingham and Tucson to register a dissenting view. Many average Americans, it turned out, didn't buy the explanations coming out of Washington, where a $135,000 salary was seen as quite reasonable, and they resented being taken for granted.

It happened again, with stunning swiftness, when Bill Clinton nominated Zoe Baird as attorney general. After *The New York Times* revealed that the $500,000-a-year corporate lawyer had hired an illegal immigrant as a baby-sitter, the editorial writers, and the talking heads on *McLaughlin* and *Capital Gang*, were quick to pooh-pooh the issue. But the talk radio switchboards lit up. Rush Limbaugh told his audience that no one should be above the law and mocked Baird for blaming the situation on her husband. "This is something the people out there just picked up on real fast," Limbaugh says. In Hartford, Judy Jarvis denounced the senators supporting Baird as "jerks." One of Larry King's callers likened the situation to naming a ticket scofflaw as head of the motor vehicle bureau. Even Diane Rehm found her calls running two to one against Baird. "People were saying 'who does she think she is?' and 'I thought Clinton was supposed to be different,' " she says. Listeners were getting information and calling their congressmen in real time. Two days after Clinton was sworn in, Zoe Baird was forced to withdraw. The audience had spoken.

Members of Congress increasingly became aware that they were operating in an environment crackling with talk radio electricity. Senator Patty Murray, a Democrat from Washington who often drew fire from Mike Siegel, worried about the effect on her young staff. "The first lesson they learn is when certain radio hosts go on the air, they have to brace themselves," Murray says. "Because people call, swearing and threatening them." When listeners "trust a nameless, faceless caller to a talk show" rather than a United States senator, she wonders, "how do you accomplish anything?"

If ever there was a proposal that would seem popular with the talk radio crowd, it was the bill to crack down on lobbyists.

High-priced lobbyists, after all, had become the Gucci-clad symbol of the powerful special interests that were paralyzing Congress. Michigan Senator Carl Levin, a Democrat, and Maine Senator William Cohen, a Republican, had produced a measure with bipartisan backing. The legislation barred lawmakers from accepting meals, travel, and gifts from paid lobbyists, a reaction to all those television exposés about lavish entertaining and junkets. And it required paid lobbyists to disclose their activities more fully. The Senate had voted 95 to 2 to approve an almost identical bill a year earlier. On September 29, 1994, the bill cleared the House.

Then Rush Limbaugh weighed in. He had received a fax from his pal Newt Gingrich, the House Republican whip, who was determined to derail the bill. Limbaugh adopted Gingrich's critique and denounced the bill on his television show that night. "I want to read you now a paragraph from a letter that Newt Gingrich sent to all Republican members," Limbaugh told his audience.

The argument, as repeated by Limbaugh, was that the bill would apply to more than just paid lobbyists. That it could require untold numbers of civic and political groups to disclose the names and addresses of their volunteers. That those who failed to comply could face fines of up to $200,000. "This is anti-American and unconstitutional, if you ask me," Limbaugh said.

"Overnight," says Tony Blankley, "there was a tremendous amount of communication from the public."

The bill's sponsors said this was merely a disinformation campaign and that Gingrich wanted to block any reform by the Democratic Congress to boost his party's chances in November. The disclosure provision, they said, was designed to prevent paid lobbyists from concealing their role in organizing grassroots protests, and in no way would require advocacy groups to reveal their membership lists.

"The phones of members of the Senate were flooded by listeners who were accepting the description they got from Limbaugh, which was a severe distortion," Levin says. "Calls have an impact. They're more immediate than mail. The turning point came when Gingrich decided to utilize the talk radio network. I assume Limbaugh was doing it to help Gingrich. The purpose of the bill was exactly the opposite of what Rush was told by Newt."

Levin sent Limbaugh a letter of protest by overnight mail. "I would like to talk to you on the show tomorrow to set the record straight," he wrote. Limbaugh agreed to take a call from the senator, and Levin argued on the air that Limbaugh's interpretation was false.

"Anybody who is just lobbying to express their own, personal view is not affected in any way," Levin told Limbaugh. "It's just if you're paid to lobby on behalf of another person."

Limbaugh remained skeptical. "Well, this is awfully confusing and vague," he said. "There are a lot of people who are scared of this because the attitude is that members of Congress are sick and tired of hearing from constituents." Levin was followed by Oklahoma Representative Ernest Istook, Jr., a Gingrich ally, who maintained that volunteers would indeed be covered by the bill.

Limbaugh had some help. Pat Robertson, who owns the Christian Broadcasting Network, said on his *700 Club* that the bill was "one of the most shocking attempts to limit your freedom of speech and the rights of Christian people and other groups concerned about out-of-control government." Conservative activist Paul Weyrich, the founder of National Empowerment Television, used his *Dateline Washington* show to urge listeners to "stop this monstrosity before it stops you, the citizens of the United States."

Once the Christian conservatives were called to battle, some congressional offices began receiving a thousand calls a day. The measure was now being attacked as a liberal ploy to undermine constituent protest. Energized by all the static on radio and television, Senate opponents launched a filibuster against the bill. An effort to break the filibuster mustered a 52 to 46 majority, far short of the required two-thirds margin. An astonishing forty-four senators switched their votes. The lobbying bill was dead.

The Republicans used similar methods to attack Clinton's $30-billion crime bill, the product of a year and a half of bipartisan negotiations. Newt Gingrich played the Limbaugh card once again.

"I briefed him on a provision of the crime bill that establishes quotas for murderers and quotas for the death penalty, and he spent twenty minutes on the air describing it," Gingrich says. "What was at first fairly obscure for millions of people now became very real."

While Limbaugh assailed the death-penalty language, Craig Shirley was coordinating an effort to paint the crime bill as a pork-laden monstrosity. Although the bill contained three times as much spending for police and prisons as for social programs, one relatively small expenditure—$40 million for midnight basketball programs —became a prime target in radio interviews. "We were calling seven hundred fifty radio stations every two hours with new items—tidbits, anything that would attract their attention," Shirley says.

Conservative think tanks did some of the heavy lifting. Scott Hodge, a fellow at the Heritage Foundation, did seventy-five radio and television interviews denouncing the crime bill. Stephen Moore of the Cato Institute did more than fifty.

"Just a few years ago we couldn't have done this . . . On the call-in shows, about 90 percent of the people were against the crime bill," Moore says.

The crime measure went down to a sudden, unexpected defeat in the House. Although Clinton salvaged the bill by agreeing to cut it by $3 billion, it was a major political setback. Voters saw that a Democratic president could barely get one of his major domestic priorities through a Democratic House. Talk radio had scored again.

On one level, of course, this was simply democracy in action. Advocates of every ideological stripe had always tried to rally their troops, and conservatives now had a surefire way to sound the alarm. If there were many more right-wing hosts eager to carry the Republican banner, well, that was also the free market at work. But there was no easy antidote to the misinformation and distortion that often accompanied lobbying campaigns and could now be broadcast coast to coast. The creaky machinery of Congress always made it easier to block some piece of legislation than to forge a consensus, and the conservatives now had a powerful weapon at their disposal. When enough radio hosts lined up behind them, they could talk a bill to death.

Howard Stern is letting Mario Cuomo have it.

"This guy is the biggest schmuck on two feet," he says. "I hate his guts."

Don Imus is also down on the New York governor.

"It's like one of those aging ballplayers who didn't know when to hang it up," he says. "It's over! Get out!"

Bob Grant dismisses Cuomo as a *sfaccimm*, an Italian word for low-life. "We get the chance to show Mario the door in '94," he says.

It is three weeks before Election Day, and the New York airwaves are filled with the sound of Cuomo-bashing. The three-term governor is not surprised at the level of vitriol. "Hate sells," he says.

Grant was once a Cuomo booster but turned against him after the governor hung up on him during a 1986 interview. He is doing everything in his power to elect George Pataki, a previously obscure Republican state senator. Days earlier, Grant had spoken at a Pataki rally in Queens. Now, standing behind the microphone in his seventeenth-floor WABC studio, the one next to Rush Limbaugh's, the nattily dressed host has Pataki on the line. Grant sets the tone by introducing him as "the next governor of the state of New York."

"You've been out making the case about how Mario Cuomo's policies have failed," Pataki says.

"This is gonna make your opponent even more desperate," Grant says.

"Well, Bob, he can't run on his record."

Grant notes that Cuomo's wife and daughter-in-law have been criticizing Pataki. "Seems like Mario Cuomo is hiding behind skirts these days," he says.

After a few more friendly exchanges, Grant says: "My best wishes always."

"Bob, thanks for your help."

A few minutes later, Liz from New Jersey calls to say that Clinton is coming to town "to boost his Mafia friend, Cuomo." Bob Grant simply chuckles.

Never before in American history had an election been so heavily influenced by talk radio. In one race after another, the issues, the attacks, and the atmosphere were shaped by the on-air discourse. Television, particularly in big cities, had always done a lousy job covering local races, while radio by its very nature was closely attuned to precinct-level politics. It was a way of expanding the political conversation beyond those who religiously read newspapers or watched Rather, Jennings, or Brokaw. Listeners could communicate with the candidates, and with each other, rather than remain passive consumers of thirty-second attack ads. It was, in a larger sense, a fundamental coming of age for talk radio. The propaganda techniques that had previously been limited to issues, such as the congressional pay raise or the Exxon oil spill, were now being unleashed against the politicians themselves.

Many Democrats felt battered by the medium. "Hate radio is playing a major role in forming political opinion," says Texas Democratic Chairman Bob Slagle, who saw his party taking a beating on the airwaves. He would launch a "Crush Rush with the Truth" campaign in an undoubtedly futile attempt to neutralize Limbaugh.

For candidates with popular hosts as their personal cheerleading squad, talk radio was a boon in 1994. For others, it was a daily nightmare.

Jon Christensen, a Nebraska insurance salesman making his first race for the House, was inspired by talk radio. "My interest in politics was partially fueled by people like Rush Limbaugh," Christensen says. When the Republican saw cars bearing RUSH IS RIGHT bumper stickers, he would leave a special campaign brochure on the windshield. "Dear Rush Fan," it began.

"Talk radio is equal time for conservatives," Christensen says. This is a bit glib, for it assumes that the rest of the media are relentlessly trying to elect liberals, which is simply not the case. But it reflects a legitimate frustration with the way the press slices and dices the words of politicians, who relish the chance to deliver their message live and unedited.

Jon Christensen won by 1,700 votes with help from a local

Limbaugh. Steve Brown of KKAR in Omaha took up his cause against the Democratic incumbent, Peter Hoagland, showing up at several Christensen campaign events. Christensen's wife, Meredith, openly courted Brown, even accompanying him on a fishing trip. When Christensen charged on the air that "Peter Hoagland is a liar," Brown played it over and over again as a promotional stunt.

"The staffers in Hoagland's campaign made it personal against me, saying I'm a lackey of Christensen," Brown says. He insists he has always been fair to Hoagland, although "I might have played a Sam Donaldson role once or twice.

"I don't preach like Rush does. I don't claim to be a pure journalist, but I try to deal in fact. I had to do my own research on Christensen, just like a voter. I spent time with his staffers. I found out who his financial backers were. I said, You have to convince me, and therefore my audience, that you're really going to make a list of budget cuts and that when you get back there you'll take our phone calls. He said, 'You can call me at midnight.' "

Not all conservative hosts were down-the-line party men. Michael Reagan, whose Los Angeles show is carried on ninety stations, occasionally dared to differ with his famous family. When Ronald Reagan endorsed the Brady gun-control bill, named for the press secretary wounded in the attempt on Reagan's life, Michael Reagan publicly dissented. When his stepmother, Nancy Reagan, criticized Oliver North's Senate candidacy in Virginia, Michael Reagan upbraided her. And when Michael Huffington, a millionaire Texas oilman, tried to unseat Democratic Senator Dianne Feinstein in California, Reagan broke ranks and backed Feinstein.

"I also believe there are stupid Republicans," Reagan says. "I think Michael Huffington was an embarrassment to the Republican Party. He should find another state to live in. I will take on people that others wouldn't think I'd take on. That's given me credibility."

Once, politicians worried about lining up support from other officeholders or business and union leaders. These days, talk show hosts are the new kingmakers, courted by candidates who need them far more than ward heelers and county chairmen.

Chuck Haytaian, the New Jersey Republican challenging Senator Frank Lautenberg, repeatedly called Howard Stern's show and pleaded for an endorsement. Stern refused because he didn't like

Haytaian's opposition to abortion. Haytaian says he needed the nod because Imus was backing Lautenberg. Nor was Haytaian the first to play the supplicant before Stern. During her 1993 campaign for governor of New Jersey, Christine Todd Whitman promised to name a highway rest stop after Stern in exchange for his support. The governor kept her word. Although the move was denounced by critics, there is now an official Howard Stern Rest Stop on Interstate 295.

"They're important players because people are in their cars in our state," Haytaian says. "I'm a superstitious guy. Stern endorsed Christie Whitman and she won."

Bob Grant also claimed credit for Whitman's victory. "I contribute more than money," he says. "Money, that's nothing. You ask some candidates who got elected thanks to me."

The candidates were clearly paying close attention to the radio. When Roe Conn of Chicago's WLS wondered whether Dawn Clark Netsch was too homely to be a successful Senate candidate, the Illinois Democrat changed her slogan to "More Then Just a Pretty Face."

The radio hosts seemed most effective as a negative force, skewering disfavored candidates in colorful, often inflammatory language. A handful of liberal hosts held their own in the name-calling department.

In Boston, Marjorie Clapprood attacked Mitt Romney, the businessman challenging Ted Kennedy, as "some stupid, wind-up, milk-drinking, Ken-doll member of the Republican right."

In New York, Lynn Samuels denounced George Pataki as "just a low-life, low-level, vulgar, sleazy, mediocre, just-trying-to-get-money-for-himself, horrid person. I cannot tell you the contempt I have for George Pataki. He's really not fit to be a school board member."

But most of the harsh attacks seemed to emanate from conservative talkmeisters. There were more of them, and many were openly aligned with the Republican Party. They did not, to put it delicately, lose much sleep over questions of taste.

On Boston's WRKO, Howie Carr ridiculed Ted Kennedy as "the fat boy" and "the world's oldest juvenile delinquent." The *Boston Herald* columnist told his listeners that Kennedy "sucks" and missed no opportunity to bring up the Chappaquiddick accident:

"What should someone get who runs a car into a pond, and leaves a woman to suffocate in the car, and doesn't bother to call the authorities for twelve hours—what do you think an appropriate penalty for that is? How do you feel about sexual harassment of women?. . . . Say, if a waitress was trying to bring some food into a private dining room in Washington, D.C. . . . and two senators who were drunk out of their minds got her in between them and pushed together and dry-humped her . . . Do you think that's legitimate behavior?"

Kirby Wilbur of Seattle's KVI went out door-knocking for Republican House candidate Randy Tate, contributed to his campaign, hosted a fund-raiser, and frequently had him on the show. Wilbur even encouraged listeners to disrupt the campaign events of Tate's Democratic opponent, Representative Mike Kreidler.

On Cincinnati's WLW, Bill Cunningham embraced Mike De-Wine, the Republican Senate nominee in Ohio, and several GOP House candidates. "I endorse those who are normal Americans," Cunningham says. "America has many domestic enemies today, and most of them are in the Democratic Party."

Cunningham was the star attraction at a fund-raiser for Republican House candidate Steve Chabot and described his opponent, Democrat David Mann, as a "loathsome beast." Mann complained that talk radio hosts often "appeal to people's worst prejudices." But Cunningham rejects the notion that radio hosts were somehow stirring up the voters.

"Americans are not easily led," he says. "Americans are not a bunch of pigs with rings in their noses. A good chunk of my listenership has been waiting for viewpoints not heard in the traditional media. The mainstream media does not reflect American values."

On the morning after the '94 election, George Pataki called Howard Stern to thank him for helping to make him governor of New York.

"Hey, Howard, you guys are the best! You did get the word out, and it was just great, and I thank you," Pataki said.

"People are like sheep sometimes," Stern said. "They've got to be told what to do."

Richard Clear played a song called "Bye Bye Tom" and accepted congratulations from listeners for toppling Foley.

"It seems just a little sunnier today knowing that Tom Foley is road kill," Howie Carr said.

"Praise the Lord, normal people are back in charge!" Bill Cunningham declared.

G. Gordon Liddy announced that the Clintons were next. "Send 'em back there to the chicken-guts, waste-fouled waters of the rivers of Arkansas," he said.

"The liberal, elitist press lost," Rush Limbaugh said.

On the morning of January 4, 1995, hours before the new Republican Congress was sworn in, Wes Minter sat beneath an ornate chandelier in Room H-233 of the United States Capitol.

The bespectacled, pudgy-looking radio host from Minneapolis was at the epicenter of the revolution. He was camped out in a burgundy-carpeted suite of offices controlled by the new House speaker, Newt Gingrich, and loving every minute. A few weeks earlier, Minter could not have broadcast from the Capitol at all, for the reporters' committee that controlled such access would not grant press credentials to mere radio talk show hosts. They were not considered journalists. But Gingrich had set aside several rooms for the radio hosts, and they had descended upon Congress—Bill Cunningham, Michael Reagan, Armstrong Williams, and others—like conquering heroes. They had fought the good conservative fight and were eager to claim the spoils of victory. Wes Minter enjoyed the most privileged perch because he had become friendly with Gingrich while hosting a show in Atlanta.

"I've always had the highest respect for him," Minter said, his WCCO microphone mounted on a big congressional desk facing a gold-plated congressional mirror. "I'm thrilled for him. Talk radio is going to provide a real strong dialogue for the Republicans to stay in touch with the public. We're a conduit for them."

At 10:00 A.M., Minter donned a pair of black headphones and opened the show: "We're live here from the speaker-to-be's offices. Congressman Newt Gingrich will join us in mere moments."

Soon Gingrich strolled in, grinning broadly, and pumped Minter's hand. The questions could not have been milder:

"When you put your head on the pillow last night, what went through your mind?"

"Your love for exotic animals—how long have you had this passion for zoos?"

"How do you see yourself in the role of speaker?"

When it was over, Minter posed for pictures with Gingrich and asked him to autograph a copy of the Contract with America. The new speaker scribbled his name and was off. Minter pronounced himself "humble and grateful" for the plush accommodations.

Wes Minter is a gentleman, and it seemed not to have occurred to him that he had been co-opted. The talk show hosts who embraced the Republicans had now snuggled up to the new ruling party on Capitol Hill, all but abandoning any pretense of detached judgment. When the GOP revolutionaries ran into rough political waters, many of their radio allies were hard-pressed to cast them adrift, having campaigned so fervently for their election. In the name of ideology, they had forfeited their role as outsiders.

"Some talk show hosts have been so deeply aligned with the Republicans that they are afraid to criticize them," Neal Boortz says. "They don't want to be shut out. They want to maintain their access. I think to a certain extent that's happened to Limbaugh."

Indeed, talk radio seemed to lose some of its punch in 1995 as the Republicans struggled with parts of the Contract with America. The balanced budget amendment failed by a single vote in the Senate, despite widespread support among talk radio listeners. The term-limits amendment, aimed at the professional politicians that so many listeners love to hate, lost by a sizable margin, despite support from Mike Siegel, G. Gordon Liddy, Michael Reagan, Neal Boortz, and other hosts. In the days leading up to the vote, the subject was curiously absent from the airwaves. The Republican proponents of term limits were squabbling among themselves. The fine print of the various proposals—whether terms should be limited to six or twelve years, whether a federal limit should override state restrictions—did not engage the audience. Many hosts were busy bashing the perennial targets.

In San Francisco, Michael Savage was talking about illegal immigrants being eligible for disaster aid after flooding in California. "Who invited them here in the first place?" he said. "They came in through the cracks. Let them fall back into the cracks."

In New York, Bob Grant was talking about a fatal gas attack on the Toyko subway. "Harry Truman was right to drop the bomb on them," he said.

In Denver, Mike Rosen was talking about a couple reported to be receiving $46,700 a year in Social Security disability payments for themselves and their children. "Democrats are not the party of the middle class," he said.

Talk radio is about what's new, what's hot, what is most likely to spark outrage from a mass audience. Term limits had become old news. The conservative hosts were tilting at the old windmills even as one of their favorite initiatives, an emotional rallying cry just a few months earlier, was going down the tubes. Talk radio was an awesome opposition force, but it was of limited help with the more difficult task of actually passing legislation.

Radio is a relentlessly opinionated medium, and the hosts who ardently embraced one party's candidates were simply being honest with their listeners. It was, in a way, a refreshing change from the bland and homogenous tone of the newspapers and the networks. Like it or not, the hosts declare each day, this is where I stand.

But there is little doubt that the sort of character assassination that routinely erupted on the airwaves had a coarsening effect on an already mean-spirited campaign. To argue about ideas, however passionately, is one thing. To denounce politicians as the "coward-in-chief" or "a waste of a vagina," to call them abnormal, to allow listeners to describe them as members of the Mafia, to question their sexuality on the basis of whispered rumors, is to soil and degrade the political process. Talk radio is a wonderful, impassioned forum for debate, but too many hosts are twisting and abusing it in the cheapest possible way. If it becomes just another part of a vast propaganda machine, a vehicle for distorting legislative proposals and smearing public figures, then something quite precious will have been lost.

CHAPTER THIRTEEN

BLURRING
THE LINES

I n the last days of 1988, David Gergen ran into Barbara Bush at
a Christmas party at the vice-presidential residence.

They had known each other for years. Gergen had worked for
George Bush's 1980 presidential campaign. He had worked with
Vice President Bush while spinning the press as Ronald Reagan's
communications director. Now Bush was the president-elect, but
Gergen had drifted into journalism. He was Mark Shields's conservative sparring partner on *The MacNeil/Lehrer NewsHour* and a
columnist for *U.S. News*. While he wished her husband well, Gergen said, he hoped she understood that he had to remain neutral.

"Well, you don't have to be too damn neutral," Mrs. Bush shot
back.

Gergen conveyed the same message to the new president. His
name had been floated in the press as a possible new director of the
U.S. Information Agency, and he wrote Bush a letter saying he was
not interested in a job. Now that he was a commentator, Gergen
added, there might be times when he would have to criticize Bush's
performance. Bush responded with a friendly note, saying that he
understood. But relations soon turned frosty.

"He assumed you were going to be 1,000 percent loyal," Gergen
says. "I knew from friends in the administration that there were
times he resented the fact I wasn't more of a cheerleader."

The resentment hardened during the 1992 campaign as Gergen
often spoke sympathetically of Bill Clinton, a personal friend for

more than a decade. Bush was livid. Shields "went right for the jugular," Bush says. "I respected that. But Gergen, who was supposed to be the Republican spokesman, would equivocate, seldom attacked Governor Clinton, and sounded almost apologetic for representing my side of the campaign. And then, after the election, what do you know? Gergen announces he isn't a Republican and he voted for Clinton. So much for fairness—and I don't respect that."

Gergen, of course, did more than merely vote for Clinton. Four months after the inauguration, he became the new president's counselor—but not before seeking assurances from friends that there was "a road back" to journalism.

It is an increasingly well-traveled road, this murky path between politics and punditry that so many talk show stars have explored. Gergen may have trekked back and forth more frequently than most, but he's had plenty of company. Mark Shields, the host of *Capital Gang,* was a Democratic campaign operative for Bobby Kennedy, Henry Jackson, and Morris Udall before launching a new career as a columnist and talking head. Tim Russert studied under Pat Moynihan and Mario Cuomo before ascending to *Meet the Press.* John McLaughlin, George Will, John Sununu, Chris Matthews, and Mary Matalin are among the dozens of prominent prognosticators who hail from the world of partisan politics.

The once-solid barrier between commentators and candidates has been so completely obliterated that the two sides have become interchangeable, even at the highest levels. Pat Buchanan, as we have seen, used *Crossfire* as a refueling stop between his Republican presidential campaigns. Ross Perot casually made the transition from '92 White House contender to '94 radio talk show host. Jesse Jackson, after twice seeking the Oval Office, juggled his dual roles as prominent black activist and CNN talk show host, even as he made noises about a third presidential bid. Gary Hart, another two-time presidential aspirant, found a new calling behind a radio microphone in Denver while plotting a possible comeback bid for the Senate.

What is most remarkable about this cultural shift is that few in the news business find it remarkable. Journalism is not a priesthood, but there had long been a fierce institutional belief that those who write and talk about public affairs should belong to no political faction. The old rules—that journalists should not sign petitions, offer political advice, or make financial contributions—now seem rather quaint. After all, some of the highest-paid talkers are recent veterans of the political wars, between campaigns or simultaneously pontificating and politicking. There is no truth-in-labeling law. Some of those who yak about politics on the air are little more than propagandists for a particular faction or viewpoint.

One of the few who has loudly decried this musical-chairs mentality is David Broder, the veteran *Washington Post* columnist who also handicaps politics on *Meet the Press* and CNN. "When someone like Buchanan or Jackson is a candidate one moment and a commentator the next, how the hell do people know which is which?" he says. "This may be a bullshit, old-geezer view, but I really think there's a sense of wanting it all. As journalists we have so many privileges, and the unwillingness to accept the limitations of the business is just fucking selfish."

Broder says he and Jack Germond left the *Today* show several years ago because NBC insisted on introducing them as part of a rotating panel of "Washington insiders." The other insiders were Robert Squier, a Democratic media consultant, and Roger Ailes, a Republican media consultant (and now, through the magic of reincarnation, the president of CNBC). Broder hated being lumped with such obvious partisans, as he repeatedly told *Today* executives. "I would ask them, when are you going to put on the goddamn screen that Roger Ailes is on the payroll of the Republican National Committee for such-and-such an amount?"

Not all of Broder's colleagues applauded his stand. Buchanan, for one, called him "a sermonizing, sanctimonious prig."

For much of this century, it was not that unusual for the most influential pundits to dabble in the political arts. Walter Lippmann wrote speeches, and even made speeches, for President Woodrow Wilson while working for *The New Republic,* then joined Wilson's War Department, then criticized Wilson upon returning to the magazine. As a newspaper columnist two decades later, Lippmann sent FDR a letter of advice on how to preserve his New Deal programs, and he later helped draft a speech for GOP presidential candidate Thomas Dewey. Arthur Krock, Washington bureau chief of *The New York Times,* was a ghostwriter for Joseph Kennedy, traveled and vacationed with him, and recommended him for jobs in the Roosevelt administration. James Reston, Krock's successor, once advised Senator Arthur Vandenberg on a major foreign policy speech. Such volunteer work was quietly accepted because the journalistic opinion makers saw themselves as part of the governing elite. But the 1960s ushered in more stringent ethical standards that deemed such behavior highly unprofessional, and moonlighting for politicians became a firing offense for any working reporter.

At the same time, the media world has long served as a launching pad for political careers. William F. Buckley made a quixotic run for mayor of New York City in 1965. Jesse Helms was a radio and television commentator in North Carolina before running for the Senate. Bob Dornan was a right-wing voice on California radio before becoming a congressman and '96 presidential candidate (and regular substitute host for Rush Limbaugh). Another California TV commentator, Bruce Herschensohn, ran for the Senate in 1992, losing to Barbara Boxer.

But the traffic has grown increasingly heavy in the other direction, undoubtedly reflecting the enhanced prestige and financial status of the talk show culture. Some of these transformations are nothing short of miraculous.

In August 1992 Mary Matalin, the pit-bull political director of the Bush campaign, put out a statement assailing "sniveling hypocritical Democrats" and poking fun at Bill Clinton's problem with "bimbo eruptions," a phrase coined by a Clinton aide. Dee Dee Myers, the Clinton campaign spokeswoman, called for Matalin to be fired and derided Bush's reprimand of her as halfhearted. "In public they denounce sleaze and behind closed doors they applaud it," she declared.

Nine months later, Matalin reemerged as the cohost of CNBC's *Equal Time*. And in 1995, ten weeks after leaving the podium as White House press secretary, Dee Dee Myers joined her for a two-week tryout as cohost. They smiled and heaped praise on each other. (Myers followed another temporary cohost, Torie Clarke, who had been the Bush campaign spokeswoman.) Myers and Matalin soon became a permanent team. Among their first guests: George Stephanopoulos, Myers's former White House colleague, and Senator Dianne Feinstein, her former boss. The message to viewers was clear: This campaign stuff is just playacting. We're all good buddies here. Yesterday's bitter political adversary is tomorrow's esteemed television colleague.

To Matalin's credit, she is unfailingly polite to Democrats (she is, after all, married to James Carville) and makes no secret of her loyalty to what she calls "God's party." She even describes herself on the air as a "slimy partisan hack." While interviewing Barbara Bush, she said: "One of the things the Democrats say which must boil your blood as much as it boils mine . . . is that they inherited so many of these problems, that it's such a more complicated world than when George Bush was president."

"That's right, that's crazy," the former First Lady replied.

On Election Night 1994, when a more traditional talk show host would have struck a pose of studied neutrality, Matalin was near tears. "It was just overwhelming," she says. "A great victory like that takes your breath away. I would have rather been with my friends." But Matalin was a new star in the talk show firmament and soon signed a contract for her own CBS radio show.

In 1984 and 1988 Jesse Jackson was a Democratic presidential candidate. In the days before the '92 convention, he was performing his quadrennial mating dance about whether to endorse the Democratic nominee. When Jackson finally decided to back Bill Clinton, he broke the news on his CNN show, *Both Sides with Jesse Jackson*. In fact, CNN held off for several hours on reporting the decision by Jackson the newsmaker so Jackson the talk show host could have the exclusive. Three years later, Jackson the talk show host started doubling as Jackson the potential candidate, declaring on *Face the Nation* that he might challenge Clinton in 1996.

In 1988 Roger Ailes was making commercials for the Bush campaign, including some very tough ads on Michael Dukakis's prison furlough policy and the pollution of Boston Harbor. In 1992 he was an informal adviser to the Bush reelection campaign. In 1995, as CNBC president and the host of *Straight Forward,* he chatted with Peggy Noonan, who had been Bush's speechwriter in the '88 campaign. Bush's convention address that year, written by Noonan, was "probably his finest speech," Ailes said. He then asked how President Clinton was faring.

"It's quite tragic what he's become," Noonan said.

"Is he a one-termer, or can he pull out of it?" Ailes asked.

"Uh! No way."

What if Clinton showed leadership in an unexpected crisis?

If that happened, Noonan said, "I'm going to be cruel now—he may be less of a joke . . . He made the government bigger, and he raised taxes. It was classically stupid." No one pointed out, of course, that Clinton had raised income taxes only on the wealthiest 1 percent of taxpayers, as he had promised during the campaign.

After Noonan predicted that Whitewater might "finish Clinton off," Ailes turned to the new Republican leadership in Congress. "I am so impressed," Noonan said.

Roger Ailes found other forums to bash the president who had beaten his man Bush. He joked on *Imus in the Morning* about how Clinton was interested in skating star Nancy Kerrigan—"she's the only one he hasn't hit on yet." And he bemoaned the sad fate of lawyers around Hillary Clinton—one was under investigation, "one was forced to resign . . . and one's dead. I wouldn't stand too close to her."

This incessant bed hopping has produced some strange spectacles. Diane Sawyer, who worked for President Nixon in the White House and during his exile in San Clemente, interviewed Nixon for the *CBS Morning News*. Tim Russert has repeatedly interviewed Moynihan and Cuomo on *Meet the Press*. "I think my record speaks for itself," Russert says. "I left politics ten years ago and I will never go back. Some people continue to dabble in politics and present themselves as media commentators. You should have one turn in the revolving door. The experience I gained from eight years in the executive and legislative branches was enormously helpful for what I'm doing now."

Those who work off-camera are no less adept at career changes. Take Dorrance Smith, the onetime Ford White House staffer who helped launch *This Week with David Brinkley* and took over as producer of *Nightline* in the late '80s. Smith, an old friend of George Bush, became the president's assistant for public affairs in 1991, plotting administration strategy on dealing with such shows as *Brinkley* and *Nightline*. In 1995 Smith was rehired as producer of the *Brinkley* show, overseeing coverage of the president who defeated George Bush.

"I don't produce the show from any sort of polemical stand-point," Smith says. In fact, he says, "It works to my advantage because I know how the game is played."

Some can hardly wait to make the transition. During the final days of the Reagan administration, Ken Adelman, the president's arms control director, called *Washington Week in Review,* said he planned to start writing a column and would soon be available to make appearances on the show. (He wasn't invited.)

Others occasionally forget that they toil on the journalistic side of the fence. Bill Safire, a former Nixon White House speechwriter, was asked on *Meet the Press* about the Republican Party's political prospects in 1994. "I'm beginning to worry that we're getting a little smug and complacent," he said.

George Will ruffled some journalistic feathers in 1995 when he joined Newt Gingrich, Dick Armey, and fifty other lawmakers from both parties to push for term limits in Congress. Some reporters covering the press conference in the Capitol groaned when Will was introduced as a featured speaker. Bob Schieffer stood in the back taking notes, one Sunday talking head covering another. Will says he has written and talked so widely about term limits that "this is not a state secret, what my views are." There was no difference, in his eyes, between television advocacy and political activism.

Chris Matthews, who sought Will's advice when he broke into journalism, attributes some of the carping to simple jealously. The host of a nightly talk show on America's Talking, periodic *McLaughlin* panelist, and regular commentator on *Good Morning America,* Matthews joined the punditocracy in 1987 after years of working for Tip O'Neill and the Carter White House. His first move was to sign on as Washington bureau chief of the *San Francisco Examiner,* a job that basically involved writing a twice-weekly column. "He needed to be a journalist to have the kind of respect-ability to be on TV," says Larry Kramer, the former *Examiner* editor who hired Matthews.

Some journalists thought Matthews was remaining a bit too cozy with the pols when Tip O'Neill, Bob Dole, and twenty-seven other members of Congress hosted a book party for him in the Capitol. "I think we're all friends after 6:00 P.M. and I don't see the problem," Matthews maintained.

But this is more than a debate over appearances. Chris Matthews argues that former flacks are superior to journalistic hacks when it comes to covering politics. It is, he says, a choice between "guys who have spent their lives in back rooms" and "guys who have spent their lives hanging out in hallways." What he fails to see is that guys who have hung out in back rooms bring with them plenty of political and ideological baggage. But that hasn't hampered his success.

"When a paper like the *San Francisco Examiner* makes Chris Matthews its Washington bureau chief," David Broder says, "the message that sends to the staff is that the best career line is not doing a good job on the police beat or in Sacramento, but taking a very different route." Still, he says, "I'm clearly spitting into the wind on this one."

Obviously, some sort of statute of limitations must apply here. Bill Moyers, who spent years making PBS specials and briefly served as an *NBC Nightly News* commentator, cannot forever be disqualified from journalism because he served as President Johnson's press secretary thirty years ago. But neither can he erase that particular episode from his résumé, which is one reason he remains a lightning rod for conservative criticism. Moyers caused a further stir when he slept at the Arkansas governor's mansion and counseled President-elect Bill Clinton on how to revitalize the White House (before flying to Washington to fill in for Larry King). "I am a journalist, but my past has never been hidden," Moyers says.

The public was briefly reminded of Moyers' Democratic pedigree, and of Tim Russert's, when Russert threw a welcoming party for the new NBC pundit. Clinton, George Stephanopoulos, Mack McLarty, Interior Secretary Bruce Babbitt, and Russert's old mentor, Pat Moynihan, all stopped by Russert's Northwest Washington home to pay their respects.

Lack of success in politics can spur the search for a new career. Ken Bode of *Washington Week* worked for Morris Udall's 1976 presidential campaign before becoming a reporter. Bob Beckel was Walter Mondale's 1984 campaign manager; after losing forty-nine states, he was not in great demand. So he became a lobbyist and went into journalism as host of Fox's short-lived *Off the Record*, commentator for *CBS This Morning*, and frequent guest host on *Crossfire* and *Larry King Live*.

"I have never said I was a journalist," Beckel says. "What I do is give opinions as a political analyst . . . Nobody ever said journalists have the market cornered on television appearances."

The list goes on. Carl Rowan was ambassador to Finland and ran the U.S. Information Agency in the Kennedy-Johnson years. His colleague on *Inside Washington,* Charles Krauthammer, wrote speeches for Walter Mondale. John Chancellor, the former NBC anchor, did a stint at USIA under Johnson. Tom Johnson, the president of CNN, also worked for LBJ. Pierre Salinger of ABC was John Kennedy's press secretary. Lesley Stahl of *60 Minutes* worked for John Lindsay. Hodding Carter of PBS was the State Department spokesman during the Carter administration. Bernard Kalb of CNN spoke for the State Department for part of the Reagan administration. Mona Charen, a regular on *Capital Gang,* worked for First Lady Nancy Reagan. Tony Snow, a frequent talk show panelist and guest host for Rush Limbaugh, was a speechwriter in the Bush White House. Pete Williams was Bush's Pentagon spokesman before Russert hired him as an NBC reporter.

"I think you get one move," says Jeff Greenfield of *Nightline,* who once worked for John Lindsay and Bobby Kennedy. "You can't reclaim your virginity a second time."

Perhaps not. But David Gergen has been born again as a journalist time and again, emerging from each political stint as an ever more prominent member of the talk show nation. The fact that he has been a paid propagandist for four presidents has merely added to his aura of celebrity.

A tall and likable figure from Durham, North Carolina, Gergen started out as a Democrat who voted for Hubert Humphrey in 1968. Yet he wound up working as a Nixon White House speechwriter and, after Watergate, moved up to become President Ford's communications director. In 1981, despite having opposed Ronald Reagan in the previous two campaigns, Gergen was hired as Reagan's communications director. He became known as both a prodigious leaker—a colleague dubbed him Assistant to the President for *The New York Times*—and world-class media manipulator. He was a key cog in the vaunted Reagan spin machine.

Upon leaving the White House in 1983, Gergen—with no previous journalistic experience beyond the *Yale Daily News*—catapulted his way into the punditocracy. He became a *MacNeil/Lehrer* commentator, paired with Democrat Alan Baron. He was, by his own admission, still a Reagan Republican.

"I felt I had an obligation to the White House to not be a hypercritical voice because I'd worked for the administration," Gergen says. "I find it indecent when people turn around and start attacking the people they had worked for. I pulled my punches and didn't mind being represented as a Republican voice."

In 1986 Mort Zuckerman hired the former political operative to be the editor of *U.S. News*. When that didn't work out, Gergen became a columnist for the magazine and decided "to try to build a voice," meaning he wanted to raise his television profile. He did *McLaughlin*. He did *Face the Nation*. He did *Brinkley*. He did *Nightline*. And he gained a wide following for his *MacNeil/Lehrer* faceoffs with Mark Shields. Both men prided themselves on refusing to be typecast as party spokesmen. Gergen was starting to leave the Reagan legacy behind.

But that didn't mean he was free of political entanglements. Gergen had struck up a friendship in the mid-'80s with Bill and Hillary Clinton, chatting them up at the Renaissance Weekend, an annual schmoozefest for movers and shakers at Hilton Head, South Carolina. When Clinton gave an embarrassingly long speech at the 1988 Democratic convention, Gergen dropped off a note saying, "Chin up. A lot of your friends out there think you're terrific."

The night that Clinton announced his presidential candidacy in 1991, he and Gergen talked for more than an hour about the coming campaign. And when Clinton's thank-you-for-saving-me-from-the-draft letter leaked out during the New Hampshire primary, he and Gergen had another private talk. "I walked through with him what the essence of the charge against him was and the essence of his response . . . and I told him what particular part in his response had made the best impression on me," Gergen says. That, to the untutored observer, sounds an awful lot like a journalist counseling a candidate. Gergen mentioned the friendship on *MacNeil/Lehrer* a few times during the campaign, but few people realized how close they were.

They would soon find out. In early May 1993, with Clinton's presidency off to a disastrous start, the president called Gergen for a long, off-the-record chat. He was speaking not to Gergen the pundit but Gergen the friend. "He just wanted to unburden himself," Gergen says. "He wanted more than anything else a sounding board. I tried to be sensitive to the notion that a journalist should not be giving private advice to public figures, unless you say something you've already said in print or on the air."

Gergen had been chiding Clinton in his commentaries, saying he was "losing his compass," "caving in under pressure," and "lurching to the left too often." Nevertheless, when the president asked Gergen to become his counselor in late May, Gergen agreed. Mort Zuckerman told him he could probably return to *U.S. News*. Gergen made clear he didn't intend to stay more than two years. This was to be a quick spin through the White House gates. Mark Shields gave Gergen a hearty sendoff in his column, calling him "a wise, thoughtful and delightful colleague" and "a man who cares passionately about public service."

Gergen's first talk show interview was, not surprisingly, with *MacNeil/Lehrer*. "Here tonight in his new role . . . David Gergen, newsmaker," Robert MacNeil said. When it was over, Mark Shields and Roger Mudd led a panel discussion on the impact of their former colleague joining the administration. A couple of minutes later, the camera pulled back to show that Gergen was still sitting at the table. He had been there all along. It was a joke, a gentle prank on the audience. Everyone chuckled. They were all good friends, the talk show panelists and their buddy who now worked for the president. It was all part of the Beltway game. Gergen would no doubt be back among them, in Pat Buchanan fashion, once he had rendered his service to the nation.

The following Sunday Gergen appeared on the *Brinkley* show, not as a pundit but as a freshly minted administration spokesman. Gone were the reservations about Clinton losing his compass. He had gotten with the program. "I don't think he needs to save his presidency," Gergen told Donaldson, Will, and the others. "This president's got a lot going for him. He's accomplished a lot. He's had good, strong leadership here."

Bob Dole, appearing on the same program, was a bit skeptical. "What does it tell me about Mr. Gergen? I think it gets him back in a very powerful position," he said.

Eighteen months later, as Gergen was about to leave the administration, he needed television once again. Gergen had been privately telling his journalistic friends that he was deeply disappointed in the Clinton presidency, and the loose talk finally caught up with him. A Reuters story quoted him as saying of Clinton, at a dinner hosted by Bill Safire, that "nobody knows what he stands for." It was a time for damage control, and nobody did damage control better than Dave Gergen. He quickly arranged to go on *Larry King Live,* where he delivered his what-I-really-meant-to-say lines with practiced ease.

"You didn't say he had no convictions?" King asked.

"Of course not," Gergen replied. "He does have convictions . . . This is a man of courage and conviction."

Gergen explains that "I wanted to kill it quickly. I thought it was going to be a story that had legs, and I had to get out front."

Still, Gergen found ways to signal his disenchantment. He appeared on *Charlie Rose,* and when Rose asked him if he would vote for Clinton in '96, Gergen said it was too early to tell. Rose asked again, and Gergen ducked again. He admitted during the break that he had ducked. It was hardly a ringing endorsement.

Once again, Gergen was repositioning himself. Once again, he told White House officials—though not Clinton, who he thought might still be steamed over his intemperate remarks—that he was "not going to be a shill for you guys" when he returned to journalism. Now, Gergen felt he needed a decontamination period. He took up residence at the Aspen Institute, a Washington think tank, and taught a course at Duke University.

"I think it'd be totally wrong to go from working in the government on Friday to commenting on the government on Monday," Gergen says. "If you say something critical, you're an ingrate. If you say something positive, you're in the tank. The audience is confused about what your role is. I didn't want to look like I was cashing in on the situation."

But there was little doubt that he would cash in again. Gergen began giving paid speeches and casting about for media opportunities. He returned to *MacNeil/Lehrer* as a commentator, and Mort Zuckerman brought him back as editor-at-large of *U.S. News.* The former Reagan staffer who made pronouncements about Reagan's '84 reelection campaign would become the former Clinton staffer occasionally dispensing wisdom about Clinton's '96 campaign. The talk show culture beckoned.

For those tossed out of office by the voters, sitting behind the mike can be a form of redemption.

Politicians, after all, have sizable egos. To be rudely rejected by the voters is a humiliating experience. The reporters, the aides, the hangers-on all drift away. What better way to stay in the public spotlight, to keep airing your views, to achieve a measure of vindication, than by joining the talk show culture?

"What does a politician do?" says Jerry Brown, the former California governor, Senate candidate, and three-time presidential contender. "They just talk. They don't do anything else. I don't know that there's a major difference."

After endlessly reciting his 800 number during the '92 campaign, Brown simply used the number on his new radio show to raise money for his political organization, We the People. From a studio on the edge of San Francisco Bay, he began railing against some familiar targets: multinational corporations, the wealthy, political parties, the press. Brown sees organized journalism as part of "a latter-day oligarchy" that includes "million-dollar TV media pundits who pontificate to themselves." His mission, he says, is to expose "bias in the media. There's a protective cover that *The New York Times, Washington Post,* and the networks give to the status quo. I see a rather narrow class organizing the information for this society. Those Sunday shows, assuming somebody watches them, they're all talking to themselves. I want to provide an outlet for a perspective I believe is definitely excluded."

The former governor, whose show is carried by forty-two stations, sees one crucial difference in his new role: He's not trying to mollify voters. "Now that I'm not a politician, I don't have to lie anymore," he says. Brown wants to get his listeners riled up because "the establishment is rotten to the core and we've got to get rid of them. Talk radio is a way to get that upheaval moving."

For the public, listening to out-of-work pols on the radio requires a certain suspension of disbelief, a willful ignorance of the fact that they were recently part of the political order they now so passionately assail. For the ex-officeholder, the host's role can be a liberating experience, the chance to sound off at length without being pestered by annoying reporters or demanding constituents. It is a way to trade up to a much bigger salary. And it is a delicious opportunity to settle old scores.

A year after he was ousted as mayor of New York, Ed Koch had some harsh things to say in his role as television panelist on WCBS's *Sunday Edition*. Koch's target was that morning's guest, Representative Charles Rangel, the veteran Democrat from Harlem. If Rangel "was so concerned about Israel," Koch said, "why did he support Congressman Gus Savage, who is not only anti-Israel but anti-Semitic? And he went out of his way to campaign actively for this anti-Semite."

Koch's choice of targets was hardly coincidental. Rangel had called him "a sick man" during the 1989 mayoral campaign, and now it was payback time.

Rangel fired off a blistering letter, accusing Koch of "malicious" and "slanderous" remarks. "Waiting to sneak in your smear until I had no chance to reply on camera was a cheap shot, even for you," Rangel said. WCBS, which had been losing patience with Koch, dropped him from the program. "They asked me to tone down my personality and thought I was too controversial," Koch says.

That was just the beginning for Ed Koch, media superstar. He had already started writing a column for the *New York Post*. WABC radio, less fearful of controversy than local television, gave Koch his own morning show, putting him on before Rush Limbaugh. Koch began broadcasting from his Sixth Avenue law office, calling people "wackos" and dumping callers who rubbed him the wrong way. The ratings went through the roof.

Koch does his Mayor Mouth routine without guests. His show is an hourlong monologue punctuated by callers. He begins by critiquing the local papers, often getting even with those who criticized him during his twelve years in the mayor's office. He dismisses former *Daily News* columnist Earl Caldwell, who is black, as a "racist." He accuses *The New York Times* of harboring a "politically correct editorial board." Reverend Louis Farrakhan is a "monster." Representative Harold Ford, also black, is a "dope."

"It's much more fun to be a critic than a victim," Koch says.

But Koch is not always negative. He endorsed Mario Cuomo,

despite their many feuds, for a fourth term as governor. He also made a commercial for Cuomo, which the Cuomo camp paid to air on his show. It was a hall of mirrors: Koch the commentator extolling Cuomo live, followed by Koch the ex-mayor endorsing Cuomo on tape.

Koch says he learned the art of brevity as a congressman in the '70s, making one-minute speeches on the House floor. He admits to "a certain amount of theatricality" and revels in his high Arbitron numbers. "This is not my shtick," he says. "My shtick is being a lawyer. To do something other people have as their prime vocation —and I beat them—gives me an enormous sense of pleasure."

No modern politician used talk shows to greater effect than Ross Perot, so it was natural that he would keep on talking after the '92 campaign. Hosting a weekly radio show from Dallas, he denounced the big shots while hailing "the wisdom from grassroots America." The Perot pitch is reminiscent of Rush Limbaugh in its indictment of the establishment.

"Washington obviously thinks you're too dumb to know what's going on," he said. "The whole purpose of this program is to make sure every American knows what's going on and cannot be manipulated by the latest distortions coming out of Washington."

Many of Perot's callers shared his worldview. John from Connecticut called one Sunday to complain about "these crazy people in the press . . . a bunch of outrageous liberals with these special agendas for these fringe groups."

"Here's the good news," Perot said. "More and more people are going to talk radio because they like to get the facts and they like to have a voice."

Perot rarely let the facts interfere with his political diatribes. On one show he declared "the word on the street" is that the United States had paid Haitian General Raoul Cedras "millions of dollars" to leave the country. No corroboration, in his view, was necessary. Perot also charged, again without offering evidence, that Haitian President Jean-Bertrand Aristide is "suspected of being a major drug dealer." On another program he interviewed economist Pat Choate about the negative effects of the GATT trade agreement.

"Some people say we're giving up part of our sovereignty. Is that true or not?" Perot asked.

"It is true," Choate replied. Perot felt no need to mention that he and Choate had coauthored a book attacking the NAFTA agreement, instead presenting him as an independent expert with "all kinds of degrees." (Choate, having gotten a taste of Perot-style publicity, has since launched his own radio show. Perot, meanwhile, tired of the radio gig and dropped it after eight months.)

The height of absurdity came when Ross Perot sat in for Larry King. It was early 1995, and the billionaire remained a potent political force, making speeches, endorsing candidates, denouncing NAFTA, and weighing another White House campaign. Perot's celebrity status made him irresistible to CNN, which already had an all-but-declared candidate, Pat Buchanan, cohosting *Crossfire*. Now, in an obvious ratings ploy, the network abandoned the notion that its interviewers should, however temporarily, work in journalism. Perot's guest was Bob Dole. It was less an interview than a love-in as Perot and Dole praised each other and recited their applause lines, hawking their wares for the cameras.

"Are you going to run for president in 1996?" Perot asked. "Well, now, what better place to announce it than on *Larry King Live*? . . . What are your plans?"

"Well, maybe I should ask you that question," Dole replied. "We could both announce it right here together."

When Dole allowed that he would probably run for president— as the whole country already knew—Perot said: "Well, that's exciting. And remember, you heard it on *Larry King Live*." CNN officials were so pleased they later tapped Dan Quayle as a substitute for King.

By 1995 an extraordinary number of defeated and retired pols were flooding the talk radio circuit. It had become a rite of passage, almost a perk of leaving office.

Six months after Mario Cuomo was ousted as governor, he launched a Saturday morning radio show from New York with about twenty stations. Brushing aside those who imagined him as the Rush Limbaugh of the left—and a huge cash offer from Sony Worldwide Networks—Cuomo refused to sign a contract for five days a week. He says he would rather have a smaller audience and deliver "complicated truths."

"People are closer to frenetic during the week, driving to work with one hand on the wheel and one hand on the cellular phone," he says. "Once a week, you have a better opportunity to reach people if your argument takes more than one sentence . . . I'm not a guy who's going to shout at you to get your attention."

Cuomo envisions a program in which he interviews welfare mothers as well as famous politicians. And while he displays an autographed picture of himself with Clinton in his Lexington Avenue law office, Cuomo insists he is not taking to the airwaves as a Democratic party spokesman. "So much of political communication is shibboleth, slogan, partial truths, mostly huge generalizations—and Democrats are just as guilty," he says.

Days before launching the show, Cuomo fretted aloud about becoming part of a wacky talk culture. "The danger is it gets to be entertainment. You start having to speak in shorthand. McLaughlin makes it because he's more histrionic than historical. Novak makes it because he's so outrageous, he looks like an aging conservative gnome."

Cuomo began to work the talk circuit. He sat in on the *Brinkley* roundtable, denouncing "Republican hypocrisy." He filled in for his old pal Larry King. One of his first radio guests was his former aide, Tim Russert, whose handling of *Meet the Press* was criticized by several hostile callers. "He took thousands of dollars to interview Bob Dole before a banking group," one said. "How can we expect him to ask fair or tough questions of Bob Dole?"

Cuomo's initial outings were flat, his tone a bit preachy as he recycled old applause lines like "we should have all the government we need but only the government we need." His first caller was a Howard Stern prankster, his second an insult artist who called him a *sfaccimm*. "You were a big supporter of these big liberal left-wing policies that ruined New York State," Jim from Washington told Cuomo. It was a rude welcome to the realities of talk radio.

In Virginia two of the three unsuccessful Senate candidates wound up on the air. Oliver North took up residence in afternoon drive time at Washington's WRC and was syndicated nationwide. And former governor Douglas Wilder settled in at Richmond's WRVA, bumping his Republican successor, Governor George Allen, to another time slot. Wilder, a party maverick, heaped praise on Allen, his first guest, and chided his former Democratic running mates and Democrats in the state legislature. The sound of grinding axes could be heard in the background. (Wilder failed to attract an audience and was dropped in the summer of 1995.)

North, who had already amassed a nationwide conservative following during his role in the Iran-contra affair, had served notice after losing to Chuck Robb that he planned to run for office again. After raising a record $20 million for his campaign, North kept on raising money, assailing the "media jackals" who his followers loved to hate. What better way to solidify his political base than by holding forth on the air fifteen hours a week? The fact that he had once misled Congress was all but forgotten. The criminal case had turned him into a celebrity, and that made him a marketable radio personality. He was picked up by 122 stations in just three months.

"This is radio with a mission," North declared on his first day, when he "shredded" a caller who raised his controversial past by turning on a mock paper shredder. Sipping coffee from a silver canteen, he attacked "the potentates of pork on the Potomac . . . This microphone is my chance to get a message out based on conservative principles and traditional values . . . I really relish this three hours a day I've got to develop an issue beyond a seven-second sound bite on the evening news." North's first telephone guest was Larry King. "Ollie, you're a terrific personality . . . You can always jump back into politics," King said.

If history is written by the victors, radio hosts also have a chance to put their spin on it. North, who was indicted in the biggest scandal of the 1980s, did not hesitate to accuse Clinton of an "unprecedented sleaze factor." As for the newspaper he called "The Washington Compost," he could not understand how its public opinion poll found less support for the Contract with America than the 90 percent of his listeners who called in to support the contract, as if that were a scientifically valid sample. "Where does *The Washington Post* find these people?" North asked.

North's station was not above exploiting his program for corporate ends. While North was interviewing Newt Gingrich, top executives arranged for WRC's No. 2 official, Warren Wright, to call the show, posing as "Bill from Fairfax." After praising North's program, "Bill" declared his opposition to House legislation that would lift federal restrictions on the number of radio stations that one company can own. When I asked North, who was not in on the scam, if he felt his listeners had been deceived, he said he was "disappointed" by the phony call but that this sort of thing goes on all the time in talk radio. "That's perhaps a disadvantage of this medium," he said.

Radio executives lusted after the kind of name recognition that politicians automatically provided. Former New York mayor David Dinkins landed a twice-weekly slot on WLIB, where he described how a taxi refused to pick him up on his way to teach a class on racism but stopped for a white person down the street. Dinkins also criticized the man who defeated him, Rudy Giuliani, just as Ed Koch had used radio to criticize Dinkins. Jim Hightower, the one-time Texas agricultural commissioner, made waves with a syndicated show that used the number 1-800-AGITATE. Marjorie Clapprood, who narrowly lost her 1990 bid for Massachusetts lieutenant governor, was part of a hot morning duo in Boston. Mike Boyle, who was recalled by the voters as mayor of Omaha, was reincarnated as a local deejay. Christine Todd Whitman, who lost a New Jersey Senate race to Bill Bradley, hosted a radio show before being elected governor. Blanquita Cullum, a former Bush administration official, was attracting attention on Washington radio. Benjamin Chavis, fired as the NAACP's executive director, settled behind the mike at Washington's WOL. They all followed in the footsteps of the late Philadelphia mayor Frank Rizzo, who recast himself as a radio host denouncing "all the liberal garbage being dispensed in this town."

Former Chicago alderman "Fast Eddie" Vrdolyak, after three crushing defeats, resurfaced on WLS in afternoon drive time. Vrdolyak slammed Mayor Richard Daley, a longtime antagonist, at every turn, urging listeners to call City Hall if they disagree with Daley's policies. He also took regular shots at the press, particularly the *Chicago Tribune,* which once called him "ol' Rasputin." "I'm there to correct most of the people in the media," Vrdolyak says.

Not every former public official hit it big. David Duke was dropped by a small station in Covington, Louisiana, his deejay career no more successful than his campaigns for governor and president. The owner, Robert Namer, a Jewish businessman, says he hired Duke because running a profitable station was more important than any qualms he had about Duke's views. But, he says, Duke spent too much time on racial issues. "David's got to loosen up, develop a wit," Namer says. Daryl Gates, the former L.A. police chief, also fizzled after a brief run. Fame, or notoriety, was not enough. A talk show host had to be able to engage the audience, and some ex-pols were just too stiff.

Still, radio remained a unique vehicle for rebuilding shattered reputations. Vincent "Buddy" Cianci resigned as mayor of Providence in 1984 after pleading no contest to assault charges for beating a contractor he believed was having an affair with his wife. The disgrace didn't stop him from becoming a popular Providence radio host. Cianci regained the mayor's office in 1990 and still runs the city.

Roger Hedgecock resigned as mayor of San Diego in 1985 after being convicted of conspiracy and perjury in a scheme to funnel $350,000 into his campaign. The conviction was later overturned on procedural grounds, but Hedgecock never forgot that the *San Diego Union-Tribune* had helped drive him from office. After becoming the morning man on KSDO, Hedgecock frequently used his new megaphone to denounce the paper for biased reporting.

"They tried to control me, and every other elected official, through the editorials and the news coverage," Hedgecock says. "We've been able to give a different side to stories the paper wanted to slant, or give facts that are completely different from what was in the paper. I think they are an anachronism."

In his first days as mayor, Hedgecock says, his private line rang. It was the *Union-Tribune*'s editorial page editor, who regularly used the hotline to call Hedgecock's predecessor, Pete Wilson. "I wanted to let you know how we feel about some items," the editor said. Hedgecock wasn't interested.

Hedgecock sees himself as broadcasting to "the great silent majority." In the late '80s, he began crusading for people to drive south and shine their headlights across the Mexican border to protest illegal immigration. "We were branded as racists in the paper," he says.

Gerald Warren, who recently stepped down as the *Union-Tribune*'s editor, says Hedgecock "very much wants to get even for what he sees as insults, slights, and attacks on him." He says Hedgecock has assailed him and owner Helen Copley in unusually personal terms, even calling her "anti-Catholic."

Warren, himself a former Nixon White House aide, says Hedgecock once lambasted him for a controversial speech. "He said I'd made these statements after three or four drinks. I haven't had a drink in nearly six years. He is willing to say something, whether it's true or not, regardless of how it hurts another person. He doesn't bother to check things if they fit his agenda."

Hedgecock, who doubles as a lobbyist for developers and gambling interests, has found other targets. He described the gay lifestyle as a "deathstyle," sparking a boycott campaign by a local gay organization that accused him of preaching hatred and intolerance. "The homosexual activists want to broad-brush this by saying that I'm homophobic, and I'm not," Hedgecock says.

Perhaps no one in talk show land has more completely transformed his identity than Jerry Springer, one of *Donahue*'s many daytime competitors. Most people have forgotten that Springer was the mayor of Cincinnati in the early '70s. Even fewer recall that he resigned after acknowledging a liaison with a prostitute in a Kentucky motel.

But in true daytime talk fashion, Springer sought forgiveness. In 1982, while running for governor of Ohio, he aired a rather unusual ad. "Some nine years ago, I spent time with a woman I shouldn't have," Springer told viewers. "I paid her with a check. I wish I hadn't done that. The truth is I wish no one would even know."

Then came the audacious appeal: "Ohio is in a world of hurt, and the next governor is going to have to take some heavy risk and face some hard truths. I'm prepared to do that. This commercial should be proof. I'm not afraid of the truth, even if it hurts." Springer finished a distant third in the primary, but he had found his true calling.

If talk radio was becoming a haven for unemployed politicians, it was hardly surprising that some hosts were succumbing to the lure of the campaign trail. It was, in a sense, a natural progression. Radio had become a conduit for public discontent with the political system, and sooner or later it was bound to give rise to a new generation of protest candidates. Buoyed by their aura of celebrity, instinctively disdainful of career politicians, they decided that running the world would be as easy as running their mouth.

They were wrong. Ten radio personalities ran for Congress or statewide office in 1994. All but one lost. The transition from the airwaves, where they could monopolize the conversation, to the stump, where they were constantly under siege, was a rocky one.

Ronna Romney, a Detroit talk show host, mounted a high-profile bid for a Senate seat in Michigan. As the former daughter-in-law of onetime Michigan governor George Romney, she combined a famous political name with talk show fame.

"Talk radio really became the vehicle that propelled me into politics," Romney says. "I have high name ID, and people know what I stand for. They know about my personal life, about my children. When I stepped from behind the mike to the political arena, many people who listened to my voice followed me."

But not enough. Despite an early lead in the polls, Romney was trounced in the GOP primary by Spencer Abraham, who went on to win the seat. Romney went back on the air in Detroit and immediately began planning another run in '96.

Janet Jeghelian, a Boston talk show host, mounted a long-shot bid against Ted Kennedy; she lost in the Republican primary. In Florida, three radio hosts—Beverly Kennedy, Wendell Griffith, and Marc Little—ran for Congress as Republicans in separate districts; all lost. In Arkansas, Indiana, and Oregon, talk show candidates also mounted losing efforts.

On one station in West Yarmouth, Massachusetts, the triumph of talk radio politics was complete. The morning man on WXTK, Republican Ed Teague, found himself running for the state legislature against the afternoon host, Democrat Cathy Brown. Both stayed on the air throughout the campaign. "It allowed people to compare and contrast us," Teague says.

Many listeners didn't realize that Teague had been a state representative for six years. He left the show an hour early each morning to drive to the capitol in Boston. Some constituents quizzed him about issues on the air. "You were exposed politically all the time," he says. "I'm sure some people disliked what I said from time to time, but they knew what they were getting."

Brown, a town selectman, found her radio fame outweighed by the on-air warfare. Teague's campaign, she says, "would set up calls. They would have people call up and throw a bomb at you, and you just learned to handle it. If someone wants to attempt to embarrass you on live radio, you just face it."

While WXTK asked both hosts not to discuss the race on the air, Teague's cohost, Peter Kenney, "campaigned for Ed on the radio," Cathy Brown says. "He would bad-mouth me on the radio time and again, calling me an idiot and saying 'what does she know, she's a girl.' " Teague admits that his partner "made mention of the race more than was necessary. It was pretty clumsy for me." Both candidates quit the station after the election. Brown went back to her restaurant business; Teague is now House minority leader.

Not everyone took politics so seriously. In New York, Howard Stern staged what appeared to be a joke candidacy for governor. It was good for some on-air ranting and raving, just like when Imus had run against Barry Goldwater Jr. a quarter century earlier. But after the Libertarian Party officially nominated Stern, some political pros said he could be a factor in drawing votes away from Republican George Pataki. Candidate Stern, whose platform consisted of reinstating the death penalty and making highway repair crews work at night, even made the front page of *The New York Times*. "He's bringing us shock politics," said Ludwig Vogel, the state Libertarian chairman. Certainly Stern's constant denunciations of Mario Cuomo didn't do the incumbent any good. Stern pulled out of the race after a judge ruled that he would have to comply with state election law by disclosing his finances. That, the millionaire deejay decided, was no joking matter.

The problem, as many broadcasters learned, is that sharp language that appeals to a loyal radio audience can backfire with the broader electorate. The goal in politics is to avoid offending a majority of voters, while talk show hosts are paid to be outrageous. "When you're a talk show host, your job is to create provocative conversation," says Mike Siegel, the Seattle radio rebel. "A politician is trying to bring people together. They're almost 180 degrees diametrically opposed." Siegel considered running for the Senate in 1994 but decided to wait for the Washington governor's race in '96.

One candidate who successfully made the leap was J. D. Hayworth of Arizona. Hayworth was known in Phoenix primarily as a TV sportscaster. But in 1990 he enjoyed a brief run as a radio host on KFYI. While running for the House four years later, the Republican kept doing a daily radio commentary for months, even as opponents tried to knock him off the air.

"Radio for me was a very good bridge into a more serious vein,"
Hayworth says. "It gave the listeners a taste of my other interests.
The whole idea of message discipline, the turn of a phrase on the
stump, you also use on the electronic stump." Now, the congressman says, "I do as much talk radio as I can."

Once conservatives had mastered the art of using talk shows for
political ends, it was probably inevitable that they would try to take
over the means of communication.

Convinced that the press was relentlessly liberal, the activists of
the right were determined to broaden their message beyond talk
radio, to reach more than just the Limbaugh and Liddy crowd.
They wanted nothing less than their own television networks. And,
to an extraordinary degree, they have been successful.

These conservatives are far too sophisticated to broadcast crude
propaganda. The new right-wing media have appropriated the para-
phernalia of the news business: anchor desks, colorful graphics,
call-in hosts, reporters doing standups. It is the ultimate fusion of
partisan politics and the talk show culture.

In a modern town house behind the Senate office buildings on
Capitol Hill, a $10-million renovation has produced the modern
studios of National Empowerment Television. Founded by Paul
Weyrich, the veteran conservative activist who runs the Free Congress Foundation, it is C-SPAN with attitude, a full-fledged menu
of call-in shows that lean to the right.

Soon after its debut in late 1993, NET was available in ten
million homes by satellite or cable. Its brand of conservative chat
quickly found an audience, drawing fifty-four thousand viewer calls
a month. Some 175 advertisers signed on.

Most of the network's political guests are Republicans, although
such liberal lawmakers as Barney Frank have also made appearances. "Almost nobody turns us down," says Burton Yale Pines,
until recently NET"s vice chairman and the host of his own nightly
show. "It's live television. You do a fifteen-minute interview with
CBS or NBC and they edit you down to thirty seconds and embarrass you. Politicians love live television because they control it. We
don't set up ambushes and we're not piranhas."

The network's biggest star is Newt Gingrich. His weekly program, *Progress Report,* is financed by the Progress and Freedom Foundation, which also pays to televise Gingrich's lectures on American civilization at Reinhardt College in Georgia. The congressman's presence gave the network instant credibility. And he has been even more valuable since becoming House speaker, appearing at a $50,000-a-plate fundraiser for NET.

"We're trying to explore the positive aspects of what's happening in America . . . We've not engaged the intellectual side enough," Gingrich says. "Network news takes nine- or twelve-second sound bites. Here's a chance to be in a person's living room for an hour in a nonconfrontational mode, which is good for the Republican Party and frankly good for me."

Gingrich's foundation is buying his way on the air for $125,000 a year, as are a host of other conservative groups: Reed Irvine's Accuracy in Media. Beverly LaHaye's Concerned Women for America. The National Rifle Association. The Cato Institute. The American Life League.

There is also a twentysomething *McLaughlin* knockoff called *Youngbloods.* The young pundits, ranging from an aide to Senator Trent Lott to a gay liberal, shoot the breeze on living room chairs and couches, dressed in jeans and miniskirts. Other big-name conservatives have flocked to NET. Bob Novak has a show. Former attorney general William Barr has a show. Weyrich, a onetime NBC correspondent, has a show. Armstrong Williams, the black conservative radio host, has a show. Arianna Huffington, the flashy socialite and wife of former Republican congressman Michael Huffington, has a show. Huffington was so upset with the "wolf-pack" press and the way it covered her husband's 1994 Senate campaign that she began planning a syndicated Sunday program called *Beat the Press,* to focus on victims of unfair media coverage. Her guest for the pilot episode would be Newt Gingrich. It sounded more like *Beat Up on the Press.*

In a cluttered marketplace, NET has successfully positioned itself as a network for those fed up with politics as usual. "The vast majority of callers are populists," Pines says. "We get a lot of Democrats. We're tapping very much into the Perot phenomenon, those who are pissed at Washington."

NET may soon have some competition. The Conservative Television Network plans to launch in 1996 with a mixture of news, entertainment, and electronic town halls. The chairman, lest anyone harbor doubts about its ideology, is Republican Senator Malcolm Wallop of Wyoming. Founded by GOP media consultant Anthony Fabrizio, the network's advisers include Floyd Brown, the creator of the infamous Willie Horton commercial, and top executives from the Heritage Foundation, *National Review,* and American Conservative Union.

The Republican Party itself has joined the television fray. GOP-TV, launched by Haley Barbour, the party chairman, is available on more than two thousand cable systems. With the help of taped appeals from Ronald Reagan and George Bush, it has been both an organizing tool and a way to showcase rising GOP governors and mayors. Young Republican staffers pose as reporters, delivering polished reports in front of the Capitol dome. Barbour's premier show, *Rising Tide,* which he hosts, is carried by WOR, the New York superstation. "We don't want it to be just talking heads sitting around chewing the fat," Barbour says. "We try to make it fast-moving. We want it to have a news look."

On one program, following a news update, "reporter" David Thibault said Clinton had been "ignoring the crisis" in Medicare. "He doesn't tell the truth, he never has," said a Florida woman interviewed by Thibault. Barbour then gently questioned Florida Senator Connie Mack, who said the president had "failed" to grapple with Medicare's slide toward bankruptcy but that the Republicans would "improve" the program. There was no mention, of course, that Republicans had blocked any action on health care for two years by insisting there was no health care crisis, or that the coming Medicare cutbacks were likely to be painful.

Barbour's next guest was former Oregon congressman Denny Smith, who launched a radio show in 1994 after losing a bid for governor. The two sang the praises of talk radio.

"We try to give people the news unfiltered," Barbour said. "Talk radio does that too."

"They know they're getting the straight stuff from the horse's mouth," Smith agreed.

"We don't need the news media to tell us what to think," Barbour said. Of course, the notion that GOP-TV is "unfiltered," when every moment is scripted for partisan effect, is laughable. But the slickly packaged shows make the Democrats look like they are communicating with tin cans and string.

Even presidential candidates have their own TV operations these days. Lamar Alexander, the former Tennessee governor, held monthly meetings with party activists in two thousand communities through a linkup called the Republican Exchange Satellite Network, broadcasting from a studio once used by *Hee Haw.* "This is the way America likes to meet in the '90s," Alexander says. "We're a media-drenched nation, and virtually all the ideas flow through Washington, D.C. It's hard for people in Nashville and Billings and Concord to be part of the national debate."

Many Democrats scoffed at these ventures as preaching to the choir, but it soon became clear that partisan television was effective. The liberals, complacent and underfunded, found themselves watching the revolution from the sidelines. The only avowedly liberal outlet, the '90s Network in Denver, had few programs and reached just six hundred thousand homes. The momentum was all on the other side. Conservatives had long felt marginalized by the talk show culture, and now they had found a way to eliminate the middleman.

What was once something of a closed shop—talk shows run by career journalists and very much reflecting their values—had been blown wide open. Candidates and strategists moved easily from political combat to the talk show arena and back again, blurring the old distinctions beyond recognition. Politicians were wresting control of the microphone from their media adversaries. The public was being exposed to a more diverse range of voices than ever before, but amid the sound and fury were all kinds of personal agendas and animosities. Viewers and listeners now had to be on guard, to decipher and decode the mixed messages from this rapidly changing media culture. It was a new era, a time when anyone could have a talk show. Anyone at all. Even me.

CHAPTER FOURTEEN

A PERSONAL ODYSSEY

O ne humid Friday afternoon, I finally lost my temper on television.

The regular weekly taping of *Reliable Sources,* the CNN show that examines the media, had just gotten under way on the opposite side of Larry King's eleventh-floor studio. Bernard Kalb, the crusty moderator with the unfashionably wide brown ties, was in his usual seat across from me, facing the everpresent TelePrompTer. Martin Schram, syndicated columnist and resident wise guy, was to Kalb's right, and Ellen Hume, the feisty analyst from the Annenberg Washington Program, was on my right.

Seated in the middle of this semicircle was a red-bearded man whose job was to bait us. Brent Bozell, a conservative activist, is an affable enough fellow in person, but gives no quarter when assailing what he sees as the hopelessly liberal media. While Bozell styles himself a media critic, he is also a political player who served as Pat Buchanan's finance chairman in the 1992 presidential campaign. On this spring day in 1994, CNN had invited Bozell to *Reliable Sources* to make sure there were some fireworks.

Our first topic was the lawsuit that Paula Jones, the former Arkansas state employee, had just filed against President Clinton, accusing him of sexually harassing her in a Little Rock hotel room three years earlier. My newspaper, *The Washington Post,* had received considerable publicity for wrestling with the allegations for three months before finally publishing a pair of front-page stories about the case.

Schram set the stage by reading from a fund-raising letter for Bozell's Media Research Center, which charged that "the liberal press is purposely withholding from the American public this information."

"Are they withholding it?" Bozell shot back. "In Howie Kurtz's paper, that's exactly what happened with the person who wanted to do a story on it and couldn't run it."

That, for some reason, set me off. "I'm not gonna let that go by," I broke in. "That was a *front-page* story last week that didn't meet your timetable, but was published on the front page!"

"It ran weeks and weeks after your reporter who had been covering the story went to his editors and said let's run this thing, and his editors wouldn't let him," Bozell said, pointing at me.

"We should let *you* decide?" I demanded, pointing back.

"Is that true or not?"

"We should let *you* decide what we publish?"

"Is that true or not, what I just said?"

"The story was published."

"Weeks later."

Kalb broke in at that point, and Hume declared that "we're not going to let some conservative-agenda person on this program attack the *Post* for doing it right for a change." It was good theater, I suppose, but to most viewers it must have seemed just another televised shouting match.

I was mad at myself for losing it on the air, but even more frustrated that the difficult issue of when newspapers should publish disputed allegations had gotten lost in the clamor. Actually, I agreed that the *Post* had been too slow to publish Paula Jones's allegations, not out of any partisan desire to protect Clinton but from an abundance of caution about airing explosive charges against a sitting president. Bozell had overstated the case in classic debater's fashion, boxing me into a corner where I had to defend my newspaper. To have tried to explain the nuances of the issue would have undercut my argument and exhausted the precious seconds allotted me before someone cut in and the discussion lurched on to the next topic.

As I've started appearing more regularly on the tube in recent years, I have been forced to confront the inescapable truth that television is the enemy of complexity. You rarely have time to express the fine points, the caveats, the context of your subject. You're always being interrupted just as you try to make a larger point. What works best on a talk show is the snappy one-liner, the artful insult, the definitive declaration. What makes you look weak and vacillating is an acknowledgment that your case is not airtight, that the other side may have a valid point. And so I have felt myself sliding into the very trap I have often criticized in my role as a media reporter, a willingness to oversimplify things to secure my spot in the talk show nation.

Let's be honest: Going on TV is a blast. Your mother thinks you're important. Your sources think you're important. The guy who fixes your car at the Exxon station recognizes you. Your friends tell you that they liked your tie, although they usually can't remember what it is you said. You reach a far wider audience than in print. The feeling you get when the red light goes on—that your babbling is somehow of interest to millions—is quite seductive.

We all devise various rationalizations for becoming what my colleague E. J. Dionne calls a "media slut." My own reasoning is that I use television to bring to a broader audience the subject that I study and write about, the media. But the truth is that there are so many iterations of the subject—from war correspondents in Bosnia to on-line communication to First Amendment lawsuits to coverage of health care or poverty or religion—that I invariably find myself sounding off about matters on which I am less than fully informed. In other words, I wing it—just like everyone else on television.

When I first started doing taped interviews for *Nightline* or *Dateline NBC* or the *Brinkley* show, I would spend a few minutes scribbling down the six or seven points I wanted to make. What a yutz! No matter how cogent or eloquent or insightful I was, the programs would use only one or two sentences, invariably the punchiest or most colorful. I learned to deduce in advance which "bite" would make it on the air. Sometimes the reporter would take some of my other comments and make those points himself. I gradually realized that my role was simply to provide a pithy declaration to go with a piece of tape, or fill a gap in the narrative, or serve up a suitable kicker. My fame, such as it was, was limited to roughly 6.8 seconds.

Once the talk show bookers got me in their Rolodexes, my

phone began to ring more often. Sometimes I would calmly protest that I didn't know much about the subject at hand; the bookers never seemed to care. If *Entertainment Tonight* needed someone to talk about how sitcoms have become more sexually explicit over the years, I would do quite nicely, although I rarely watch sitcoms anymore. Glibness and instant availability are prized above all. After all, how much knowledge do you need to provide a few seconds for John Tesh and Mary Hart on the subject of *Roseanne*?

The phrase "pack journalism" takes on a new resonance when you're interviewed over and over on the same subject. ABC didn't particularly care if I'd said the same thing on CBS or NPR a couple of days earlier; in fact, that seemed only to add to my aura of marketability. Talk show producers watch other talk shows for ideas, and your appearance on one somehow certifies you as an expert for the others. What's more, they like knowing in advance what your "take" is on the subject. In one stretch during the '92 presidential primaries, I appeared on a half-dozen shows to discuss, yes, how talk shows had taken over the campaign. When O. J. Simpson was arrested in June 1994, every talk show in America decided within days to do the "media circus" angle, even as they eagerly plunged into the three-ring extravaganza themselves. I did O.J. on *48 Hours,* O.J. on *Nightline,* O.J. on *Dateline NBC,* O.J. on *Larry King Live,* O.J. on *Equal Time,* O.J. on *Entertainment Tonight,* O.J. on *Brinkley.* All these interviews were free of charge. The only payment is in ego gratification.

Strange things started to happen. Viewers who had seen me on some program would call me at work and insist on continuing the discussion, as if I had nothing better to do and life was just one long talk show. Obscure radio stations, some as far away as Australia, would call me at home at odd hours. Desperate TV bookers would ask if I knew a woman—any woman—to fill out a panel on this or that topic. Knowledge was secondary; wearing a skirt is what mattered when producers wanted to break up the row of dark suits and power ties. They found it particularly hard to line up conservative women. Affirmative action, I learned, is not just a talk show topic but a talk show way of life.

I didn't fully understand the game in the late '80s, my pre-TV era, when a booker for *Crossfire* called about an article I had written about my love-hate relationship with New York City. Would I be willing to debate, say, Ed Koch, by arguing that the city had turned into a hopeless, stinking sewer? Well, I explained, it was a bit more complicated than that, the news wasn't all bad, and so on. I never got a call back. I later heard the producer thought I was too "intellectual" for the show. Kind of a compliment, I guess.

More recently, I was invited on *Under Scrutiny with Jane Wallace* to talk about the trend toward tabloid journalism. Tabloid news, it turns out, is one of the favorite topics for talk shows because it allows them to devote an entire program to Lorena Bobbitt or Heidi Fleiss or Bill Clinton's sex life under the banner of high-minded analysis. The day after I agreed to do the show, I got a call back from the booker. They were now planning to bring on Joey Buttafuoco, the Long Island lowlife whose sole claim to fame was that he had been boffing a teenage girl who later shot his wife in the head. Would I mind appearing with this esteemed gentleman? I quickly begged off the show (as it turned out, so did Buttafuoco). One must have standards, you know.

But it wasn't until *Reliable Sources* was launched in 1992 that I got a more complete education in the realities of talking head television. The staff at CNN works hard at putting together a good program, and some of the shows really clicked. But I couldn't help but notice that any topic deemed too esoteric—how the press covers the environment, or the Supreme Court, or news on the Internet—was generally rejected in favor of segments on Bill Clinton, Hillary Clinton, Newt Gingrich, O. J. Simpson, Tonya Harding, or our all-purpose fallback, cynicism in the media. Stories involving newspapers in Hartford or Pittsburgh were invariably bumped for that week's big Beltway issue, the same issue that all the other talk shows were talking about. The staff often worked at getting big-name talkers on the show—Sam Donaldson, Jack Germond, Cokie Roberts, Fred Barnes, Michael Barone, Eleanor Clift—rather than beat reporters who specialized in the subject at hand. The producers liked stories on major public figures the audience would instantly recognize, especially if there was some recent videotape of the person for the little setup package at the top of the segment. One time we kicked around an ESPN interview in which an angry athlete knocked over a table—something none of us knew a damn thing about—just so CNN could replay the tape for the forty-ninth time.

On a weekly panel show, one quickly becomes acquainted with the everpresent danger of saying something dumb. Or contradictory. Or incomprehensible. The topics race by and the words come tumbling out, with no chance to modify or soften or erase them. One time Bernie Kalb asked me a question I couldn't quite follow and the camera went to a tight shot just as my face filled with befuddlement. I soon learned the politician's trick of ignoring the actual question and answering the question you wished you'd been asked ("The real issue here, Bernie, is . . .").

Low blows come with the territory. Fred Barnes joined our panel one week during a discussion of the coverage of the extraordinarily nasty Virginia senate race between Oliver North and Chuck Robb. The media had certainly been beating up on North, but Barnes ratcheted up the argument about five levels by turning to me and calling *The Washington Post* "a wholly owned subsidiary of the Robb campaign." I mumbled something about how this was unfair and moved on, but I later told Barnes he had really overstated his case.

"It's television," he said with a shrug. By *McLaughlin* standards, I suppose, it was pretty mild stuff.

The biggest adjustment in doing a panel show has to do with the time constraints. With three or four other panelists, and perhaps a guest or two appearing by satellite, nobody has more than a few seconds to make a point and someone is always cutting you off. CNN favors an uptempo style, apparently fearing that any discourse that lasts more than fourteen seconds will send viewers lunging for the clicker. Cram in three or four topics per show and you've got what sometimes feels like an exercise in superficiality. We didn't hurl insults at each other, but we often had the potential for a more enlightening debate than the twenty-two minute format permitted.

The segment I resented most was dubbed "The Good, the Bad and the Ugly," a ripoff of *McLaughlin*'s predictions and *Capital Gang*'s outrage of the week (and itself soon copied by *Capital Gang Sunday*'s "Hall of Fame" and "Hall of Shame"). Marty Schram, Ellen Hume, and I all argued against this obvious gimmick, to no avail. Many of the news items I was reporting for my media column couldn't be used because there was no way to explain them in the allotted fifteen to twenty seconds. One or more of us would frequently arrive at the studio with no suitable tidbit and would have to scramble to come up with something. It was, in a word, ugly. (In fairness, however, viewers seemed to like it.)

We may have reached the height of absurdity when Charles Murray and Richard Herrnstein published their book, *The Bell Curve: Intelligence and Class Structure in American Life,* with its controversial theory linking race and IQ. The book was receiving an avalanche of publicity—cover stories in *Newsweek, The New Republic, The New York Times Magazine*—and Schram and I argued for cutting back on the day's other subjects so we'd have enough time for a decent discussion.

But when the other topics had run their course, Bernie Kalb repeated the producer's admonition on the remaining time. "A minute forty-five," he said. I was stunned. One minute and forty-five seconds for four people to examine whether IQ is inherited or the product of environmental differences and whether that could explain low test scores among blacks.

The music came up, and we went into our once-around. Schram called the coverage of *The Bell Curve* "at least as destructive as it was provocative." I defended the reporting by saying "if you don't talk about it and you don't write about it, you leave it to the talk shows, you leave it to the whispering campaigns." Ellen Hume said the book "has been hyped way out of proportion to the quality of the work."

"Ellen, you have the last word," Kalb said, and that was that. Coming up next: Two minutes on the superficiality of the media.

The media food chain at work:

The *National Enquirer* publishes an explosive story about O. J. Simpson, attributed to an unnamed jail "insider." It seems that Simpson, in a session with his minister, former football star Rosey Grier, was urged to seek God's forgiveness. Clutching a Bible, Simpson shouted: "I did it!" His outburst was overheard by a sheriff's deputy, the December 1994 article says.

Incredible story, if true. The unattributed account hits the journalistic echo chamber and makes its way into *The New York Times.* The paper's legal correspondent, David Margolick, uses the *Enquirer* report in the seventh paragraph of a story about the double murder case.

The unusual sight of the august *Times* quoting a supermarket tabloid that often buys its information is clearly a juicy media story. After all, no one knows who the anonymous source is, or whether any money changed hands. We briefly kick it around on *Reliable Sources,* and a few days later I write about the controversy in my "Media Notes" column in *The Washington Post.* Margolick defends his story, saying the *Enquirer* has been quite accurate in covering the Simpson case. The *Chicago Tribune* also picks up the tabloid report. But Linda Deutsch, the Associated Press reporter at the trial, threatens to remove her byline until her editors back off from their demand that she cite the *Enquirer.*

On the morning my story is published, I get a call from a producer for *Extra,* the new Time Warner entertainment show. A crew is dispatched to my office to obtain the requisite sound bites on the controversy. Margolick is also interviewed. "Our top story tonight: Has the gray lady gone senile?" says host Arthel Neville. "Now even *The New York Times* has an Enquiring mind . . ."

That afternoon, a *Today* show producer calls from Los Angeles and invites me to appear on the program. At 7:36 the next morning, still somewhat bleary-eyed, I am in NBC's Washington studio, staring at a lone camera and being questioned by Bryant Gumbel. Margolick does the segment from L.A., where it is still the middle of the night. Two minutes before airtime, the producer says in my ear that I shouldn't refer to Simpson allegedly saying "I did it!" because NBC doesn't want to air the unproven allegation. A minute later someone has countermanded the order and the producer says I can say what I want. Gumbel opens the segment. "The revered *New York Times* has taken to using the *National Enquirer* as a source, a bit like finding out Pavarotti was getting singing tips from Cher," he says. We each field a couple of questions and it's over.

When I arrive at work, the phone rings again. It is a New York booker for the Talk Channel, a new network owned by Multimedia, which syndicates *Donahue, Sally,* and Rush Limbaugh's television show. "We saw you on the *Today* show this morning, and we're going to be doing the same topic today on our show," she says. What a surprise.

When I arrive at the studio—actually a conference room at a downtown office building—host Denise Richardson is saying: "Could your child end up being a member of a religious cult while

they're away at college? It's not that far-fetched." After the cult
segment winds up, we do half an hour on the *New York Times* flap,
with *Enquirer* editor David Perel and *Village Voice* media critic
James Ledbetter. Every few minutes, a disembodied voice in my
ear says, "Howard, jump in!"

After dinner, I flip on the television and see my article flashed
on the screen. *Crossfire* is doing the story. "Is the O. J. Simpson
case dragging responsible journalism into the tabloid slime?" Mike
Kinsley asks. "Or is it time for so-called responsible journalism to
stop looking down its nose at the *National Enquirer?*" Bill O'Reilly,
the host of *Inside Edition,* says there's no reason for the *Times* to
"censor" the information. John Sununu takes a cheap shot at me,
suggesting that I wrote the piece solely to stick it to the *Post*'s
biggest rival. I shout at the set from my living room couch.

Kinsley says Margolick, after agreeing to appear on *Crossfire,*
had called back to say his editors didn't want him doing any more
TV interviews. The following morning, the *Times* itself weighs in
with a story on the uproar.

The circle is complete when Mike Walker, a *National Enquirer*
columnist (and coauthor of the tell-all book by Nicole Simpson's
friend Faye Resnick), invites me on his syndicated radio show for
one more go-round. "My job is to bring you cutting-edge gossip,"
he tells his audience. "Never be ashamed of your love for gossip . . .
I did the history-making story that Roseanne and Tom had tattooed
each other's names on their butts." Talk about a tough act to follow.

Why did my column cause such a brief sensation on the talk
circuit? Well, it came out in the traditionally slow week before
Christmas. Television loves simple morality tales with recognizable
names that can be explained in a short sentence: the mighty *New
York Times* deigns to recognize the lowly *National Enquirer.* For a
few brief moments, it filled a yawning void in the O.J. news cycle.

Talk shows routinely feed off each other because their members
live in the same electronic hothouse, breathing the same super-
charged air. They are always searching for controversy, for ever
more prominent targets upon which to open fire. If Phil Donahue
wants to televise executions, that's a juicy debate for *Crossfire.* If
Jenny Jones is seen as the unwitting backdrop for murder, it is
perfect fodder for *Nightline.*

Newspapers also serve as a lightning rod. When *The Washington Post*, with support from *The New York Times*, bowed to the Unabomber's threat of further violence and published his 35,000-word manifesto, the second-guessers had a field day. The papers were denounced and defended on *Crossfire*, on *Nightline*, on *Reliable Sources*, on *This Week with David Brinkley*, and the rest.

Sometimes, as a media reporter and part-time talking head, I found myself caught in the middle.

In the spring of 1995, Rush Limbaugh began denouncing the notion that incendiary talk radio hosts were contributing to the ugly climate that produced the Oklahoma City bombing. The immediate focus of his wrath were certain liberal pundits on the weekend talk shows. Carl Rowan, on *Inside Washington*, had attributed the bombing to "the angriest of the angry white men" and the debate over affirmative action. Juan Williams, on *Capital Gang*, had said the bombing showed white men "in their natural state" and was "the essence of the angry white man taken to some extreme, some fanatic extreme." Limbaugh, as it happens, was on target; these were off-the-wall statements.

I was writing a front-page story that day about President Clinton's denunciation of "the purveyors of hatred and division," and quoted Limbaugh's comments right after Clinton's. My fax machine soon spit out part of a recent transcript from a Limbaugh broadcast, courtesy of the *Flush Rush Quarterly*. Limbaugh had been talking about growing anger in the west against federal restrictions on property rights and policies pushed by "environmental wackos." He said that "the second violent American revolution is just about—I got my fingers about a quarter of an inch apart—is just about *that* far away. Because these people are sick and tired of a bunch of bureaucrats in Washington driving into town and telling them what they can and can't do with their land . . ."

Now I don't believe for a second that Rush Limbaugh, whatever his rhetorical excesses, encourages violence. But his prediction of a violent revolution, without the slightest expression of disapproval, was well worth noting. I used the quote, without comment, in the last paragraph of my story. The next day Limbaugh said on the air that he could not find such a tape.

That evening I was invited on *Equal Time* with Mary Matalin to talk about the role of talk radio. Matalin, who had spoken to Limbaugh that morning, was determined to defend "the man, the legend, the way of life," as she called Limbaugh. "I loathe when Rush is lumped in with the irresponsible ones," she said. I repeated my contention that Limbaugh was not encouraging violence.

At the same moment, *Crossfire* was debating the merits of talk radio with G. Gordon Liddy, who was being pressed on his comments about shooting federal firearms agents in the head. Mike Kinsley had argued against giving Liddy a televised forum to launch his tirades, but to no avail. Kinsley, who had gotten the same fax as I did from the *Flush Rush Quarterly,* read Limbaugh's two-month-old quote on the air. John Sununu saw nothing wrong with it.

"When Rush Limbaugh says there's a violent revolution coming because people are sick of federal bureaucrats," Kinsley said, "and he says it in a tone of approval, or at least shrugging . . . Rush Limbaugh says irresponsible things, and it does, in my view, contribute to an atmosphere of hatred and paranoia about the government."

On the radio the next day, Limbaugh returned fire. He took his cue from a caller, Randall from Bloomington, Indiana, who accused "the liberals" of "character assassination. Such occurred last night when I tuned into the meeting of the mindless on *Crossfire*." The quote attributed to Limbaugh, if true, surely must have been out of context, Randall said.

Limbaugh accused Kinsley of "ranting and raving." He explained that the quote came from "yesterday's *Washington Post* story by our old buddy Howard Kurtz. Kurtz wrote a number of things about this business that talk radio might be responsible in some way, shape, manner, or form for the evil in Oklahoma City . . . Now Kinsley made a huge error by not calling Howie Kurtz and saying, 'Howie, what the hell are you talking about?' Kinsley just took it and ran with it, assuming the worst, because he wanted to. Because I've made jokes about how you can see Kinsley's little veins in his neck when he gets mad. So he's got an animus."

(This is an interesting piece of logic: Kinsley had "an animus" against Limbaugh because Limbaugh had made fun of the way he looks. Kinsley later told me he was totally unaware of this bit of ridicule. "Many people have standing to criticize the way I look, but Rush Limbaugh is not one of them," he said. "I certainly have no vendetta against Rush. He's clearly more obsessed with me than I am with him.")

Limbaugh turned his attention back to me. "He clearly leaves the impression that I on this radio program fomented and encouraged this so-called second American revolution," he declared. Limbaugh then noted that I had been on *Equal Time* the previous night (he must watch a lot of television). Mary Matalin had been "brilliant," he said. He then proceeded to imitate me in a crybaby voice: *"I-I-I didn't mean Limbaugh was encouraging revolution, I-I-I didn't mean that."* (There's no pleasing some people.)

Limbaugh insisted he had been quoted out of context. Never mind that I had merely reprinted his words and said precisely what he was referring to—property rights and environmental issues—without criticism. He played a three-minute tape of his original comments. First he had spoken of a Montana rancher who had been fined $4,000 for shooting a grizzly bear that charged him. Then there was the family that was jailed for putting nineteen loads of sand on a property deemed to be wetlands. And finally the comment about being a quarter of an inch from a violent revolution, sounding pretty much the way it did the first time.

Randall from Bloomington was still on the line. "Did that clip make it sound like I was advocating a violent revolution?" Limbaugh asked.

"Of course not," Randall replied. "Merely an observation."

"Do you think the quote that Mr. Kinsley attributed to me was in any way, shape, manner, or form a position of advocacy of armed revolution?"

"Oh, not at all."

(Just for good measure, Limbaugh attacked Kinsley and me again on his television show that night, playing a clip from *Crossfire*. He asked his studio audience if it sounded like he was fomenting a revolution. "No!" the crowd shouted.)

Minutes after Limbaugh began his radio diatribe, my voice mail began to fill up with messages from angry dittoheads. These were people who had not read what I had written; indeed, some lived thousands of miles from *The Washington Post*'s circulation area. All they had was Limbaugh's description of my supposed sins. And, in a talk show nation, that was enough.

"Get your facts straight!" one demanded.

"Howard, you bagel-eating little rat," another said. "Are you listening to Rush Limbaugh? Maybe you'd learn something."

My radio career began as something of a lark.

I had heard from a friend that a popular Washington rock station, WRQX-FM, had an opening for a talk show host. The previous host of the Sunday night show, called *Liveline,* had been let go, and the station was casting around for a replacement. What the hell, I thought, it might be fun. When I called the station manager, Lorrin Palagi, he agreed to give me an on-air tryout that very Sunday. It was sink or swim.

I had done plenty of radio as a guest, but I soon learned that sitting in the host's chair was a whole different experience. The time . . . goes . . . very . . . slowly. Unlike television, where you have to blab everything quickly, yakking your way through a two-hour show can give your lungs a workout. You tell a long, rambling story; the clock barely moves. You tell another anecdote, give the time, backtrack, mention the 800 number, reel off a couple of jokes, give the time again, and hope some calls come trickling in.

My performance seemed rather rough, but Palagi said I sounded natural and offered me the job. I later learned that I had beaten out Ed Rollins, the Republican political consultant, who within weeks touched off a firestorm by charging (and then recanting) that the campaign he managed for New Jersey Governor Christine Todd Whitman had paid black ministers to discourage their followers from voting.

The station, known to its mostly young fans as Mix 107.3, usually played the likes of Genesis, Springsteen, and Madonna, but reserved this one rather undesirable time slot for talk. The following Sunday I found myself sitting behind a control panel that, with the flick of a finger, could give someone the floor—"Tom from Rockville, you're on the air"—or, just as important, cut them off. My engineer, Peter Finkhauser, would talk to the callers in the adjoining control room and rush out with little slips of paper bearing their names and topics. A high-tech system it wasn't.

The phrase "hot button issue" takes on a whole new resonance when you're waiting for the buttons to light up. Mention crime, race, welfare, taxes, O.J., gun control, or Bill Clinton and boom, people rush to sound off. Talk about economics, global trade, or foreign affairs and the lines go dead.

When you're parked behind the mike for two hours at a stretch, giving out that toll-free number every few minutes, you begin to feel the subtle pressure to say something provocative, to ratchet up your rhetoric. I saw myself mainly as a moderator, tossing out topics with a little analysis and trying to get a conversation started. But it was the red meat of passionate opinion that would get listeners riled up enough to call.

There were, to be sure, plenty of nice moments. On just about every show, two or three people would call with intelligent, thought-provoking comments, and they were often folks with whom I would not normally have much contact. When I mentioned an article about teenagers having sex at a younger age, the lines were flooded with junior high and high school kids who never called on any other subject. When the issue was tensions between local blacks and Hispanics, many members of the Hispanic community suddenly called the show. Police officers called in from their squad cars during a debate about gun control. When we were debating the need for the Food and Drug Administration, a teenager whose father is an FDA milk inspector called to defend his dad's work. And when the talk turned to tobacco regulation, lots of smokers (and former smokers) had something to say.

Talk radio, it seems, provides the connective tissue for people of different ethnic groups and subcultures. The first-name anonymity emboldens those who might otherwise be reticent about sounding off publicly. And there's a fascinating chain reaction when a caller says something provocative. Four or five people will quickly phone in to take issue with the caller, a person they have never met. In a community of strangers, radio has become a substitute for the back-fence discussions of a bygone age.

Although I shied away from the self-help stuff, some people invariably would pour out their personal problems and ask for advice about getting a job, picking a college, dealing with depression. I was spectacularly unqualified to address any of this and secretly appalled that they would be desperate enough to ask some radio guy for help.

There is something depressing, too, about the overheated and polarized nature of public debate these days. Lots of angry folks out there just want to talk back: to the media, to the authorities, to anyone who will listen. For them, talk radio is a sort of airwaves therapy, a socially acceptable way to vent their spleen or simply to feel connected in a fragmented world. I developed a hardy core of regulars, people who would call in week after week, regardless of the topic, perhaps comforted by the notion that someone cared enough to listen.

And yet, to be brutally candid, some of my callers had a stunningly simplistic view of the world. They knew what they believed and didn't want to be confused by the facts. Welfare is a huge giveaway program. Clinton is a dishonest bum. Crime is out of control, and all criminals should be locked up for life, and perhaps sentenced to Singapore-style caning. Many of the callers were diehard conservatives, but the disgust and frustration transcended ideology. You couldn't change their minds by bringing up qualifying details—say, that two-thirds of welfare recipients are children, or that incarcerating hundreds of thousands of prisoners at huge public expense has done little to reduce the crime rate. For them, talk radio was not about dialogue; it was simply a chance to rant.

I was on the air the night that Clinton launched a military invasion of Haiti, only to order U.S. warplanes to return home after Jimmy Carter struck a last-minute deal with Haitian military leader Raoul Cedras. Clinton had just gone on national television to explain what had happened. And yet some of my listeners were so cynical, so distrustful of the president, that they dismissed the invasion as a hoax.

David, from Waldorf, Maryland: "My private little theory on this is I think the fixeroo was in from the beginning. I think they cut this deal with the Haitian leadership before the big armada went down and it was basically a face-saving for both of them."

I suggested that this was far-fetched: "You don't send sixty-one aircraft into battle if you've already cut the deal. You just don't do it, there would be no need."

"That was part of the show: 'We can make it sound like he backed down at the last minute,' " David insisted.

After a couple of callers defended Clinton and one dismissed David's argument as "absurd and idiotic," Mark from D.C. came on the line. "I still haven't heard those planes were actually going to be dropping people," he said. "It's just a bit too much to hear these pro-Clinton people screaming about what a great victory this is. We have to find out what those planes were actually doing while they were in the air."

How do you argue with people who don't believe anything the government says? I tried in vain another evening when Pauline from Alexandria, Virginia, called with what she called "my two cents."

"I voted for President Clinton. I don't mind saying I'm sorry I did," she said.

"Why?"

"Number one, homosexuals. Number two, no jobs."

"You say no jobs. It seems the unemployment rate is the lowest that it's been in four years."

"That's what they say," she retorted.

"And something like six or seven million jobs have been created."

"I don't believe that."

I was briefly speechless. "You don't believe that? You think it's a lie?"

"I don't believe that."

"If official government statistics say that six or seven million jobs have been created since 1992, you think that is simply not true?"

"Yes. I simply think that is not true."

Any discussion of the finer points of economic policy was lost on part of the audience. Ryan, from Glen Burnie, Maryland: "I'll tell you how we take care of it all. We just do away with all the taxes. Let's do away with all the aid. Let's go back to free enterprise."

And then there was Larry from Waldorf, Maryland, a man to the right of Attila the Hun, who called in regularly to harangue me. He was in classic form after incoming House Speaker Newt Gingrich charged on *Meet the Press* that up to a quarter of the White House staff had used drugs four or five years before joining the Clinton administration (the actual figure during that period turned out to be 1 percent).

"You have to hear the exact same things coming out of the White House about massive drug use there," Larry said.

"Massive drug use?" I said. "What do you base that on?"

"Rumors that are floating around inside the Beltway . . . It's fairly clear that, one, they have been using, and two, they probably still are. Most people don't stop using drugs."

Even Gingrich, who has admitted inhaling in his youth, would probably quarrel with that, but Larry was just warming up: "I'm sure you've heard all the stuff about Bill Clinton, that he doesn't really have an allergy problem. His problem with his nostrils is they're burned out from cocaine."

I placed my finger above the cutoff switch. "I think that's a little irresponsible to make that charge without evidence," I said.

"When he comes up with his medical records, which he's never done, maybe we can put that aside," Larry said. He then reprised a previous rant about "all the homicides that are occurring down in Arkansas, swirling around Whitewater," which, according to far-fetched conspiracy theory, were tied to the Clinton White House.

So much for the presumption of innocence.

But there is also an uplifting side to talk radio, as I discovered one night when Lisa, a rather arrogant young woman on Capitol Hill, complained that "the government is becoming a big, fat pork pig" and that all social programs—Social Security, Medicare, Medicaid, you name it—should be done away with or left to the states. "It should be the old-fashioned way: hard work, earn your living. If you can't make it, don't ask for it . . . I don't think a lot of people have the brains to realize what's going on."

The switchboard lit up with callers who put a human face on the debate. Tracy, a nurse from Virginia, talked about how she has supported her four children since her husband became disabled. "We lost just about everything," she said. Susan, a thirteen-year-old from Silver Spring, Maryland, who said she was from "a lower-class family" and that "the people who are calling you on this Social Security issue are basically rich snobs." Lynn from Manassas, Virginia, whose husband had lost his job and whose seventy-year-old father just had bypass surgery. "If he didn't have Medicare, how could he afford it?" she asked. Luis from D.C., who said he was receiving Social Security disability payments for emotional problems. Paul from Arlington, Virginia, a Salvadoran immigrant who said he had never taken a penny in government benefits. Bill from Gaithersburg, Maryland, whose 105-year-old grandmother was living in a nursing home financed by Medicare. "What would the people who don't want these programs suggest be done with her?" he said. He couldn't afford to help her because "I've got six kids, and I've put four of them through college and I've got two more to go. It's a struggle."

It was as moving a series of stories as I'd ever heard. These were not the kind of people who would normally appear on television or be quoted in the newspapers. It reminded me of the way talk radio broadens the circle of public debate.

But the radio audience can also convict someone of being a drug addict, faking a military invasion, fabricating economic statistics, or being an accessory to murder. There is no right of rebuttal, no editorial filter, no mechanism to keep outlandish or unsupported opinions off the air. Everyone's an expert, whether they know anything or not. Talk radio can be wonderfully illuminating and, a moment later, infuriatingly unfair.

After sixteen months, my radio career ended as abruptly as it had begun. Lorrin Palagi moved to Chicago, and a new station manager, Randy James, was brought in from Dayton, Ohio. He peppered the jocks with memos saying, "We need to take a serious look at the verbiage amount we use in our talk breaks . . . Let's look at ways we can cut back on the chatter . . . Mix 107.3 will air 'the NEW Night Mix, a special blend of dedications, requests and your favorite songs.' This is the way it will always be referred to as. No variations." He didn't see why a rock station should have a talk show on Sunday nights. It didn't appeal to his "core audience." He pulled the plug on *Liveline*. After one hundred forty hours of radio talk, I no longer had to have an opinion on every subject that came up every week. It was, in an odd sort of way, a relief.

CHAPTER FIFTEEN

THE FUTURE
OF TALK

I t's a talk show jungle out there.

On *Capital Gang*, Bob Novak says that Mark Shields "has always got the latest fax from the Democratic headquarters to tell him what the proper line is."

"You've sat here and lied through your teeth," Shields snaps.

"I think that's beyond the pale to call me a liar on the air," Novak says.

"I resent the fact that you're calling me some sort of spokesman for a political party," Shields says. The following week, Shields apologizes.

On *Inside Washington*, Evan Thomas calls Paula Jones "some sleazy woman with big hair coming out of the trailer parks." The following week he says: "I got a lot of letters and comments that said I was sexist and elitist and a jerk. And I don't know about the sexist, but it was elitist and I was a jerk, so I apologize."

On *48 Hours*, Dan Rather quizzes three lawyers about the latest twist in the O. J. Simpson case. "What's your speculation: a knife is in that envelope or not?" Rather says. "Well, I think it's kind of silly to speculate on it, Dan," says Richard "Racehorse" Haynes. "Well, we really don't know for sure," says Laurie Levenson.

On *Brinkley*, Sam Donaldson says to Newt Gingrich: "A lot of people are afraid of you. They think you're a bomb thrower. Worse, you're an intolerant bigot. Speak to them."

On *Maury Povich,* Connie Hamzy, who claims to have slept

with Bill Clinton, says: "I may be a slut and a whore, but I'm not a liar."

On *Eye to Eye,* Connie Chung says: "Why don't you whisper it to me, just between you and me."

"She's a bitch," says Kathleen Gingrich.

On *Crossfire,* Mike Kinsley says: "That's a very cheap, dishonest—"

"It's what we call a clean hit," Pat Buchanan says.

"It's called a spin! That's exactly what's wrong with American politics, and you're responsible for a lot of it!"

On *McLaughlin,* Fred Barnes praises candidate Pat Buchanan for being "decisive."

"Hitler was decisive, too," says Eleanor Clift.

"I resent this Hitler stuff!" Barnes says.

"I didn't call you Hitler, Fred!"

If the airwaves are crackling with insults, arguments, spin, and speculation, it may be because there's so much damn time to fill. Hit the clicker and chances are you'll find talking heads rambling on with varying degrees of insight and invective. There are so many daily servings of talk soup that the broth is diluted with the same warmed-over journalistic opinions. Mort Zuckerman says on *McLaughlin* that Colin Powell will run for president in 1996. Mort Kondracke says on the same show that Colin Powell won't run. And neither of them has the faintest idea.

Hour after hour, the talkers just keep on coming. In the spring of 1995, CNBC trotted out its "Talk All-Stars" for a promotional extravaganza. There they were, every known species, shoulder to shoulder on the same stage: Tim Russert and Geraldo Rivera, Mary Matalin and Phil Donahue, Dick Cavett and sex-advice guru Bob Berkowitz, weatherman Al Roker and actor Charles Grodin, former Moral Majority spokesman Cal Thomas and former Soviet spokesman Vladimir Pozner, with Tom Snyder calling in. They spent much of the time debating talk shows and whether the press was lavishing too much attention on the O. J. spectacle. At each break was a commercial for CNBC's 11:30 special on, yes, O. J. Simpson.

Perhaps no single day more vividly illustrated the absurdity of pointless punditry than October 2, 1995, when the Simpson jury returned a sealed verdict that would not be announced until the following day. With hours of O.J. airtime to fill, the talk show types began spewing forth predictions, blithely ignoring the fact that none of them had the faintest idea what the twelve jurors had done.

The boldest commentators had been taking a stand for days. Rush Limbaugh predicted that Simpson would be convicted. Fred Barnes predicted that Simpson would be convicted. John McLaughlin and Jack Germond and Morton Kondracke said there would be a hung jury.

As that Monday evening wore on, the speculation grew more fevered and the sense of certainty deepened, as if the talk show environment were feeding on itself. Michael Kinsley predicted that Simpson would be convicted. Geraldo Rivera predicted that Simpson would be convicted. "I think it's a guilty verdict, probably first degree," attorney Gerald Lefcourt told Dan Rather.

On *Larry King Live,* former judge Jack Tenner and Jeffrey Toobin of *The New Yorker* said a conviction was likely. King's panel of experts proceeded to ponder what kind of sentence Simpson would receive and what prison he would serve in.

On *Rivera Live,* four of the five analysts agreed that Simpson would be found guilty. "I think it's a conviction," attorney Jay Monahan said.

"Guilty," agreed former prosecutor Joseph diGenova.

Those who refused to play the crystal-ball game were ridiculed. On *Crossfire,* Kinsley said: "Let's go to our talking heads. Barry Tarlow, what's the verdict?"

"How in the world would I know what the verdict is?" the Los Angeles lawyer replied.

"Then what the heck are you doing here?" Kinsley demanded.

The mere fact that the jury had decided Simpson's fate in less than four hours confounded most of the smart-aleck set. "We look kind of silly . . . We said the jury would be out three weeks," Leslie Abramson admitted on *Nightline.*

"If these jurors voted to convict this man . . . all of us are made to seem the fools we probably are," Geraldo Rivera said.

When Simpson was acquitted the following day, many of the same experts promptly began speculating about the reasons for the verdict, despite the fact that the jurors had initially refused to talk to the press. It was simply more hot air.

Within twenty-four hours the talk culture had moved on. "O.J.

the Hollywood celebrity: Does he have a future in Tinseltown?"
Mary Hart asked on *Entertainment Tonight*.

Every producer feels the pressure to juice up the news. I once
sat in on an editorial meeting at *Now with Tom Brokaw and Katie
Couric* as the staff kicked around possible stories. Someone
mentioned the Whitewater affair, then very much in the news.
"It's just so boring," said Jeff Zucker, the twenty-eight-year-
old executive producer. "I don't even understand it . . . Nobody
cares about Bernie Nussbaum." Then he came up with an
angle on "the Hillary thing. We should do the Rose Law Firm.
This is *The Firm*, and it should be played off the movie. They all
have fancy houses and fancy cars. I want this to be *The Firm*. Got
it?"

Zucker later produced a sheaf of minute-by-minute ratings for
each program. The numbers had jumped for one of *Now*'s five
segments on Tonya Harding. "That's how we knew to keep doing
it," he said.

The market is clearly glutted. CNN alone fields a dozen talk
shows. A certain sameness creeps in as the same participants rehash
the same topics. Unlike Brian Lamb, who has the luxury of ignoring
ratings, the imperative on commercial television is always the same:
Hook the viewer. In an age of channel surfing, CNN viewers tend
to glide in for ten or twelve minutes at a time. "We used to really
wring our hands about the fact that we did something earlier in the
day, or we did it yesterday," Rick Davis says. "But viewers don't
watch nonstop."

And what are viewers learning as they dip in and out, grazing at
the talk show smorgasbord? "If you look at it in a nutrition sense,"
Shields says, "ours is not a diet on which people are going to meet
the minimum daily requirements of citizenship. It's no substitute
for reading a newspaper."

It is the low-calorie elements—the sneer, the put-down, the
stinging denunciation—that give many talk shows their distinctive
identity. Panelists are brought on to disagree, to confront, to *blurt*,
in McLaughlin's memorable phrase. *Blurting is good!* Inevitably,
the clash of ideas gives way to the clash of personalities.

On one edition of *Capital Gang*, there was an embarrassing
moment when Bob Novak kept trying to talk over Margaret Carlson
for a full twenty seconds until Carlson finally yielded. It was a clear

reminder why men dominate the talk show world, for the combat is played out according to their rules.

"I disagree with Bob on most things, but I don't have the stomach for going higher and higher till I prevail," Carlson says. "Women don't have the room to behave like men because they're slapped down for it a lot sooner. Women are not expected to be yelling and screaming and totally domineering. You're seen as a wild woman."

"Sometimes it gets a little out of hand," Novak admits. "When you disagree with a person once a week for six years, sometimes things get rubbed a little raw."

The pugilistic approach to television talk is spreading like a virus. "You get a highly partisan Democrat and a highly partisan Republican and they duke it out," says Norman Ornstein. "It's careening out of control. The notion is that TV is like a courtroom, and you have a Robert Shapiro type and a Marcia Clark type, and people take more and more outrageous positions. When people call to book me, they'll say, 'Are you willing to take this hard-line position?' If I wanted to give the Congress a B or C, there would be much less interest than if I said an A-plus or an F. Chances are they'll get some guy who will say A and another who will say F.

"I see it on *CBS This Morning,* with Fred Barnes and Bob Beckel. They're entertaining guys. But when they were analyzing the election, it was Fred saying all these right-wingers would win and Bob saying all these left-wingers would win, and zinging each other."

The food-fight approach seems to be spreading around the world. On the Russian talk show *One on One,* the regional governor from Nizhny Novgorod called right-wing extremist Vladimir Zhirinovsky a "scumbag" and a "bastard." Zhirinovsky promptly threw a glass of orange juice in his face, and the governor responded by emptying his fruit juice over Zhirinovsky. All that was missing was Geraldo.

While stopping short of such histrionics, most programs this side of *MacNeil/Lehrer* seem to enjoy a certain degree of arm-waving confrontation. Everyone knows the game, and plenty of journalists are willing to perform like "dancing bears," as Jack Germond puts it, to get on stage. Even the most erudite writers can succumb to the temptation. "All of us, when we start appearing on these shows and pontificate and feel the competition to say something stronger than Fred Barnes, you inevitably become very full of yourself," says Ken Auletta, media critic for *The New Yorker*.

A powerful House committee chairman is indicted on a laundry list of fraud charges. He is the perfect symbol of Washington corruption, a beefy, deal-making, backroom pol who seems to have lost sight of the distinction between public money and private enrichment. Surely such a man would be roundly denounced on the talk show circuit.

Not if the congressman is Dan Rostenkowski, who has cultivated a backslapping relationship with reporters over three decades. He is colorful copy. He's a good source. In a moment that reveals much about the incestuous relationship between the talking heads and the politicians, many journalists rush to Rostenkowski's defense after his 1994 indictment.

"Anybody who thinks that what Rostenkowski did deserves a prison sentence, I think they've got a distortion of reality," Bob Novak says.

David Broder, who like Rostenkowski hails from Chicago, describes him as a "warrior" and "someone who is willing to take on tough fights."

"I have a real bias on this one," Broder says. "I would hate to see Rosty end up in jail. My sympathies are entirely with Rosty."

"The idea that we're even considering sending someone to prison for [no-show employees] strikes me as kind of a bizarre perversion of the judicial process, it's so widespread," Jon Margolis of the *Chicago Tribune* says on *Washington Week*.

"By way of full disclosure, I've known Dan Rostenkowski for more than thirty years and consider him a friend, so I am not completely impartial about this," Cokie Roberts says on National Public Radio.

Rostenkowski, it must be remembered, was charged with defrauding the taxpayers of more than $500,000, including such offenses as hiring ghost payrollers, misappropriating government furniture, and embezzling House postage stamps.

For all their posturing as tough-minded critics of the system, many reporters and commentators, as we have seen, are very much part of the governing elite. There is a natural affinity with politicians, a lofty sense of doing the people's business together. Perhaps the *Capital Gang* format, in which the congressman joshes around alongside the journalists, accurately reflects the relationship.

John McLaughlin dines at the White House with Ronald Reagan. Rush Limbaugh joins George Bush in his box at the Republican convention. David Gergen talks with candidate Clinton about how to handle the draft issue. Bill Moyers reviews his LBJ days with president-elect Clinton in Little Rock. Mort Kondracke writes Clinton a letter on how to rescue his presidency and joins him for iced tea on the White House patio. Howard Fineman plays touch football with Clinton at a Renaissance Weekend. Chris Matthews's book party is hosted by Tip O'Neill. Larry King spends weekends with Mario Cuomo at the governor's mansion. Bob Schieffer plays golf with Sam Nunn. Cokie Roberts moderates a Clinton administration awards ceremony with an old family friend, Al Gore. George Will is an usher at Judge Robert Bork's wedding. Will questions Bob Dole on *Brinkley* even as his wife, Mari, becomes communications director for Dole's '96 presidential campaign. Bob Novak charges admission to off-the-record seminars with Ted Kennedy and Bob Dole. Novak's daughter worked for Dan Quayle. Tim Russert makes a paid appearance at a banking convention with Dole. Clinton stops by a party at Russert's house. David Brinkley dines with Dole at their Florida retreat. Chris Matthews interviews Sam Donaldson and writer Sally Quinn and mentions that he's bumped into Colin Powell at parties at their homes. Sam Donaldson gives a glowing introduction for a Kennedy Center speech by Powell. It is a cozy little village in which many of the players see each other on the party circuit and the speaking circuit and trade gossip over the phone.

New alliances are forming all the time. After Will criticized Newt Gingrich on *Brinkley* for suggesting that the poor be given tax credits to buy laptop computers, Gingrich called to say he was right. The House speaker admitted he had gone too far in tossing out new proposals.

"He was just being friendly," Will says. A couple of years earlier, Will had called Gingrich "a case study in the primacy of career-ism in the life of the modern congressman." But the two men had buried the hatchet over lunch shortly before the '94 election. In his next appearance on the show, while testing the presidential waters in New Hampshire, Gingrich answered a question from Will with praise: "As you said brilliantly in a speech the weekend after President Clinton was sworn in . . ." The political tides were shifting.

The reason for this symbiotic relationship between the journalists and the politicians is simple: They both need the talk shows. They both benefit from the exposure. The talker needs big-shot guests, and the politician needs the national platform. They are mutual enablers, fueling the illusion of each other's importance.

In the early 1980s, Mark Shields gave up his Saturday radio show on Washington's WRC after five years.

"I got tired of listening to myself," he says. "At the end of the year, I'd said just about everything I wanted to say."

This is a stunning and dangerous admission that threatens the very fabric of the talk culture as we know it. A talking head tired of talking? Preposterous! There is always something clever or caustic to say on every topic under the sun.

Not long ago, I came upon a videotape of a 1984 appearance I made on *Meet the Press,* the only time I've ever been on that show. It was like discovering some faded black-and-white footage in the *I Love Lucy* archives. I was covering urban affairs at the time, and the show was broadcasting from a mayors' conference in Philadelphia. I sat with NBC's Bill Monroe and two other print journalists behind one long table; two mayors, Dianne Feinstein of San Francisco and Wilson Goode of Philadelphia, sat at the opposite table. We asked two questions apiece, the politicians gave lengthy answers and then a new round ensued. No one interrupted. But it was rather dull, and no one challenged the mayors on what they said. They were free to give brief campaign speeches without being pressed on evasions or contradictions. Perhaps most important, no one cared what we thought. It was a televised press conference. The era of journalists as performers and opinionators—as box-office stars—was still being born.

In just fifteen years, the explosion of television and radio talk shows has transformed the political and cultural landscape. Every presidential speech, every congressional hearing, every campaign event is now seen through the talk show filter. What the talkers say —Shields and Gergen and Donaldson and Will and Barnes and Clift and Limbaugh and Liddy—often drowns out our elected leaders. What the talkers ignore is marginalized by a political system that can digest only two or three issues at once. In a world of all talk all the time, the sheer volume of punditry echoes in our collective consciousness long after the president or House speaker or Senate majority leader has had his say.

The talk ritual is so deeply embedded in our culture that public figures in crisis are now expected to make the rounds, whether to plead their case, confess their mistakes, or expiate their sins. When Michael Jackson was struggling to put allegations of child molestation behind him and promote a new double album, he sat down with Diane Sawyer (having already done *Oprah* two years earlier). Jackson was accompanied by his wife, Lisa Marie Presley, who assured Sawyer that yes, they did have sex together.

When actor Hugh Grant was busted for utilizing the services of a Los Angeles hooker, he quickly fessed up with Jay Leno, followed by similar mea culpas with Larry King, Katie Couric, David Letterman, and Regis Philbin and Kathie Lee Gifford. Leno helped defuse the situation by asking the squirming Grant: "What the hell were you thinking?"

"I did a bad thing, and there you have it," Grant replied with charming embarrassment before proceeding to promote his new film, which was buoyed by the wave of publicity.

When Robert McNamara finally admitted in a book that he had been tragically wrong about the Vietnam War, the ritual required him to say so over and over on the talk show circuit. And so the former Pentagon chief trooped from studio to studio, fielding the same questions from Ted Koppel, from Diane Sawyer, from Charlie Rose, from Larry King, from Brian Lamb, growing teary-eyed at difficult moments, seeking forgiveness before the cameras. Writing a book was not enough. McNamara had to be subjected to trial by talk show.

In early 1994, more than a year after *The Washington Post* reported that Bob Packwood had made unwanted sexual advances toward twenty-three women, the Oregon senator went on *20/20* (right before Lorena Bobbitt), told Barbara Walters he couldn't remember most of the incidents because he was drunk, and apologized for "any misconduct that I might have done, whether I could remember it or not." He repeated the same message on *Larry King Live*.

In September 1995, on the day the Senate Ethics Committee urged that he be expelled for sexual misconduct, altering evidence and seeking favors from lobbyists, Packwood returned to the *King* show, lashed out at his accusers and vowed he would not resign. The following afternoon, he resigned. That night, Packwood went on *20/20* to plead for sympathy with Barbara Walters, saying his diary entries about sleeping with twenty-two staff members and seventy-five other women were an "exaggeration" and "wishful thinking." Two days later he awkwardly repeated the ritual with Bob Schieffer on *Face the Nation*.

There is, as we have seen, a healthy dimension to the spread of talk as it obliterates the rules and restrictions of organized journalism. All kinds of views, from the guns-are-good lectures of G. Gordon Liddy to the anticorporate harangues of Jim Hightower, are in play. Those who have been shut out by the big networks and newspapers now have a turn at the microphone.

The mushrooming of the talk show culture has broadened the audience for serious (and less than serious) talk about public affairs. The new programs have proven that news doesn't have to be dull. Millions of Americans, after all, have managed to live productive lives without watching *Meet the Press* or C-SPAN. To the extent that McLaughlin or King or Donahue jazz up the news with a little showmanship, they are doing their part to boost public awareness.

Clearly, the talk phenomenon helps viewers and listeners feel connected to a political world that seems increasingly remote from their daily existence. Call-in shows spur a national conversation, offer a voice to the powerless, provide an outlet for anger and frustration. Strangers can commiserate about common problems or seek guidance in the wake of tragedy. Politicians are subjected to skeptical questioning from real people. In short, talk shows have begun to open a window on the interactive media of the twenty-first century.

That's the good news.

The not-so-good news is that the entire country is being buried by a volcano of verbiage. The talk is frequently repetitive, inane, uninformed, unbearably shrill. Argument has become an end in itself. Complex issues are boiled down to punchy one-liners, artificially squeezed into left-right debating formulas, pompously graded on a scale of zero to ten. Too many talk shows have become an exercise in self-importance by overpaid infotainers who have little in common with their audience.

Time and again, as I have attempted to show, these talkers make snap judgments that turn out to be flat wrong, only to be discarded when the winds of consensus shift direction. By the time President Clinton's "disastrous" invasion of Haiti turns out to be successful in restoring democracy, the talkers have moved on to the next crisis. By the time a Republican takeover of Congress no longer seems far-fetched, the talkers have regrouped and are pronouncing last rites for the Democratic Party. Pretending to great wisdom, they often regurgitate what they read in the morning papers. Much of the playacting and posturing seems to carry a strong whiff of consumer fraud, but people tune in nonetheless, and producers faithfully peddle that which will sell.

I will forgo here the usual ten-point plan to improve the subject at hand. This is not nuclear physics. We already know how to create quality talk shows; there are a number of them around. We know how to deal with substance and tone down the shouting matches and keep uncorroborated rumors off the air. The real question is whether there is a significant market for talk that is not driven by bluster, sensationalism, and superficiality. Viewers vote each day with their remote controls. Perhaps, in the end, people get the talk shows they deserve.

The upper reaches of the talk industry, from the Sunday morning shows to *Washington Week* to *Charlie Rose,* have the luxury of playing to the elite. These programs don't have to yell and argue to draw an audience because their fans, much prized by advertisers, are affluent opinion-maker types. In that sense the elite shows are comparable to *The New York Times,* which reaches only 10 percent of newspaper readers in its metropolitan area but has a lock on the most demographically desirable fraction of the market.

The bulk of the talk business is in the position of the *New York*

Post or *Daily News.* These shows need to reach the masses to survive, and they know that much of their audience has only a passing interest in the latest political intrigue or legislative wrangling. Such programs, from *Larry King* to *McLaughlin* to *Donahue,* are in the business of marketing news as entertainment. If that means indulging in a bit of hype, in slick packaging, in shouting-head journalism, well, there's plenty of competition out there. The commercial imperative is to grab the viewer by the lapels and refuse to let go.

Somewhere in between are an array of niche programs that, like *The American Spectator* or *The Nation,* appeal to a carefully targeted group of like-minded folks. They may be aimed at gun enthusiasts (G. Gordon Liddy) or O.J. aficionados (*Rivera Live*), at angry white men (Bob Grant) or politically attuned women (*Equal Time*). Many openly trumpet their ideology, and they don't need huge ratings to survive. They simply need to connect with members of their particular subculture.

It is the combined lung power of these hundreds of shows that creates the deafening roar that so often overwhelms intelligent public discourse. In this static-filled environment, it is the loudest, the most extreme, the most twisted pronouncements that break through the din. As some of the talkers themselves have conceded, the opposition argument—why some proposal is terrible, alarming, or outrageous—is the easiest to communicate to an already cynical audience. The defense of the same policy is necessarily more complicated, more muddled, less suited to a sound-bite culture. The talk that resonates most powerfully in the talk show world is negative talk.

Thus, it is easier for Fred Barnes to declare the health care crisis a myth than for Michael Kinsley to defend the intricacies of a 1,364-page plan. It is easier for Rush Limbaugh to demonize a lobbying-reform bill as a threat to civil liberties than for the Senate sponsors to insist that it is not aimed at ordinary volunteers. It is easier for Ross Perot to denounce a bipartisan crime measure as a "hug-a-mugger bill" than for supporters to explain that programs like midnight basketball, a minuscule portion of the measure, are supported by most police chiefs.

After two years in which the Republicans repeatedly won the talk show battle against the Clinton administration, they found themselves on the receiving end in 1995. Their balanced-budget amendment was defeated by Democrats who portrayed it as an assault on Social Security, an argument based on the transparent fiction that the retirement fund remains sacrosanct. Federal loan guarantees to Mexico, supported by the leadership of both parties, failed in Congress because critics branded it a "bailout." The GOP proposal to return the school lunch program to the states was successfully depicted by Democrats as swiping bread from the mouths of starving children. It was, in fact, an intellectually defensible plan for greater local control over social spending, albeit at a lesser rate of budgetary increase. But such fine print is meaningless in the lightning-quick world of talk show politics. Once the Republicans were stamped the party of ketchup-as-a-vegetable, they had lost the media war. On the airwaves, simplification rules.

As for the issues that generate so much emotion on call-in shows, such as welfare and affirmative action, there remains a huge gap between angry talk and real problem-solving. Would cutting off aid to pregnant teenagers really reduce illegitimacy? Should poor whites be favored over middle-class blacks in college admission programs? Should veterans' preferences be tossed out along with other forms of affirmative action? These kinds of thorny questions tend to get lost in all the overheated arguments.

What is lost as well is the kind of stimulating debate that, as we have seen, simply falls outside the tried-and-true talk show formulas. There is, for example, no real left wing in today's talk show environment, largely because the left has faded as a political force in America. When was the last time anyone stood up on a talk show and said the country should spend more money on the inner cities? Or that corporate executives are overpaid? Or that businesses are too quick to lay off innocent workers to compensate for management blunders and ill-advised mergers? During the health care debate, little attention was given to a Canadian-style single-payer insurance plan because it was seen as an example of dreaded "big government." The point is not that these are great ideas but that they have become non-ideas, ignored by producers and bookers. Those who pass for "liberals" on the talk shows are panelists who halfheartedly defend the Clinton administration, which itself has been lurching toward the center.

This narrowing of the talk show arteries has hurt the right as well. In all the years before the Republicans won control of Congress in 1994, how many talk shows seriously explored Newt Gingrich's ideas on welfare reform or food stamps or urban renewal? Gingrich the partisan bomb thrower got plenty of attention, but most of the talk culture did not take him seriously as an intellectual force. He filled a limited need—an opposition leader who provided incendiary sound bites—but beyond that he was merely a minority spokesman in a fiefdom controlled by Democrats for decades. This was not so much liberal bias as shortsighted pragmatism. The talk shows had no need to grapple with Gingrich's proposals because, all the experts agreed, they had no chance of passing. Now Gingrich's ideas dominate the national agenda, and the talk shows, along with the rest of the media, are still scrambling to catch up.

The sad reality is that much of today's endless talk may be falling on deaf ears. After the first one hundred days of the Republican Congress, polls showed that six in ten people still were not familiar with the Contract with America, despite the fact that it had been chewed over on every television and radio talk show in creation and given saturation coverage by the newspapers and networks. People are so deeply skeptical of the political system that they regard all the talk about cleaning up Washington as just that, talk. The pundits and the politicians are seen as distant figures chattering away in some foreign language. The ultimate irony in this talk show age is that so many people are simply tuning it out.

Some liberal reformers want to revive the Fairness Doctrine in hopes of elevating the tone of on-air debate. But that antiquated 1949 rule, written at a time of limited broadcast frequencies, is ill suited to today's multimedia world. For one thing, it required only reasonable balance in overall programming, over a perod of weeks or months, when a controversial issue was debated. More important, the heavy hand of government regulation is simply not the answer. Station executives ought to provide airtime for competing points of view, but another level of bureaucratic review in Washington will merely keep some communications lawyers busy.

The futility of trying to deploy content cops on the information highway is becoming increasingly clear. Thanks to the magic of technology, the talk culture is again being transformed as it spreads to the on-line community that links millions of people around the globe. They can download raw data, tap into the latest headlines, and debate one another in thousands of newsgroups and bulletin boards. But in a mirror image of television and radio shows, much of this cybertalk is garbage. Facts are often mangled. Unfounded rumors race by at 14,400 bits per second. Entire bulletin boards are devoted to showbiz and other gossip. Much of the on-line chatter is boring, banal, or insanely repetitive. And the talk often degenerates into a volley of anonymous flames and personal insults. No one need take responsibility for inflammatory remarks. The computer has made every user the star of his own talk show before a vast unseen audience linked by telephone wires.

Fringe characters and conspiracy theorists thrive in such an argumentative atmosphere. Months after the Vince Foster debate faded from talk radio, it remained a sizzling on-line topic.

"Anyone who thinks that Vincent Foster's death was a simple suicide in Fort Marcy Park is nuts . . . The blood stains and the fact that no dirt was found on his shoes prove this," says one America Online subscriber.

"Who knows, maybe Hillary called in a hit on Vince because he made a crack about how big her ass was getting . . . I think Vince got plunked because he was about to spill the beans," says another.

"Vince Foster was probably a homosexual who was out cruising and got shot," says a third.

"Just prior to Foster's death, Hillary reportedly told Foster that his spying for Israel was known, that he was about to be indicted on charges bordering on treason," says the publisher of *Conspiracy Nation,* an Internet newsletter.

After the Oklahoma City federal building was blown apart, a Concord, California, businessman posted a message asking: "Did CLINTON order the bombing?" He warned that the president might use the tragedy to declare martial law and shut down conservative radio stations. "Ways to cope: Buy weapons and ammunition," he counseled. Some flooded the Internet with detailed instructions on how to mix fertilizer and fuel oil to construct a similar bomb. "I want to make bombs and kill evil Zionist people in the government," one person wrote. "Teach me. Give me text files." Others flocked to a World Wide Web site called the White Nationalist CyberHate page.

Every conceivable taste is accommodated. Discussions range from the physical attributes of certain anchorwomen (the computer community is a largely male preserve) to vicious political invective, much of it shielded by on-line pseudonyms. Clinton-bashing is a favorite pastime, just like on the radio. "Remember when America had a real commander-in-chief and not a draft-dodging, pot-smoking, gay-loving womanizer in office," one disgruntled citizen says. "The Clintons will serve several terms," another says. "Unfortunately they will be prison terms."

The computer universe is also becoming a potent marketing tool for those in the media. *Crossfire* has a debating group on Compu-Serve where viewers continue the televised arguments. Oprah Winfrey has an *Oprah Online* enclave on America Online, with chat groups ("Relationships," "Parenting," "Talking to the Dead") and polls ("Would you leave your spouse if you discovered that he or she was having an affair?"). Prominent personalities appear in cyberspace "auditoriums" to answer typed questions from their fans. Jay Leno, Joan Rivers, Sally Jessy Raphael, Conan O'Brien, Ed Koch, and Michael Reagan are among the talk show stars who have worked the electronic arena. Sometimes verbal warfare breaks out among audience members, just like on call-in shows. It may be virtual reality, but it provides what feels like real contact with big-name talk show-offs.

Not surprisingly, much of the discourse in this community involves the talk show world itself. After the *Jenny Jones* "ambush" show that led to a murder, daytime talk was subjected to withering on-line criticism. One viewer called the *Jones* program "just an example of trash television that invades our homes . . . They glorify disgusting subjects and the lifestyles of freaks." Another called Jenny Jones a "pig." A more thoughtful viewer declared that "these shows are symbolic of the sickness that exists in our society."

Each talk show personality is cheered and jeered. *The McLaughlin Group* has attracted more than 2,600 messages on America Online, with more than a hundred weighing on whether Eleanor Clift Must Go. Howard Stern and Don Imus fans exchange slurs in less than inspiring fashion. ("Howard is the one and only king, you stupid fucks! Get a grip!!!") Rush Limbaugh, who has his own America Online fan group and receives five hundred messages a day on CompuServe, is one of the most hotly debated figures in cyberspace.

"Limbaugh is truly a talented disinfotainer, and he earns his millions feeding the viscera of the resentful," one critic says.

"Thank God for Rush, he takes the heat for just telling the truth," a defender proclaims.

A third observer simply dismisses him as "a fat, lying bastard."

This is clearly a game that anyone can play; you don't need access to the airwaves to sound off in Limbaugh-like fashion. It is perhaps the ultimate democratization of the conversation that emanates from millions of radios and television sets, with the audience atomized into endless fragments according to interest and obsession. Anyone with a keyboard and a modem is empowered, but the explorers are floating in a galaxy of half-truths and one-sided rhetoric. The absence of editorial control means that each cyber-surfer is on his own.

In this sense, the talk shows are merely part of a larger media phenomenon in which unconfirmed speculation crowds out verifiable fact. A bogus report on a single L.A. television station—say, that police have found a bloody ski mask near O. J. Simpson's house —ricochets into thousands of news outlets before it is retracted. Press ethics melt away in the heat of fevered competition. Salacious stories—the naming of accuser Patty Bowman in the William Kennedy Smith rape case, or *Rolling Stone* publisher Jann Wenner leaving his wife for a male Calvin Klein model—make their way from the tabloids to television to *The New York Times* and *The Wall Street Journal*. Talk shows feed off this sort of sensationalism, legitimize it, and carry it to a mass audience. Even the high-minded programs get into the act by analyzing the sleazy behavior of the rest of the media. In this hot-air environment, nothing is out of bounds.

For all its many forms, the world of talk is still dominated by a few dozen media celebrities who preach and provoke the rest of us. This round-the-clock punditry has turned the political arena into a pressure-cooker environment in which there is little time for thoughtful deliberation. The goal is to drown out the opposition, to win the week, to spin the news cycle in your direction until the issue has faded from the airwaves. Whether a particular approach to military spending or law enforcement or downsizing government actually works is almost meaningless, for by the time the results are in the talkers will have long since rendered their verdict and moved on. Policy outcomes are for the history books. The talk shows want to know what you did today and how you'll be faring in the polls next week. The clock is ticking: Good, bad, or ugly?

It is a surreal world in which Larry King and Sam Donaldson and Cokie Roberts make more for an hour-long speech to a corporate group than many Americans earn in a year. It is a mirror-image world in which Pat Buchanan and Jerry Brown and David Gergen and Jesse Jackson magically morph themselves from politicos to pundits and back again. It is an exhibitionist world in which poorly educated Americans pour out their sexual and emotional problems for the amusement of Phil and Oprah and Geraldo and their massive audiences. It is an aging, white-guy world in which the *McLaughlin* regulars are over fifty, King and Donahue and Novak are over sixty, and Brinkley has passed seventy-five.

The talk circuit these days is rife with private alliances—Rush Limbaugh and Newt Gingrich, Bob Grant and George Pataki—that color much of the public commentary. Sunday morning pontificators blithely predict the future. The old prohibitions against making unfounded or inflammatory charges have vanished into the ether. Richard Clear can ask Tom Foley whether he is gay, J. Paul Emerson can rail about shooting immigrants, and other radio hosts can bash blacks and gays in the most hateful terms. Listeners, too, crank up the rhetorical temperature, repeating the latest Whitewater rumor or calling Mario Cuomo a gangster or urging white people to "oil your guns." In this vast sea of gab, ripples of wit and wisdom float alongside errors and idiocy. The old checks and balances are gone forever. It is up to the audience to sort it all out.

From Imus in the morning to Koppel late at night, America has become a talk show nation, a boob-tube civilization, a run-at-the-mouth culture in which anyone can say anything at any time as long as they pull some ratings.

As for me, it's time for a break. I'm all talked out.

S O U R C E S _____

*All interviews were conducted by
the author unless otherwise noted.*

Chapter 1. The Talkathon Culture

6 Abraham Lincoln was called . . . : *Executive Privilege,* Jack Mitchell, Hippocrene Books, 1992.

7 Irving Kristol, the neoconservative writer . . . : William Chapman, *The Washington Post,* April 15, 1973.

7 "You probably never heard of him . . .": Ann Devroy and Bill McAllister, *The Washington Post,* November 4, 1994.

16 "bad judgment": Tom Shales, *The Washington Post,* October 26, 1991.

18 The source of the false report . . . : Brett D. Fromson, *The Washington Post,* March 11, 1994.

Chapter 2. The Art of the Blurt

24 "There were four stages . . .": Christopher Hitchens, *Prepared for the Worst,* Hill and Wang, 1988.

29 "the greatest moral leader . . .": Eric Alterman, *Sound and Fury,* HarperCollins, 1992.

32 "the facile charge . . .": Rowland Evans and Robert Novak, *New York Post,* January 15, 1975.

32 "Deepening dependence . . .": William Greider, *The Washington Post,* June 17, 1979.

33 "looking as warm and friendly . . .": Tom Shales, *The Washington Post,* October 30, 1985.

34 "a foolish argument . . .": Patrick Buchanan, *Right from the Beginning,* Little, Brown, 1988.

34 "unapologetic" attack on the networks . . . : E. J. Dionne, Jr., *The Washington Post,* February 15, 1992.

36 "a rather mousy secretary": Charlotte Hays, *Washingtonian,* July 1992.

Chapter 3. Daytime Dysfunction

49 "Phil, come on": Walter Goodman, *The New York Times,* June 13, 1994.

50 "old-fashioned, bring-'em-in-the-tent . . .": Raleigh *News & Observer,* April 26, 1994.

50 "Years ago, when we were doing stories . . .": Simi Horwitz, *The Washington Post,* November 15, 1992.

52 "You can no longer just put prostitutes . . .": Paula Span, *The Washington Post,* April 16, 1992.

52 "It's not enough to have . . .": Cherie Burns, *New York,* December 5, 1994.

52 "I'm not going to be able to spend . . .": *People,* September 12, 1994.

53 "We are dangerously close . . .": Tom Shales, *The Washington Post,* November 18, 1988.

55 "I'm convinced you don't . . .": Tom Shales, *The Washington Post,* July 15, 1978.

55 "I don't know anyone better . . .": Tom Shales, *The Washington Post,* January 14, 1984.

55 "I'd get a standing ovation . . .": Tom Sherwood, *The Washington Post,* July 23, 1987.

55 "proud to make a contribution . . .": Peter J. Boyer, *The New York Times,* June 16, 1988.

57 "If you want to know . . .": Larry King with Mark Stencel, *On the Line,* Harcourt Brace Jovanovich, 1993.

58 "Why did you want your husband dead?": Howard Rosenberg, *Los Angeles Times,* March 2, 1988.

59 "Has TV gone too far?" Harry F. Waters, *Newsweek,* November 18, 1988.

60 "You're a mass-murderin' dog . . .": Charles Leerhsen, *Newsweek,* November 14, 1988.

60 "Coming up next . . .": Tom Shales, *The Washington Post,* October 27, 1988.

60 "I have every ratings record . . .": Harry F. Waters, *Newsweek,* November 18, 1988.

60 "I went too far . . .": Diane Haithman, *Los Angeles Times,* January 18, 1990.

60 a "spic" and a "dirty Jew": Michele Greppi, *New York Post,* August 18, 1992.

60 "I feel embarrassed . . .": John Carmody, *The Washington Post,* May 16, 1995.

61 a woman named Christine . . . : Cherie Burns, *New York,* December 5, 1994.

61 "We've been accused of showing . . .": Harry F. Waters, *Newsweek,* November 18, 1988.

62 Sherrol Miller, a self-described . . . : Rush Limbaugh, *See I Told You So,* Pocket Books, 1993.

63 as a man named Dr. Ron . . . : Wendy Kaminer, *I'm Dysfunctional, You're Dysfunctional,* Vintage Books, 1992.

64 "A seventeen-year-old girl at Michigan State . . .": Marc Gunther, *Detroit Free Press,* March 19, 1995.

64 Miriam Booher, a domestic worker . . . : Meryl Gordon, *The Washington Post,* May 22, 1993.

65 "cheap publicity": *New York Post,* October 1, 1993.

65 "I had sex with him . . .": Howard Rosenberg, *Los Angeles Times,* May 11, 1994.

65 her life had been "destroyed": Janice Kaplan, *TV Guide,* April 1, 1995.

66 "Trashy stuff sells": Patricia Winters, New York *Daily News,* March 30, 1995.

66 "The idea of having somebody . . .": Richard Huff, New York *Daily News,* March 11, 1995.

66 "We originated same-sex . . .": Francine Russo, New York *Daily News,* March 26, 1995.

67 "I was devastated": Michelle Green, *People,* March 27, 1995.

67 "a vast, scary wasteland . . .": Linda Stasi, New York *Daily News,* March 12, 1995.

68 "They sought to spread . . .": Patricia J. Priest, *The Washington Post,* January 10, 1993.

69 "It certainly seems that . . .": Vicki Abt and Mel Seesholtz, *Journal of Pop Culture,* Summer 1994.

71 "What we are trying to change . . .": Barbara Grizzuti Harrison, *The New York Times Magazine,* June 11, 1989.

71 "When I think of sex . . .": Tom Shales, *The Washington Post,* November 15, 1993.

Chapter 4. The King of Schmooze

76 "King may need to develop . . .": Tom Shales, *The Washington Post,* June 8, 1985.

78 "I don't want to get into that": Ellen Edwards, *The Washington Post,* November 8, 1993.

79 "I'm as nice to Dan Quayle": Larry King with Mark Stencel, *On the Line,* Harcourt Brace Jovanovich, 1993.

79 "I always get a good reaction": Ellen Edwards, *The Washington Post,* November 8, 1993.

80 "He doesn't try to embarrass . . .": Thomas J. Meyer, *The New York Times Magazine,* May 26, 1991.

80 "I want to start even . . .": Laurence Laurent, *The Washington Post,* December 14, 1980.

80 "There's a whole pack of them . . .": Larry King with Mark Stencel, *On the Line,* Harcourt Brace Jovanovich, 1993.

82 "fighting a ghost": Cindy Skrzycki, *The Washington Post,* February 3 and February 9, 1993.

83 "To be in your presence . . .": Larry King with Peter Occhiogrosso, *Tell it to the King,* Putnam, 1988.

84 "He'll run and win": Gay Sands Miller, *The Wall Street Journal,* November 15, 1979.

89 "It's very personal": David Finkel, *The Washington Post Magazine,* January 31, 1991.

89 "the beginning of a beautiful friendship": Larry King with Mark Stencel, *On the Line,* Harcourt Brace Jovanovich, 1993.

90 "gave me an indication": Michael Isikoff, *The Washington Post*, May 31, 1992.

93 "You're a long way . . .": Paul Hendrickson, *The Washington Post*, January 28, 1993.

Chapter 5. Caught in the Crossfire

100 "giant web of hypocrisy": *The New Republic,* October 6, 1979.

101 "I've served as a summer replacement . . .": Michael Kinsley, *Curse of the Giant Muffins,* Summit Books, 1987.

102 Rockefeller had loaned Braden . . . : Tom Kelly, *Washingtonian,* August 1978.

103 "No one cares about Ronald Reagan": Joann Stevens, *The Washington Post,* December 27, 1979.

103 "I don't think he understands . . .": Stephanie Mansfield, *The Washington Post,* July 2, 1981.

104 "I felt like I was in a barroom brawl": Stephanie Mansfield, *The Washington Post,* July 2, 1981.

104 "a form of ideological masturbation . . .": Stephanie Mansfield, *The Washington Post,* July 2, 1981.

108 "This single staff selection . . .": Rowland Evans and Robert Novak, *The Washington Post,* February 8, 1985.

109 "polecat" and "McCarthyite bum": Eric Alterman, *Sound and Fury,* HarperCollins, 1992.

112 "Someone is trying to make an ass . . .": Nancy Collins, *Vanity Fair,* November 1994.

112 "certain intellectual compromises . . .": Barbara Matusow, *Washingtonian,* February 1990.

113 "croaky voice": David Shenk, *The Washington Post,* August 8, 1993.

119 "Simple honesty requires . . .": Michael Kinsley, *The New Republic,* December 22, 1986.

120 "Get serious": Michael Kinsley, *The Washington Post,* March 19, 1992.

120 "Big Boobs . . .": Michael Kinsley, *The Wall Street Journal,* July 17, 1986.

120 "In our sound-bite-and-spin . . .": Michael Kinsley, *The New Yorker,* March 27, 1995.

121 "playing along with the hoax": Michael Kinsley, *The Washington Post,* January 14, 1993.

121 "it is very hard to believe . . .": Michael Kinsley, *The Washington Post,* May 12, 1993.

123 "masterful" performance: Robert D. Novak, *The Washington Post,* June 15, 1995.

Chapter 6. Toe to Toe with Ted

137 "Stop the O. J. stuff . . .": Bill Carter, *The New York Times,* March 27, 1995.

142 "That's when I knew . . .": Jacob Weisberg, *New York,* January 9, 1995.

Chapter 7. Video Vérité

158 "the anti-Geraldo": Wes Smith, *Chicago Tribune,* September 29, 1994.

158 "a guy so square . . .": Richard B. Woodward, *Mirabella,* August 1994.

158 "All the charisma . . .": Thomas J. Meyer, *The New York Times Magazine,* March 15, 1992.

163 "C-SPAN is more real . . .": Jim Auchmutey, *Atlanta Journal-Constitution,* February 7, 1985.

165 "Maybe two minutes was incendiary . . .": Thomas J. Meyer, *The New York Times Magazine,* March 15, 1992.

166 "You can't imagine . . .": James Lardner, *The New Yorker,* March 14, 1994.

Chapter 8. Sunday Ritual

175 Days after President Kennedy's funeral . . .: *David Brinkley,* David Brinkley, Alfred A. Knopf, 1995.

175 "one of my closest friends": Tom Shales, *The Washington Post,* November 12, 1982.

176 "Dinosaurs from prehistoric times": Marc Gunther, *The House that Roone Built,* Little, Brown, 1994.

177 "Does this mean I have to stop . . .": Eleanor Randolph, *The Washington Post,* September 26, 1986.

179 He asked Defense Secretary Caspar Weinberger . . . : Sam Donaldson, *Hold On Mr. President!,* Random House, 1987.

182 "I just love the institution": Paul Hendrickson, *The Washington Post Magazine,* June 20, 1993.

184 "cheap shot": Ann Devroy, *The Washington Post,* November 8, 1993.

187 "the most tough-minded panel show": William Safire, *The New York Times,* May 14, 1992.

187 "a thin-smiling punching bag . . .": Robert Novak, *Chicago Sun-Times,* April 14, 1994.

194 During the Iran-contra furor . . . : Eleanor Randolph, *The Washington Post,* December 22, 1986.

198 "It's kind of sad . . .": Lyric Wallwork Winic, *Washingtonian,* July 1995.

Chapter 9. Talking for Dollars

203 "Members of the House . . .": James J. Kilpatrick, *The Washington Post,* December 26, 1988.

203 "I think that's my own personal . . .": Eleanor Randolph, *The Washington Post,* April 14, 1989.

204 "I just got on the gravy train . . .": Ken Auletta, *The New Yorker,* September 12, 1994.

204 "We are private . . .": Ken Auletta, *The New Yorker,* September 12, 1994.

204 "I'm not an elected . . .": Ken Auletta, *The New Yorker,* September 12, 1994.

204 "I'm a totally private . . .": Ken Auletta, *The New Yorker,* September 12, 1994.

205 "I'm not going to disclose . . .": Alicia C. Shepard, *American Journalism Review,* May 1994.

205 "A private matter": Alicia C. Shepard, *American Journalism Review,* May 1994.

205 "That's private": Eleanor Randolph, *The Washington Post,* April 14, 1989.

205 "Their audience deserves . . .": Eleanor Randolph, *The Washington Post,* April 14, 1989.

205 "What I find most offensive . . .": Ken Auletta, *The New Yorker,* September 12, 1994.

207 "It's hard to imagine . . .": James M. Perry, *The Wall Street Journal,* April 15, 1994.

211 "media-generated myths": Fred Barnes, *Forbes MediaCritic,* Fall 1993.

212 Kinsley also split . . . : James Warren, *Chicago Tribune,* December 4, 1994.

212 And, in a Crossfire roadshow . . . : James Warren, *Chicago Tribune,* March 5, 1995.

213 Cokie Roberts has spoken to . . . : Marc Gunther, *TV Guide,* December 11, 1993.

213 She and her husband, Steve Roberts . . . : James Warren, *Chicago Tribune,* October 2, 1994.

214 "We are like monkeys . . .": Ken Auletta, *The New Yorker,* September 12, 1994.

215 Tim Russert has staged . . . : James Warren, *Chicago Tribune,* October 30, 1994.

216 "I would have to agree . . .": Alicia C. Shepard, *American Journalism Review,* May 1994.

217 "I don't like to say no . . .": Marc Gunther, *TV Guide,* December 11, 1993.

219 cohost Joan Lunden was . . . : Peter Johnson, *USA Today,* April 4, 1995.

224 television news "is increasingly dishonest": Stephen Hess, *The Washington Post,* October 22, 1989.

225 "You're the former governor . . .": Sherri Kimmel, *The Pennsylvania Lawyer,* January 1995.

Chapter 10. The Rush Hour

229 "I'm not out to save . . .": Claudia Puig, *Los Angeles Times,* November 25, 1989.

229 "I'm not doing this to reshape . . .": Rick Dubrow, *Los Angeles Times,* September 11, 1992.

231 "These are the people whose . . .": Rush Limbaugh, *Policy Review,* Fall 1994.

233 "The shit that hit the fan . . .": Paul D. Colford, *The Rush Limbaugh Story,* St. Martin's Press, 1993.

233 "would do well to imitate . . .": Rowland Evans and Robert Novak, *The Washington Post,* May 20, 1992.

234 "ask me for my views . . .": Jeffrey Yorke, *The Washington Post,* June 9, 1992.

234 "Rush is a very sound man . . .": Paul D. Colford, *The Rush Limbaugh Story,* St. Martin's Press, 1993.

234 "You are on a high . . .": Paul D. Colford, *The Rush Limbaugh Story,* St. Martin's Press, 1993.

234 "He's a gift from God": Henry Allen, *The Washington Post,* August 20, 1992.

235 "He was incredibly deferential": Mary Matalin and James Carville, *All's Fair,* Random House/Simon and Schuster, 1994.

235 "I was not wrong about anything . . .": Paul D. Colford, *The Rush Limbaugh Story,* St. Martin's Press, 1993.

236 a self-described "dork": Steven V. Roberts, *U.S. News & World Report,* August 16, 1993.

237 "will be the most-listened-to . . .": Paul D. Colford, *The Rush Limbaugh Story,* St. Martin's Press, 1993.

237 "The purpose of a call . . .": Rick Dubrow, *Los Angeles Times,* September 11, 1992.

237 "It's the single most regretful . . .": Lewis Grossberger, *The New York Times Magazine,* December 16, 1990.

238 "in an interminable funk": *Frontline,* PBS, February 28, 1995.

238 "I listen to Rush regularly . . .": D. Howard King and Geoffrey Morris, *Rush to Us,* Pinnacle Books, 1994.

238 "Mr. Limbaugh is in . . .": Walter Goodman, *The New York Times,* July 22, 1990.

238 "The poor in this country . . .": Rush Limbaugh, *The Way Things Ought to Be,* Pocket Books, 1992.

239 One critic counted . . . : Howard Rosenberg, *Los Angeles Times,* September 3, 1993.

239 "I don't think I'll ever like TV . . .": Margaret Carlson, *Time,* unpublished.

239 "a powerhouse antidote . . .": James Bowman, *National Review,* September 6, 1993.

240 "at powerless people . . .": Molly Ivins, *The Washington Post,* October 14, 1993.

240 "to throw dirt on government . . .": Anthony Lewis, *The New York Times,* July 18, 1994.

240 "Talk shows like Limbaugh's . . .": Larry King with Marc Stencel, *On the Line,* Harcourt Brace Jovanovich, 1993.

240 "This guy is starting to believe . . .": *Playboy,* April 1994.

240 "He calls women like me . . .": Peter Laufer, *Inside Talk Radio,* Birch Lane Press, 1995.

241 "For the past six months . . .": James Bowman, *National Review,* September 6, 1993.

241 "all the liberal groups were panicked . . .": Margaret Carlson, *Time,* unpublished.

241 "along with a thousand million other . . .": Margaret Carlson, *Time,* unpublished.

242 "Are you upset . . .": Brian Keliher, *Flush Rush Quarterly,* Winter 1995.

243 "This administration's policies . . .": Rush Limbaugh, *Policy Review,* Fall 1994.

245 "You in the press . . .": Rush Limbaugh, *Limbaugh Letter.*

249 "The days where it's not as much fun . . .": Margaret Carlson, *Time,* unpublished.

251 "a very close symbiotic relationship": Steven V. Roberts, *U.S. News & World Report,* August 16, 1993.

251 "Rush has made it significantly . . .": D. Howard King and Geoffrey Morris, *Rush to Us,* Pinnacle Books, 1994.

252 "You know, all this stuff . . .": Brian Keliher, *Flush Rush Quarterly,* Winter 1995.

253 "It has never been the express . . .": Thomas Byrne Edsall, *The New York Review of Books,* October 6, 1994.

254 "Liberals fear me . . .": Rush Limbaugh, *Policy Review,* Fall 1994.

Chapter 11. Radio Rebels

259 "opportunistic twits": Richard Corliss, *Time,* January 23, 1995.

262 "We ought to slap . . .": Gary Gerkhardt, *Rocky Mountain News,* November 17, 1994.

262 "ought to be put down . . .": Timothy Egan, *The New York Times,* January 1, 1995.

262 "Everybody in California . . .": John Tierney, *The New York Times,* February 14, 1995.

263 "ugly bitch": Peter Laufer, *Inside Talk Radio,* Birch Lane Press, 1995.

263 "The problem we have right now . . .": Bob Herbert, *The New York Times,* April 29, 1995.

263 "the jerk, the wacko . . .": Gary Gerkhardt, *Rocky Mountain News,* November 17, 1994.

263 Steve Cokely, who once worked . . . : Sheli Teitlebaum, *The Jerusalem Report,* March 19, 1992.

263 "You would vote for Hitler . . .": Ed Siegel, *The Boston Globe,* November 3, 1994.

264 "I listen to my tapes . . .": Marc Fisher, *The Washington Post,* March 6, 1995.

264 "actually killing these cops . . .": Paul D. Colford, *Newsday,* November 3, 1994.

265 "I say to white people . . .": Philip Gourevitch, *New York,* October 24, 1994.

265 He has called the Reverend . . . : Philip Gourevitch, *New York,* October 24, 1994.

266 "As long as they're black . . .": Gwen Florio, Nancy Phillips, and Kevin L. Carter, *The Philadelphia Inquirer,* October 28, 1994.

266 "He is extremely angry . . .": Gwen Florio, Nancy Phillips, and Kevin L. Carter, *The Philadelphia Inquirer,* October 28, 1994.

267 "Mr. Liddy . . . how many techniques . . .": Randall Bloomquist, *The Washington Post Magazine,* May 24, 1992.

268 In a *Washington Post* poll . . . : Richard Morin, *The Washington Post,* May 18, 1995.

268 They range from William Cooper . . . : Sara Rimer, *The New York Times,* April 27, 1995.

269 "There is no doubt in my mind . . .": Kevin Berger, *San Francisco Examiner,* May 1, 1995.

269 "I would bet my last cent . . .": Nell Henderson, *The Washington Post,* April 26, 1995.

270 "a following of drowsy worshippers . . .": Fred Rayfield, *The Compass,* October 1, 1951.

271 The most celebrated radio personality . . . : Betsy Carter, *Newsweek,* October 29, 1979.

272 "Radio is a scuzzy . . .": *Playboy,* April 1994.

272 "You have to train . . .": Richard Harrington, *The Washington Post,* July 31, 1981.

273 "Stern's show is like being caught . . .": Richard Harrington, *The Washington Post,* July 31, 1981.

273 "They didn't explain . . .": Howard Stern, *Private Parts,* Simon and Schuster, 1993.

273 "No jokes or sketches . . .": Howard Stern, *Private Parts,* Simon and Schuster, 1993.

275 "All journalists are lying skunks": Rebecca Johnson, *Esquire,* May 1992.

275 expanding the definition of "indecent" speech . . . : Jeanie Kasindorf, *New York,* November 23, 1992.

275 He described a rape scene . . . : Paul Farhi, *The Washington Post,* October 28, 1992.

275 "Soon-Yi enjoys . . .": Paul Farhi, *The Washington Post Magazine,* May 21, 1995.

276 "Penis out of my mouth . . .": *Playboy,* April 1994.

276 "a little bit of a nut": Robert O'Harrow, Jr., *The Washington Post,* April 30, 1994.

276 "I don't think you can go . . .": Richard Harrington, *The Washington Post,* October 28, 1993.

277 "a goofball . . .": Howard Stern, *Private Parts,* Simon and Schuster, 1993.

277 "should be evaluated psychiatrically": *Playboy,* April 1994.

277 "I'm just another asshole . . .": Bruce Fretts, *Entertainment Weekly,* October 15, 1993.

279 "Everybody knew I was a drunk . . .": Paula Span, *The Washington Post,* July 28, 1993.

280 "needs to be on this show . . .": Martha Sherill, *Esquire,* October 1994.

280 "It's not some tribal ritual . . .": Martha Sherill, *Esquire,* October 1994.

280 "I'm not Ted Koppel . . .": Paula Span, *The Washington Post,* July 28, 1993.

280 "You're not going to be governor . . .": Joseph F. Sullivan, *The New York Times,* February 6, 1993.

282 "a weird, manic-depressive genius": Rob Sunde, *Communicator,* May 1995.

282 "a tight-ass wussy": Andrew Ferguson, *Washingtonian,* October 1994.

282 "I listen. And I cringe . . .": Leonard Shapiro, *The Washington Post,* May 13, 1994.

284 "I got tired of hearing . . .": Marc Fisher, *The Washington Post,* March 6, 1995.

Chapter 12. The Influence Game

289 President Bush had branded "disgusting" . . . : Ann Devroy and Tom Kenworthy, *The Washington Post,* June 8, 1989.

291 "the nation's new hero": Neal Gabler, *Winchell,* Knopf, 1994.

294 "a liar, a faker . . .": *Frontline,* PBS, January 31, 1995.

294 "They wake up every day . . .": Leslie Phillips, *USA Today,* October 26, 1994.

295 "Arthur, cut out the letters!": Micki Siegel, *Parade,* December 31, 1978.

295 "That was my first taste . . .": Richard Harrington, *The Washington Post,* July 31, 1981.

296 "The talk show hosts and Ralph Nader . . .": Tom Kenworthy and Don Phillips, *The Washington Post,* February 7, 1989.

298 "The first lesson they learn . . .": Kim Masters, *The Washington Post,* November 7, 1994.

298 "This is anti-American . . .": Christopher Drew, *Chicago Tribune,* October 7, 1994.

299 "one of the most shocking . . .": Christopher Drew, *Chicago Tribune,* October 7, 1994

299 "stop this monstrosity . . .": Michael Weisskopf, *The Washington Post,* October 6, 1994.

300 "I briefed him on a provision . . .": D. Howard King and Geoffrey Morris, *Rush to Us,* Pinnacle Books, 1994.

300 "We were calling seven hundred fifty . . .": Alan Vanneman, *Youth Today,* November-December 1994.

300 "Just a few years ago . . .": Alan Vanneman, *Youth Today,* November-December 1994.

301 "Hate sells": Philip Gourevitch, *New York,* October 24, 1994.

302 "Crush Rush with the Truth": Sam Attlesey, *Dallas Morning News*, January 11, 1995.

302 "My interest in politics was . . .": Kevin Merida, *The Washington Post*, December 11, 1994.

302 "Talk radio is equal time . . .": John Fund, *Forbes MediaCritic*, Spring 1995.

303 "Peter Hoagland is a liar": David Finkel, *The Washington Post Magazine*, January 15, 1995.

304 "Money, that's nothing": Leslie Phillips, *USA Today*, October 26, 1994.

304 "some stupid, wind-up . . .": Ed Siegel, *The Boston Globe*, November 3, 1994.

305 Kirby Wilbur of Seattle's KVI . . . : Leslie Phillips, *USA Today*, October 26, 1994.

305 "loathsome beast": Leslie Phillips, *USA Today*, October 26, 1994.

Chapter 13. Blurring the Lines

310 "went right for the jugular": Vic Gold, *Washingtonian*, February 1994.

311 "a sermonizing, sanctimonious prig": Charles Trueheart, *The Washington Post*, January 4, 1989.

311 Walter Lippmann wrote speeches . . . : Ronald Steel, *Walter Lippman and the American Century*, Little, Brown, 1980.

311 Arthur Krock, Washington bureau chief . . . : Nigel Hamilton, *JFK—Reckless Youth*, Random House, 1992.

314 "she's the only one he hasn't . . .": Lois Romano, *The Washington Post*, March 11, 1994.

315 "He needed to be a journalist . . .": Thomas B. Rosenstiel, *Los Angeles Times*, April 26, 1989.

315 "I think we're all friends . . .": Eleanor Randolph, *The Washington Post*, June 10, 1988.

316 "guys who have spent their lives . . .": Charles Trueheart, *The Washington Post*, January 4, 1989.

317 "You can't reclaim your virginity . . .": Charles Trueheart, *The Washington Post*, January 4, 1989.

318 "Chin up . . .": Dan Balz, *The Washington Post*, May 30, 1993.

318 "I walked through with him . . .": Michael Kelly, *The New York Times Magazine,* October 31, 1993.

319 "a wise, thoughtful and delightful . . .": Mark Shields, *The Washington Post,* May 5, 1993.

319 "Here tonight in his new role . . .": Michael Kelly, *The New York Times Magazine,* October 31, 1993.

319 "What does it tell me . . .": Ruth Marcus, *The Washington Post,* May 30, 1993.

321 "million-dollar TV media pundits": William B. Hamilton, *The Washington Post,* February 13, 1994.

325 "You were a big supporter . . .": Kevin Sack, *The New York Times,* June 25, 1995.

327 described how a taxi refused to pick him up . . . : Dennis Hevesi, *The New York Times,* December 4, 1994.

327 "all the liberal garbage . . .": Paula Span, *The Washington Post,* November 10, 1988.

327 "I'm there to correct . . .": Paul Galloway, *Chicago Tribune,* April 4, 1993.

328 "David's got to loosen up . . .": Paul E. Bourgoyne, *New Orleans Times-Picayune,* July 24, 1993.

329 "Some nine years ago . . .": Bill Peterson, *The Washington Post,* May 24, 1982.

330 In Florida, three radio hosts . . . : Katharine Q. Seelye, *The New York Times,* April 16, 1994.

331 "He's bringing us shock politics": Todd S. Purdum, *The New York Times,* April 3, 1994.

Chapter 15. The Future of Talk

355 "I may be a slut . . .": Thomas B. Rosenstiel, *Los Angeles Times,* May 13, 1994.

355 "Hitler was decisive . . .": Charlotte Hays, *Washingtonian,* July 1992.

368 "Just prior to Foster's death . . .": Susan Schmidt, *The Washington Post,* July 4, 1995.

368 "I want to make bombs . . .": Michael Janofsky, *The New York Times,* May 12, 1995.

INDEX

ABOUT THE AUTHOR

HOWARD KURTZ is the media reporter for *The Washington Post*. He is the author of *Media Circus: The Trouble with America's Newspapers,* which in 1995 was voted the best recent book about the news media by *American Journalism Review*. His writing has appeared in *The New Republic, The Washington Monthly, New York* magazine, and *Columbia Journalism Review*. Kurtz often appears on CNN's *Reliable Sources* and has made the talk show rounds on television and radio. He lives in Washington, D.C., with his wife and two daughters.